Global Economic Modeling

A Volume in Honor of
Lawrence R. Klein

Global Economic Modeling

A Volume in Honor of
Lawrence R. Klein

editor

Peter Pauly

University of Toronto, Canada

 World Scientific

NEW JERSEY · LONDON · SINGAPORE · BEIJING · SHANGHAI · HONG KONG · TAIPEI · CHENNAI · TOKYO

Published by

World Scientific Publishing Co. Pte. Ltd.

5 Toh Tuck Link, Singapore 596224

USA office: 27 Warren Street, Suite 401-402, Hackensack, NJ 07601

UK office: 57 Shelton Street, Covent Garden, London WC2H 9HE

Library of Congress Cataloging-in-Publication Data

Names: Pauly, Peter H., 1947–   author. | Klein, Lawrence R. (Lawrence Robert), 1920–2013, honoree.

Title: Global economic modeling : a volume in honor of Lawrence R. Klein /
   [edited by] Peter Pauly, Rotman School of Management, University of Toronto.

Description: New Jersey : World Scientific, [2018] | Includes bibliographical references.

Identifiers: LCCN 2018009776 | ISBN 9789813220430 (hardcover)

Subjects: LCSH: Econometric models. | Econometrics.

Classification: LCC HB141 .G576 2018 | DDC 330.01/5195--dc23

LC record available at https://lccn.loc.gov/2018009776

British Library Cataloguing-in-Publication Data

A catalogue record for this book is available from the British Library.

For any available supplementary material, please visit
http://www.worldscientific.com/worldscibooks/10.1142/10459#t=suppl

Desk Editor: Jiang Yulin

Printed in Singapore

Contents

Introduction

Peter Pauly

Rotman School of Management, University of Toronto
105 St. George Street
Toronto, ON M5S 3E6, Canada
E-mail: pauly@rotman.utoronto.ca

Applied econometrics, in particular econometric modeling, has evolved and matured significantly since its early days in the late 1940s. Along the way, the field has been met with its share of challenges that have proved to be catalytic for important subsequent improvements. More than 40 years ago, the first global oil shock and the following recession exposed significant design flaws in early econometric models and spawned a re-orientation of applied econometrics. Similarly, in this century, almost a decade after the global financial crisis economists and politicians are still struggling to agree on the lessons from the experience. Whatever advances in economic theory will ultimately emerge, they are likely to be accompanied by supporting empirical research. It seems obvious to many observers that in support of a better understanding of the global economy, the present time should be a time of resurgence for national and international applied econometrics. And nobody embodied that tradition of careful, yet ambitious research more than Lawrence R. Klein, whose pioneering work laid the foundation for the field. He has been a life-long contributor to, observer of, and commentator on the continuous development and improvement of applied econometrics. Throughout all the challenges he witnessed, he never wavered in his conviction that model-based economic research would be essential for evidence-based public policy and would ultimately provide the pathway to an improved economic well-being of society. It is this maxim that has been the foundation of Klein's scholarly commitment, and the contributions in this volume seek to offer new insights in that tradition.

The life of an academic is reflected in many different ways: his or her scholarly achievements, often the recognition from one's peers, or the impact on the direction of research in one's chosen field, a significant public policy impact, and many others. Klein has indeed been a giant among his peers, by any of these dimensions. During his illustrious career, he achieved everything anybody could aspire to, every academic recognition imaginable, and the love and admiration of the profession. Most fittingly, the press release issued by the Royal Swedish Academy of Sciences to announce the award of the 1980 Nobel Prize in Economic Science to Klein asserts that "...(F)ew, if any, research workers in the empirical field of economic science, have had so many successors and such a large impact ....".

Klein was, obviously, a prolific author with hundreds of papers and scores of books to his credit. His published work is voluminous and monumental. He obtained every academic recognition possible, from his early recognition of the American Economic Association's John Bates Clark Medal, the appointment to a University Professorship at the University of Pennsylvania, the presidencies of the American Economic Association, the Econometric Society, and the American Academy of Sciences, among others, to more than thirty honorary degrees. The culmination of all of this was, of course, the awarding of the Nobel Prize in Economics. His contributions are indeed immense and have been expertly acknowledged and appreciated by many others[a].

But more than that, he was cherished by his students, colleagues, and collaborators for a uniquely personal devotion to the community of scholars in his orbit, perhaps more so than any other academic economist was. In particular, he practiced the wonderful age-old academic tradition of providing hands-on guidance to impart his academic experience. In his homage, Ignazio Visco, who worked and interacted with Klein for many years, expresses the experience of working with Klein very thoughtfully, when he writes:

> *"In many ways his role can be likened to that of a master craftsman, whose workplace was a beehive of constant activity. His was a 'workshop', or rather several workshops, in which those who had the good fortune to take part ended up acquiring the 'craft', learning not only how to view the economic system using the instruments of theory, but also, and perhaps above all, how to create and utilize new quantitative tools for analyzing its operation, to design forecasting scenarios and to derive practical indications for economic policy."*

And, quite possibly most important, he combined a manifestly towering academic excellence and a pioneering vision for the field with a deeply caring and humble personality. Scores of young scholars from all over the world were drawn to his community of researchers not just by his academic stature, but by his fundamental humanity and concern and respect for the personalities and diverse backgrounds of every individual he interacted with. Indeed, many of the authors in this volume have worked with Klein, experienced him as a co-author, colleague, or mentor, and owe their academic interests to his guidance. And those who were not directly linked to him will readily acknowledge his impact on the field they are working in.

It is with his unique impact on the field in mind that we bring together in this volume a set of papers that are related to the broad spectrum of Klein's contributions to economics. During his long and illustrious career, he contributed to a wide range of areas: early Keynesian economic theory, econometric theory, applied econometrics, and macroeconomic modeling. Beyond his academic footprint, his impact on public policy was

---

[a] The most comprehensive and informative discussions of Klein's academic contributions and his impact on the field of applied econometrics are I Visco, Lawrence R. Klein: Macroeconomics, econometrics, and economic policy, *Journal of Policy Modeling* **36**(4), 605-628 (2014), and O. Bjerkholt, Lawrence R. Klein 1920-2013: Notes on the early years, *Journal of Policy Modeling* **36**(5), 767-784 (2014).

equally broad, domestically as advisor to numerous (democratic) administrations and, possibly even more important, to policy makers and international organizations around the world. He was a protagonist in so many areas of economic analysis, from early Keynesian theory, tools and techniques for applied economic analysis to the application of these insights to actual policy concerns. The breadth of his contributions is astonishing and arguably unmatched to this day by any of his peers. Following that tradition, the four sections in this volume explore developments in areas that are reflective of his wide-ranging scholarly interest and public policy involvement: (I) international econometric modeling, (II) the international financial system, (III) trade and development, and (IV) new dimensions of modeling.

Arguably the most significant aspect of his role as spiritus rector of the field of applied econometrics is in laying the groundwork for the field of large-scale econometric modeling. He guided numerous national and international modeling projects, from the US model at the University of Pennsylvania's Wharton Econometrics (WEFA) to his pioneering creation of the first multi-country model at Project LINK. Late in his career, Klein became increasingly involved with attempts at high-frequency modeling. *Mariano and Ozmucur* take his work forward significantly in an application to the Philippines. The paper brings together various strands of development in modern dynamic time-series analysis that are of particular importance to mixed-frequency problems such as the combination of current with lower-frequency information.

The large multi-lateral organizations — the International Monetary Fund (IMF), the Organization for Economic Cooperation and Development (OECD), and the United Nations (UN, through Project LINK) – have a long history of economic forecasting on a global scale. These forecasts were never purely model-based, but enhanced routinely by the expertise of resident or national experts. To paraphrase Yogi Berra, it is indeed not easy to make predictions, especially about the future. However, it helps to systematically analyze the forecast record ex post. Arguably, no organizations have been more assiduous in doing so than the OECD. For this volume, *Turner* provides a comprehensive and most instructive review of the forecasting operations and forensic efforts at the institution.

The most significant and enduring impact of Klein's scholarly work has been in the area of applied econometrics, with a focus on international modeling. The consortium of Project LINK, which he initiated and which ultimately brought together hundreds of modelers from around the world, was a pioneering effort at the time. It remained, as he often confirmed, his *"...true love in research and substance"*, and over the years it influenced countless other modeling efforts. The survey paper by *Pauly* attempts to take stock of what applied macro-modelers, both nationally and internationally, have achieved over more than half a century, and lays out the challenges still ahead.

Over the recent two or three decades, Dynamic Structural General Equilibrium (DSGE) models have emerged as the favorite paradigm of the academic modeling community. They grew out of a challenge of the perceived ad-hoc character of early-generation econometric models and the DSGE modeling community has made great advances in developing ever more sophisticated structures. Probably more successfully than any other international organization, the IMF has long been central to a range of different modeling efforts. With many central banks around the world, the IMF embarked on DSGE modeling at a very early stage. There is no doubt that the IMF research department has now for several decades been at the forefront of the development of ever more sophisticated multi-country models. This reflects a strong research ethos of the institution and an admirable closeness to the academic world. The paper by *Benes, Laxton, and Mongardini* is another outstanding example of the frontier research coming out of the IMF. Specifically, with the use of one of the more recent IMF models the authors examine the effectiveness of macroprudential regulations in view of the experiences during the Global Financial Crisis.

One of the many lessons for modelers from that crisis was the need to incorporate more important nonlinearities into their model. Specifically, it is generally accepted now that most, if not all, of the existing models were unsatisfactory in their treatment of measures of risk. *Gibson, Hall and Tavlas* in their paper examine in particular the dynamics of risk spreads among European economies. They take the analysis further by examining the feedback mechanisms between those risk spreads and equity prices, which obviously should play an important role in any macroeconometric model of the monetary sector. They note in particular the potential instabilities, which can be generated by 'Doom Loops', i.e. the irrational mutual reinforcement of risk and return measures that can destabilize an economy.

One has to go back in history quite a long time, probably to the first oil shock of the 1970s, to find an event that has dislodged the basic tenets of the modeling profession as profoundly as the global financial crisis that unfolded in 2008/2009. Virtually no model was equipped to capture the critical transmission mechanisms in a way that would allow an observer to predict, and then analyze, financial crises caused by a credit crunch and bank runs. In addition, the international regulatory environment was incomplete as well. It is hard to underestimate how close the world economy came to a real collapse at that time. In his remarks, delivered as a luncheon address to conference participants, *Macklem* provides a fascinating glimpse of the challenges policy-makers were facing. At the time, he served as Senior Deputy Governor of the Bank of Canada, and was at the table when the most consequential decisions were made. In this address, he shares his memories of those turbulent days, but also reviews the elements of reform to the international regulatory environment that he was intimately involved with as Chair of the Stabilization Board's Standing Committee, and reviews the successes of, and outstanding challenges, of the regime that emerged in the aftermath of the crisis.

One of the striking characteristics of national and international financial markets these days is the extent to which they are dominated by institutional investors, including large pension funds. That, combined with the globally diversified portfolios of these institutions, is obviously a challenge for our understanding of the transmission of shocks through the system, as well as the risks in individual markets. *Richardson and Larcher* in their paper take up the issue of what the relations are between market valuations and deficits in defined-pension plans. There is an important linkage between this finding and widespread worries about insufficient macroprudential oversight in insurance markets, which can easily disrupt fragile international financial markets.

Development issues have always been central to applied modeling. In the course of his career, Klein earned particular respect and admiration for his research and personal involvement in the developing and emerging world. Incidentally, he was the driving force behind the enlargement of Project LINK to incorporate individual country models for several dozen emerging and developing countries, a path-breaking effort at the time. Perhaps no country has been as much at the center of his concerns as China. Not accidentally, in 1980 he led the first delegation of North American social scientists to China, and the 'Summer Palace Workshop on Econometrics' he organized spawned a whole generation of applied econometricians in China. The focus on the rapid emergence of China on the world economic stage in the paper by *Lau*, one of Klein's earliest co-operators, is very much in the tradition of this work. The paper takes stock of the country's economic achievements to date as well as of remaining challenges, and provides an outlook on future developments.

From its very early beginnings, the structural representation of bilateral trade on a global scale was at the heart of multi-country modeling. The focus was on merchandise trade, and elaborate models based on consumer demand theory emerged to capture trade linkages at the disaggregated (SITC) level. Those were the early days, and modeling was fully in the tradition of trying to capture comparative advantage trade of finished goods. The framework was quite appropriate to analyze trade liberalization through tariff reductions. However, since then, rapid globalization has transformed trade relations radically. The break-up of the production process into individual tasks and the resulting creation of intricate value-added chains have transformed the nature of merchandise trade as well as the driving forces behind its direction and growth. The paper by *Gangnes and Van Assche* reviews critically many of these developments and in addition seeks to unravel the puzzling stagnation of world trade in manufactures in the aftermath of the crisis.

Few issues have received as much attention in the international economic community as the rising trends in national and international income and wealth inequality. With an increasing amount of available data on a global scale, it has become possible to examine trends both within and across countries in much finer granularity than ever before. Incidentally, the early pioneers of applied econometrics such as *Tinbergen, Theil*, or *Klein* were very much concerned with matters of income distribution, but the emphasis faded over time. There is a plethora of hypotheses about the underlying causes for the widening income and wealth gaps. *Darvas* in this volume examines the role of technical progress in a cross-country study using a large data set encompassing most advanced industrial countries. He recognizes some effects that could be traced to technical progress, which are exacerbated by increased globalization, but concludes that the major drivers of inequality are likely to be found elsewhere.

Apart from China, no other country has captured Klein's scholarly and public policy interest as enduringly as India. He recognized it as a large, peaceful and democratic country that however faced enormous developmental challenges. In a research program for, and supported by, the United Nations Commission for Trade and Development (UNCTAD) he championed the development of quality-of-life indicators that could help to sharpen economic development strategies. In the tradition of that work, the survey by *Basu* in this volume reviews many of the development policy proposals that have been brought forward over the past decade. His primary focus is on the development of a methodology to support sustainable development efforts, i.e. policies that recognize the intricate linkages between economic, social, political, and environmental dimensions of the development challenge.

It was recognized very early on that global econometric models focusing solely on economic linkages and transmissions were inadequate, in particular for the analysis of longer-term global dynamics. This became even more obvious with the growing concern about global climate change and its economic and environmental implications. There now are several highly sophisticated 'integrative assessment models', models that integrate environmental and global modeling. In his paper, *Schleicher* takes the next step and spells out the need for 'deepened' structural modeling that would improve the linkages between the different components of an integrated model with a detailed analysis of the full value chain of the energy system at the microeconomic level. This, it is argued, would facilitate the analysis of radical technological innovations and the design of appropriate regulatory environments.

Late in his life, Klein witnessed the onset and early devastation created by the global financial crisis, but not all of its aftermath. Nonetheless, he very early on diagnosed the prolonged recession as what we now all know it was: a long period of insufficient demand as a result of households, firms and governments (to some extent) going through a protracted process of deleveraging. In that situation, austerity policies were exactly the wrong medicine, and in the final paper of the volume *Stiblar* delivers a passionate 'cri de coeur' highlighting the painful consequences of misguided policies from the perspective of a small open economy at the periphery of the European economic zone.

Earlier versions of most of the papers in this monograph have been presented at a symposium on 'Global Economic Modeling', honoring the work of Lawrence R. Klein, and hosted by the Rotman School of Management at the University of Toronto. We are grateful for financial support to the conference from the Rotman School of Management, the federal Department of Finance, Ontario's Ministry of Finance, Industry Canada, and the Bank of Canada. Thomas Wilson, who has been working with Klein and Project LINK for many years, was instrumental in securing that support. Wendy Dobson and Ig Horstmann, co-Directors of the Institute for International Business, generously agreed to the conference being hosted and supported by the IIB. Most of all, we are deeply indebted to Erin Bell, Administrator of the Project LINK Centre at the University of Toronto, for her tireless work. She oversaw the organization of the conference as well as the production of this volume with great skill and diligence, endless patience, and unflagging humor. Her enduring commitment to this project has indeed been absolutely essential.

Peter Pauly
University of Toronto

I.   International Econometric Modeling

High-mixed-frequency forecasting models for GDP and inflation

Roberto S. Mariano[a] and Suleyman Ozmucur

University of Pennsylvania,
Department of Economics,
3718 Locust Walk, Philadelphia Pa 19104-6297
E-mails: mariano@upenn.edu, ozmucur@sas.upenn.edu

This paper analyzes the technical and practical issues involved in the use of data at mixed frequencies (quarterly and monthly and, possibly, weekly and daily) to forecast monthly and quarterly economic activity in a country. In particular, it considers alternative high-frequency forecasting models for GDP growth and inflation in the Philippines, utilizing indicators that are observable at different frequencies and with particular focus on dynamic time-series models that involve latent factors. The study compares the forecasting performance of this approach with more commonly used data-intensive methods that have been developed in applications in the U.S. and Europe. These alternative approaches include Mixed Data Sampling (MIDAS) Regression and Current Quarter Modeling (CQM) with Bridge Equations. While these alternatives are mostly data-intensive, the dynamic latent factor modeling with mixed frequencies presents a parsimonious approach which depends on a much smaller data set that needs to be updated regularly. But it also faces additional complications in methodology and calculations as mixed-frequency data are included in the analysis.

Regarding high-frequency forecasting of GDP growth in the Philippines, our preliminary results based on static simulations and turning point analysis indicate that the mixed dynamic latent factor model (MDLFM) performs better than the MIDAS regression, bridge equations with and without principal components, and the benchmark autoregressive models. For the GDP deflator, MIDAS exhibits the best performance. Further comparison analysis and empirical applications are needed to settle this issue more definitively – especially in the direction of introducing more elaborate error structures, multiple latent common factors, and other exogenous indicators in the high-frequency models for Philippine GDP growth and inflation. Future work also will cover dynamic multi-period simulations of the estimated models as well as extensions to other selected countries in Southeast Asia.

JEL Classification: C53, C58

1. Introduction

Building on earlier results reported in Mariano and Ozmucur[1,2], this paper analyzes the technical and practical issues involved in the use of data at mixed and high frequencies to forecast monthly economic activity in the Philippines. In particular, it considers constructing high-frequency forecasting models for GDP growth and inflation in the Philippines, in the form of dynamic time-series models that combine latent factors with a parsimonious set of indicators that are observable at different frequencies.

---

[a] Earlier versions of this paper were presented the United Nations DESA Expert Group Meeting on the World Economy (LINK Project) — October 21-23, 2015 in New York, the 12th National Convention of Statistics in Manila — October 2013, the Asian Meeting of the Econometric Society in Singapore — August 2013, and at the ADB conference in Manila in May 2012.

The authors acknowledge partial funding support from the Sim Kee Boon Institute for Financial Economics at Singapore Management University and the School of Arts and Sciences at the University of Pennsylvania.

The econometric issue of combining mixed high-frequency data for short-term forecasting was a research area of extreme interest to Lawrence Klein. In the context of macroeconometric models, his works on this topic started over 25 years ago – e.g., as reported in his presentations in international meetings in the 1980s, Klein and Sojo[3,4], Klein and Park[5,6], Klein and Ozmucur[7-9], and Mariano and Tse[10] — and continued to his dying days – through his weekly reports on updated forecasts from his Current Quarter Model (CQM) of the U.S. economy. To quote from Klein and Ozmucur[9], "Our long-standing conviction stands intact that detailed structural model building is the best kind of system for understanding the macroeconomy through its causal dynamic relationships, specified by received economic analysis." There are, however some related approaches, based on indicator analysis that are complementary for use in high frequency analysis. For most economies, the necessary data base for structural model building, guided by consistent social accounting systems (national income and product accounts, input-output accounts, national balance sheets) are, at best, available only at annual frequencies. Many advanced industrial countries can provide the accounts at quarterly frequencies, but few, if any, can provide them at monthly frequencies.

"A more complete understanding of cyclical and other turbulent dynamic movements might need even higher frequency observation, i.e. weekly, daily, or real time." It would not be impossible to construct a structural model from monthly data, but a great deal of interpolation and use of short cut procedures would have to be used; so, we have turned to a specific kind of indicator method to construct econometric models at this high frequency. "In step with new technological developments in the information sector of modern economies, attention has been paid to the use of newly available computer power, data resources, telecommunication facilities and other technical changes that made higher frequency analysis of economic statistics available."

This topic also has generated considerable interest currently, especially in financial econometrics, as more observable data have become available at different and higher frequencies. This is especially so for government policy planners as well as monitors of financial market developments, who would be interested in timely utilization of high-frequency indicators to update their market assessments and forecasts.

The mixed-frequency models of the type we consider for forecasting purposes in this paper have been used in the construction of business condition indices in the econometrics literature. From a methodological perspective, the combination of mixed-frequency data and latent factors in the dynamic model introduces complexities in the estimation of the model. Algorithms have been developed to address these complexities and applied in BCI construction for the U.S. and Europe.

This paper investigates the potential gains in applying this approach to high-frequency forecasting of GDP growth and inflation in the Philippines. Extensions of the approach, introducing richer error structures in the model and use of multiple factors, are also investigated. For purposes of application to the Philippines, we take "high-frequency" forecasting to refer to either month or quarter, with updates on the forecast as information becomes available within the forecasting period.

Compared to other forecasting approaches that have been applied in the literature, which are mostly data-intensive, the dynamic factor modeling procedure in BCI construction presents an interesting and parsimonious approach which depends on a much smaller data set that needs to be updated regularly.   But it also faces additional complications in methodology and calculations as mixed-frequency data are included in the analysis.

The forecast performance of the estimated models is also compared with other alternative current modeling approaches – e.g., Mixed Data Sampling Regression or MIDAS[11-13], Factor Analytic Models[14], and Current Quarterly Modelling (CQM) with Bridge Equations[4,8,9,15].

Earlier published references dealing with dynamic factor modeling for construction of business conditions indices (BCI) in the U.S. and Europe provide the starting point for the application to the Philippines that is presented in the paper.   The current efforts towards constructing and maintaining economic index indicators in the Philippines are tapped to jump-start the specifications for the empirical component of the project. Estimation and validation of the empirical models presented in the paper rely on filtering algorithms that can be set up within software packages that are commercially available, such as EVIEWS, MATLAB, or OX.

Regarding high-frequency forecasting of GDP growth in the Philippines, the preliminary results reported in the paper, which are based on static simulations of the estimated models, indicate that the dynamic latent factor model performs better than the unrestricted MIDAS regression, the bridge equations with and without principal components, and the benchmark autoregressive models. For the GDP deflator, MIDAS exhibits the best performance. Further comparison analysis and empirical applications are needed to settle this issue more definitively – especially in the direction of introducing more elaborate error structures, multiple latent common factors, and other exogenous factors in the high-frequency models for Philippine GDP growth and inflation. Future work also will cover out-of-sample and dynamic simulations and turning point analysis of the estimated models as well as extensions to other selected countries in Southeast Asia.

2.   Methodology for Dynamic Latent Factor Models with Mixed Frequencies (MDLFM)

The approach is intertwined with analyzing the business cycles in an economy. The basic philosophy that drives the approach is that macroeconomic fluctuations are driven by a small number of common shocks or factors and an idiosyncratic component peculiar to each economic time series. The seminal papers on this are Geweke[16], Sargent and Sims[17] and Stock and Watson[18]. We also introduce another feature - use of mixed-frequency data. This further complicates the analysis, but also enhances the potential for further gains in forecast performance. More recently the approach has received renewed interest for forecasting purposes in the U.S. and larger European countries (e.g., see Foroni & Marcellino[19,20]). The earlier works (e.g., Stock and Watson[18]) develop single factor models to construct composite indices of economic activity based on a handful of coincident indicators. A related approach (e.g., Chow & Choy[14]) uses the model to extract unobserved common factors from a large collection of observable indicator variables. Furthermore, the estimated factor model, properly validated, also may be used to forecast macroeconomic variables of interest.

The common factors are latent, explained by their joint dynamics and, possibly, interactions with observable indicators. The dynamics of the target variable output depends on own lags, the unobservable common factors, and, possibly, exogenous factors. The system may also have other observable variables that serve as indicators for the latent common factors.

A similar modeling approach is used in

- Mariano and Murasawa[21,22] in constructing an improved coincident economic index indicator for the U.S. using mixed frequencies. Here, quarterly GDP is included in the standard list of monthly coincident indicators, namely
    o Employees on non-agricultural payrolls
    o Personal income less transfer payments
    o Index of industrial production
    o Manufacturing and trade sales

- Aruoba, Diebold & Scotti[23], ADS for short, in constructing a "real-time" (daily) BCI for the US, using four indicators
    o GDP – Quarterly
    o Employment – Monthly
    o Initial jobless claims – Weekly
    o Yield curve premium rate – Daily

Here the business economic condition of a country is treated as a latent (unobservable) entity for which there are observable variables or indicators. As ADS remarked, "Latency of business conditions is consistent with economic theory, … which emphasizes that the business cycle is not about any single variable, whether GDP, industrial production, sales, employment, or anything else. Rather, the business cycle is about the dynamics and interactions ("co-movements") of many variables."

From this perspective, it becomes natural to use a state-space formulation for the latent factor model. Kalman filtering procedures (linear and nonlinear – e.g., see Kalman[24]; Kalman & Busy[25]; Cuthbertson, Hall, and Taylor[26]; Durbin & Koopman[27]; Hamilton[28]; Harvey[29]; Kim & Nelson[30]; Tanizaki[31]; Bai, Ghysels, and Wright[32]; Banbura, Giannone, and Reichlin [33]; Banbura and Runstler[34]; Brauning and Koopman[35]; Koopman and van der Wel[36]; Stock and Watson[37]) are then applied to estimate unknown model parameters and perform signal extraction for the calculation of the latent factors.

The Kalman filtering approach needs to be adapted to special complicating features of the problem. In particular, using mixed frequency data for the indicators introduces inherent nonlinearities and missing data in the "measured" variables. Also, additional attention is needed and further complications in calculations arise when dealing with indicators that are flow variables. All these are accounted for in the specific way in which the state-space representation is set up for the analysis.

In terms of dynamic factor modeling with mixed frequencies for BCI construction, there are earlier published references dealing with the topic and related issues as applied to the U.S. and to Europe (e.g., Stock and Watson[18]: Liu and Hall[38]; Mariano and Murasawa,[21,22]; ADS[23]; and Foroni and Marcellino[19,20]). These provide the starting point for the analysis of the methodology in the paper and its application in this paper to the Philippines and other selected Southeast Asian countries.

The model structure for the analysis is as follows. Let

x_t = latent business condition at time t
y_t^i = ith business / economic indicator at time t
w_t^k = kth exogenous variable at time t
$\tilde{y}_t^i$ = ith observable business / economic indicator at time t

Note that y_t^i may not be observable at all values of t when observations are available at lower frequency (e.g., quarterly or semester or annual, instead of monthly). In this case, there would be missing data for $\tilde{y}_t^i$. When available, $\tilde{y}_t^i$ would equal y_t^i if it is a stock variable, but would equal the intra-period sum of corresponding monthly values if it is a flow variable.

For the dynamic latent factor model for x_t and its interaction with y_t^i, we assume that x_t follows an autoregressive process of order p, AR(p):

$$\rho(L) x_t = \varepsilon_t, \ \varepsilon_t \sim \text{iid } N(0,1), \ \rho(L) = 1 + \rho L + \rho^2 L^2 + \ldots + \rho^p L^p.$$

In turn, the indicators y_t^i are linearly related to their own lags (internal dynamics), to x_t, as well as to some exogenous variables w_t^k:

$$y_t^i = \chi_i + \beta_i x_t + \Sigma \left(\delta_{ik} w_t^k + \gamma(L) y_t^i + u_t^i \right)$$

where, u_t^i are contemporaneously uncorrelated (for different i) and iid N(0,1) and uncorrelated with ε_t. $\gamma(L)$ is a polynomial lag operator of some finite degree, with an additional idiosyncratic structure due to the time-spacing of available observable indicators (see ADS[23], p. 418).

This model can be recast in the standard state-space form (e.g., see ADS[23] p. 419 or Mariano and Murasawa[21,22]):

$$y_t = Z_t \alpha_t + \Gamma w_t + \varepsilon_t$$

$$\alpha_{t+1} = T_t + R v_t$$

$$\varepsilon_t \sim (0, H_t)$$

$$v_t \sim (0, Q)$$

where

    y_t = vector of observed variables

    α_t = vector of state variables

    Z_t = matrix of parameters for state variables

    w_t = vector of predetermined variables such as constant term, trends, and lagged dependent variables

    Γ = matrix of parameters for predetermined variables

    ε_t = measurement shocks

    v_t = transition shocks

Kalman filtering procedures can then be applied to estimate unknown parameters in this state-space formulation and perform signal extraction to calculate estimates of the latent factor. This Kalman filtering approach needs to be adapted to special complicating features of the problem. In particular, using mixed frequency data for the indicators introduces missing data in the "measured" variables y_t. Details for formulating the state space model to accommodate this are in Mariano and Murasawa[21,22]. Also, additional attention is needed and further complications in calculations arise when dealing with indicators that are flow variables (see Harvey[29], and ADS[23]). All these are accounted for in the specific way in which the state-space representation is set up for the analysis. It should be pointed out that specific expressions for the variables and parameters in the measurement and state equations depend on the mixed frequencies appearing in the model. The formulas get more complex and numerical treatment of the model gets more computer intensive as higher and higher frequencies are introduced into the model.

3.   Alternative Modeling Approaches

3.1.   *Benchmark – AR (p) and VAR (p)*

For this paper, we use univariate and vector autoregressive processes as benchmark models for the target variables under discussion. For quarterly observable target variables, alternative models could be used: unrestricted quarterly AR(p) or VAR(p) or multi-frequency monthly AR(p) or monthly VAR(p) with missing observations – see Zadrozny[39] Abeysinghe[40,41], and Mariano and Murasawa[22]. In the monthly models with missing observations, the model can be re-cast with a state-space representation and Kalman filtering technology can then be applied to the state-space formulation to estimate the model.

3.2.   *Current Quarter Model (CQM): Bridge equations and principal components*

In an effort to develop an alternative full-blown structural modeling of the economy which at the same time harnesses key information available at different frequencies, Klein and Sojo[3,4] proposed a high-frequency macro-econometric or current quarter model (CQM) for the U.S, which uses bridge equations and principal components. This concept and modeling approach has been applied to other countries and studied in various subsequent publications – e.g., Klein and Park[5,6], Klein and Ozmucur[8,9], Baffigi, Golinelli and Parigi[15], Howrey[42] and Ozmucur[43]. Now, CQM models have been developed for updating quarterly forecasts in China, Hong Kong, Japan, Mexico, Russia and Turkey[43-49]. CQMs are now under construction for Malaysia, the Philippines, and Thailand.

The main objective is to forecast in a timely fashion the national income components – typically available quarterly – utilizing quarterly and higher-frequency data as they become available. For the U.S., real GDP components are considered from the production, expenditure and income sides.

To establish statistical relationships, CQM uses "bridge equations" relating GDP components to quarterly and monthly "indicator" variables. Indicator variables are observable, with sufficient correlation to the GDP component; and with enough lead time relative to the GDP components. For monthly indicators, averages are used over the quarter – averages (or estimates of them) are updated as more monthly observations become available. For purposes of forecasting the monthly and quarterly indicators, ARIMA models are used as well. If no indicators are available, an ARIMA model would be estimated for the GDP component itself.

Since data for the production side are released with a longer lag in the United States (about 3 months), the method of principal components is used as the third way of estimating GDP. Monthly indicators are used to extract principal components. Quarterly average of the first principal component is used as the first determinant of real GDP, and GDP deflator. The remaining principal components (quarterly averages since they are available monthly) enter the equation in a stepwise fashion provided they are significant at the five percent level.

More details for the U.S. CQM are provided in Klein and Park[5,6] and Klein and Ozmucur[8,9].

3.3.   *MIDAS (Mixed Data Sampling) regressions*

A typical bridge equation relates a quarterly variable to three month averages of monthly variables. This implicitly imposes a restriction on parameters for the months of the quarter, which introduces asymptotic biases and inefficiencies[13]. In contrast, MIDAS estimates a monthly regression of GDP on monthly (and possibly quarterly) indicators using parsimonious distributed lags to represent missing observations. The initial reference is Ghysels, Santa-Clara, and Valkanov[11]. One typical lag structure that is used is the exponential Almon lag structure. Alternative lag structures that have been used in empirical work include Beta, Linear, Hyperbolic, and Geometric lag coefficients. The model is estimated by nonlinear least squares using actual observed data at mixed frequencies[50-52].

The approach also has been extended to Unrestricted (Truncated) MIDAS; Autoregressive MIDAS, which adds a lagged y to the regressors; Factor-MIDAS – which includes latent factors; Markov-Switching MIDAS; and explicit combination of MIDAS and MF-DLFM.

4.   Empirical Results for the Philippines

The current efforts towards constructing and maintaining economic index indicators in the Philippines (e.g., Bersales et al[53]; Virola and Polistico[54]; Zhang and Zhuang[55]; and OECD[56]) are tapped to jump-start the empirical component of the paper.

The Leading Economic Indicator Index[56] which is quarterly, was developed jointly by the Philippine Statistics Authority National Statistical Coordination Board and the National Economic and Development Authority (NEDA).   The computation of the composite leading economic indicator involves the use of a reference series (the non-agriculture component of GDP) and eleven leading economic indicators, which reflect the importance of the openness and emerging nature of the economy. These indicators are: consumer price index, electric energy consumption, exchange rate, hotel occupancy rate, money supply, number of new business incorporations, stock price index, terms of trade index, total merchandise imports, visitor arrivals, and wholesale price index. We excluded some variables from the list because of data limitations and included some other variables which proved to be useful in other studies.

Initially, sixteen monthly indicators are considered in our analysis. As in Klein & Sojo[4], these indicators are grouped into two. There are ten indicators used in the prediction of real GDP and eight indicators are used in the prediction of GDP deflator. All variables, including quarterly GDP, were tested for unit roots using critical values provided by MacKinnon[58]. All variables were transformed to obtain year-on-year growth rates or year-on-year differences. Furthermore, before estimating equations, these variables were standardized to have zero means and unit variances. These variables are listed below:

Monthly indicators for real GDP (Fig.1)

    Y01 --- Industrial production index growth rate (year-on-year)
    Y02 --- Merchandise Imports growth rate (year-on-year)
    Y03 --- Merchandise Exports growth rate (year-on-year)
    Y04 --- Real government expenditure growth rate (year-on-year)
    Y05 --- Real Money supply (M1) growth rate (year-on-year)
    Y06 --- World trade volume growth rate (year-on-year)

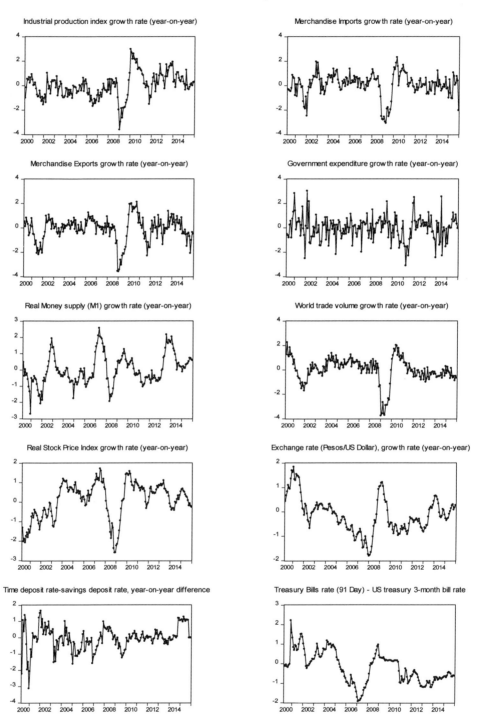

Fig. 1. Standardized Monthly Indicators for Real GDP Growth (2000M01-2015M12).

Y07 --- Real Stock Price Index growth rate (year-on-year)

Y08 --- Real exchange rate, growth rate (year-on-year)

Y09 --- Time deposit rate-savings deposit rate, year-on-year difference

Y10 --- Treasury Bills rate (91 Day) - US treasury 3-month bill rate, year-on-year difference

Monthly indicators for GDP Deflator   (Fig. 2)

Y21 --- Consumer Price Index growth rate (year-on-year)

Y22 --- Producer Price Index, growth rate (year-on-year)

Y23 --- Wholesale Price Index (Metro Manila) growth rate (year-on-year)

Y24 --- Retail Price Index growth rate (year-on-year)

Y25 --- Exchange rate, growth rate (year-on-year)

Y26 --- Money supply (M1) growth rate (year-on-year)

Y29 --- Time deposit rate-savings deposit rate, year-on-year difference (same as Y09)

Y30 --- Treasury Bills rate (91 Day) - US treasury 3-month bill rate, year-on-year difference (same as Y10) get variables (Fig. 3)

Y51 --- Gross Domestic Product growth rate (year-on-year)

Y52 --- Real Gross Domestic Product growth rate (year-on-year)

Y53 --- GDP Deflator growth rate (year-on-year)

Data for the 2000 to 2015 period are used in all estimations. In addition to the mixed-frequency dynamic latent factor model, four other modeling approaches are included – the benchmark Autoregressive Process, Bridge Equations, Principal Components, and MIDAS (see Anderson[59], Clements and Hendry[60,61], Diebold and Rudebusch[62]; Engle and Granger[63,64]; Klein and Ozmucur[64] for various methods and issues).

Specifically, the following nine models are estimated in this empirical exercise (listed in Table 1 below). The model variations in the categories of benchmark autoregressive process, bridge equations, and principal components – models 1 – 6 in the list below - are based on quarterly observations (actual or aggregated from monthly data) while variations of MIDAS and MF-DLFM – models 7 – 9 - are monthly models using mixed actual monthly and quarterly data.

1. AR - The selected model for real GDP growth (Y52) is an AR (1) – based on Box-Jenkins methodology. For the GDP deflator growth rate (Y53), the estimated model is an AR (2). All coefficients are significant at the five percent level. Determination coefficients are 0.49 for real GDP, and 0.67 for the GDP deflator.

2. VAR - The estimated bivariate model for Y52 and Y53 keeps lags 1 and 2. Likelihood ratio test, final prediction error, Akaike information criterion, Schwarz information criterion, Hannan-Quinn information criterion all select lag order of 2.

3. LEI - This includes the Leading Economic Indicator Index for the Philippines in separate autoregressive distributed lag (ARDL) models for Y52 and Y53. Schwarz

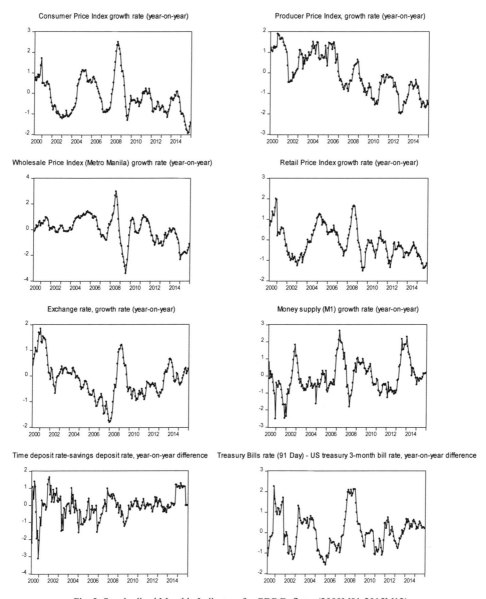

Fig. 2. Standardized Monthly Indicators for GDP Deflator (2000M01-2015M12).

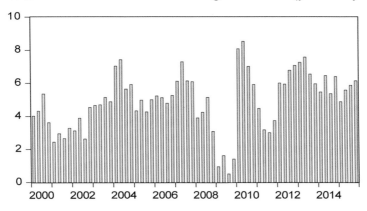

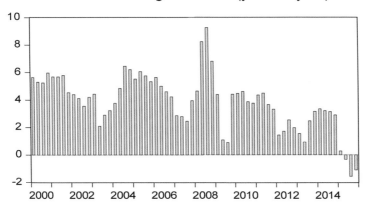

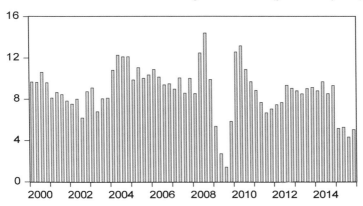

Fig. 3. Real GDP Growth and GDP Deflator Growth (2000Q1-2015Q4).

Table 1. Performance Indicators (mean absolute error, root mean square error, Theil inequality coefficient (U), and the correlation between actual and predicted)

One-period in-sample simulation, 2000Q2 – 2015Q4

Model	MAE	RMSE	THEIL	CORRELATION
Real Gross domestic product growth rate (year-on-year)				
AR	0.89	1.24	0.66	0.39
VAR	0.86	1.06	0.49	0.62
LEI	0.84	1.11	0.53	0.56
Bridge Equations	0.69	0.88	0.37	0.76
PCA_2groups	0.68	0.87	0.63	0.77
Bridge with PCA	0.68	0.87	0.63	0.77
MIDAS	0.44	0.54	0.21	0.92
MIDAS_PCA	0.44	0.57	0.22	0.91
DLFM	0.40	0.50	0.19	0.96
	MAE	RMSE	THEIL	CORRELATION
GDP deflator growth rate (year-on-year)				
AR	0.73	1.05	0.62	0.47
VAR	0.76	1.04	0.61	0.48
LEI	0.73	1.04	0.60	0.49
Bridge Equations	0.50	0.65	0.30	0.84
PCA_2groups	0.48	0.61	0.28	0.86
Bridge with PCA	0.44	0.54	0.24	0.89
MIDAS	0.35	0.43	0.19	0.93
MIDAS_PCA	0.34	0.41	0.18	0.94
DLFM	0.47	0.55	0.23	0.97
	MAE	RMSE	THEIL	CORRELATION
Gross domestic product (GDP) growth rate (year-on-year)				
AR	1.17	1.57	0.63	0.63
VAR	1.12	1.41	0.46	0.66
LEI	1.11	1.43	0.51	0.68
Bridge	0.78	0.96	0.28	0.86
PCA_2groups	0.79	0.97	0.28	0.86
Bridge with PCA	0.64	0.83	0.24	0.90
MIDAS	0.51	0.66	0.18	0.94
MIDAS_PCA	0.49	0.61	0.17	0.95
DLFM	0.33	0.44	0.12	0.98

criterion is used to select the model with a possible maximum lag of 8 quarters. Selected models are ARDL(1, 1) for real GDP growth, and ARDL (2, 0) for GDP deflator. Determination coefficients are 0.58 for real GDP growth, and 0.67 for GDP deflator growth.

4. Bridge - Separate regressions are done for Y52 and Y53 on the indicator variables described earlier, with correction for error serial correlation. The monthly data for the indicators are converted to quarterly figures by averaging, which are then used in estimating the bridge equations. Monthly indicators entering into the equations are

selected using forward stepwise method with stopping criterion of a p-value of 0.1. Real GDP equation includes Y01 (industrial production), Y03 (exports), Y04 (government expenditures), Y07 (real stock prices), and Y09 (time deposit rate-savings deposit rate), in addition to lagged real GDP and a constant term. On the other hand, in addition to lagged GDP deflator and a constant term, Y21 (consumer price index) and Y23 (wholesale price index) are selected in the equation for GDP deflator. Determination coefficients are 0.74 for real GDP growth, and 0.89 for GDP deflator growth.

5. PCA with Two Groups - Principal components are calculated separately from the two groups of monthly indicators for real GDP growth and the GDP deflator growth, as in Klein & Park[5,6], Klein & Ozmucur[7-9], and Mariano & Ozmucur[1,2]. Separate regressions are then performed for Y52 and Y53 on the corresponding group of principal components. The first principal component explains 31% of the variation in 10 indicators for real GDP growth. First seven principal components can explain over 90% of the variation in those ten indicators. Factor loadings indicate that the first principal component stands for international trade, exports (Y02) and imports (Y03), the second principal component for real exchange rate (Y08), the third principal component for the difference between time deposit rate and savings deposit rate (Y09), the fourth component for real government expenditures (Y04), the fifth component for real money supply (Y05), the sixth component for gross international reserves (Y06), and the seventh component for industrial production (Y01).

On the other hand, the first principal component explains 40% of the variation in the 8 indicators for GDP deflator growth and the first five principal components can explain over 90% of the variation in those indicators. Factor loadings indicate that the first principal component stands for consumer prices (Y21), producer prices (Y22), wholesale prices (Y23), and retail prices (Y24), the second component for the exchange rate (Y25), the fourth component for the difference between time deposit rate and savings deposit rate (Y29), and the fifth component for money supply (Y26). The third principal component stands for three indicators, namely money supply (Y26), the difference between time deposit rate and savings deposit rate (Y29) and the difference between the Treasury bill rate and the US Treasury bill rate (Y30).

The relationship between real GDP growth and the principal components was established with the stepwise least squares. The first principal component and the first lag of the dependent variable are included in the equation. Other principal components and the dependent variable with lags 2 to 4 lags are selected using forward selection method. Those indicators which are significant at the 10% level are kept in the equation. It should be noted that those who did not make the first cut (those who account for 90% of the variation in indicators) may turn out to be significant in these bridge equations. For example, real GDP growth equation includes Z09 (ninth principal component), in addition to Z01, Z03 and Z04. This equation, which also includes the first and third lags of Y52, has a determination coefficient of 0.75. GDP deflator growth equation includes sixth and seventh principal components (Z26 and z29), in addition to first and second principal components (Z21, Z22). The equation, which also includes the first and fourth lags of Y53, has a determination coefficient of 0.90.

1.   Bridge with PCA - This is a variation of #5, using as regressors the principal components of all indicator variables grouped together. Real GDP growth equation, now, includes Z30, in addition to Z01, Z03, Z04, Z09 and Y52 (-1). There is a little change in the determination coefficient compared with the one in equation with two groups (0.7595 and 0.7549). However, GDP deflator growth equation is slightly improved with similar additions. This equation, which includes eight principal components and 2 lagged values of the dependent variable, has a determination coefficient of 0.94. Adjusted determination coefficient is 0.92, compared with 0.89 in the equation with two groups.

2.   MIDAS - MIDAS regressions are estimated separately for Y52 and Y53, using actual monthly data for the indicator variables. Eviews, version 9.5, software[66] allows one to use Almon, exponential Almon, Beta, and step options. Almon lags (polynomial distributed lags) are used in this paper. This option had several advantages for the particular data set at hand. It yielded higher determination coefficients, and also required less computation time. Somewhat more common options, exponential Almon lags and beta functions, may lead to highly nonlinear equations with convergence and computation time issues. Almon lag[67,68] with a polynomial degree of 3 is used, and a maximum of 6 lags are allowed[66]. Both real GDP and GDP deflator equations has eight monthly indicators. For all 8 variables a lag of 3 or more is chosen. This is an improvement on our earlier papers[1,2], which used unrestricted MIDAS with 2 lags. Almon type of restrictions enable the use of more lags without increasing the number of right hand variables hence reducing the number of degrees of freedom. Determination coefficients are 0.90 for real GDP growth and 0.95 for GDP deflator growth. It should be noted that, in both equations, there are quite few coefficients which are insignificant. However, alternative equations with fewer variables (omitting variables which are not significant) gave forecast results which were inferior to the ones provided from these equations. Therefore, these equations with better forecasting power were kept as the final set of equations.

3.   MIDAS_PCA - Variation of #7, with principal components of the indicator variables as regressors. Results are not very different than the previous model (MIDAS) in terms of determination coefficients, but there are some differences in forecasting performance.

4.   DLFM - A bivariate mixed-frequency dynamic latent factor model is estimated for Y52 and Y53, with two unobserved common factors. As the first step of dynamic factor modeling, all monthly variables are grouped into one. Real exchange rate and real money supply are deleted from the first since nominal magnitudes of these variables are already in the second group. There were also two interest rate differential variables, which appear in both groups. This reduces the total number of indicators from 18 in two groups to 14 variables in a single group. Real government expenditures (Y04), and time deposit rate and savings rate difference (Y09) are also excluded from the original list because of data

issues. The final list contains the two quarterly variables of interest (Y52 and Y53) and 12 monthly indicator variables: Y01, Y02, Y03, Y06, Y07, Y10, Y21, Y22, Y23, Y24, Y25, and Y26.

The system closely follows Mariano & Murasawa[21], and extends it by including variables related to the general price level. There are 14 target variables (12 monthly, 2 quarterly, listed above), and two unobserved common factors (S1 and S6), and two specific factors (S11 and S16). Common factors are included in all 14 measurement or observation equations, while specific factors (idiosyncratic components) are included in the related equation. For example, specific factor S11 appears in real GDP equation, while specific factor S16 appears in GDP deflator equation. Derivation of the form of the lags in equations with quarterly and monthly target variables are given in Mariano & Murasawa[21]. All variables are standardized before estimating the model. This has the advantage of reducing the number of parameters to be estimated, and determining the initial values of some of the variables as zeros (average for the period). Here, exact maximum likelihood estimators are computed, despite the longer time required compared with some short-cut methods such as the EM algorithm. BFGS (Broyden-Fletcher-Goldfarb-Shannon) algorithm with Marquart steps are utilized to maximize the likelihood function. Convergence was achieved after 82 iterations. Equations for monthly indicators also include exogenous variables (lagged dependent variables), in addition to common factors. The number of lags is determined with the help of autoregressive equations prior to building the state space model. For example, Y01 (industrial production) includes lags 1 and 2, and Y02 (merchandise imports) include lags 1, 4, and 5. Results indicate that common factors with lags and specific factors are significant in the model. Lagged dependent variables also play an important role.

The estimated models are used to calculate one-period ahead forecasts over the sample period. For illustrative purposes, the actual values and one-step ahead forecasts for the mixed-frequency dynamic latent factor model are presented in Figs. 4, 5, and 6.

Table 1 summarizes the mean absolute errors, root mean square errors, Theil inequality coefficients (U), and the correlation between actual and predicted of the alternative estimated models based on one-period-ahead static forecasts. The results indicate that the mixed-frequency dynamic latent factor model has the lowest mean absolute error - .40% for real GDP growth rate, and 0.33% for the nominal GDP growth rate. Corresponding statistics are 0.43%, and 0.49% for MIDAS_PCA, which ranks the second. On the other

One-step-ahead Y52

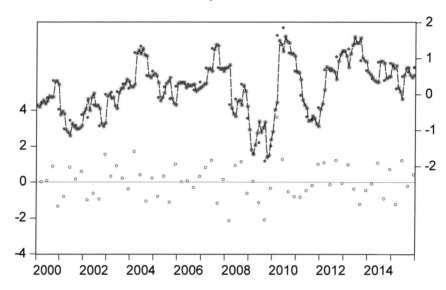

One-step-ahead Y53

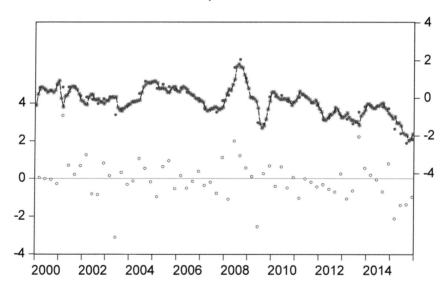

Fig. 4. DLFM One-Step-Ahead Growth Forecasts (••••-actual, ****-predicted, °°°°-residuals) for Real GDP (Y52) and GDP Deflator (Y53), 2000 – 2015.

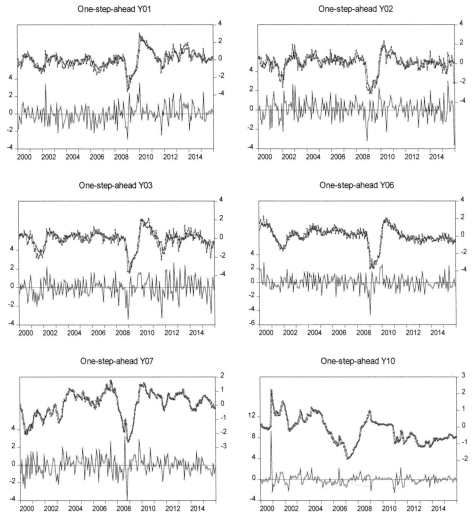

Fig. 5. DLFM One-Step-Ahead Growth Forecasts (••••-actual, ****-predicted, °°°°-residual).

hand, MIDAS_PCA has the lowest mean absolute error for the GDP deflator (0.34%), while DLFM has a mean absolute error of 0.47%. Principal components, and bridge equations follow these two models. The benchmark AR and VAR models show the biggest errors. Note also LEI shows little improvement, in performance relative to the benchmark models. DLFM has the lowest Theil inequality coefficients for real GDP growth (0.19) and nominal GDP growth (0.12), while MIDAS_PCA has the lowest coefficient for GDP deflator (0.18). DLFM has the highest correlation coefficient between actual and predicted for all the variables.

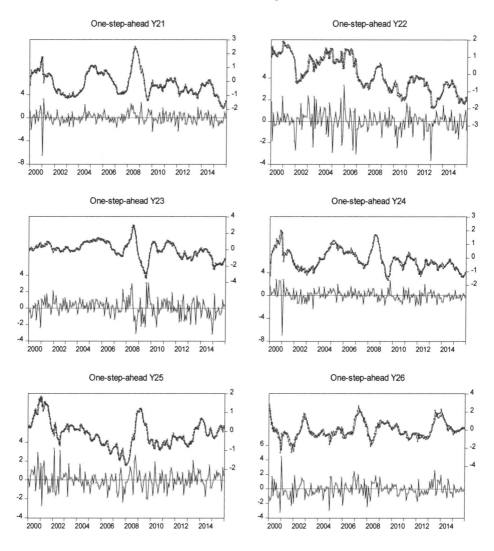

Fig. 6. DLFM One-Step-Ahead Growth Forecasts (••••-actual, ****-predicted, °°°°-residual).

To test the statistical significance of the superior forecasting performance of MF-DLFM relative to the other models, we apply the Diebold-Mariano test[69] to compare the forecast accuracy of MF-DLFM relative to the alternative models, taken one at a time (see also Mariano[70] for comparisons of various tests, and Mariano and Preve[71] for multiple forecasts comparisons).   The test results are indicative of the significantly lower errors (less than -1.96 for a 5% level of significance) for the dynamic factor model (Table 2), with the exception of MIDAS models for the real GDP growth rate. However, MIDAS models seem to perform better in the prediction of the GDP deflator growth. Bridge equations and principal components are also relatively successful. There are no significant differences between predictions made with the DLFM and bridge equations and principal components. On the other hand, DLFM performs better than others for nominal GDP growth.

More work is required for a more definite conclusion on this issue. Further analysis and empirical applications are needed to settle this issue more definitively – especially in the direction of introducing more elaborate error structures, multiple latent common factors, and other exogenous indicators in the dynamic latent factor model. Alternative variations of MIDAS will also be explored and the specification of the other modeling strategies can also be refined further for improved forecasting performance.

It is also important for a model to predict turning points. Therefore, several statistics are used to see the models' success in predicting turning point points. Changes in model forecast $(P(t)-P(t-1))$ and the actual $A(t)-A(t-1))$ are compared to analyze the prediction accuracy. These changes are grouped into four[72,73], as shown below:

- Actual is decreasing, and the model predicts a decrease (correct prediction of a turning point, n11 out of a total number of n predictions),
- Actual is decreasing, and the model predicts an increase (false prediction of a turning point, n12 out of a total number of n predictions),
- Actual is increasing, and the model predicts a decrease (false prediction of a turning point, n21 out of a total number of n predictions),
- Actual is increasing, and the model predicts an increase (correct prediction of a turning point, n22 out of a total number of n predictions).

		predicted Down (-)	predicted Up(+)	
Actual	Down(-)	n11	n12	n1.
Actual	Up (+)	n21	n22	n2.
		n.1	n.2	n

The ratio of total correct prediction of turning points= (n11+n22)/n.

The ratio of correct prediction of downturns= n11/n1.

The ratio of correct prediction of upturns= n22/n2.

All models do relatively well, if the prediction is for the level of GDP, real GDP or the GDP deflator. However, not all of them fare well in predicting the turning point in the growth rate of these indicators (Table 3). For example, DLFM and MIDAS models correctly predicts 90% of turning points in real GDP, while MIDAS_PCA predicts 94% of them (Table 3). The ratio is 87% and 89% for the bridge equation model, and the PCA model, respectively. On the other hand, DLFM correctly predicts 80% of downturns, and 97% of upturns. Corresponding ratios for the MIDAS model are 93% and 94%.

Pearson χ^2, which is a measure of overall independence between changes in "actual" and "prediction" indicate independence for almost all the models (critical value for 95%

confidence and 1 degree of freedom, for a 2x2 table, is 3.841). Pearson's Phi coefficient (mean square contingency coefficient), which gives the degree of association between two dichotomous variables, actual and predicted changes here, is higher for the DLFM model. For example, for real GDP growth, Phi coefficient is 0.78 for DLFM, compared with 0.87 for the MIDAS_PCA model. Phi coefficient for DLFM is 0.66 for GDP deflator, compared with 0.71 for the MIDAS model.

Table 2. Diebold-Mariano Statistics

Diebold-Mariano Statistics (errors in dynamic factor model compared with errors in an alternative model)		
Real gross domestic product growth rate (year-on-year)		
Model	Absolute value of errors	Squares of errors
AR	-4.43	-2.45
VAR	-5.39	-4.02
LEI	-4.59	-2.70
Bridge Equations	-3.81	-3.90
PCA_2groups	-4.17	-3.92
Bridge with PCA	-4.17	-3.92
MIDAS	-1.21	-0.96
MIDAS_PCA	-0.97	-1.16
GDP deflator growth rate (year-on-year)		
	Absolute value of errors	Squares of errors
AR	-2.86	-3.05
VAR	-3.15	-3.23
LEI	-2.86	-3.04
Bridge Equations	-1.05	-1.70
PCA_2groups	-0.83	-1.40
Bridge with PCA	0.05	-0.35
MIDAS	1.89	1.81
MIDAS_PCA	2.09	2.07
Gross domestic product (GDP) growth rate (year-on-year)		
	Absolute value of errors	Squares of errors
AR	-6.93	-4.63
VAR	-7.64	-5.21
LEI	-7.31	-4.81
Bridge Equations	-5.06	-4.25
PCA_2groups	-6.23	-5.18
Bridge with PCA	-4.40	-3.67
MIDAS	-2.93	-2.70
MIDAS_PCA	-2.69	-2.72

Table 3. Turning Point Errors (2000Q3-2015Q4)

Alternative models	Correct total	Correct	Correct	Pearson χ^2	Phi
Real Gross Domestic Product Growth (y-o-y)					
AR	0.81	0.83	0.78	23.4	0.61
VAR	0.77	0.70	0.84	18.8	0.55
LEI	0.73	0.73	0.72	12.7	0.45
Bridge Equations	0.87	0.93	0.81	34.8	0.75
PCA_2groups	0.89	0.97	0.81	38.2	0.79
Bridge with PCA	0.89	0.97	0.81	38.2	0.79
MIDAS	0.90	0.93	0.88	40.5	0.81
MIDAS_PCA	0.94	0.93	0.94	47.0	0.87
DLFM	0.90	0.80	0.97	38.0	0.78
GDP Deflator Growth (y-o-y)					
AR	0.68	0.71	0.65	7.8	0.36
VAR	0.68	0.68	0.68	7.8	0.35
LEI	0.69	0.74	0.65	9.4	0.39
Bridge Equations	0.77	0.77	0.77	18.6	0.55
PCA_2groups	0.81	0.84	0.77	23.4	0.61
Bridge with PCA	0.81	0.84	0.77	23.4	0.61
MIDAS	0.85	0.90	0.81	31.5	0.71
MIDAS_PCA	0.85	0.87	0.84	31.3	0.71
DLFM	0.81	1.00	0.61	27.4	0.66
Gross Domestic Product Growth (y-o-y)					
AR	0.76	0.77	0.74	16.5	0.52
VAR	0.77	0.71	0.84	19.0	0.55
LEI	0.74	0.71	0.77	14.6	0.48
Bridge Equations	0.87	0.84	0.90	34.3	0.74
PCA_2groups	0.82	0.77	0.87	26.1	0.65
Bridge with PCA	0.85	0.81	0.90	31.5	0.71
MIDAS	0.89	0.94	0.84	37.5	0.78
MIDAS_PCA	0.92	0.90	0.94	43.7	0.84
DLFM	0.94	0.97	0.90	47.2	0.87

In order to gauge the out-of-sample performance, estimations were done using rolling samples with 44 observations, which gave 20 quarterly and 80 monthly forecasts. A model is first estimated using 2000Q1-2010Q4 period data, and a forecast is obtained for 2011Q1. Then, the same model is estimated using 2000Q2-2011Q1 period, and a forecast for 2011Q2 is obtained. These rolling calculations continued to get to the final data point 2015Q4 (using the estimation period 2005Q1-2015Q3). Results are given in Table 4. The dynamic latent factor model has lowest errors in out-of-sample forecasts also.

5.   Conclusion

This paper uses mixed-frequency data to estimate dynamic latent factor models for high-frequency forecasting of GDP growth and inflation in the Philippines. Kalman filtering procedures are then applied to estimate unknown parameters in this state-space formulation and perform signal extraction to calculate estimates of the latent factor. Our results for the real and nominal GDP growth rates indicate that the mixed dynamic latent factor model performs better than the MIDAS regression, bridge equations with and without principal components, and the benchmark autoregressive models. However, MIDAS is better than the other models in the case of the GDP deflator. Further comparison analysis and empirical applications are needed to settle this issue more definitively – especially in the direction of introducing more elaborate error structures, multiple latent common factors, and other exogenous indicators in the high-frequency models for the Philippines. Future work also will cover dynamic multi-period simulations of the estimated models as well as extensions to other selected countries in Southeast Asia.

Table 4. Performance Indicators (out-of-sample, mean absolute error and root mean square error)

		Real GDP growth	GDP deflator growth	GDP growth
AR	MAE	0.81	1.30	1.00
AR	RMSE	0.97	1.60	1.41
VAR	MAE	0.78	1.35	1.41
VAR	RMSE	0.90	1.63	1.89
LEI	MAE	1.06	1.33	1.07
LEI	RMSE	1.23	1.62	1.44
MIDAS	MAE	0.41	0.35	0.56
MIDAS	RMSE	0.56	0.43	0.72
MIDAS_PCA	MAE	0.52	0.54	0.61
MIDAS_PCA	RMSE	0.73	0.64	0.78
DLFM	MAE	0.23	0.29	0.38
DLFM	RMSE	0.28	0.36	0.47

References

1.   R. S. Mariano and S. Ozmucur, High-mixed-frequency Dynamic latent factor forecasting models for GDP in the Philippines, *Estudios de Economia Aplicada,* **33**(2), 451-462 (2015a).

2.   R. S Mariano and S. Ozmucur *High-Mixed-Frequency Forecasting Models for GDP and Inflation in Selected Southeast Asian Countries,* Paper presented at the Project LINK Meeting (New York, October 21-23, 2015) (2015b).

3.   L. R. Klein and E. Sojo, *Combinations of High and Low Frequency Data in Macroeconometric Models*, Paper presented at the American Economic Association Meeting (Chicago, Illinois, December, 1987).

4.   L. R. Klein and E. Sojo, *Combinations of High and Low Frequency Data in Macroeconometric Models*, in *Economics in Theory and Practice: An Eclectic Approach,* eds. L.R. Klein and J. Marquez. (Kluwer Academic Publishers, 1989), pp. 3-16.

5.   L. R. Klein and J. Y. Park, Economic forecasting at high-frequency intervals, *Journal of Forecasting* **12**, 301-319 (1993).

6.   L. R. Klein and J. Y. Park, The University of Pennsylvania model for high-frequency economic forecasting, *Economic and Financial Modelling,* 95-146 (1995).

7.   L. R. Klein and S. Ozmucur, *Some Possibilities for Indicator Analysis in Economic Forecasting*, Paper presented at the Project LINK Fall Meeting (Bologna, October, 2002).

8.   L. R. Klein and S. Ozmucur, *University of Pennsylvania Current Quarterly Model of the United States Economy Forecast Summary.* Project LINK website http://www.chass.utoronto.ca/LINK (April, 2004).

9.   L. R. Klein and S. Ozmucur, *University of Pennsylvania High Frequency Macroeconomic Modeling* in *Econometric Forecasting and High-Frequency Data Analysis,* eds. R. S. Mariano & Y.-K. Tse (World Scientific Publishers, Singapore, 2008), pp. 53-91.

10. R. S. Mariano and Y.-K. Tse (eds.), *Econometric Forecasting and High-Frequency Data Analysis*, (World Scientific Publishers, Singapore, 2008).

11. E. Ghysels, P. Santa-Clara, and R. Valkanov, *The MIDAS Touch: Mixed Data Sampling Regression Models*, (mimeo, Chapel Hill, NC, 2004).

12. E. Ghysels, A. Sinko, and R. Valkanov, MIDAS regressions: Further results and new directions, *Econometric Reviews* **26**(1), 53-90 (2007).

13. E. Ghysels, *Matlab Toolbox for Mixed Sampling Frequency Data Analysis Using MIDAS Regression Models* (mimeo, Version 5, May, 2013).

14. H. K. Chow and K. M. Choy, Analysing and forecasting business cycles in a small open economy, a dynamic factor model for Singapore, *OECD Journal of Business Cycle Measurement and Analysis* **1**, 19-41 (2009).

15. A. Baffigi, R. Golinelli and G. Parigi, Bridge models to forecast the Euro Area GDP, *International Journal of Forecasting* **20**(3), 447-460 (2004).

16. J. Geweke, *The Dynamic Factor Analysis of Economic Time Series* in *Latent Variables in Socio-Economic Models*, eds. D. J. Aigner and A.S. Goldberger (North-Holland, Amsterdam, 1977), pp. 365-383.

17. T. Sargent and C. Sims, *Business Cycle Modeling Without Pretending To Have Too Much A Priori Economic Theory,* in *New Methods in Business Cycle Research*, ed. C. Sims. (Minneapolis, Federal Reserve Bank of Minneapolis, 1977).

18. J. H. Stock and M. W. Watson, *New Indexes of Coincident and Leading Economic Indicators*, in *NBER Macroeconomics Annual 4*, eds. O. J. Blanchard and S. Fischer (Cambridge, Massachusetts, MIT Press, 1989).

19. C. Foroni and M. Marcellino, *A Comparison of Mixed Frequency Approaches for Modelling Euro Area Macroeconomic Variables*, Economics Working Papers ECO 2012/07, European University Institute (2012).

20. C. Foroni and M. Marcellino, *A Survey of Econometric Methods for Mixed Frequency Data*, Economics Working Papers ECO 2013/02, European University Institute, (2013).

21. R. S. Mariano, R. S. and Y. Murasawa, A New Coincident Index of Business Cycles Based on Monthly and Quarterly Series, *Journal of Applied Econometrics* **18**(4), 427-443 (2003).

22. R. S. Mariano and Y. Murasawa, A coincident index, common factors, and monthly real GDP, *Oxford Bulletin of Economics and Statistics* **72**(1), 27-46 (2010).

23. S. B. Aruoba, F. X. Diebold and C. Scotti, Real-time measurement of business conditions, *Journal of Business & Economic Statistics* **27**(4), 417-427 (2009).

24. R. E. Kalman, A new approach to linear filtering and prediction problems, *Transactions of the ASME-Journal of Basic Engineering* **82** Series D, 35-45 (1960).

25. R. E. Kalman and R. S. Bucy, New results in linear filtering and prediction theory, *Transactions of the ASME-Journal of Basic Engineering* **83**, 95-108 (1961).

26. K. Cuthbertson, S. G. Hall, M. P. Taylor, *Applied Econometric Techniques* (The University of Michigan Press, Ann Arbor, Michigan, 1992).

27. J. Durbin and S. J. Koopman, *Time Series Analysis by State Space Methods*, 2nd ed. (Oxford University Press, 2012).

28. J. D. Hamilton, *Time Series Analysis* (Princeton University Press, Princeton, New Jersey, 1994).

29. A. C. Harvey, *Forecasting, Structural Time Series Models and the Kalman Filter*, (Cambridge University Press, Cambridge, 1989).

30. M. J. Kim and C. R. Nelson, *State-Space Models with Regime Switching* (MIT Press, Cambridge, Massachusetts, 1999).

31. H. Tanizaki, *Nonlinear Filters, Estimation and Applications* 2nd ed. (Springer-Verlag. Berlin, Heidelberg, New York, 1996).

32. J. Bai, E. Ghysels, and J. Wright, State space models and MIDAS regressions, *Econometric Reviews* (2011).

33. M. Banbura, D. Giannone, and L. Reichlin, *Nowcasting* in *Oxford Handbook on Economic Forecasting,* eds. M. P. Clements and D. F. Hendry (Oxford University Press, 2012).

34. M. Banbura and G. Runstler, A Look into the factor model black box: Publication lags and the role of hard and soft data in forecasting GDP, *International Journal of Forecasting*, **27**, 333-346 (2011).

35. F. Brauning and S. J. Koopman, Forecasting macroeconomic variables using collapsed dynamic factor analysis, *International Journal of Forecasting*, **30** 572-584 (2014).

36. S. J. Koopman and M. van der Wel, Forecasting the US term structure of interest rates using a macroeconomic smooth dynamic factor analysis, *International Journal of Forecasting*, **29** (2013).

37. J. H. Stock and M. W. Watson, *Implications of Dynamic Factor Models for VAR Analysis*. National Bureau of Economic Research Working Paper 11467 (June 2005).

38. H. Liu and S. G. Hall, Creating high-frequency national accounts with state-space modelling: A Monte Carlo experiment. *Journal of Forecasting* **20**, 441-449 (2001).

39. P. Zadrozny, Gaussian-likelihood of continuous-time ARMAX models when data are stocks and flows at different frequencies, *Econometric Theory* **4**(1), 108-124 (1988).

40. T. Abeysinghe, Forecasting Singapore's quarterly GDP with monthly external trade. *International Journal of Forecasting* **14**, 505-513 (1998).

41. T. Abeysinghe, Modeling variables of different frequencies, *International Journal of Forecasting* **16**, 117-119 (2000).

42. E. P. Howrey, *New Methods for Using Monthly data to Improve Forecast Accuracy*, in *Comparative Performance of U.S. Econometric Models*, ed. L. R. Klein. (Oxford University Press, New York and Oxford, 1991), pp. 227-249.

43. S. Ozmucur, *Current Quarter Model for Turkey* in *The Making of National Economic Forecasts*, ed. L. R. Klein (Edward Elgar Publishing Ltd., Cheltenham, UK, and Northampton, MA, USA, 2009), pp.245-264.

44. A. Coutino, *A High-Frequency Model for Mexico.* Project LINK, 2005, website. http://www.chass.utoronto.ca/LINK.

45. Y. Inada, *A High-Frequency Model for Japan.* Project LINK, 2005, website. <http://www.chass.utoronto.ca/LINK.

46. L. R. Klein, V. Eskin and A. Roudoi, *Empirical Regularities in the Russian Economy.* Project LINK Spring Meeting. United Nations, New York, April 23-25 (2003).

47. L. R. Klein, V. Eskin and A. Roudoi, *University of Pennsylvania and Global Insight Current Quarter Model of the Russian Economy. Forecast Summary.* Project LINK, 2005, website. http://www.chass.utoronto.ca/LINK.

48. L. R. Klein. and W. Mak, *University of Pennsylvania Current Quarter Model of the Chinese Economy. Forecast Summary.* Project LINK, 2005, website. http://www.chass.utoronto.ca/LINK.

49. Kumasaka's ITEconomy.com .

50. M. Armesto, K. Engemann and M. Owyang, Forecasting with mixed frequencies, *Federal Reserve Bank of St. Louis Review*, November / December (2010).

51. C. Foroni, C. M. Marcellino, and C. Schumacher, U-MIDAS: MIDAS Regressions with Unrestricted Lag Polynomials, Discussion paper, Deutsche Bundesbank and European University Institute, 2011.

52. M. Marcellino and C. Schumacher, Factor-MIDAS for now- and forecasting with ragged-edge data: A model comparison for German GDP, *Oxford Bulletin of Economics and Statistics* **72**, 518-550 (2010).

53. L. G. Bersales, R. Reyes and J. de Guia, *A Composite Leading Economic Indicator for the Philippines*. Paper presented at the 9th National Convention of Statistics (Manila, Philippines, 2004).

54. R. Virola, R. Reyes, and F. Polistico, *The Leading Economic Indicator System (LEIS) in the Philippines*. Presented at the Third International Seminar on Early Warning and Business Cycle Indicators (Moscow, November 2010).

55. W. Zhang and J. Zhuang, *Leading Indicators of Business Cycles in Malaysia and the Philippines,* Economic and Research Department (ERD) Working Paper # 32, Asian Development Bank (December, 2002).

56. OECD Development Centre Asian Business Cycles Quarterly (2011) www.oecd.org/std/cli .

57. Philippine Statistics Authority National Statistical Coordination Board, *Leading Economic Indicators, First Quarter 2014*, (2014) http://www.nscb.gov.ph/lei/publication/PSA-NSCB_LEI%20Q12014.pdf

58. J. G. MacKinnon, *Critical Values for Co-integration Tests* in *Long-Run Economic Relationships*, eds. R. Engle and C. W. Granger, (Oxford University Press. Oxford, 1991).

59. T. W. Anderson, *An Introduction to Multivariate Statistical Analysis,* 2nd ed. (John Wiley, New York, 1984).

60. M. P. Clements and D. F. Hendry, *Forecasting Economic Time Series* (Cambridge University Press. Cambridge, 1998).

61. M. P. Clements and D. F. Hendry (eds.), *A Companion to Economic Forecasting* (Blackwell, Oxford, 2002).

62. F. X. Diebold and G. D. Rudebusch, Scoring the leading indicators, *Journal of Business* **62**, 369-391 (1989).

63. R. F. Engle and C. W. J. Granger, Cointegration and error-correction: representation, estimation, and testing, *Econometrica* **55**, 251-276 (1987).

64. R. F. Engle and C. W. J. Granger (eds.), *Long-Run Economic Relationships* (Oxford University Press, Oxford, 1991).

65. L. R. Klein and S. Ozmucur, *The Use of Surveys in Macroeconomic Forecasting* in *Macromodels'2001*, ed. W. Welfe (University of Lodz. Poland, 2001).

66. IHS Global Inc. *Eviews, 9.5*, (Irvine California, 2016). <www.eviews.com>.

67. S. Almon, The distributed lag between capital appropriations and net expenditures, *Econometrica* **33**, 178-196 (1965).

68. S. Almon, Lags between investment decisions and their causes, *Review of Economics and Statistics* **50**, 193-206 (1968).

69. F. X. Diebold and R. S. Mariano, Comparing predictive accuracy, *Journal of Business and Economic Statistics* **13**, 253-265 (1995).
70. H. Theil, *Economic Forecasts and Policy* (North-Holland, Amsterdam, 1958).
71. R. S. Mariano, *Testing Forecast Accuracy*, in *A Companion to Economic Forecasting* Clements, eds. M. P. and D. F. Hendry, (Blackwell. Oxford, 2002).
72. R. S. Mariano and D. Preve, Statistical tests for multiple forecast comparison, *Journal of Econometrics* **169**(1), 123-130 (2012).
73. R. S. Tsay, *Analysis of Financial Time Series,* 2nd ed., (John Wiley & Sons, Hoboken, New Jersey, 2005).

The use of models in macroeconomic forecasting at the OECD[a]

David Turner

Macroeconomic Analysis Division, Economics Department, OECD
Paris, France
E-mail: david.turner@oecd.org

This paper firstly describes the role of models in producing OECD global macroeconomic forecasts; secondly, reviews the OECD's forecasting track record; and finally, considers the relationship between forecast performance and models. OECD forecasts are not directly generated from a single global model, but instead rely heavily on expert judgment which is informed by inputs from a range of different models, with forecasts subjected to repeated peer review. For the major OECD economies, current year GDP growth forecasts exhibit a number of desirable properties including that they are unbiased, outperform naïve forecasts and mostly identify turning points. Moreover, there is a trend improvement in current-year forecasting performance which is partly attributed to the increasing use of high frequency 'now-casting' indicator models to forecast the current and next quarter's GDP. Conversely, the track record of one-year-ahead forecasts is much less impressive; such forecasts are biased, often little better than naïve forecasts and are poor at anticipating downturns. Forecasts tend to cluster around those from other international organizations and consensus forecasts; it is particularly striking that differences in one-year-ahead forecasts between forecasters are relatively minor in comparison with the size of average errors made by all of them. This may reflect herding behaviour by forecasters as well as the mean reversion properties of models. These weaknesses in forecasting performance beyond the current year underline the importance of increased efforts to use models to characterize the risk distribution around the baseline forecast, including through the increased use of model-based scenario analysis.

Keywords: Forecasting; Economic outlook; Models; GDP growth; Proceedings; World Scientific Publishing.

·

---

[a] The views expressed in this paper should not be reported as representing the official views of the OECD or of its member countries. The opinions expressed and arguments employed are those of the author. This paper is based on a presentation given at a conference on 'Global Economic Modelling' in honour of Lawrence Klein in Toronto in June 2015, with comments from the conference participants, especially Ken Wallis, gratefully acknowledged. The author has worked in the Economics Department at the OECD since 1991, since which time he has been involved in OECD forecasts in a variety of capacities; since 2009 he has been Head of the Macroeconomic Analysis Division, which is the division responsible for most of the models which are described in this chapter. The work of numerous colleagues at the OECD, on which this chapter heavily draws are gratefully acknowledged as well as thoughtful comments on an earlier draft from Nigel Pain and Cyrille Schwellnus. Thanks are also due both to the Independent Evaluation Office of the IMF and to the National Institute for Economic and Social Research for sharing data on forecast errors. My particular thanks to statistical analysis from Jeroen Meyer and Gil Parola and help in document preparation from Veronica Humi.

1. Introduction

The award of the Nobel Prize for Economics to Lawrence Klein in 1980 recognized his general contribution to macroeconomic modelling, including his role as the leader of the LINK project aiming to produce the world's first global economic forecasting model and in doing so opening up *"a completely new line of development of great theoretical and practical value"*[1,b] In the light of Klein's pioneering work on global macro modelling, this paper reviews the use of models, broadly defined, as they are currently used at the OECD in producing global macroeconomic forecasts. It is worth emphasizing at the outset that OECD forecasts are not directly generated from a single global model, which might appear more in keeping with Klein's legacy. While a global model does play a role, OECD forecasts are instead produced using a combination of different models combined with expert judgement and peer review by both insiders and outsiders. This process can be characterized as a means to reconcile a 'bottom-up' approach, in which country forecasts are based largely on the judgement of experts with detailed knowledge of that country, and a more model-based 'top-down' approach, which ensures that forecasts are based on common assumptions and that linkages between countries are properly accounted for.

The rest of the paper describes the role of models in OECD forecasts, reviews the forecasting track record and considers the relationship between the two. It is organized as follows: the next section provides an overview of the forecasting round at the OECD, since an appreciation of this context is essential for understanding the role of models in the process; in Section 3 the various modelling tools which are used in generating OECD forecasts are discussed; in Section 4 the OECD's forecasting track record is reviewed; Section 5 provides some concluding remarks, including speculation on how the use of models may have influenced forecast performance as well as highlighting recent changes in the forecast process.

2. The Forecasting Round

The forecasts published twice a year in the OECD *Economic Outlook* are the outcome of a forecasting round which lasts seven to eight weeks. The length of this process is necessitated by the series of reviews to which the forecasts are subjected and so is a reflection of the relative weight which is attached to judgement, rather than relying on the mechanical outcome from a single model. In between the publication of OECD *Economic Outlooks*, an interim update of the forecasts is published. However, the procedures underlying this interim update, including the use of models, are less intensive, with the main focus on GDP and developments in the largest economies. Nevertheless, these interim updates are important, not least because they provide a more up-to-date 'baseline' for the following *Economic Outlook* Forecast Round.

---

[b] Klein was particularly passionate about his work on global macro modelling; in reviewing the modelling work in which he was involved, he commented "… my true love for both research and substance remains the LINK system"[2].

The *Economic Outlook* forecast round starts with a scene-setting meeting known as the General Internal Meeting (or 'GIM') of all economists involved in the forecasts.[c] The purpose of this meeting is to provide guidance on how the forecasts should be revised relative to the previous published forecasts. This will involve taking stock of new information which has become available since the last forecast, particularly new data and the implications of the most recent high frequency monthly data. It will also involve an evaluation of the main changes in the 'forces acting', for example due to changes in commodity prices, exchange rates, monetary policy, other financial variables and fiscal policy.

The central guidance from the GIM has become more specific, formalized and been given greater weight in recent years reflecting a perception that cross-country spillovers from shocks have become increasingly important and may have contributed to similar forecasting errors across many OECD countries.[d,e] Following the GIM, economists with specialized knowledge of particular countries, known internally as 'Country Desks', are responsible for submitting a preliminary forecast for individual countries. Country Desks have experience of monitoring specific OECD or non-OECD economies in order to produce a regular *Economic Survey* of that country and the expertise and contacts which they gain through this monitoring process means they are well placed to provide a macroeconomic forecast for 'their' country.

Once a preliminary set of forecasts have been generated for each country, the responsible Country Desks present their forecasts and are cross-examined on various aspects of them at the 'Internal Departmental Meeting' (or 'IDM'). On the basis of this internal scrutiny, the country forecasts are revised before being subject to external scrutiny at the meeting for 'Short Term Economic Prospects' (or 'STEP'), where (the still preliminary) OECD forecasts are systematically compared with national forecasts at a meeting attended by external country delegates with experience of forecasting, most often from Finance Ministries. Following discussion at the STEP meeting, and also to reflect new information which has since become available, the forecasts are revised a final time before being published in the OECD *Economic Outlook*. The forecast provides a focus for a narrative on the world economy and so a basis for policy assessment and advice which are also elaborated in the *Economic Outlook*.

---

[c] Each meeting of the forecasting round is commonly referred to by an obscure acronym (GIM, IDM, STEP) which confuses newcomers, but to which insiders become quickly accustomed.

[d] In a review of forecasting errors over the crisis period, Pain et al.[3] found that growth was typically weaker and errors higher in countries that were more open to external developments and exposed to shocks from other economies.

[e] The degree of centralisation in terms of top-down guidance that OECD Directors issue to Country Desks, is arguably now greater than in the forecast procedures of most other international organisations[4].

3.   The Role of Models

The most important modelling tools which contribute to OECD forecasts include: a global macroeconomic model; now-casting models; a trade model; and a 'Forecast Entry' model by which Country Desks enter their forecasts into a central database. The emphasis here is less on the detailed specifications underlying these models than on how they contribute to the forecasting process, although readers interested in the former should find further details in the appended references.

3.1.   *Global macroeconomic models*

While global macroeconomic models do not directly generate OECD forecasts they do contribute to the process. For this purpose, a succession of global models has, until recently, been constructed and maintained 'in-house' since the 1980s (Table 1). However, given the resource-cost of updating and maintaining a global model, the OECD decided from around 2010 to make use of the NIGEM global model which is provided by the National Institute for Economic and Social Research (NIESR) in the United Kingdom.

Table 1.   Global Macro Models Used in the Forecasting Process at the OECD

	Date from	No. countries/ regions	No. vars in large country sub-model	Frequency	Wealth variables?	Forward-looking?
INTERLINK[*]	Early 1980s	30	250	Semi-annual	No	No
Small Global Model[**]	2001	4	<20	Quarterly	No	Yes
OECD Global Model[***]	2006	9	300	Quarterly	Yes	No
NiGEM[****]	2010*	50	500	Quarterly	Yes	Yes

Notes:
[*]See Richardson[5] and Daalsgard et al.[6]
[**]See Rae and Turner[7].
[***]See Hervé et al.[8]
[****]See NIESR[9].

The INTERLINK model[5] — a large global model on a semi-annual frequency with distinct models for each OECD country and regional models covering the non-OECD — was used throughout much of the 1980s and 1990s. A number of trends in the subsequent global models used by the OECD can be identified: reflecting a similar change in the published forecasts, there has been a move to a quarterly frequency; increased importance has been attached to the possibility of being able to run the model with forward-looking model-consistent expectations particularly to model the transmission of shocks through financial markets; and increased importance has been attached to modelling wealth in the transmission of shocks. The trend in the size of successive model is less obvious (Table 1): following INTERLINK there was a short-lived flirtation with a small global model with few regions and few variables in each region[7]; a new OECD global model[8] then focused on modelling only the largest countries and regions, although with a large number of variables particularly to capture wealth effects; finally, NIGEM[9] is the largest of the global models which has been used by the OECD, both in terms of the number of countries and variables covered in a typical country.

NIGEM separately distinguishes most OECD countries and the largest non-OECD countries, with other countries modelled in terms of regional blocks. It is based around a 'New-Keynesian' framework, with the long-run properties of equations imposed consistent with theory, but with dynamic adjustment estimated using historical data, so striking a balance between theory and data. Financial markets are presumed to be forward-looking, but with liquidity constraints, myopic behaviour and nominal rigidities in other sectors slowing the process of adjustment to shocks, although the model is also designed to be flexible so that assumptions regarding behaviour and policy can be readily changed.

The 'rental' and use in the forecasting round of a model from outside the OECD has the advantage of avoiding the heavy development and maintenance costs associated with a large scale global model. It also has the advantage that it comes with an established reputation given a wide user base – which in the case of NIGEM includes many users from central banks and finance ministries – and comes with a body of published papers describing the use of the model in policy exercises. The disadvantages of using an 'outside model' is that when model properties are queried (as, is inevitable with any large-scale macro model) those responsible for running the model are less willing and able to defend it, as it is "not their baby". Moreover, modifying the model in response to such criticism is difficult, whereas if the model was maintained "in-house" then critical feedback could more easily be channelled into amending and improving the model. [f]

3.1.1. The role of the global model in assessing changes in 'forces acting' since the previous forecast

The global model plays a role in "setting the scene" at the start of each forecast round, by evaluating the macroeconomic effect of changes since the last published projections in commodity prices exchange rates, interest rates, fiscal policy, the path of economic activity and other key conditioning variables. The effects of the new elements and revised judgments are typically assessed on the basis of model simulations using the global model and their effects on GDP and inflation are evaluated. These results are only one input to inform central guidance at the GIM, which in turn influences the Desks who are responsible for submitting country forecasts.

---

[f] A recent example of this is the tendency for NIGEM to generate more pronounced changes in inflation in model simulations than seems to be consistent with recent experience of the relative stability of inflation in the wake of the financial crisis[10], which may be explained by the fact that the NIGEM model equations are estimated over a longer sample in which inflation was more volatile.

3.1.2. *The role of the global model in constructing alternative scenarios*

Probably the most important use of the global model is to consider variant scenarios around the central forecast, based on alternative assumptions about policy or key conditioning variables such as commodity prices. The scenarios are often published alongside a commentary on the central forecast in the *General Assessment* overview chapter of the *Economic Outlook* and have been given greater emphasis since the financial crisis, as a means of illustrating uncertainty and risks surrounding the central forecast. Past scenarios have covered a range of issues, which have recently included:

- A stylized downside scenario in the euro area [Box 1.6[11]];
- Quantifying the macroeconomic effects of a binding US debt ceiling [Box 1.4[12]];
- Risks in China's financial system and potential spillovers [Box 1.1[13]];
- Potential energy market spillovers from events in Ukraine [Box 1.2[14]];
- The global impact of weaker demand growth in China [Box 1.2[15]];
- The impact of an increase in public investment in OECD economies [Box 1.6,[15]];
- Financial market shocks from Brexit [Box 1.1[16]].

3.2. *Financial Conditions Indices*

With the onset of the financial crisis, greater effort has been made to quantify forces acting through financial markets with the development of financial conditions indices for the major OECD countries[17]. These capture the effect of broadly defined financial conditions on economic activity and include not only standard text-book measures of policy interest rates and exchange rates, but also survey measures of bank lending conditions and interest rate spreads (the difference between government interest rates and the rates at which companies can borrow). The latter, less conventional, components are typically less well captured, if at all, in large macroeconomic models, but have been important in tracking the adverse effects of the financial crisis. Changes in these FCIs provide information, in addition to that provided by global model simulations, on the 'forces acting' since the last publication forecast and so provide further guidance as to how the forecasts should be revised.

3.3. *Now-casting models*

For the major OECD and non-OECD economies, the near-term assessment also takes account of projections from a suite of statistical models using high frequency indicators to provide estimates of near-term quarterly GDP growth, typically for the current and next quarter.[g] These OECD models were first used in the forecasting process after 2000 and build on the work of Sédillot and Pain[19], Mourougane[20] and Chalaux and Schwellnus[21] in using short term economic indicators to predict quarterly movements in GDP by efficiently exploiting monthly and quarterly information. The models combine information from both

---

[g] The development of the high-frequency short-term forecasting models was another aspect of macro modelling which Klein actively pursued, particularly in the later stages of his career, see for example Klein and Ozmucur[18].

"soft" indicators, such as business sentiment and consumer surveys, and "hard" indicators, such as industrial production and retail sales, with use being made of different frequencies of data and a variety of estimation techniques. The procedures are relatively automated and can be run whenever major monthly data are released, allowing updating and choice of model according to the information set available.

The most important gains from using these models are found to be for current-quarter forecasts made at or immediately after the start of the quarter in question, where estimated indicator models appear to outperform autoregressive time series models, both in terms of size of error and directional accuracy. The main gains from using a monthly approach arise once one month of data is available for the quarter being forecast, typically two to three months before the publication of the first official outturn estimate for GDP. For one-quarter-ahead projections, the performance of the estimated indicator models is noticeably better than simpler time series models once one or two months of information become available for the quarter preceding that being forecast. The recent performance of these statistical indicator models, suggest that in 'normal times' without any information for the quarter, the 70% confidence band around the quarter-on-quarter GDP forecast (non-annualized) averages plus or minus 0.4 percentage points for the major OECD economies, declining to plus or minus 0.3 percentage points when a complete set of monthly indicators is available.[h]

Outside of 'normal times', a post-mortem evaluation of forecasts over the period of the financial crisis, concluded the OECD's indicator models for GDP *provided a very useful real-time signal of a significant slowdown and then major contraction*[3]. The models were slow to predict the strength of the contraction in the third quarter of 2008, but thereafter the downturn and bounce-back were highlighted relatively quickly (Figure 1).

3.4. *The forecast entry system*

The physical input of OECD forecasts is achieved through a purpose-built 'Forecast Entry' system which for the user resembles an elaborate spreadsheet. The system both centralizes the forecast data management process and allows Country Desks to view most recent data outcomes, new information and common assumptions as well as to input and revise the projections for the countries for which they are responsible in a consistent manner. Typically, a Country Desk will be responsible for: quarterly forecasts of about 60 macroeconomic variables, with another 150 or so variables being built-up by identities and about 60 variables such as exchange rates or commodity prices being set exogenously according to centrally agreed assumptions. At the same time, the system maintains the consistency and coherence of the data set by incorporating all the relevant national accounts, trade and other accounting identities linking the various concepts. Thus, as individual forecast components are updated and submitted, all identities are automatically

---

[h] The figures quoted are for an average of the United States, Germany, the United Kingdom, France and Italy over the period 2005-14, but excluding the volatile period of the financial crisis 2008-9. They also exclude Japan, for which GDP data is notably more volatile and so the confidence bands correspondingly wider.

re-evaluated to provide a fully consistent data set. The system also provides guidelines in the form of equation-based estimates or rules of thumb for more than half of the variables which the Country Desk is responsible for forecasting. Desks are at liberty to use these guidelines, ignore them or replace them with their own equations.

Annualized quarter-on-quarter percentage changes, 2007q1 – 2012q4

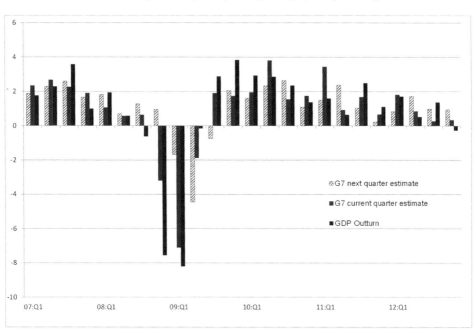

Fig. 1. OECD Indicator Model Estimates and G7 GDP Growth.

Note: Outturn is defined as the published figure at the following Economic Outlook. Indicator model estimates shown are real-time estimates, typically from the last month of the quarter. Data are weighted using nominal GDP at PPP rates in 2010.
Source: Pain et al. [3]

3.5. *The trade model and global consistency*

A small Trade Team is tasked with monitoring the global consistency of trade and the balance of payments throughout the forecast round. While errors and omissions mean that global exports are not equal to global imports in historical data, an objective of the Trade Team is to ensure that these inconsistencies do not grow over the forecast period. A growing global balance-of-payments discrepancy over the forecast horizon would be problematic for the consistency of the forecasts; for example, as a matter of accounting, not all countries can simultaneously gain from a boost to net exports. This is of particular relevance when one of the issues which has most exercised policy-makers in recent years is increasing imbalances between countries, as it would imply an increasing imbalance of the world with Mars.[i] Where there are signs of an increasing global inconsistency, the Trade Team endeavours to correct it, usually by interacting with the Desks responsible for the country forecasts which depart from the trade model in a direction which contributes to the global imbalance. The trade model provides projections for the key aggregate national accounts trade variables for each country, which take account of domestic activity, export weighted markets, relative price competitiveness and trend developments[23].

While the OECD's world trade forecast is built as the aggregation of individual country import and export forecasts, additional tools are used to assess the short term evolution of world trade. Two types of indicator models have been developed to forecast world trade in the short term: one approach uses a bridge equation model based on world industrial production, export orders, technology indicators, oil prices and the Baltic dry index; a second approach is based on a dynamic factor model using an extended dataset (see Guichard and Rusticelli[24]). In addition, a global equation linking world trade growth to world GDP growth is used to assess the consistency of world trade and world GDP forecasts, drawing on the work of Ollivaud and Schwellnus[25]. To the extent that possible inconsistencies are identified, this information is used iteratively by the Trade Team in guiding the more detailed forecast components at country and regional levels.

4.   The Forecasting Track Record

The OECD has regularly published reviews of its forecasting performance[3,26,27], this section provides a summary of some of the key findings from these reviews.

4.1.   *Forecast performance for the current year is much better than for the following year*

It is not surprising that forecast errors tend to increase with the length of the forecast horizon, but current year forecasts also display a number of desirable properties which are not present in one-year–ahead forecasts.[j] Vogel[27] analyses GDP growth forecasts for the G7 over the pre-crisis period 1991-2006 and finds:

- Current-year projections are unbiased, whereas one-year-ahead projections tend to persistently overestimate outcomes during low-growth episodes and show little sensitivity to initial cyclical conditions;
- Current-year projections add value to naïve forecasts, such as the sample means or previous realizations, but this is not the case for one-year-ahead forecasts, for which on average naïve forecasts were found to be a more accurate guide;
- Current-year forecasts: correctly predict turning points in about three-quarters of cases, but only 6% of cases in one-year-ahead forecasts.

---

[i]*The Economist* magazine, in an article titled '*Export to Mars*'[22], highlighted a recent IMF forecast in which the global current account surplus doubled over the forecast horizon, raising the question "*Are aliens buying Louis Vuitton handbags?*"

[j] For the purposes of this paper, current-year forecasts refer to those published in May of the same year, whereas one-year-ahead forecasts refer to the May forecast for the following year.

Pain et al.[3] analyze GDP growth forecasts over the period 2007-2012, including the crisis, and find:

- Formal tests of bias, suggest that both current-year and one-year-ahead forecasts tended to be systematically over estimated over the period 2007-2012, but the average over prediction for OECD countries for the current year was only 0.15 percentage points, whereas for the one-year-ahead forecast it was 1.5 percentage points, i.e. ten times greater.
- Formal statistical tests suggest that both current-year and one-year ahead forecasts do not 'encompass' a naïve forecast, although the magnitude of the estimated coefficients are such as to suggest that, for practical purposes, current-year forecasts come close to encompassing a naïve forecast.[k]
- Analyzing the directional accuracy of G7 growth forecasts over a longer period (1971-2012), current-year forecasts are found to correctly predict growth accelerations and decelerations in 80-90% of cases, but one-year-ahead forecasts correctly identify growth decelerations in less than 50% of cases.

4.2.   Current-year forecast performance has improved over time

Abstracting from the immediate impact years of the financial crisis, the forecast performance of GDP growth for the current year published in May of the same year has exhibited a trend improvement over time. Thus, the root mean square forecast error of GDP growth for the G7 countries for the current year has tended to fall both in absolute terms (Figure 2) and when normalized on the volatility of GDP growth (Table 2). The decline in the RMSE probably partly reflects a decline in the volatility of GDP growth, however the RMSE has continued to decline even though the volatility of growth has picked up after the crisis. On the other hand, there is no obvious sign of any trend improvement in the corresponding one-year-ahead forecasts.

4.3.   Forecasts are strikingly similar to the consensus and other international organizations

There is a close correlation in forecast errors between the OECD, other international organizations and consensus forecasts. This synchronicity of errors is most striking for the one-year-ahead forecasts, especially given the paucity of these forecasts in other respects,

---

[k]The formal test involves regressing the outcome on an intercept, lagged outcome and official forecast with the official forecast 'encompassing' a naïve forecast if the regression coefficients on the intercept and lagged outcome are insignificantly different from zero. While the current-year coefficient on the lagged outcome is statistically significant, its value is only -0.07 whereas the coefficient on the forecast (0.95) is close to unity and the intercept term is insignificant.

as discussed previously in section 4.1. For the major seven economies, over the period 1991-2011, the average absolute difference in one-year-ahead forecasts between the OECD and IMF, or OECD and consensus, is 0.2 – 0.4 percentage points, which is typically about one-quarter of the size of the average absolute error across all forecasts for the respective country, with the latter varying from 1.1 percentage points for France to 2.1 percentage points for Japan (Figure 3).[1] Over the entire period 1991-2011 and for all G7 countries, the difference between OECD and IMF, or OECD and consensus forecasts has never exceeded the average absolute forecast error for that country.

Table 2. The Root-Mean-Square Error of OECD GDP Growth Forecasts

Unweighted mean of G7 countries

	Percentage points of GDP		Ratio to standard deviation of growth	
	May projection for current year	May projection for next year	May projection for current year	May projection for next year
1971-2012	1.0	n.a.	0.4	n.a.
1971-1981	1.3	n.a	0.5	n.a.
1982-1990	1.0	1.7	0.6	1.0
1991-2006	0.7	1.6	0.5	1.2
2007-2012	0.7	2.7	0.3	1.1

Note: Errors are calculated as actual growth less projected growth at each forecast horizon, where actual growth is the published outturn as at May the following year. May projections for the following year are only available from 1982.
Source: Pain et al.[3]

4.4.   *Forecasts are still particularly vulnerable around major global shocks*

Forecast errors of the OECD and other international organizations were unusually large around the financial crisis with the largest errors occurring at the height of the financial crisis; the average unweighted error (over-prediction) across all OECD countries of GDP growth forecasts made in May 2008 for calendar year 2009 was more than 5 percentage points (see Figure 11 of Pain et al.[3]). Such forecast failings are, however, not unprecedented, with forecast errors being of a similar order of magnitude to those experienced around the first oil price shock in the early 1970s.

Indeed, Klein was particularly exercised by the forecast failures that occurred around the time of the first oil shock, noting: "*The turbulent period of the second half (or two-thirds) of the 1970s was very difficult for forecasters,*"[28]. He further argued that "*the principal issue is that models did not properly integrate food, fuel and flexible exchange rates into their equation systems*", but that the experience was also a learning opportunity which should lead to the subsequent improvement of models. Similarly, a review of the forecasting failures around the financial crisis has led to changes in forecasting models and

---

[1.]Comparisons of OECD forecasts with those of the European Commission, as well as the IMF and consensus, over the period 2007-12 find similar synchronicity of errors, see in particular Figure 11 of Pain et al.[3]

procedures[3], which hopefully will improve forecasting performance. Nevertheless, their poor performance over the period of the financial crisis serves as a reminder of the limitation of macroeconomic forecasts in the face of major global shocks. It also reinforces the case for scenario analysis to examine the implications of costly tail risks, especially because their precise timing is usually hard to predict.

Unweighted G7 average, 5 year-windows

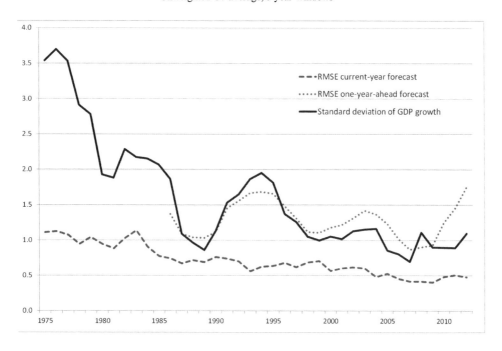

Fig. 2. Forecast Accuracy and Volatility of GDP Growth.

Note: Data points are for 5-year averages of rolling windows, but exclude the immediate impact of the financial crisis by excluding 2008 from the calculation of the RMSE of the current-year forecast and by excluding 2009 from the calculation of the one-year-ahead forecast and the standard deviation of growth.
Source: Authors calculations based on data in Pain et al.[3]

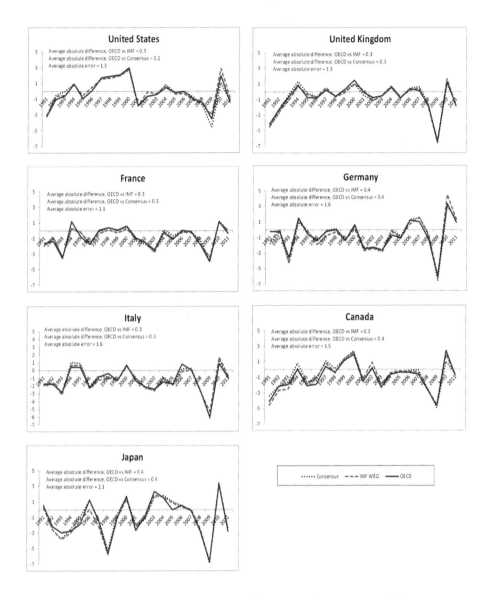

Fig. 3. One-Year-Ahead Forecast Errors for GDP Growth (percentage points).

Note: One-year-ahead forecast errors are calculated from the May forecast of the preceding year. The outturn for GDP growth is taken as the realization two years later (to allow for data revisions). Given the similarity in errors, the average absolute error shown for each country is the average across OECD, IMF and consensus forecasts.
Source: Independent Evaluation Committee of the IMF[4] and OECD calculations.

5. Concluding Remarks

Any macroeconomic forecast is likely to be partly model-based and partly judgement-based. Indeed, Klein recognized the importance of the combination of both model and judgement, asserting that the forecast record of such a combination has been *"superior to pure model applications or pure-human-judgement applications"*[28]. The forecasting process at the OECD is designed to give a high weight to expert judgement, subject to close and repeated scrutiny. The approach is similar to that adopted in other international organizations such as the IMF and European Commission[4,29]. The advantage of this approach is that it places much of the responsibility for forecasting on country experts who follow day-to-day economic developments in that country and allows them to adopt whatever model (formal or otherwise) that they judge best suited to capture the particular features of the economy in question. While OECD forecasts cannot be traced back to a single global model, in the way that LINK forecasts could be, a variety of models do play a role in the forecast process as described in Section 3.

What would be the potential benefits and costs of generating OECD forecasts directly from a single global model more in keeping with the LINK approach? An advantage of model-based forecasts is that it is possible to separate out the extent to which forecast errors reflect model errors, incorrect judgements about exogenous factors or errors of judgement by forecasters (see Wallis et al.[30-33]). Such feedback might possibly lead to future improvements in forecasting performance, including in model specification. A more model-based forecast might also enhance consistency with a narrative on the global economy and scenario analysis, particularly if some important developments are likely to play out beyond the short-term forecast horizon. On the other hand, greater reliance on a global model would risk leading to a loss of accountability and ownership by the country experts who deal on a bilateral basis with national governments. This would be particularly unfortunate to the extent that the macroeconomic outlook provides an important context for policy analysis and recommendations in OECD country surveys. The remaining remarks speculate on how the particular combination of models and judgement involved in OECD forecasts may have influenced the forecasting track record, however, as explained below, it would be surprising if switching to a more model-based approach were to lead to significant improvements in forecasting performance.

The track record of OECD forecasts as summarized in Section 4, is mixed; the record for current-year forecasts appears more positive, being unbiased, encompassing naïve forecasts and mostly identifying turning points. There are also some signs of a trend improvement with a gradual decline in the root-mean-square error of current-year forecasts. Conversely, one-year-ahead forecasts are often little better than naïve forecasts and display no obvious signs of trend improvement. Perhaps of greater concern — given that the forecasts are the basis for policy assessment and advice — is that one-year-ahead forecasts are biased and particularly poor at anticipating downturns. This record is, however, consistent with Klein's views about the time frame for reliable forecasting: *"…one year horizons are quite sensible for useful economic forecasting, but errors are much larger over longer stretches of time"*[28] and is also consistent with more recent analyses of both statistical models and professional forecasters which suggest that forecast performance of GDP growth is poor beyond horizons further ahead than one quarter[34,35]. This in turn probably reflects the complex, dynamic and non-linear nature of the processes underlying economic growth, so that unforeseen future events or small differences in initial conditions can have large unforeseen consequences[39].

The longer-run trend improvement in current-year forecasting performance is probably partly explained by a decline in the volatility of GDP growth and possibly the increased accessibility and timeliness of national accounts data and other hard indicators. However, more recent improvements in forecast performance, despite increased volatility of post-crisis growth, are likely due to the introduction of, increasing weight given to, and improved performance of, high frequency now-casting indicator models to forecast the current and next quarter GDP. For the May current-year GDP forecast, an outturn for the first quarter will sometimes be available, with the indicator models providing guidance for the second and third quarter growth rates, while the fourth quarter growth rate has relatively little weight in the calculation of the calendar year-on-year growth rate[37]. In these circumstances, accurate predictions from the indicator models virtually guarantee a reasonable forecast of year-over-year GDP growth for the current calendar year (notwithstanding subsequent data revisions). Research at the OECD is ongoing to further improve these models,[m] and future developments, including the possibility of making use of 'big data', suggest further improvements in short-term forecasting performance might be possible.

As well as the poor performance of one-year-ahead forecasts, it is disconcerting that errors are so similar across international organizations and consensus forecasts, not just on average, but on a period-by-period basis (as illustrated in Figure 3).[n] To some degree this is the inevitable consequence of all forecasters failing to anticipate major future economic events, such as oil shocks or financial crises coupled with forecasters' tendency to predict a relatively rapid reversion to long-run trend growth rates. This may be reinforced by herding behaviour among forecasters as "it is always safer to be wrong in a crowd"[36]. Such herding behaviour is discussed in a recent review of IMF forecasts: *"desk economists may hesitate to deviate from consensus forecasts, because "rocking the boat" in this way would call for lengthy and elaborate justifications in the course of the departmental and interdepartmental review process"*[4]. An interesting question is whether dispersion is likely to be greater among forecasts which are more model-based than judgement-based. An example of the greater dispersion of more model-based forecasts are the published forecasts of UK GDP growth over the 1980s generated on rival models analyzed in detail

---

[m] Recent OECD research[38] has compared the forecasting performance of state-of the-art' Dynamic Factor Models that synthesize information from a large number of indicators against small-scale bridge models which are currently used at the OECD. It concludes that monitoring a large number of indicators adds noise rather than relevant information and so there is no gain from switching from the models currently being used.

[n] While there is also a high degree of synchronicity among current-year forecasts it is less disconcerting. Firstly, this is because current-year forecasts exhibit many desirable properties (unbiasedness, identification of turning points and bettering of naïve forecasts) which year-ahead forecasts do not. Secondly, relative to average forecasts errors, the dispersion in current-year forecasts is greater than that of a year-ahead forecasts.

by the ESRC Macroeconomic Modelling Bureau, see for example Figure 1 in Wallis[40] and Table 4.7 of Wallis et al.[33]. On the other hand, forecasts for the G7 countries of one-year-ahead GDP growth (comparable to those shown in Figure 3) published by the *National Institute for Economic and Social Research* and generated on the NIGEM model exhibit a similar synchronicity of forecast errors with consensus, IMF and OECD forecasts.[o] This may be because macroeconomic models typically have an intrinsic property towards mean reversion[36]. A corollary is that it would be surprising if greater reliance on a global model to generate OECD forecasts led to a significant improvement in forecast performance.

After reviewing the experience of forecasting over the crisis period, most international organizations have made a greater effort to characterize the risk distribution around their baseline forecast[3]. In the case of the OECD, this has been through giving greater emphasis to commentary as to whether risks are balanced around the central forecast and through the increased use of model-based scenario analysis to illustrate key risks. The importance of models in this role was recognized by Klein who noted that: *"Policy alternatives may be studied on the basis of validated models. That is surely one of the most important applications (policy alternatives), more important in many respects than pure generation of forecasts"*[28]. Other international organizations, such as the IMF, have gone further in publishing forecast ranges, fan charts and assessments of the likelihood of the occurrence of particular events, such as recession or deflation. The OECD has also recently been carrying out work to evaluate the usefulness of early warning indicators which can signal the probability of an imminent severe recession or crisis[43,44], although this has not yet been incorporated as part of the regular commentary around the central forecast. Such developments, which explicitly recognize the inevitable uncertainty around global macroeconomic forecasts, appear particularly appropriate given the paucity of the forecast track-record of all international organizations beyond the current year. Such developments also represent another way in which different models, broadly defined, can have an important influence on global macroeconomic forecasts and their presentation.

References

1. Royal Swedish Academy of Sciences, *The Prize in Economics 1980* – Press release, http://nobelpeaceprize.org/ (1980).
2. L. R. Klein, *The Link Model and its Use in International Scenario Analysis, in Economic Modelling in the OECD Countries*, ed. H. Motamen (Chapman and Hall, London, 1988), pp. 1-10.

---

[o] The average absolute difference of one-year-ahead NIESR forecasts of GDP growth and those of the OECD, IMF and consensus is within 0.1 percentage points of the average absolute difference between the OECD, IMF and consensus for every G7 country over the period 1991-2011. See Kirby et al.[42] for an evaluation of NIESR's forecast performance for the United Kingdom, United States and euro area.

3. N. Pain, C. Lewis, T.-T. Dang, Y. Ji and P. Richardson, *OECD Forecasts During and After the Financial Crisis: A Post-Mortem*, OECD Economics Department Working Papers, No. 1107 (OECD Publishing, Paris, 2014).

4. IEO, IMF Forecasts: *Process, Quality, and Country Perspectives*, Independent Evaluation (IEO) of the International Fund, (2014), http://www.ieo-imf.org/ieo/pages/EvaluationImages181.aspx.

5. P. Richardson, *The Structure and Simulation Properties of the OECD's INTERLINK Model*, OECD Economic Department Working Papers, No. 10 (OECD Publishing, Paris, 1988), http://www.oecd.org/eco/outlook/31705400.pdf.

6. T. Daalsgard, C. Andre, P. Richardson, *Standard Shocks in the OECD Interlink Model*, OECD Economic Department Working Papers, No. 306 (OECD Publishing, Paris, 2001).

7. D. Rae, and D. Turner, *A Small Global Forecasting Model*, OECD Economics Department Working Papers, No. 286 (OECD Publishing, Paris, 2001).

8. K. Hervé, N. Pain, P. Richardson, F. Sedillot and P.-O. Beffy, *The OECD's New Global Model*, OECD Economics Department Working Papers, No. 768, OECD Publishing, (Paris, 2010).

9. NIESR, *NiGEM Overview*, National Institute of Economic and Social Research, (London, 2016) https://nimodel.niesr.ac.uk/

10. IMF, *The Dog That Didn't Bark: Has Inflation Been Muzzled or Was It Just Sleeping* in *World Economic Outlook*, April. (IMF, 2013).

11. OECD, *OECD Economic Outlook*, No. 92, November (OECD Publishing, Paris, 2012).

12. OECD, *OECD Economic Outlook*, No. 93, May (OECD Publishing, Paris. 2013).

13. OECD, *OECD Economic Outlook*, No. 95, May (OECD Publishing, Paris, 2014a).

14. OECD, *OECD Economic Outlook*, No. 96, November (OECD Publishing, Paris, 2014b).

15. OECD, *OECD Economic Outlook*, No. 98, November (OECD Publishing, Paris, 2015).

16. OECD, *OECD Economic Outlook*, No. 99, May (OECD Publishing, Paris, 2016).

17. S. Guichard, D. Haugh and D. Turner, *Quantifying the Effect of Financial Conditions in the Euro Area, Japan, United Kingdom and United States*, OECD Economics Department Working Papers, No. 677 (OECD Publishing, Paris, 2009).

18. L. R. Klein, and S. Ozmucur, *The University of Pennsylvania Models for High Frequency Macroeconomic Modelling in Econometric Forecasting and High-frequency Data Analysis*, eds. R. Mariano and Y. K. Tse, (World Scientific Publishing, 1991).

19. F. Sedillot and N. Pain, *Indicator Models of Real GDP Growth in Selected OECD Countries*, OECD Economics Department Working Papers, No. 364, (OECD Publishing, Paris, 2003), http://EconPapers.repec.org/RePEc:oec:ecoaaa:364-en.

20. Mourougane, *Forecasting Monthly GDP for Canada*, OECD Economics Department Working Papers, No. 515, OECD Publishing (Paris, 2006).

21. T. Chalaux and C. Schwellnus, *Short-term Indicator Models for Quarterly GDP Growth in the BRIICS: A Small-scale Bridge Model Approach*, OECD Economics Department Working Papers, No. 1109 (OECD Publishing, Paris, 2014).

22. The Economist, *Exports to Mars* (The Economist, Nov 12, 2011), http://www.economist.com/node/21538100?fsrc=scn/tw/te/ar/exportstomars

23. M. Morin and C. Schwellnus, *An Update of the OECD International Trade Equations*, OECD Economics Department Working Papers, No. 1129 (OECD Publishing, Paris, 2014), http://dx.doi.org/10.1787/5jz2bxbkrxmv-en.

24. S. Guichard and E. Rusticelli, *A Dynamic Factor Model for World Trade Growth*, OECD Economics Department Working Papers, No. 874 (OECD Publishing, Paris, 2011). DOI: http://dx.doi.org/10.1787/5kg9zbvvwqq2-en.

25. P. Ollivaud, and C. Schwellnus, *Does the Post-crisis Weakness of Global Trade Solely Reflect Weak Demand?* OECD Economics Department Working Papers, No. 1216 (OECD Publishing, Paris, 2015).

26. V. Koutsogeorgopoulou, *A Post-mortem on Economic Outlook Projections*, OECD Economics Department Working Papers, No. 274, (OECD Publishing, Paris, 2014) DOI: http://dx.doi.org/10.1787/351822846618.

27. L. Vogel, *How Do the OECD Growth Projections for the G7 Economies Perform: A Post-mortem*, OECD Economics Department Working Papers, No. 573 (OECD Publishing, Paris, 2007).

28. L. R. Klein, *Econometric Models as Guides for Decision-making* (Free Press, New York, 1982).

29. ADE and DIW, *Evaluation of Forecasting Services of the Directorate General Economic and Financial Affairs*, Final Report (Berlin, 2007).

30. K. F. Wallis, (ed.) *Models of the Economy* (Oxford University Press, Oxford, 1984).

31. K. F. Wallis, (ed.) *Models of the Economy* (Oxford University Press, Oxford, 1985).

32. K. F. Wallis, (ed.) *Models of the Economy* (Oxford University Press, Oxford, 1986).

33. K. F. Wallis, (ed.) *Models of the Economy* (Oxford University Press, Oxford, 1987).

34. T. Stark, Realistic *Evaluation of Real-time Forecasts in the Survey of Professional Forecasters, Research Rap Special Report*, Federal Reserve Bank of Philadelphia (Philadelphia, PA, 2010), http://www.philadelphiafed.org/research-and-data/publications/research-rap/2010/realistic-evaluation-of-real-time-forecasts.pdf.

35. W. J. Jansen, X. Jin and J. M. de Winter, Forecasting and nowcasting real GDP: comparing statistical models and subjective forecasts, *International Journal of Forecasting* **32**(2), 411-436 (2016).

36. J. Kay, Economic forecasting will never be an exact science, *Financial Times* October (2003), http://www.johnkay.com/2003/10/29/economic-forecasting-will-never-be-an-exact-science.

37. P. Cross. and O. Wyman, The relationship between monthly, quarterly and annual growth rates, *Canadian Economic Observer*, December (2012), http://www.statcan.gc.ca/pub/11-010-x/2011006/part-partie3-eng.htm.

38. P. Ollivaud, P.-A. Pionnier, E. Rusticelli, C. Schwellnus & S.-H. Koh, *Forecasting GDP During and After The Great Recession: A Contest Between Small-Scale Bridge And Large-Scale Dynamic Factor Models*, OECD Economics Department Working Papers 1313 (OECD Publishing, Paris, 2016).

39. J. Kay, *The Failures of Economic Forecasting*, 25 September (1995), http://www.johnkay.com/1995/09/25/the-failures-of-economic-forecasting.

40. K. F. Wallis, Macroeconomic forecasting: A survey, *The Economic Journal*, March, (1989), pp. 28-61.

41. Turner, D. S., The role of judgement in macroeconomic forecasting, *Journal of Forecasting* **9**, (1990), pp. 314-345.

42. Kirby, S., K. Paramaguru and J. Warren, The accuracy of NIESR's GDP growth forecasts, *National Institute Economic Review* **232**, May (2015).

43. Hermansen, M. and O. Röhn, *Economic Resilience: The Usefulness of Early Warning Indicators in OECD Countries*, OECD Economics Department Working Papers, No. 1250, (OECD Publishing, Paris, 2015).

44. O. Röhn, A. Caldera Sánchez, M. Hermansen, M. Rasmussen, *Economic Resilience: A New Set of Vulnerability Indicators for OECD Countries*, OECD Economics Department Working Papers, No. 1249 (OECD Publishing, Paris, 2015).

Reflections on global modeling: The state of the art

Peter Pauly

Rotman School of Management, University of Toronto
105 St. George Street
Toronto, On M5S 3E6, Canada
E-mail: pauly@rotman.utoronto.ca

From their early beginnings in the 1970s, global econometric models have developed in very diverse directions. From the early demand-driven model structures in the Cowles Commission tradition to today's highly sophisticated Dynamic Structural General Equilibrium (DSGE) models, they have become the primary tool for forecasting and policy analysis at most national and international agencies. Both economic theory and econometric techniques have advanced considerably since the early days of econometric modeling, and a critical examination of the decades-long development of multi-country econometric modeling appears in order. This paper seeks to provide a selective review of both achievements and shortcomings in the field of international econometric modeling, and to suggest possible areas of future research.

1.   Introduction

It has been about seven decades since the first attempts at applied econometric analysis, soon after the end of the Second World War. Early pioneers, such as Jan Tinbergen and Lawrence Klein, developed a rudimentary toolkit for structural model-based macroeconomic analysis, known as econometric modeling. After initial single country efforts, the attention of econometric modelers, based on the recognition of the increased importance of cross-country interactions, turned to multi-country modeling. These efforts have pioneered a vast research agenda, which led the profession from simplistic accounting frameworks to highly sophisticated structural models, from small exercises to most demanding and data-intensive large-scale efforts, and through several waves of advances in economic theory that are reflected in these models. What has the profession achieved, and can the attempt to capture the global economy in a consistent, as well as comprehensive, framework ever be successful? Over the many years of model development, the world economy has experienced the ups and downs of business cycles, several serious crises, and profound structural changes. Have modelers, on the national and international level, learned from these shocks and adapted their tool kit appropriately? What is still missing? Those and other questions are even more a apropos in the aftermath of what turned out to be a major world-wide recession whose long-run implications are still being analyzed, and that in many ways has altered the professions confidence in its tools.

Obviously, any review of global modeling activities must start with an assessment of the state of affairs in the area of econometric modeling generally. A most valuable survey text on the broad range of developments in the field summarizes the relevant academic history as follows:[a]

"Macroeconometric models, in many ways the flagship of the economics profession in the 1960s, came under increasing attack from both theoretical economics and practitioners in the late 1970s. The onslaught came on a wide front: lack of microeconomic theoretical foundations, ad hoc modelling of expectations, lack of identification, neglect of dynamics and non-stationarity, and poor forecasting properties. As a result, by the start of the 1990s, the status of macroeconometric models had declined markedly ... Nevertheless, unlike the dinosaurs which they often have been likened to, macroeconometric models never completely disappeared from the scene... (I)t is fair to say that such models continue to play a role in economic policy. Model building and maintenance, and model based economic analyses, continue to be an important part of many economists' working week, either as a producer (e.g. member of modelling staff) or as a consumer (e.g. chief economists or consultants). Thus, the discipline of macroeconometric modelling has been able to adapt to changing demands, both with regards to what kind of problems users expect that models can help them answer, and with regard to quality and reliability."

This excerpt quite fittingly describes the history of macro-econometric modeling in general. Large sections of this survey will address the response of modelers to these critiques in terms of macroeconomic theory, modeling technique, and the applications of quantitative models to data-based policy analysis at the national, single-country level. But, obviously, much of it applies just as well to international macro-econometric models, their development and uses. After all, the ideal international model is in essence just a construct of appropriate national models, connected via a comprehensive set of cross-country linkages. The primary purpose of this review then is to provide a selective summary of the history of macro-econometric modeling in general, but with a particular focus on multi-country models, a subjective assessment of its successes and failures, as well as some thoughts on future challenges.

Reflections like this one can never be all-encompassing, encyclopedic and comprehensive. Rather, the intent is to take stock of achievements to date and to offer a very selective set of suggestions for future developments. The underlying premise of this effort is that indeed international econometric models have a future as instruments of forecasts, policy analysis and policy design, but they need to adjust significantly by addressing heretofore neglected issues and by exploring new data, techniques, and tools of analysis.

---

[a] Bårdsen[1], pp.1-2.

2.   The Early Years

And by now there is a fairly long history to review. Not long after the first-large scale models became available, the thoughts of some researchers turned to multi-country modeling. Lawrence Klein was obviously the driving force behind this effort, but the merry 'band of brothers' that participated in this effort brought together distinguished economists and economic modelers. In addition to Klein himself, Rudi Rhomberg at the IMF, Aaron Gordon at Northwestern, and Bert Hickman at Stanford, met for an initial planning meeting at Stanford in August 1968. Subsequently, many others joined the group for a core group of participating modelers: James Ball in London, Otto Eckstein at Harvard, Giorgio Basevi in Bologna, Wilhelm Krelle in Bonn, Jean Waelbroeck in Brussels, and John Sawyer in Toronto, among others. The effort was initially supported by the U.S. Social Science Research Council and other funding organizations. It was clear to the original group that an ever more interdependent world economy, with increasing size and frequency of international transactions, capital flows, and migration, needed a tool to look at the world as an integrated system. Similarly, the recognition on the part of many nations of the potential advantages to meaningfully coordinate international economic policy added further urgency to the budding modeling effort. Hence, the motivation in the late 1960s was straightforward, and the mandate to address these concerns became even more urgent as many of the most important exchange rates moved to a regime of floating rates in 1973.

For the most part, the models that originated from this initial effort were in the tradition of the time: reduced-form structures, based on decision rules, and demand-driven. Arguably, Project LINK, which grew out of the efforts started by the individuals listed above, was the pioneering effort, although many others followed in its footsteps. With the exception of LINK, they remained centrally designed and operated, often with a uniform national model structure. Project LINK[b] pursued an extreme version of disaggregation and national variability: it relied on existing and independently operated national models, which were maintained at LINK's national centers and then integrated into a framework modeling inter-country linkages at LINK Central. It sought to exploit the expertise from national partners around the world on the premise that they know best how to model, analyze, and forecast their economies. And the project was, laudably, way ahead of other models in terms of seeking broad international coverage, including developing counties, emerging markets, and what was then still the group of centrally planned economies. As a result, the LINK model was characterized by extreme size and heterogeneity, comprising eighty models ranging from a few equations to more than a thousand, for an overall size of more than twenty thousand.

---

[b] There is, of course, a long list of papers describing the structure and functioning of the LINK system. Representative examples, among many others, are Klein[2,3], Hickman[4] or Hickman and Ruffing[5].

Over the ensuing years, significant international modeling activities took hold in most international organizations. Leading international research institutions were among the first to engage; the International Monetary Fund (IMF)and the Organization for Economic Cooperation of Developing Countries (OECD) were among the most active institutions[c], while the World Bank (WB), though quite active on the modeling front (mostly on the fiscal side, as in the MFMod class of models) kept most of the discussion and documentation in-house. Over time, regional institutions like the Commission of the European Communities (EC) or, later, the European Central Bank (ECB) entered the scene[d]. Important policy-making national institutions, such as the US Federal Reserve Bank or the Japanese Economic Planning Agency (EPA) soon also started model-building projects[e], as did various other research institutes[f]. Finally, a wide range of multi-country models, of different degrees of coverage, size, and specification, were developed at commercial operations,[g] and as individual efforts of university researchers[h].

As a result of all these activities over the initially very fertile early decades of multi-country modeling a diverse landscape emerged. Models of vastly different sizes, coverage, and level of disaggregation co-existed. While all, or at least most, of the models were developed within the parameters of the reigning paradigm of demand-driven models based on reduced-form decision rules, the models showed nonetheless great variety of structural specification.[i]

While that diversity was just a reflection of important, yet sometimes subtle, differences in model assumptions and a consequence of the richness of economic theory, it also pointed to an increasingly worrying other aspect of the proliferation of (national and international) models. As a result of their structural differences, the models also

---

[c] Both these institutions have documented their modeling efforts over time quite extensively. An early version of the OECD model can be found in Richardson[6], and Hervé et al.[7] is representative for subsequent generations of models. Similarly, the IMF modeling activities have undergone numerous iterations, as documented, among others, in Masson et al.[8], Bayoumi et al.[9], Laxton[10], or Anderson et al.[11]

[d] Good documentations of these efforts are Bekx et al.[12] for the EC and Fagan et al.[13] for the ECB. Both institutions have, of course, expanded and modernized their models over time.

[e] See the discussion of early FED modeling activities in Edison et al.[14], or a description of the EPA system in Economic Planning Agency[15].

[f] For example, the British National Institute of Economic and Social Research[16].

[g] Large multi-country models were also developed at a few private firms devoted to international economic analysis. The most prominent examples were probably Wharton Econometrics, which morphed through numerous incarnations into what is today Global Insight, Michael Evans' Chase Econometrics, and Oxford Economics, among many others.

[h] Good examples are McKibbin and Sachs[17], Fair[18,19,20], or Taylor[21].

[i] Comprehensive overviews of many of the traditional first-generation models can be found in Klein and Lo[22], Bodkin et al.[23], or Mitchell et al.[24] A good survey of the landscape after about two decades of international modeling, with a focus on second-generation models, is contained in chapter 8 of Whitley[25].

exhibited disturbingly large differences in their response characteristics to common shocks. That, of course, increasingly called into question the usefulness of these models for policy analysis. How was one to draw policy conclusions from a set of often contradictory recommendations obtained by different models? This fundamental conundrum sparked a series of model comparison exercises, which sought to at least understand the reasons for these conflicting responses.[j] Perhaps not surprisingly, while these efforts advanced both the theory and practice of modeling quite significantly, they were never fully satisfactory in the sense that they often proved impossible to unambiguously link certain structural differences across models to differences in response characteristics. It is thus quite correct to conclude that these models never reached consensus on the most important policy questions that were posed to them.

3.   Criticism and Decline

Following the initial heydays of international modeling, as early as the mid- to late 1970s a certain disillusion began to take hold. In retrospect, it is easy to see how large international models became too big and impenetrable for their own good. They became hard to update and maintain, they were complicated to operate, and to the outsider they remained black boxes: their results were hard to explain and over time lost credibility because they were seen as arbitrary. And it was difficult to make the models respond to significant structural changes (the collapse of the communist bloc, German unification, European Union, are good examples, and there are more), as well as to changes in the number and definition of countries and regions. Large models collapsed, if you will, under their own weight. And, ultimately many of them died or morphed into something else.

But arguably more important than these technical issues were, for national and international models of that vintage alike, four fundamental conceptual critiques that challenged the foundation of empirical macroeconomics at the time:

- First-generation demand-driven models, owing to the lack of a well-developed supply side, failed dramatically to adequately deal with the commodity (oil) price shocks of the 1970s and 1980s. The importance of supply side modeling was soon understood, and it led to a second generation of 'traditional' structural models that paid assiduous attention to an appropriate role of supply factors[28].
- The rational expectations (RE) revolution obviously presented a major challenge to traditional models, which relied on (backward-looking) adaptive or

---

[j] It has been one of the many laudable contributions from the Brookings Institution, many years after they were actively involved in the very first large-scale modeling projects, to support a multi-year effort of systematic model comparison exercises which included many of the multi-country models at the time; the results of this project are summarized in two waves published by Bryant et al.[26,27]

extrapolative treatments of expectations.[k] The notion that economic agents had more information about expected future events was intuitively appealing and needed to be addressed in some way. For example, it was obviously inappropriate to examine pre-announced or rule-based policies in a framework that was completely extrapolative. The resulting RE hypothesis, however, was radical. The assumption that agents had sufficient knowledge of the data-generating process of both endogenous and exogenous variables in the system to correctly anticipate, and potentially counteract, policy actions and their effects destroyed the basis of traditional modeling. The same was true if one were to think of strict rationality as applying not to individual agents, but to the medium outcome of the market process.

- Intimately related to the concern about the effects of forward-looking expectations was, of course, the Lucas critique which questioned the validity of structural models which were based on reduced-form decision rules rather than identifying deep structural parameters and non-rational expectations[31]. As a consequence, it was argued that policy prescriptions based on traditional econometric models were inadmissible since they would ignore endogenous changes to the model structure. This was closely linked to the demand for micro-foundations in aggregate econometric models. A representative agent framework that was derived rigorously from first principles was seen as necessary condition for a usable policy model. At a very fundamental level, the Lucas-critique was, of course, correct, although it needed to be interpreted more broadly as applying to all market participants, including policy makers. It quite appropriately challenged the traditional models' bias in favor of policy activism.
- Last, the challenge presented by time-series econometricians questioned another pillar of traditional structural modeling. Sims'[32] critique of the exclusion restrictions imposed by structural models, as well as the lack of identification of the models and their dynamic structure, tackled a deeply troubling aspect of first-generation models. Too often these models were either under-identified or they relied for identification on the dynamic structure, i.e. the time lags incorporated in the models. Hence, Sims' logical conclusion was that the research program of structural econometric modeling of the time was fundamentally misguided.

Obviously, since those fundamental critiques were articulated, national econometric models have made great progress in addressing these issues. Modelers have learned from the experience of first-generation models and become less ambitious in scope and scale, yet more demanding with regard to theoretical and econometric rigor, as well as

---

[k] The hypothesis had indeed a fairly long gestation, with many antecedents along the way. The canonical reference is, of course, Lucas[29], while Lucas and Sargent[30] collect the most important papers.

practicality of their models. Fully-specified supply-sides are appropriately incorporated in later-generation structural econometric models. Similarly, it is quite evident that the treatment of expectations in traditional structural models has become much more sophisticated. Rational expectations are routinely allowed for, generally as options among other schemes such as extrapolative or active learning mechanisms. Moreover, the co-integration and error-correction revolution has provided a toolkit to combine adequately long-run economic theory with short-run time series techniques. Finally, it can also be argued that aspects of representative agent modeling have always been part of even traditional models. Obviously, they have not been implemented as rigorously as it is the case in more recent models, but it is somewhat misguided to label reduced-form models as atheoretical. Rather, microeconomic foundations in these models were used as approximate guides to an appropriate final form, but not as firm restrictions on model specification. Lastly, many of these concerns have been addressed in revisions and new constructions of international econometric models as well.

The criticism also had quite a powerful effect on multi-country modeling, leading to significant advancements in two directions: first, the construction of elaborate multi-equation and multi-country time series models, and second, a vast research program that sought to separate long-term structural modeling from the representation of short-term dynamics. In retrospect, it is indeed very important to acknowledge the progress that was made subsequently, in a relatively short time span, in multi-country modeling in response to the multi-pronged assault on modeling in general that dominated the 1970s. Note, for example, that the models participating in the Brookings model comparison exercises, as documented in Bryant et al.[26,27] already exhibit many of these refined properties.

4.   Second-Generation Macro-Econometric Models

Not surprisingly, econometric modeling has changed substantially since the advent of those first-generation models. In fact, several distinct branches developed in response to different aspects of the critiques outlined above. Dynamic structural general equilibrium (DSGE) models emerged as the primary vehicle for modelers who sought to improve the theoretical foundations of models. Vector-autoregressive models (VARs) were advanced to give primary attention to the time-series properties of the underlying variables. And a class of newer structural econometric models (SEMs)[1] sought to combine long-term, theory-based structures equilibrium structures with short-term time-series oriented adjustment processes. The subsequent discussion attempts to evaluate in broad strokes the relative advantages and disadvantages of these competing modeling paradigms.

---

[1] Fair[20] introduced the term for modern versions of what was referred to in earlier days as Cowles Commission models, i.e. models that incorporate an eclectic mix of theory and data, without the strict theoretical rigor.

4.1. *DSGE models*

From early real business cycle (RBC) and computable general equilibrium (CGE) models to their descendants, today's DSGE models, there now exists a class of models that have strong microeconomic foundations, impose equilibrium conditions, are forward-looking, exhibit explicit production structures, and incorporate policy reaction functions, to name just a few of the defining properties of these models.[m] DSGE models have been adopted successfully, and are being used regularly, by many central banks around the world. To many critics the underlying assumptions of the DSGE paradigm are still unconvincing and at times starkly at odds with known behavior of economic agents; but they have defined a framework that has strong theoretical appeal. Earlier versions of these models have obviously paid insufficient attention to financial factors (asset prices, money and credit), but significant progress has been made in this regard since the global financial crisis, most notably through the incorporation of financial frictions into the general equilibrium framework. In a separate section the discussion will focus below on how much micro-foundation good macroeconomic forecasting and policy analysis needs, but it is obvious that a much more coherent story can be told when there is a strong theoretical architecture undergirding the model. Nonetheless, the challenges posed by aggregation issues are present in the DSGE world as well. Hence it remains questionable whether the strong theoretical constraints that are imposed (e.g. optimizing behavior, rational expectation, perfect observability) can be justified in a framework that deals with highly aggregate data, after all.

Finally, following an initial period of fairly simple-minded calibration of these models, it is also noteworthy that the econometrics of DSGE models have become much more sophisticated. Many of the parameters of these models are still based on calibration, with occasionally weak empirical support, but larger parts of the structure are being estimated. Typically, the technique of choice is a Bayesian estimation of the full model, as classical estimation is generally non-informative in the specific parameter space of DSGE models. Yet, as is often noted, full-model estimation can be non-robust to specification errors, and the reliability of results suffers when only loose priors are available.

Last, long-established tenets of the philosophy of science remind us that not all forms of evidence have equal validity. It would still appear that the specification tests that are applied to these models (e.g. matching moments) are less demanding that those applied to a standard structural econometric model. A recent review of these methods by an active practitioner of DSGE modeling[36]offers an interesting, and sobering, perspective. The paper quite rightfully questions the scientific rigor of the empirical validations underlying

---

[m] There probably is no "standard" DSGE model, reflecting the wide variety of approaches pursued under the label, but a canonical reference is Smets and Wouters[33]. An accessible description of DSGE models for policy analysis can be found in Sbordone et al.[34] A very useful survey is provided by Christiano et al.[35]

today's DSGE research, which still relies on eyeballing moment characteristics without proper statistical decision theory.

Blanchard[37], among others, has tried to summarize these and other concerns about DSGEs. He considers the approach to be an extremely valuable tool for normative economic analysis, in particular the systematic analysis of economic distortions. In his discussion, he notes, however, that the types of distortions that are being considered in current-generation DSGE models (nominal rigidities and financial frictions) are still too limited and lists many others that an empirically oriented model should encompass, such as real rigidities, non-rational expectations, behavioral anomalies, incomplete markets, and imperfect observability. Arguably, to many traditional modelers a model that seeks to incorporate just these properties would seem to look very much like the prototype of modern-day SMEs.

With the benefit of hindsight, it is also clear that all equilibrium, Lucas-type (DSGE) models failed the test of reality spectacularly, never more so than during the global recession of 2008/2009 and its aftermath. Their proprietors argued against precisely the medicine most traditional econometric models would have prescribed: active countercyclical monetary and fiscal policy to fight a pronounced and extended global slump. Furthermore, DSGE models go into great detail and theoretical sophistication modeling the domestic economy, but they have very little to offer when it comes to international linkages and cross-country spillovers. And thus, the need for a new generation of multi-country models,) is obvious. To date, the IMF[n] and the ECB (with a regional focus) are virtually the only protagonists of having developed and propagated multi-country versions of these structures; more research is urgently needed. In that endeavor, much can be learned from several critical assessments of the correct use contained in a recent volume by Gürkaynak and Tille[38], as well as from the empirical challenges that DSGE models encountered in recent years.[o]

4.2.   Vector-autoregressive models (VARs)

The disappointment with first-generation econometric models, both as forecasting tools and instruments for systematic policy analysis, provided the opportunity for Sims' fundamental critique to take hold very quickly. VAR modeling promised the development of theory-free models that would not generate forecasts that were conditional on model assumptions. Yet, with the explosion of work on VARs it soon became clear that there was no free lunch. VARs could easily be used as forecasting tools, just as generations of earlier time-series models had successfully demonstrated. Yet the application of these structures for purposes of policy analysis required a causal ordering, which was non-unique. Cooley and LeRoy[40] were the first to diagnose the problem, and others elaborated

---

[n] Good examples of the evolution of the DSGE approach at the institution are, as indicated before, among many others[8-11].
[o] An interesting survey of the challenges to DSGE models evidenced by the financial recession is Lindé et al.[39]

on the issue[41,42]. Subsequent refinements allowed for some simultaneity, but with the increased focus on the implications of non-stationarity identification became even more difficult.

Despite these difficulties, VAR modeling has become a valuable tool for certain types of economic analysis. VAR modelers have led us to a much better understanding of how to capture the dynamics of economic variables and, more importantly, how to model the dynamic interactions between a set of variables. From the perspective of multi-country economic analysis, in particular the work that Hashem Pesaran and his partners[p] have done over the last two decades to extend this framework to a truly multi-country model is indeed quite impressive. It provides an alternative set of tools to engage in economic forecasting on a global scale. It is less clear whether the framework can be employed usefully as a tool for policy analysis. The methodology of 'impulse response functions' has been applied widely, even in international policy analysis. Yet VARs do not lend themselves easily to policy analysis, in particular the analysis of complicated policy packages. The reliance on individual response characteristics to exogenous shocks seems unsatisfactory as they are only a poor substitute to full-model policy modeling and simulation, as they are routinely applied in SEMs.

4.3.   *Co-integration and error correction*

Last, with the advent of the concept of co-integration — summarized in Engle and Granger[46], Hendry[47], or Engle and White[48] — and of increasingly sophisticated error-correction techniques traditional structural modelers were given proper tools to explicitly separate long-run equilibrium structures from the short-run dynamics of the business cycle. Most importantly, the paradigm provided modelers with a sophisticated theoretical framework to incorporate a well-developed equilibrium supply side. I would argue that the class of well-developed structural models that have emerged over the last two decades or so within the co-integration/error-correction framework have progressed a long way towards addressing the basic critiques leveled against structural modeling, while avoiding the constricting theoretical rigor that so often plagues DSGE models. Indeed, the best of the newest generation of SEMs are built around a strong, theory-based long-run equilibrium core with a superimposed flexible dynamic structure. In these models, economic theory guides the specification, but it does not completely constrain the ultimate parametrization.

---

[p]Informative references on the projects progress through the years are Pesaran et al.[43] and Pesaran and Smith[44]. A more recent and very useful comprehensive overview over the entire GVAR research program can be found in Chudik and Pesaran[45].

4.4.   *A comparative assessment*

Elements of all three paradigms discussed below come together in newer-generation SMEs[q]. The approach seeks to build on important developments in the time series literature and clearly recognizes that the distinction between long-run (equilibrium) and short-run adjustment is important and can be incorporated properly. It also allows for a full specification of both demand- and supply-factors: the long-run (equilibrium) part of the model is strongly constrained by economic theory. For example, the explicit form of the supply side is determined by long-run theory, while the short-run utilization of that supply potential is the result of disequilibrium factors determined on the demand side.[r] Theory constrains the long run, while the properties of the data shape the short-run (disequilibrium) dynamics around the long-run equilibrium.

It is this third direction that I still consider to be the most fruitful one for empirically informative and politically useful large-scale macro-econometric modeling efforts, both nationally and internationally. More than twenty years ago, Hall[51] (and more broadly elaborated in a wider context in Hall[52]) wrote a paper titled 'Macroeconomics and a Bit More Reality' where he discussed the challenges that time-series (VAR) models and the required focus on forward-looking expectations presented to traditional structural econometrics. He went on to outline the ways how econometric techniques and theoretical developments had evolved to response to these challenges: stronger theory to underlie a priori exclusion restrictions, and co-integration and error-correction modeling to separate out the equilibrium from the short-run dynamics. He went on to say: "*These developments all point to a convergence of methodology, with the emergence of a best practice model…*". I believe that assessment has essentially been borne out by the developments since then.

It is also important in this context to recall the conditions put forward by Pesaran and Smith[53] that conscientious modelers were expected to meet. They highlighted three properties that any model should satisfy: relevance, consistency, and adequacy. These criteria demand that the model should be able to produce the necessary information (relevance), based on a framework that reflects accepted theory (consistency), and that is has predictive or explanatory power (adequacy). Not surprisingly, Pagan[54], in his comprehensive review of modeling activities at the Bank of England, touches on the same issues. How do these competing modeling paradigms fare against that set of expectations? In my view, only the third approach comes anywhere close to satisfying all three conditions. VARs are by definition atheoretical and DSGEs emphasize theoretical consistency over predictive accuracy. Any serious modeling effort must strive to be both

---

[q] Many of the characteristics of the SMEs of the late 1980s and 1990s are reviewed in summary volumes such as Allen and Hall[49] or Bårdsen et al.[1] Willman et al.[50] is a very good and instructive representative example of the kind of model developed and used at the time in many countries, such as the UK (London Business School), Italy (Prometeia), France (Metric), and Germany (Sysifo), as well as in multi-country models (NIESR).

[r] The resulting notion of an 'output gap' has shown to be a useful indicator of business cycle conditions, both nationally and internationally.

empirically relevant, as evidenced through a minimum level of predictive power, and allow for an unambiguous interpretation of the results in view of the underlying structure.

That, in my view, is the standard that must be applied to modern macro-econometric modeling. Many of the observations made in this section were primarily directed at the construction of national (single-country) models. Yet, at its core, whether it relies on a uniform structure across countries or accommodates, as Project LINK does, different structures for different countries, a good international model is composed of good country models. By extension, most of these remarks apply to multi-country models as well.

5.   Where Do International Models Stand Now?

In this section I want to turn to some thoughts about several aspects that are specific to multi-country models, primarily in order to take stock of how far we have come – or not. It goes without saying that the central benefit from multi-country modeling is expected from a capture of international linkages and transmission mechanisms that is consistent, transparent, and comprehensive. How are we – or have we been – doing on that score, as the world economy became vastly more integrated further over the decades?

5.1.   *International linkages*

5.1.1. *Trade flows*

Not surprisingly, the early modeling of international transmission mechanisms focused on merchandise trade, both because it still was the dominant concern at the time, and because merchandise trade data were better and more complete than those covering services. Project LINK did path-breaking work on using expenditure models to capture the essence of bilateral price- and activity-based trade flows. Those models worked quite well, but they were dependent on good bilateral trade and trade price information. And the bilateral data were just not too good.

Early multi-country models, such as Project LINK, sought to represent location-based relative trade competitiveness in the tradition of Armington[55]. The availability of trade matrices on an SITC basis made possible a fairly detailed treatment of bilateral trade shares.[s] Since then, in my view, international modelers have not kept up with the explosion of theoretical research on trade. Over the last twenty of thirty years, our understanding of the complexities of trade relations has expanded enormously. The expansion of intra-industry trade, the establishment and dynamic nature of value chains, the outsourcing of parts or the whole of the production process (in manufacturing and services), rendered many of the traditional approaches inappropriate.

---

[s] During the early years, the pioneering research for the LINK model went through several iterations; a good example of the work can be found in Gana et al.[56] See also the very comprehensive survey in Italianer[57], covering many other international modeling efforts, including an ambitious effort at the Commission of the European Community.

The most fundamental shift in the theory of trade was, of course, the emergence of "new trade theory" focusing on increasing returns and imperfect competition, as in Krugman[58] and Helpman and Krugman[59], two of the most cited seminal works. Even more importantly, subsequent trade research focused increasingly on the determinants of trade at the firm or plant level, as well as the recognition of a fundamental change to production processes in a globalizing world.[t] Based on this work, much of the attention turned to understanding the importance of emerging value-chains for global trade relations. Obviously, the analysis of international trade has been made more complicated by the emergence of global value chains. The disaggregation of the production process into a sequence of steps that can be undertaking in different countries renders the Armington perspective of trade mostly obsolete. Furthermore, official statistical systems still are geared towards measuring the gross value of trade (and the attendant price indices), rather than focusing of value added per country.

So, where are we today? While trade theorists talk about "trade in tasks"[u] as the dominating paradigm, not much of that can be found in international macro-econometric models. The studies looking at the effects of the globalization of production have in general, not been conducted in a multi-country, general-equilibrium framework. Data on the value added traded among, at least, the major economies are now available for about two decades. Yet, the new knowledge has not yet informed or stimulated a new modeling strategy for multi-country models.

For some researchers, gravity models have provided useful forecasting tools[v], yet they remain imperfect tools for policy analysis. While attractive in their simplicity as a forecasting tool, the lack of connection to underlying structural and behavioral fundamentals, such as prices, productive potential and preferences, renders gravity models unsuitable for detailed policy analysis. The fundamental challenge, then, is for trade modeling to catch up with trade theory; there is a significant need to bring truly dynamic global modeling, warts and all, with all its multitude of interdependencies, to the task.

A good example of how fragile our understanding of trade determinants in practice still is has also been the emerging puzzle about the post-crisis slowdown in international trade. What has caused the apparent breakdown in the trade/GDP relations? Much has been written about the causes, cyclical or structural, of the marked slowdown in the growth of global trade in recent years, most prominently following the great recession,

---

[t] For more than a decade, a core group of researchers has advanced our thinking about the determinants of trade at the micro level. Good examples of this research program are Bernard et al. [60,61]

[u] See, for example, Grossman and Rossi-Hansberg[62].

[v] Representative for a vast literature, Anderson and van Wincoop[63] provide an excellent survey of advantages and disadvantages of the approach.

but possibly dating back quite a bit further.[w] With the notable exception of the OECD, it appears that little of that work has been done within the context of global econometric models. One suspects that, at least in part, is a reflection of the lack of structural detail in these models discussed above.[x]

Last, until very recently, the unavailability of bilateral data also made it infinitely more complicated to specify comparable models for service trade. That created an increasing vulnerability as the importance of international trade in services grew enormously. Despite the fact that vastly better statistics have in the interim improved our understanding of international linkages through transport, travel, banking services, etc., to this day none of the leading multi-country models have developed a satisfactory representation of the dynamics of service trade.

5.1.2. *Capital flows, monetary linkages, and exchange rates*

It is probably fair to say that from the very beginning the modeling of international capital flows and exchange rates, that is of international monetary linkages in general, has been the weakest part of most multi-country models. To a large extent, that reflected the sparseness of available data. In the early years, there were no data on bilateral capital, let alone reliable aggregate data. And stocks of assets and liabilities, domestic as well as international, were hard to come by. Hence, several ambitious attempts of international flow-of-funds models were severely hampered by data limitations and never really took off.

Nonetheless, over the years, as international macroeconomic theory flourished, enormous progress was made on the partial equilibrium theory and empirics of capital flows and exchange rates. Yet relatively little of it found its way into multi-country models. If you looked around, in most of these models you saw reliance on simple transmission mechanisms: interest parity conditions (IP), versions of purchasing power parity (PPP), and simplified direct interest linkages. All, or most, of the advances in international finance remained unutilized by modelers. Just as the national models failed to modernize their financial sectors to incorporate more sophisticated banking and credit channels, multi-country models failed to adjust to the complexity of the rapidly evolving international financial system. That became, of course, painfully obvious in the great financial crisis when, I believe, it turned out that monetary theory, with few exceptions was incapable of providing sufficient insights into the causes and consequences of a breakdown in monetary transmission mechanisms.[y]

---

[w] Much of the focus of this discussion has been on the nature of trade, in particular the establishment, over the years, of intricate global value chains. Modern DSGE models link merchandise trade to the production side more closely, but not in terms of value-added and not bilaterally.

[x] Examples of the burgeoning literature are Hoekman[64], Eaton et al.[65], Haugh et al.[66], or the discussion by Gangnes and Van Assche in this volume, among many others.

[y] There was, of course, a well-developed literature on bank runs and liquidity crises, going back as far as Minsky's Austrian business cycle theory, but more recently to the pioneering work of

It is now, of course, universally recognized that adequate banking sector characteristics, which would allow for debt and credit crises to be possible, were missing in most national models. In fact, were few models had a banking sector at all. Most models, DSGE models and SMEs alike, relied on simple central bank reaction functions or other reduced form mechanisms that linked real sector developments to nominal interest rates. Complications, such as credit crunches, bank runs, or liquidity crises, were not modeled. That, of course, was just as much a problem for the few existing international models. Furthermore, the international models of the time were incapable of reflecting the most important channels of contagion, let alone to characterize the determinants of systemic risks. But the crisis has stimulated an avalanche of good work on financial economics, domestically and internationally. It looks like as a result of the crisis the profession is now getting close to developing a new generation of models that incorporate new mechanisms of international spillage.

Arguably, no aspect of modeling international transmission mechanisms has been – at least since the advent of mostly flexible exchange rates in the 1970s – as vexing and frustrating as the appropriate representation of exchange rate flexibility. There is no question that much of the cross-country transmission of economic policies or external shocks is conditional on the endogenous response of exchange rates. And, in my view, many of the pitfalls of international models can be traced back to their inability to capture exchange rate dynamics. Over many decades, economic theory has, of course, offered a plethora of exchange rate theories[z]. From long-run equilibrium conditions such as purchasing power parity (PPP) or (covered and uncovered) interest parity (IP) to short-run frameworks like the monetary theory of exchange rates, the portfolio-balance model, or Dornbusch's overshooting model, to name just a few, the menu of choices of extremely varied. Yet none of them have been shown to be superior to simple time series models, be it random walk models or more sophisticated linear or non-linear representations. They have turned out to be structurally unstable, highly time-dependent, and generally unreliable in policy simulations and as forecasting tools, at high as well as low frequencies.[aa] As a result, most modelers have resorted to following simple rules such as PPP or IP or, probably preferable, to implement more elaborate assessments of equilibrium exchange rates as in Isard[75] or Cline and Williamson[76]. That, it appears, is still the state-of-the art.

Diamond and Dybvig[67]. Yet none of these played any significant role in the consensus macroeconomic model of the time.

[z] A voluminous theory has documented the breadth of exchange rate theories. Good examples are, among many others, Isard[68], Taylor[69], or MacDonald and Marsh[70].

[aa] The literature exploring exchange rate forecastability is extremely large. From the early results obtained in Meese and Rogoff[71], through updates such as Cheung et al.[72], the evidence is somewhat mixed, but generally unsupportive of sustainable forecasting successes. More recent surveys can be found in Rossi[73] or Cheung et al.[74]

5.1.3. *Other linkages*

Little progress has, until very recently, been made in multi-country models in terms of getting a handle on other longer-term international linkages: migration, technology transfer, and foreign direct investments (FDI). All those are clearly of more longer-term import and of relatively little importance for our understanding of business cycle transmissions, yet they are vital to understanding long-term trends in growth and development: the location of production, the effects of technical progress on global market shares as well as the feedback into national economies (outsourcing, hollowing out discussions), and the direction of trade and investment. All these issues have, of course, received great attention in the economics literature. Research in economic theory and trade on the issue of international technology transfer has been particularly intense[77-82]. Yet, despite much fruitful research in these areas, it has not found its way into integrated international models in a meaningful way. Nonetheless, there are good examples of promising analyses in the real business cycle literature, as well as in the applied VAR tradition, which should in principle be applicable to empirical cross-country analysis.

5.2. *Global markets and commodities*

Despite the vast amount of modeling of national and international commodity markets (oil, minerals, and agriculture), it has been surprisingly difficult to integrate these models into global macro-models. There are well-developed international modeling efforts for individual markets – a good example is the successful work at the Center for Global Trade Analysis with the GTAP system of linked CGE models.[bb] Of note are also the many global oil market models, including the one developed within Project LINK, as in Kaufmann[85]. But for the most part these models run off a macroeconomic model, and it still appears to be challenging to actually feed back the results of these models into an integrated global model.

That state of affairs is indeed unsatisfactory. Obviously, for much of the commodity-producing developing world commodity cycles are of vital importance. They determine income flows, growth cycles and balance-of-payments constraints, among many others. Similarly, the macroeconomic and political implications of commodity price swing are globally important. It is thus imperative that international models incorporate better treatments of commodity models per se, but also more detailed integration into the systems. Commodity markets are almost by definition international and cannot be examined satisfactorily in isolation. Interestingly, there are also important linkages between individual commodities, either directly or by their joint interaction with certain

---

[bb] A vast literature has grown around the design and operation of international CGE models, certainly beyond the scope of this selective survey. An immensely useful reference is the handbook edited by Dixon and Jorgenson[83]. A more recent assessment of successes and remaining challenges of that line of research can be found in Kehoe et al.[84]

industries. Based on a global network analysis. Diebold et al.[86] document convincingly the extent of connectedness among commodities. International modelers ignore that web of linkages at their peril.

5.3. *Forecast accuracy*

As soon as national and international econometric models had a sufficiently long track record and accumulated a significant forecast record, they have been subject to numerous assessments of their forecast performance. Most of these evaluations were conducted by the modelers themselves as part of regular validation exercises, but in particular the forecasts issued by international agencies that received wide public attention, such as regular forecasts of the IMF or the OECD, were publicly reviewed.[cc]

Unquestionably, the forecasts generated at international organizations which are, at least to some extent model-based, have therefore attained special prominence, as evidenced by the broad impact of the OECD and IMF forecasts, among others, in the public debate. The quality of these forecasts is often on par with, if not better, than national forecasts. They can lay claim to being less politically influenced and not obviously biased; over time, they have often been recognized as arbiters in the public debate. But they also share a few unfortunate properties with many other national forecasts. Too often, they miss turning points and they are, obviously, not good at predicting systemic risks. Their performance in the run-up to the global financial crisis has been as unsatisfactory as that of many other institutions. Yet, thanks to their explicit structure they provide the opportunity to perform systematic informative post-mortem analyses of prediction failures.

As is well known, all these forecasts — whether produced at national or international organizations, in academia, or by commercial entities — incorporate a certain amount of adjustment of the pure model-based forecast. All forecasters constantly evaluate the trade-off between strict adherence to the model structure and the frequent need to superimpose personal judgment or new information, as well as to correct for the possibility of structural changes not reflected in the models. These adjustments are necessary to improve the forecast while maintaining the core message of the model. They become onerous of the override or even determine the model properties; there is a thin line all modelers need to be cognizant of.

Finally, both VARs and DSGE models tend to be in some ways inferior forecasting tools, although for vastly different reasons. While the short-term forecast performance of pure time series models is generally on par with well-maintained SEMs, and sometimes even better, their comparative advantage declines with the length of the forecast horizon. High-frequency time-series models are thus often the preferred tool of forecasting and

---

[cc] See, for example, studies such as Mitchell et al.[24] or Pons[87], or more recent efforts such as Wieland and Wolters[88] or Genberg and Martinez[89]. Particularly laudable in this context are ex-post forensic efforts that seek to understand the sources of forecasting errors, such as the OECD study prepared by Pain et al.[90] following the global financial recession.

analysis on financial markets, yet found less success over medium- tom long-term horizons. On the other hand, since their comparative advantage is the analysis of economic equilibria under various distortions to the economy. DSGE models were, of course, never really meant to be forecasting tools, and should have never been used for that purpose. But unfortunately, they were increasingly applied in forecasting exercises, and not surprisingly they failed at the task of producing reliable short-term forecast. To take just one example, the rational expectations assumption by definition forces all forecast errors into the very short-run. It is no wonder then that the DSGE paradigm failed as a forecasting tool.

6.   A Research Agenda

The purpose of this section is to review some recently prominent discussion of research strategy for the construction of econometric models. These issues are being discussed almost exclusively in the context of national model building efforts, but they are, of course, just as relevant in the multi-country context.

6.1.   *Theory vs. relevance: Microfoundations*

In the aftermath of the great recession, and triggered by the obvious failure of the dominant model paradigm at the time, namely DSGE models, a furious debate ensued. These models were not able to explain (which was unexpected) or predict (which should have been obvious) the huge disturbance to the world economy caused by events in the financial sector. With increased intensity, the debate focused on the rationale for the extreme theoretical rigor that was brought to bear on DSGE models. The critique culminated in just one question: how much micro-foundation is necessary in an econometric model?

A perceptive summary of the ensuing debate was contained in Smith[91], and the debate has not abated since then. Strong opponents of DSGE modeling maintain that 'serious' macroeconomic (and international) analysis requires complete macro-foundation. Many observers find that position to be untenable in a world where models are built to represent the dynamics of macroeconomic aggregates, rather than individual behavior. Yet there are somewhat more nuanced assessments, such as in Ghironi[92] who posits, with a focus on trade theory, that "… *macro needs more micro than the benchmark setup has been incorporating*". Effectively, that reflects the notion expressed by many others that the DSGE model patches that have been put forward to date (adding finance, allowing for a zero lower bound on interest rates, meaningful modeling nonlinearities) may still prove to be insufficient and a different microeconomic approach may be called for.

So, the issue remains unresolved, and probably for a good reason. At a very fundamental level, the discussion reflects different roles assigned to econometric models. Should they serve a normative or prescriptive function? Normative economics may reasonably require a strong and restrictive theoretical basis so as to be able to make unambiguous conditional statements. Models that have prescriptive priorities may well be derived with a certain amount of flexibility around some basic fundamental theoretical guiding principles. In the extreme, one does not always need a structural model, whether SEM or DSGE, to make quantitative predictions, as many generations of successful VARs have demonstrated.

6.2.   *Forecasting vs. policy analysis*

Just as much as national model builders, international modelers have struggled with the puzzle of 'forecasting vs. policy analysis'. It certainly appears as if there has been some divergence on the issue. Clearly, the comparative advantage of DSGE models is their tractability and clarity in the analysis of policy options; yet, as pointed out, they lack the flexibility to generate acceptable short-term forecasts. On the other hand, VARs may have the capacity to generate superior short-term forecasts, but it remains difficult to conduct reliable policy analysis with them, in particular in the presence of complex policy packages.

But it is premature to throw in the towel yet. With others, I continue to believe that a carefully specified structural model, built with sound theoretical structure and appropriate econometrics, can and should be delivering on both counts. After all, all forecasts are conditional and fundamentally no different from a policy scenario. Every forecast based on a formal model — whether it is Keynesian or monetary, general or partial equilibrium, structural or atheoretical, static or dynamic — is conditional on that particular structure and those design principles are reflected in the output, i.e. in the forecast. Fundamentally, that is no different from a policy recommendation derived from a model simulation (or from a reading of response characteristics).

And the need for forecasts isn't going away anytime soon. What has to be put aside is the misunderstanding of economic forecasting as being unconditional. All models face the challenge of (lack of) invariance to the changes in exogenous conditions. How far outside the sample distribution can a model be seen as representative, or are non-linearities too strong? Qualitatively, that caveat is the same as the issue whether a set of policy assumptions drives the model beyond its representative validity.

In a recent blog post Blanchard[93] makes the case for different classes of macroeconomic models to be used. In all, he distinguishes between five different types of models, but in the current context I want to follow his particular focus on the long debate over the coexistence of 'theory models' "... *aimed at clarifying theoretical issues within a general equilibrium setting*"[dd] and 'policy models' "... *aimed at analyzing actual macroeconomic policy i*ssues". Many national and international macro-modelers have always maintained that a well-developed structural model need not sacrifice one objective

---

[dd] Of particular note in this context is also a recent paper by Stiglitz[94]. In it, he takes another tack at specifying, from his perspective and based on his analysis of the shortcomings of current macroeconomics, the characteristics that the next generation of macroeconomic 'theory' models should have, in order for them to be useful in answering a whole class of new challenges. A 'next-generation' multi-country model would, of course, have to incorporate those national characteristics as well, combined with possibly enhanced cross-country linkages.

for the other. Indeed, Hall[52] makes exactly that case. Yet Blanchard is skeptical: "*It would be nice if a model did both, namely have a tight, elegant, theoretical structure and fit the data well. But this is a pipe dream.*"

This assessment is obviously linked to the earlier discussion about the usefulness of the representative-agent paradigm in a world where aggregate dynamics are typically both complicated and unstable over time. And Blanchard comes to a somewhat resigned conclusion:

> "*My suggestion is that the two classes should go their separate ways. ... DSGE modelers should accept the fact that theoretical models cannot, and thus should not, fit reality closely. The models should capture what we believe are the macro-essential characteristics of the behavior of firms and people, and not try to capture all relevant dynamics. ... Policy modelers should affect the fact that equations that truly fit the data can have only a loose theoretical justification. In that, early macroeconomic models had it right: the permanent income theory, the life cycle theory, the Q theory provided guidance for the specification of consumption and investment behavior, but the data then determined the final specification. ... Both classes should clearly interact and benefit from each other.*"

With a hat-tip to Ricardo Reis, Blanchard concludes:

> "*...there should be scientific cointegration. But the goal of full integration has, I believe, proven counterproductive. No model can be all things to all people.*"

No doubt, a similar assessment would apply to pure time-series models (VARs). And, to bring us back to the topic of this overview, similar observations will just as well be appropriate for different paradigms that undergird past and current multi-country modeling efforts. Yet, while Blanchard's suggestion has some intuitive appeal, it remains unsatisfactory. Could it not be that some models are more useful than others, after all? For example, how can we trust a policy recommendation that is based on a model that cannot fit historical data, or only in a loose, calibrated sense? Such a model may provide normative guidance based on a particular theoretical framework. But the experience of the financial crisis has demonstrated beyond any doubt the folly of trying to apply insights from models that are weakly supported by historical data to real world problems.

Finally, the modelers community will no doubt benefit from a new round suitable model comparison projects. As indicated above, several decades ago the Brookings Institution provided an invaluable service to the research community by supporting a model comparison project that covered a wide range of international models, as documented in Bryant et al.[26,27] A similar effort at the present time would be most timely.[ee]

[ee] It would appear that the Centre for Economic Policy Research is in the process of establishing such a model comparison network, in cooperation with the University of Frankfurt, with focus on DSGE models, based on early work summarized in Wieland et al.[95] and Wieland and Wolters[88].

6.3. *Policy design*

During the 1970s and 1980s, great hopes were attached to large econometric models being used for the design of optimal policies. While there are few attempts to apply optimal control techniques to large multi-country models[ff], there is a voluminous literature on optimal control techniques and experiments with national econometric models.[gg] In principle, of course, the inversion of a model to solve for instrument options to achieve a pre-set vector of policy objectives flows directly from the original Tinbergen approach to policy making. But the enthusiasm dissipated, despite the considerable sophistication of the effort, such as e.g. the application of stochastic control techniques, developed in engineering and the natural sciences, in the work of Kendrick[100] and others.

Additionally, the rational expectations revolution posed additional challenges to earlier, naïve optimal control methods. Specifically, the recognition that non-rational expectations implied the dynamic inconsistency of active policies appeared to deal a fatal blow to econometric policy analysis. Yet the technology advanced quite rapidly. Frameworks to generate optimal policies under rational expectations were soon developed, using mostly Nash equilibrium algorithms. And within the optimal control community, techniques of adaptive control allowed the incorporation of learning algorithms into the optimization routines. Hall[101] and Hall and Garratt[102] document many of these conceptual developments, and these tools for the modeling of expectations are now standard for both national and international models. To nobody's surprise, with the computing powers at the time, truly multi-country optimal control proved to be technically hard, yet vastly improved hardware and software should by now have made these issues much more tractable. In recent years, the theoretical analysis of optimal policy design under various expectation assumptions has advanced rapidly. Unfortunately, that theoretical work as, for example, reviewed in Hansen and Sargent[103] has not found its way into national or international SEM research

In addition, following the first wave of optimal control applications, concerns were raised about the arbitrary nature of the specification of preference functions, although there were several suggestions regarding techniques to deduce economic agents' (or policymakers') revealed preferences. Common to all these concerns was the recognition that the Lucas critique had made it obvious that optimization exercises with fixed structural models that are not based on invariant deep structural parameters would always be problematic. But the challenge to develop optimal control solutions in policy-invariant

---

The data base for the project at present contains 82 distinct models, of which 8 models are (to some extent) multi-country in character.

[ff] A notable exception is Petersen[96], a PhD thesis based on the Project LINK system, whose primary operational manager he was during much of the 1980s.

[gg] In addition to a vast journal literature (see many volumes of the *Journal for Economic Dynamics and Control* and the earlier *Annals of Economic and Social Measurement*), many monographs were devoted to the subjects. Representative of many others are, e.g. Chow[97], Holly and Hughes Hallett[98], or Petit[99].

model frameworks with learning behavior on the part of private and public market participants still exists, and future research in that area may well prove fruitful after all.

There is, potentially, another role for national and international models. They could be used as tools to complement the vast theoretical work on policy design. Hurwicz and Reiter[104] provide an instructive overview of this line of research into design mechanisms, and the award of the 2007 Nobel Prize to Hurwicz, Maskin, and Myerson has highlighted its importance. To date, though, mechanism design, as opposed to macro-policy design, has completely remained a theoretical rather than empirical exercise. There is no reason for this to be the case, and there is ample opportunity for applied modelers to contribute to that line of exploration through data-based optimization.

6.4. *International policy coordination*

If there is one area where one should find at least a beginning of empirically-based policy design, it is in the realm of international policy making. Yet Blanchard et al.[105] have referred to international policy coordination as the "...*Loch Ness monster of international macroeconomics: much discussed by rarely seen*". Given the undeniable global benefits of successful implementation of international policy coordination, surely it would seem a priori to be one of, if not the, comparative advantages of international econometric models to explore the possibilities and pitfalls of such actions. Indeed, the obvious driving force behind the creation of multi-national models was the recognition that there are important spillover effects across countries, which would seem to indicate gains from coordination. Multi-country models should own the field of international economic policy design, in particular matters of international policy coordination. There can be no doubt about the importance of international spillovers anymore; vastly increased trade and financial integration have generated a truly interconnected global economy.

That literature probably had, at least with regard to theory, its heyday in the 1980s.[hh] There were also a number of pioneering studies with international scope.[ii] But for international models this area is, after all, to a large extent their 'raison d'etre'. But it would seem to be incumbent on international modelers to become more vocal. If it needed any reminder, cross-border spillovers during the financial crisis were swift and dramatic. The well-known shortage of instruments at the national level rendered national governments largely helpless. As Blanchard et al. (2013) noted: "The legacy of the global financial crisis – high public debt, near zero interest rates, and at times what looks like domestic political dysfunction – suggests that nowadays policy makers have fewer policy tools to achieve their manifold objectives. In such circumstances, gains from policy

---

[hh] The theory is surveyed quite comprehensively in Ghosh and Masson[106]; more recent reviews can be found in Blanchard et al.[105], or in Ostry and Ghosh[107].
[ii] Representative samples of empirical studies are, among others, Oudiz and Sachs[108], Frenkel et al.[109], and Barrell et al.[110]

coordination across countries are likely to be greater than during the Great Moderation." The challenge to international modelers is obvious.

And we have learned more about international interdependencies. For example, Rey[111,112] focuses on evidence of effects of global volatility on international asset prices and capital flows, which also have implications for our understanding of the traditional policy trilemma in open economies, and also strengthens the need for policy coordination. And yet it is true that with one or two celebrated exceptions, such as the 1985 Plaza Accord, which created a coordinated action by five governments to engineer an orderly depreciation of the US dollar, and the joint action of central banks to prevent a global recession in the aftermath of the financial meltdown in 2008/2009, there has never been a serious attempt at coordinated policies. The politics of it are enormously complicated. Nonetheless, recent attempts to revive these efforts, though incomplete, deserve all the support they can get.[jj]

Some regulatory post-crisis efforts can be thought of as examples of successful policy coordination, even though they are not explicitly called that. The Financial Stability Board, created in response to the near-death experience for the global financial system during the crisis, monitors regulatory practices around the world to ensure that they meet globally-agreed standards. It remains to be seen whether there also is a willingness to implement enforcement mechanism to eliminate remaining forms of shadow banking that represent the most acute concern regarding the systemic stability of the world's financial markets. With increased financial integration the need for greater international regulatory coordination among national financial regulators is obvious, even though it conflicts with desires for bespoke national regulations. No doubt there are latent objections to regulatory coordination, as outlined by Lupo-Pasini and Buckley[116], but also significant opportunities[117].

Finally, as many critics of globalization have pointed out[kk], there are systemic properties shaped by the international policy environment that are hard, if not impossible to capture by economic modelers. For example, over the past few decades, national deregulation has often occurred without the necessary international regulatory framework to provide boundaries to firms' actions being in place. Obviously, those are also coordination failures, based on a lack of recognition of spillovers of national regulatory actions. At any rate, international modelers have to find a way to incorporate more successfully structural shifts in the national and international regulatory environment into their structures.

[jj] Obviously, the call for internationally coordinated policy responses has been revived in recent years, as in, for example, Eichengreen[113] or Frankel[114]. At the same time, the obstacles to effective coordination have not disappeared, as a recent overview of the history of 'coordination' documents quite comprehensively; see Ghosh and Qureshi[115].

[kk] Rodrik[118] is one of many publications, many inspired by Rodrik's long-standing leadership in the area, that laid out the case against unfettered globalization.

But above all, little in the way of coordinated macro-policy has actually taken place.[ll] That is most unfortunate, not the least because by all accounts the policy environment is becoming increasingly hostile to coordination. As in many countries we seem to be observing a move towards populist retreat from international cooperation to a regime of zero-sum global competition, the benefits from rigorous model-based cooperation as well as theoretical exercises are larger than ever.

6.5. *Broadening the scope*

Economic modelers have always recognized that there existed numerous promising opportunities to improve the relevance of traditional economic models by incorporating non-economic variables into a structure that focusses on economic interactions, or alternatively, link economic models with modeling efforts directed at other factors. One of the most satisfying developments over the last few decades is therefore how much progress has been made to successfully link economic models with other modeling frameworks.

The most obvious, and in many ways most advanced, instance is the creation of global integrated climate models. Among the very first attempts to build bridges between the economists' modeling community and climate researchers was the Energy Modeling Forum (EMF), organized at Stanford University.[mm] Those initial attempts of getting economic modelers and climate modelers to talk to each other were difficult for reasons that all interdisciplinary research is dealing with. Social scientist and hard scientists did not speak the same language. The terminology of econometric modeling did not match up well with the technical jargon of climate scientists. Social scientists were quite familiar with uncertainty and incomplete observability, while at the time climate models were purely deterministic. But things changed rapidly.

From that very modest beginning we have witnessed the emergence of truly integrated multi-country models that seek to capture in great detail the interactions between economic activity and natural developments on a global scale. It is enormously gratifying to see truly integrated frameworks such as Bill Nordhaus' DICE model, or the

---

[ll] Arguably, one recent case of a missed opportunity has been the conduct of monetary policy in the aftermath of the financial crisis. Met with significant controversy, the US Federal Reserve started its quantitative easing in 2010, while the European Central Bank did maintain its austerity policy. In the intervening years a widening gap in economic performance in favor of the US materialized. In retrospect, not only would the European economies have benefitted from an earlier move to expansionary monetary policy in Europe (which eventually happened), so would the world economy have received an additional stimulus from an actively coordinated expansionary monetary policy at the earliest possible time. Similarly, the Eurozone's fiscal coordination failure of 2012 has been recognized widely as another example of a lost opportunity for gains from coordination.

[mm] The program is active to this day and has stimulated an impressive amount of research over the years. The initial work of the EMF was presented in Hickman and Huntington[119].

research program of McKibbin and his co-authors, which has for many years been solidly educating the fight against global warming, at least by those who conduct the argument with empirical model-based substance rather than ideology.[nn]

7.   Some Speculative Thoughts

Finally, I want to touch on a few issues that are not all necessarily specific to multi-country models, if at all high on the research agenda of international macro-modelers. They are however, while mostly speculative, in my view germane to the fundamental advancement of any economic modeling effort, whether it is national or multi-country.

7.1.   *The strength of interdependencies*

One of the important concerns in the context of large multi-country models, as early as in the pioneering effort of Project LINK, has always been the size and complexity of international linkages. The approach pursued within LINK, namely to construct large bilateral trade matrices, possibly even disaggregated by product categories (for example SITC categories) is extremely cumbersome and becomes almost unworkable with a large number of countries. Any attempt to fully capture bilateral trade linkages in a model with, at the time, almost 80 countries (i.e. more than 6,000 trade shares per category) is obviously daunting, if not a priori hopeless, if only because of data limitations.

But are all bilateral trade relations systemically important? Many bilateral coefficients are zero, or close to it. Hence, trade matrices tend to be fairly sparse. Moreover, trade is often regionally concentrated and thus these matrices have a block structure. But it is very important to realize that, even if trade matrices cannot exactly be decomposed, there may be a promising route to solutions that dates back to a decades-old discussion about aggregation and exogeneity in dynamic systems.

The theory of nearly-completely decomposable dynamic systems[oo] evolved in the context of the aggregation debate in economics. It was shown that aggregation of variables in nearly completely decomposable systems must separate the analysis of the short-run from that of the long-run dynamics, an insight that incidentally also paved the way for co-integration analysis many years later. Along the way, it was proved that, provided that inter-group dependencies are sufficiently weak as compared to intra-group ones, in the short run interdependent systems will behave approximately as if they were completely

---

[nn]Of particular merit in this context are 'Integrative Assessment Models', such as Nordhaus' DICE framework, described in detail in Nordhaus[120], which also provides a superb summary of various approaches. The notion has, of course, also been fully embraced by CGE models, see e.g. the comprehensive overview in Dixon and Jorgenson[83]. Another well-known and broadly applied framework is the family of G-Cubed models, as in McKibbin and Wilcoxen[121].

[oo] See the discussions in Courtois[122] and Courtois and Ashenhurst[123]; the latter provides a comprehensive description of the theory. Early versions of the idea are known as the Ando-Fisher-Simon model of decomposable systems, and the relevant papers are collected in a volume by Ando et al.[124]

decomposable.[pp] The analogy to international interdependencies is obvious: international linkages can be dealt with approximately by triangularization of trade matrices (in goods and services), i.e. by partial exogenization of linkages. The approach remains, however, to this day unexplored in the context of international models. As the density of international linkages has, if anything, only become more important, it is as promising as ever to explore sparse matrix techniques to simplify the task.[qq]

7.2.   Global systemic analysis

If anybody needed another reminder of the wide-ranging implications of globalization, the experience of the past years has been unambiguous. Across all channels of transmission — goods, capital migration, technology transfer – the world has become significantly more interconnected, and with it more fragile. Shocks anywhere in the world have systemic implications, and consequently the need for multi-country models has only intensified.

On the side of trade in goods and services, we have already discussed the changing composition of trade, from final goods trade to trade in intermediate goods. The material in WB[126] provides a fascinating and in-depth analysis of the extent of the current global value chain system, as well as of the implied international interdependence of trade and production. Yet, as indicated earlier, the modeling of trade in multi-country econometric models is not representative of these trends. Consequently, existing models are ill-suited to address questions of systemic risk in the international trading system.

There is, of course, much more awareness of, and attention to, the systemic risks in the global financial system. Much of it has, of course, been driven by the observed market failures of the last decade. Numerous studies, such as Weiss et al.[127] or Gottesman and Leibrock[128], have emphasized the necessary focus on the characteristics of regulatory regimes, but also the importance of prudent macroeconomic management. Obviously, it should be the role of multi-country models to assist in the latter exercise. There are still substantial data challenges, as documented by Cerrutti et al.[129] and others, but the need to incorporate indicators of systemic risk into international macro-models is widely acknowledged. There is no question that much more research is required to fully understand the aggregate and distributional effects of financial globalization.

Finally, it has been established for a long time that the bulk of the volatility in economic activity across countries is due to common shocks. And in fact, the recent global recession has re-emphasized that financial market integration has been one of the major factors behind what was an unexpectedly large and fast diffusion of the original shocks

---

[pp] In addition, results obtained in the short run will remain approximately valid in the long run with regard to the relative behavior of the variables of the same group.
[qq] Another parallel research development is the focus on network connectivity. A good example, with focus on the international financial (banking) system is Diebold and Yilmaz[125].

across borders. This has found much attention in the literature. Rey[111,112] demonstrates convincingly the presence of a global financial cycle, as an international credit channel.

It is common knowledge by now that in terms of dollar values and inherent volatility, financial flows dominate the shape of international linkages and hence the extent of fragility of the global economy. That alone calls for a renewed effort to identify global systemic risks. Beyond that, the evidence is strong that more financially integrated economies have more synchronize business cycles, as suggested by, e.g., Kose et al.[130] and Crucini et al.[131] Short- and long-term international forecasting and policy analyses must by necessity be undertaken within frameworks that capture these features.

7.3.   *Volatility and high-order moments*

For a long time, the predominant tendency in forecasting and policy analysis among modelers, including multi-country modelers, has been to generate point forecasts of expected values, in some cases with confidence intervals. Forecasters have, of course, always realized that any future random variable should ideally be represented in terms of the entire conditional distribution. And Engle and White[48], as well as the vast ARCH/GARCH literature took us a step towards that objective by focusing, in addition to the mean, on the conditional variance. While obviously for a quadratic loss function the certainty equivalence result provides some comfort, in many cases the loss function is unlikely to be quadratic (or even symmetric). The practice of many institutions, most notably Central Banks (and the IMF) of providing fan charts goes some ways towards recognizing and addressing the vulnerability. But more could be done. In finance, much work has been done to explore the potential of 'density forecasts',[π] which attempt to explain higher-order moments as well, but not much of it has materialized in the traditional applied macroeconomics area, and certainly not in international models.

It may well not be technically achievable in a large-scale modeling framework to deal directly with the full predictive distribution. But, in particular in the aftermath of a highly disruptive global disturbance such as the great recession, there certainly is increasing interest to provide predictions of various confidence intervals around the prediction, be it mean or median or interval, and furthermore, a sense of how the implied uncertainties may change over time. That is by now routine in many agencies that provide confidence intervals around a central forecast (as in now familiar 'fan charts'), but the scope for similar information to be provided more broadly is immense.

But even more important than that is the need to feed back these higher-order moments into the basic model structure. Among the many things we have learned from the global financial meltdown of 2008/2009 is certainly the importance of non-linearities, the need to focus on risk measures, both sectoral and in the aggregate, as well as on global measures of systemic risk and vulnerability. A very instructive recent example is the work

---

[π] Valuable surveys of density forecast techniques, including the combination of multiple such forecasts, can be found in Tay and Wallis[132] as well as Hall and Mitchell[133], among others.

of Adrian et al.[134] on 'vulnerable growth'. They seek to exploit the asymmetries in the conditional distribution of GDP growth to construct measures that could be described as 'GDP at risk', as in the value-at-risk measures that are prominent in the finance literature. The approach is promising; there is clear evidence that the upside risks to GDP growth are generally small, while downside risks are more substantial and at the same time more variable. It remains to be seen whether these ideas can be integrated usefully into macro-models. Some promising work is already under way.[ss]

7.4.   Micro/Macro combination

Over the years, there has been a veritable explosion of quantitative and qualitative economic information at the micro level: survey data, experimental results, individual measurements of all sorts. The obvious challenge to modelers is, of course, to combine that wealth of micro-information with an overarching macro-economic or even multi-country framework. In the first instance, there is often a way to exploit micro-economic information to exogenously improve the structural characteristics of the model.

In recent years it has become abundantly obvious that many of the important issues of the day involve concerns not just about overall macro-aggregates, but also matters of distribution. Just consider the dramatic increase in interest in issues of inequality, of income and wealth distributions. This is an issue of enormous importance both within countries and across countries. Researchers are painfully aware that at a fundamental level for these questions frameworks that are based on representative agent assumptions are inadequate. This is so because the challenge is not just to derive distributional implications of the dynamics of macroeconomic aggregates, and of policies aimed at influencing these aggregates. Rather, it is by now well understood that changes in income and wealth distributions have important implications for agents' behavior, and thus for the short- and long-run dynamics of an economy.[tt] It is therefore essential that macro-econometric models also provide for multiple feedback channels from indicators of inequality to the demand and supply sides of models, as well as to adjustment mechanisms in these models, to be able to address the subsidiary questions of whether or not there are discernible effects of inequality on business cycles and/or long-run growth. It would be a great achievement if international modelers could enter that debate as well.

[ss] See, for example, the Benes, Laxton and Mongardini paper in this volume.
[tt] A detailed discussion of these effects is beyond the scope of this survey, but there is growing evidence that inequalities strongly affect not only individual behavior, but also intergenerational mobility as well as the institutional dynamics of an economy (regulatory capture).

7.5. *High-frequency information*

Modelers have long sought techniques to merge models of different frequencies to improve short-term accuracy.[uu] Indeed, economic policy happens in real time and requires rapid and up-to-date input. During the latter parts of his career, Lawrence Klein became increasingly convinced that what was needed was much timelier economic analysis, and he built what he called "current quarter models" of the US economy.[vv] With his customary zeal, he also convinced many other groups round the world to build similar structures for other countries. These structures exploited fairly simple correlations across macro-aggregates which would then allow updating of the forecast at higher frequencies. The approach no doubt addressed a need, but remained technically somewhat modest. But then much more sophisticated structures based on large data sets – combined with advanced time-series techniques were developed. The research group headed by Lucrezia Reichlin and her team at the London Business School has made most significant progress in this area.[ww]

Today, the practice of 'nowcasting' is fairly advanced, well-aligned with the general focus on (and availability of) big data, and in widespread use. Bok et al.[139] provide a useful survey of the state-of-the-art of incorporating high-frequency information into an econometric forecasting framework in the era of big data, with focus on their forecasting praxis at the Federal Reserve Bank of New York. Many national and international agencies have incorporated similar approaches into their toolkit, and the academic literature has enlarged the scope of techniques significantly.[xx] More is to come here: there are great strides being made in incorporating qualitative data, text analysis, and other tools into the mix. That is, in my view, a most exciting field. It should be noted here that in recent years there have also been significant, and in some cases quite successful, developments of VARs and (single-country) DSGEs that incorporate mixed-frequencies or real-time data.[yy]

7.6. *Agent-based models*

For many years, there has been a call for the advancement of agent-based models, arguably though in a fairly separate community.[zz] The argument rests primarily on the assumption that network interactions can potentially be an important source of economic

---

[uu] Representative early studies are, for example, Corrado and Greene[135] or Howrey et al.[136]

[vv] Over the years, he produced a voluminous output, with a diverse cast of co-authors. The first comprehensive summary of the approach is probably Klein and Sojo[133]

[ww] For one of the most recent surveys of their work see Bånbura et al.[138]

[xx] See, for example, the excellent survey in Castle et al.[140]

[yy] Good examples are Smets et al.[141], Schorfheide and Song[142].

[zz] A very comprehensive survey, covering both social sciences and hard sciences contexts, can be found in Hamill and Gilbert[143]. Advocates of the approach with fairly long standing are, among others, Farmer and Foley[144].

distortions, which are not taken into account in traditional models and cannot be modeled in a representative agent framework. The availability of 'Big Data' and vastly improved computing powers have, despite the obvious conceptual challenges, broadened the interest in the concept.

Haldane[145] is one of the first applied economists raising the possibility of an agent-based modeling strategy, not as a "... panacea for the modelling ills of economics...not that they should replace DSGE models, lock, stock, and barrel. Rather, their value comes from providing a different, complementary lens to make sense of our dappled economic and financial world ..." And he sees the world in need of a new perspective (p.21):

> *"Flows of goods and services along global supply chains have never been larger. Flows of people across borders have probably never been greater. Flows of capital across borders have certainly never been greater. And, most striking of all, flows of information across agents and borders are occurring on an altogether different scale than at any time in the past. All of these trends increase the importance of taking seriously interactions between agents when modelling an economy's dynamics."*

The statement addresses the same challenges international modelers have faced since the very early days of macro-econometric modeling, yet the urgency of new approaches has never been greater.[aaa] The exponential growth of the availability of quantitative and qualitative data presents enormous opportunities for making econometric models both more realistic and more representative of deviations from the 'homo oeconomicus' paradigm. Data have not just expanded in scope and quantity, but also in quality. New sources of information, and new techniques to exploit that information, can only enhance econometric models. As with high-frequency techniques, agent-based approaches are greatly facilitated by the new abundance of data and techniques to exploit massive data sets.

Agent-based models also appear to offer an attractive framework to incorporate behavioral anomalies and other wide-ranging deviations from rationality into the models. Computational models in which large numbers of interacting agents are endowed with behavioral rules that map the driving environmental forces into actions provide a tantalizing opportunity to move beyond simple traditional models that essentially are based on reduced-form decision rules, as well as models that must rely on representative-agent representations to incorporate deep structural driving forces such as tastes and technologies. Against that promise, huge and hard to overcome challenges regarding, for example, the robustness and identification of these models remain. Furthermore, it is

---

[aaa] It is worth noting that there is an extensive literature on heterogeneous-agent DSGE models; see the recent survey contained in Ahn et al.[146] However, while these models allow for differential responses to exogenous shocks, the do not provide mechanisms for endogenous interactions among heterogeneous agents, and thus fail to address the most interesting problem, an issue that was already touched upon above in the context of micro/macro linkages.

unclear at the present time how to solve obvious problems of quality control, such as the guarantee of external validity and appropriate signal extraction at the individual level in agent-based models. But the field offers tantalizing opportunities.

8. Summary

What then are the prospects for national and global econometric modeling? The attempt to survey the landscape from a historical perspective as undertaken in this survey supports, I believe, a cautiously optimistic view. There was a time when modeling was seen as either outdated or useless and nearly left for dead, first in the 1980s and then following the more recent global financial recession. I indeed believe that was quite premature, and it would appear that recent developments bear out that assessment. In particular the experience of the great financial latter has opened up significant opportunities for future research, as outlined in this survey. It is certainly true that a certain type of modeling as exemplified by the earliest demand-driven reduced-form models has run its course, although those models show some resilience in the commercial forecasting community. But in the academic and wider research community there are very encouraging signs of a revival and refinement of SEMs. In fact, I see many indications that paradigms are merging. As should be obvious, at a very fundamental level there is a common aspiration and common core that motivate today's DSGE models just as much as modern structural econometric models. There are important differences with regard to the degree to which strong micro foundations are critical, how advantageous or limiting the assumption of strong rational expectations is, or how to trade off reliance on reduced form parameter estimation against the identification of deep structural parameters, which leads one in the direction of the DSGE paradigm. But it would appear that modelers across the divide can indeed at least still talk to each other. It should also be obvious that, as national boundaries are becoming increasingly obsolete for economic analysis, the necessity for – and superiority of – multi-country analysis must be increasing. It is incumbent to international modelers to provide adequate tools for an increasingly challenging analysis.

Sixteen years ago, Adrian Pagan[147] called what the modelers community is trying to do the search for 'Macroeconomic Wisdom'. That, I submit, to this day remains a very apt characterization of the endeavor of national and international applied econometricians. With these enormous abstractions that we call macro-models we are trying to make sense of a highly nonlinear, interdependent, unstable and incompletely observed environment. There is no doubt that the pursuit of that objective becomes infinitely more daunting once one attempts to do so on a global scale. Undoubtedly, it involves trade-offs. Pagan himself has introduced a framework where he positions different types of models along a transformation curve, with the axes 'degree of theoretical coherence' and 'degree of empirical coherence'[54]. He goes on to position DSGE models at one end of the spectrum, and VARs at the other end. In between, there is a wide range of different types of hybrid models.

This intermediate range is where I tend to position modern structural econometric models, at the national and multi-national level, and where I believe real and actionable progress is being made. With this assessment, however, comes the recognition that optimism about paradigm convergence is quite frequently contradicted by events and/or stubborn persistence of thought. It is instructive in this context to remember the long-ranging debate between Neo-Keynesians and classical economists about macroeconomic theory. No sooner had Blanchard[148] in a paper on the state of the art of macroeconomics declared that the profession was moving towards a successful consensus model did that model fail spectacularly in the Great Recession of 2008/2009. So, pronouncements of this sort must be read with the requisite caution.

At the end of this review, however, in my view there remains a cautious, but optimistic, conclusion. It is probably fair to say the progress of international econometric models has been stalled; few, if any, significant improvements have been made. To some extent, this lack of progress in the theory and practice of truly global models is surprising, given that computing powers are vastly improved. At the same time, I am indeed deeply convinced — and I trust many modeling practitioners around the world share that conviction — that econometric models, whether at the national level or as multi-country frameworks, remain vitally important tools in that quest for 'economic wisdom'. Admittedly, the financial crisis has dramatically challenged modelers' consensus views, and the lessons from the past decade are still difficult to decipher, yet the research must be intensified. There is, no doubt, an urgent need to reinvest.

The profession should be deeply appreciative of the efforts of those early pioneers who, almost 50 years ago, had the ambition, although not the sophisticated tools, to embark on an international modeling research program. Much time has gone by since those very early days, but I believe that in the decades since then, despite its most recent relative stagnation, overall immeasurable progress has been made with regard to international macroeconomic theory, econometric technique, and model application. There are many potentially fruitful avenues of further exploration left, as outlined in this review. One can only hope that the many challenges that obviously do remain will over time be addressed with the same unbounded ambition and with continued optimism about the potential of international modeling.

References

1. G. Bårdsen, O. Eitrheim, E. S. Jansen, and R. Nymoen, *The Econometrics of Macroeconomic Modelling* (Oxford University Press, Oxford, U.K., 2003).
2. L. R. Klein, *Project LINK*, Center of Planning and Economic Research, Lecture Series No. 30 (Athens, 1977).
3. L. R. Klein, *The Project LINK Model in Integrated Global Models of Sustainable Development*, ed. A. Onishi, Vol 1 (EOLSS Publishing, Oxford, 2009), pp. 132-150.
4. B. G. Hickman, *Project LINK and Multi-Country Modeling*, in *A History of Macroeconometric Model-Building*, eds. R. Bodkin, L. R. Klein, and K. Marwah, (Edward Elgar, Aldershot, 1991), pp. 482 - 506.

5.   B. G. Hickman and K.G. Ruffing, *Project LINK: Past, Present, and Future*, in: *Modelling Global Change*, eds. L. R. Klein and F. C. Lo (UN University Press: Tokyo, 1995), pp. 13-60.

6.   P. Richardson, The structure and simulation properties of OECD's INTERLINK model, *OECD Economic Studies* **10**, Spring (1988).

7.   K. Hervé, N. Pain, P. Richardson, F. Sédillot and P.-O. Beffy, *The OECD's New Global Model*, OECD Economics Department, Working Paper No. 768 (2010).

8.   P. Masson, S. Symanski, R. Haas, and M. Dooley, *MULTIMOD - A Multi-Region Econometric Model*, IMF Staff Studies for the World Economic Outlook, July (1988).

9.   T. Bayoumi, J. Faruqee, D. Laxton, P. Karam, A. Rebucci, J. Lee, B. Hunt and I. Tchakarov, *GEM: A New International Macroeconomic Model*, IMF Occasional Paper No. 239 (Washington, 2004).

10. D. Laxton, Getting to know the global economy model and its philosophy, *IMF Staff Papers* **55**(2), 213-242 (Washington, 2008).

11. D. Anderson, B. Hunt, M. Kortelainen, M. Kumhof, D. Laxton, D. Muir, S. Mursula and S. Snudden, Getting to know GIMF: The simulation properties of the global integrated monetary and fiscal model, *IMF Working Papers* **13**(55), (2013).

12. P. Bekx, A. Bucher, A. Italianer, and M. Mors, The QUEST Model (Version 1988), *Commission of the European Communities, Economic Papers* **75**, March (1989).

13. G. Fagan, J. Henry, and R. Mestre, *Structural Modelling of the Euro Area*, in *Macroeconometric Models and the European Monetary Union*, eds. Hall, S.G., Heilemann, U. and P. Pauly, (Duncker, Humblot, Berlin, 2004).

14. H. Edison, J. R. Marquez, and R. W. Tryon, The structure and properties of the Federal Reserve Board Multicountry Model, *Economic Modelling* **4**, 115-315 (1987).

15. Economic Planning Agency, *The EPA World Economic Model - An Overview*, (UN University Press, Tokyo, 1986).

16. National Institute of Economic and Social Research, *NIGEM – The National Institute's Global Econometric Model*, (London, UK. 1996).

17. W. J. McKibbin and J. D. Sachs, *Global Linkages: Macroeconomic Interdependence and Cooperation in the World Economy*, (Brookings Institution, Washington, 1991).

18. R. C. Fair, *Specification, Estimation, and Analysis of Macroeconometric Models* (Harvard University Press, Cambridge, 1984).

19. R. C. Fair, *Testing Macroeconometric Models* (Harvard University Press: Cambridge, 1994).

20. R. C. Fair, Reflections on macroeconometric modeling, *B.E. Journal of Macroeconomics* **15**, 445-466 (2015).

21. J. B. Taylor, *Macroeconomic Policy in a World Economy*, (Wiley, New York, 1993).

22. L. R. Klein, and F.C. Lo (eds.), *Modelling Global Change* (UN University Press, Tokyo, 1995).

23. R. Bodkin, L. R. Klein and K. Marwah (eds.), *A History of Macroeconometric Model-Building* (Edward Elgar Publishing, Aldershot, 1991).
24. P. R. Mitchell, J. E. Sault, P. N. Smith and K. F. Wallis, Comparing global economic models, *Economic Modelling* **15**, 1-48 (1998).
25. J. Whitley, *A Course in Macroeconomic Modelling and Forecasting* (Harvester Wheatsheaf, Hemel Hempstead, 1994).
26. R. C. Bryant, D. S. Henderson, G. Holtham, and S. Symansky (eds.), *Empirical Macroeconomics for Independent Economies* (The Brookings Institution, Washington, DC, 1998).
27. R. C. Bryant, P. Hooper and C. L. Mann (eds.), *Evaluating Policy Regimes: New Research in Empirical Macroeconomics* (The Brookings Institution, Washington, DC, 1993).
28. S. Nickell, *The Supply Side and Macroeconomic Modeling,* in *Empirical Macroeconomics for Interdependent Economies*, eds. R.C Bryant, P. Hooper and C.L. Mann (The Brookings Institution, Washington, 1988) pp. 202-221.
29. R. E. Lucas, Expectations and the neutrality of money, *Journal of Economic Theory* **4**, pp. 103-124 (1972).
30. R. E. Lucas and T. J. Sargent (eds.), *Rational Expectations and Econometric Practice* (University of Minnesota Press, Minneapolis, 1981).
31. R. E. Lucas, Econometric policy evaluation: A critique, *Carnegie-Rochester Conference Series on Public Policy* **1**, 19-46 (1976).
32. C. Sims, Macroeconomics and reality, *Econometrica* **48**, 1-48 (1980).
33. F. Smets and R. Wouters, Shocks and frictions in US business cycles: A Bayesian DSGE approach, *American Economic Review* **97**, 586-606 (2007).
34. A. M. Sbordone, A. Tambalotti, K. Rao and K. Walsh, Policy analysis using DSGE models: An introduction, *Federal Reserve Bank of New York Economic Policy Review* **2**, 23-43 (2010).
35. L. Christiano, M. Trabandt and K. Walentin, *DSGE Models for Monetary Policy Analysis* in *Handbook of Monetary Economics*, (eds.) B.M. Friedman and M. Woodford (North-Holland, Amsterdam, 2011) pp. 285-367.
36. A. Korinek, *Thoughts on DSGE Macroeconomics: Matching the Moment, But Missing the Point?* manuscript, July 15, 2017.
37. O. Blanchard, *Do DSGE Models Have a Future? Policy Brief 16-11*, (Peterson Institute for International Economics, Washington, 2016).
38. R. Gürkaynak, and C. Tille (eds.) *DSGE Models in the Conduct of Policy: Use as Intended*, (VOX eBook, London, April 2017).
39. J. Lindé, F. Smets and R. Wouters, *Challenges for Central Banks' Macro Models*, Sveriges Riksbank Working Paper 323, May 2016.
40. T. F. Cooley and S. F. LeRoy, Atheoretical macroeconometrics: A critique, *Journal of Monetary Economics* **16**, 283-308 (1985).

41. R. Fry and A. Pagan, *Some Issues in Using VARs for Macroeconometric Research*, Australian National University, Center for Applied Macroeconomic Analysis, Working Paper No. 19. (2005).

42. R. Fry and A. Pagan, Sign restrictions in structural vector autoregressions: A critical review, *Journal of Economic Literature* **49**, 938-960 (2011).

43. M. H. Pesaran, T. Schuermann and S. M. Weiner, Modelling regional interdependencies using a global error-correcting macroeconometric model, *Journal of Business and Economics Statistics* **22**, 129-162 (2004).

44. M. H. Pesaran, and R. P. Smith, Macroeconometric modelling with a global perspective, *Manchester School* **74**, 24-49 (2006).

45. A. Chudik and M. H. Pesaran, Theory and practice of GVAR modeling, *Journal of Economic Surveys* **30**, 165-197 (2016).

46. R. F. Engle, and C. W. J. Granger, *Long-Run Economic Relationships*, (Oxford University Press, Oxford, 1991).

47. D. F. Hendry, *Dynamic Econometrics*, (Oxford University Press, Oxford, 1995).

48. R. F. Engle and H. White, *Cointegration, Causality, and Forecasting* (Oxford University Press, Oxford, 1999).

49. C. Allen and S. G. Hall, *Macroeconomic Modelling in a Changing World* (Wiley, Chichester, 1995).

50. A. M. Willman, M Kortelainen, H.-L. Mannistö, and M. Tujula, The BOF5 macroeconomic model of Finland, structure and dynamic microfoundations, *Economic Modeling* **17**, 275-303 (2000).

51. S. G. Hall, Macroeconomics and a bit more reality, *The Economic Journal* **105**, 974-988 (1995).

52. S. G. Hall, *Macroeconomic Modelling: A Perspective in Macroeconomic Modelling* in *A Changing World* (eds.) C. Allen and S. G. Hall (Wiley, New York, 1997), pp. 1-13.

53. M. H. Pesaran and R. P. Smith, Evaluation of macroeconometric models, *Economic Modelling* **2**, 125-134 (1985).

54. A. Pagan, Report on modelling and forecasting at the Bank of England, *Bank of England Quarterly Bulletin Spring*, 60-88 (2003).

55. P. Armington, A theory of demand for products distinguished by place of production, *IMF Staff Papers* **16**, 159-171 (1969).

56. J. L. Gana, B. G. Hickman, J. L. Lau and L. R. Jacobson, *Alternative Approaches to the Linkage of National Econometric Models* in *Modeling the International Transmission Mechanism*, ed. J. A. Sawyer, (North-Holland, Amsterdam, 1979), pp. 9-43.

57. A. Italianer, *Theory and Practice of International Trade Linkage Models* (Kluwer, Dordrecht, 1986).

58. P. Krugman, Scale economies, product differentiation, and the pattern of trade, *American Economic Review* **70**, 950-959 (1980).

59. E. Helpman and P. R Krugman, Market Structure and Foreign Trade, (MIT Press, Cambridge, 1985).

60. A. B. Bernard, J. Eaton, J.B. Jensen and S. Kortum, Plants and productivity in international trade, *American Economic Review* **93**, 1268-1290 (2003).

61. A. B. Bernard, J.B. Jensen, S.J. Redding, and P.K. Schott, *Global Firms*, NBER Working Paper, 22727, October (2016).

62. G. Grossman and E. Rossi-Hansberg, Trading tasks: A simple theory of offshoring, *American Economic Review* **98**, 1978-1997 (2006).

63. J. E. Anderson and E. van Wincoop, Gravity with gravitas: A solution to the border puzzle, *American Economic Review* **93**, 170-192 (2003).

64. B. Hoekman (ed.), *The Global Trade Slowdown: A New Normal* (VoxEU E-Book, Centre for Economic Policy Research, London, 2015).

65. J. Eaton, S. Kortum, B. Neiman and J. Romalis, Trade and the global recession, *American Economic Review* **106**, 3401-3438 (2016).

66. D. Haugh, A. Kopoin, E. Rusticelli, D. Turner and R. Dutu, *Cardiac Arrest or Dizzy Spell: Why Is World Trade So Weak and What Can Policy Do About It?* OECD Economic Policy Paper No. 18. (2016).

67. D. W. Diamond and P. H. Dybvig, Bank runs, deposit insurance, and liquidity, *Journal of Political Economy* **91**, 401-419 (1983).

68. P. Isard, *Exchange Rate Economics* (Cambridge University Press, Cambridge, 1995).

69. M. P. Taylor, The economics of exchange rates, *Journal of Economic Literature* **33**, 13-47 (1995).

70. R. MacDonald and I. Marsh, *Exchange Rate Modeling* (Kluwer, Boston, 1999).

71. R. Meese and K. Rogoff, Empirical exchange rate models of the seventies: Do they fit out of sample?, *Journal of International Economics* **14**, 3-24 (1983).

72. Y.-W. Cheung, M. Chinn, and A. G. Pascual, Empirical exchange rate models of the nineties: Are any fit to survive? *Journal of International Money and Finance* **24**, 1150-1175 (2005).

73. B. Rossi, Exchange rate predictability, *Journal of Economic Literature* **51**, 1063-1119 (2013).

74. Y.-W. Cheung, Y-W., M. Chinn, A.G. Pascual and Y. Zhang, *Exchange Rate Prediction Redux: New Models, New Data, New Currencies*, NBER Working Paper 23267, March (2017).

75. P. Isard, *Equilibrium Exchange Rates: Assessment Methodologies*, IMF Working Paper 07/296, December (2007).

76. W. R. Cline and J. Williamson, *New Estimates of Fundamental Equilibrium Exchange Rates*, Policy Brief 08-7, (Peterson Institute for International Economics, Washington, 2008).

77. D. T. Coe and E. Helpman, International R&D spillovers, *European Economic Review* **39**, 59-87 (1995).

78. G. M. Grossman and E. Helpman, Trade, knowledge spillovers, and growth, *European Economic Review* **35**, 517-526 (1991).

79. G. M. Grossman and E. Helpman (1995), *Technology and Trade* in *Handbook of International Economics* **3**, (eds.) G. Grossman and K.G. Rogoff (Elsevier, Amsterdam, 1995), pp. 1279-1337.

80. W. Keller, International trade, foreign direct investment, and technology spillovers, *Handbook of the Economy of Innovation* **2**, 793-829 (2010).

81. S. Holly and I. Petrella, Factor demand, technology shocks, and the business cycle, *Review of Economics and Statistics* **94**, 948-963 (2012).

82. S. Holly, I. Petrella and E. Santoro, Aggregate fluctuations and the cross-sectional dynamics of firm growth, *Journal of the Royal Statistical Society* **A**(176), 459-479 (2013).

83. P. Dixon and D. Jorgenson (eds.) *Handbook of Computable General Equilibrium Modeling* (Elsevier, Amsterdam, 2013).

84. T. J. Kehoe, P. S. Pujolas and J. Rossbach, *Quantitative Trade Models: Developments and Challenges*, NBER Working Paper 22706, September (2016).

85. R. Kaufmann, A model of the world oil market for Project LINK: Integrating economics, geology, and politics, *Economic Modelling* **12**, 165-178 (1995).

86. F. X. Diebold, L. Liu and K. Yilmaz, *Commodity Connectedness*, Discussion Paper, June (2017).

87. J. Pons, The accuracy of IMF and OECD forecasts, *Journal of Forecasting* **19**, 53-63 (2000).

88. V. Wieland and M. Wolters, *Macroeconomic Model Comparisons and Forecast Competitions*, VOXEU Note, February 13 (2012).

89. H. Genberg and A. Martinez, *On the Accuracy and Efficiency of IMF Forecasts: A Survey and Some Extensions*, IEO Background Paper BP/14/04, February 12 (2014).

90. N, Pain, C. Lewis, T.-T. Dang, Y. Jin, and P. Richardson, *OECD Forecasts During and After the Financial Crisis: A Post Mortem*, OECD Economics Department Working Paper, March (2014).

91. N. Smith, *Why Bother with Microfoundations?*, Noahpinion blog, March 3 (2012).

92. F. Ghironi, *Macro Needs Micro*, NBER Working Paper 23836, September (2017).

93. O. Blanchard, *The Need for Different Classes of Macroeconomic Models*, Peterson Institute for International Economics, blog post January 12 (2017).

94. J. E. Stiglitz, *Where Modern Macroeconomics Went Wrong*, NBER Working Paper 23795, September (2017).

95. V. Wieland, T. Cwik, G.J. Müller, S. Schmidt and M. Wolters, *A New Comparative Approach to Macroeconomic Modeling and Policy Analysis*, University of Frankfurt Discussion Paper, April (2009).

96. C. E. Petersen, *Dynamic Bilateral Tariff Games: An Econometric Analysis, (PhD Thesis*, University of Pennsylvania, 1988).

97. G. C. Chow, *Econometric Analysis by Control Methods* (Wiley, New York, 1981).

98. S. Holly and A. Hughes Hallett, *Optimal Control, Expectations, and Uncertainty* (Cambridge University Press, Cambridge, 1989).

99. M. L. Petit, *Control Theory and Dynamic Games in Economic Policy Analysis* (Cambridge University Press, Cambridge, 1990).

100. D. A. Kendrick, *Stochastic Control for Economic Models* (McGraw-Hill, New York, 1981).

101. S. G. Hall. and A. Garratt, *The Treatment of Expectations Effects* in *Large-Scale Models in LINK Proceedings 1991-1992* (eds.) B. G. Hickman and L. R. Klein (World Scientific Publishing, Singapore, 1998) pp. 247-275.

102. S. G. Hall, Time inconsistency and optimal policy formation in the presence of rational expectations, *Journal of Economic Dynamics and Control* **10**, 323-326 (1986).

103. L. P. Hansen and T. J. Sargent, *Uncertainty Within Economic Models* (World Scientific Publishing, Singapore, 2014).

104. L. Hurwicz and S. Reiter, *Designing Economic Mechanisms* (Cambridge University Press, Cambridge, 2006).

105. O. Blanchard, J. D. Ostry and A. R. Ghosh, *International Policy Coordination: The Loch Ness Monster*, IMF direct blog post, December 15 (2013).

106. A. R. Ghosh and P. R. Masson, *Economic Cooperation in an Uncertain World* (Oxford University Press, Oxford, 1994).

107. J. D. Ostry and A. R. Ghosh, *Obstacles to International Policy Coordination, and How to Overcome Them*, IMF Staff Discussion Note 13/11, December (2013).

108. G. Oudiz and J. Sachs, Macroeconomic policy coordination among industrial countries, *Brookings Papers on Economic Activity* **1**, 1-75 (1984).

109. J. M. Frenkel, M. Goldstein and P. Masson, *Coordinated Versus Uncoordinated Policy Rules* in *Macroeconomic Policies in an Interdependent World* (eds.) R. Bryant, D. Currie, J. Frenkel, P. Masson, R. Portes (The Brookings Institution, Washington, 1989) pp. 203-239.

110. R. Barrell, K. Dury and I. Hurst, International monetary policy coordination: an evaluation using a large econometric model, *Economic Modelling* **20**, 507-527 (2003).

111. H. Rey, *Dilemma Not Trilemma: The Global Financial Cycle and Monetary Policy Interdependence*, NBER Working Paper 21162, May (2015).

112. H. Rey, *International Channels of Transmission of Monetary Policy and the Mundellian Trilemma*, NBER Working Paper 21852, January (2016).

113. B. Eichengreen, *International Policy Coordination: The Long View*, NBER Working Paper 17665, December (2011).

114. J. A. Frankel, International Coordination, NBER Working Paper 21878, January (2016).

115. A. R. Ghosh and M. S. Qureshi, *From Great Depression to Great Recession*, International Monetary Fund, Washington, forthcoming (2017).

116. F. Lupo-Pasini and R. P. Buckley, Global systemic risk and international regulatory coordination: Squaring sovereignty and financial stability, *American University International Law Review* **30**(4) (2015).

117. O. Jeanne, Macroprudential policies in a global perspective 2014, IMES Discussion Paper No. 2014-E-1, *Institute for Monetary and Economic Studies*, Bank of Japan (2014).

118. D. Rodrik, *The Globalization Paradox: Democracy and the Future of the World Economy* (W.W. Norton, New York, 2011).

119. B. G. Hickman and H. Huntington (eds.), *Macroeconomic Impacts of Energy Shocks*, EMF7 Report, Vol. III, (Stanford, Energy Modeling Forum, 1987).

120. W. Nordhaus, *Integrated Economic and Climate Modeling* in *Handbook of Computable General Equilibrium Modeling*, eds. P. Dixon and D. Jorgenson, (Elsevier, Amsterdam, 2013), pp. 1069-1131.

121. W. J. McKibbin and P. Wilcoxen, *A Global Approach to Energy and the Environment: The G-Cubed Model* in *Handbook of Computable General Equilibrium Modeling*, eds. P. Dixon and D. Jorgenson (Elsevier, Amsterdam, 2013), pp. 995-1068.

122. P. J. Courtois, Error analysis in nearly-completely decomposable stochastic systems, *Econometrica* **43**, 691-709 (1975).

123. P. J. Courtois and R. L. Ashenhurst, *Decomposability* (Academic Press, New York, 1977).

124. A. Ando, F. M. Fisher, and H. A. Simon, *Essays on the Structure of Social Science Models* (Cambridge, MIT Press, 1963).

125. F. X. Diebold and K. Yilmaz, On the network topology of variance decompositions: Measuring the connectedness of financial firms, *Journal of Econometrics* **182**, 119-134 (2014).

126. World Bank, *Measuring and Analyzing the Impact of GVCs on Economic Development* (The World Bank, Washington, 2017).

127. G. N. F. Weiss, D. Bostandzic and S. Neumann, What factors drive systemic risk during international financial crises? *Journal of Banking and Finance* **41**, 78-96 (2014).

128. A. Gottesman and M. Leiblock, *Understanding Systemic Risk in Global Financial Markets* (Wiley, New York, 2017).

129. E. Cerruti, S. Claessens and P. McGuire, *Systemic Risk in Global Banking: What Can Available Data Tell us and What More Data Are Needed?*, Bank for International Settlements, Basel, Working Paper No. 376, April (2012).

130. M. A. Kose, C. Otrok and C.H. Whiteman, International business cycles: World, region, and country-specific factors, *American Economic Review* **93**, 1216-1239 (2003).

131. A. Crucini, M. A. Kose and C. Otrok, What are the driving forces of international business cycles, *Review of Economic Dynamics* **14**, 156-175 (2011).

132. A. S. Tay and K. F. Wallis, Density forecasting: A survey, *Journal of Forecasting* **19**, 235-254 (2000).
133. S. G. Hall and J. Mitchell, Combining density forecasts, *International Journal of Forecasting* **23**, 1-13 (2007).
134. T. Adrian, N. Boyarchenko, and D. Giannone, *Vulnerable Growth*, Federal Reserve Bank of New York Staff Report No. 794, rev. November (2017).
135. C. Corrado, and M. Greene, Reducing uncertainty in short-term projections: Linkage of monthly and quarterly models, *Journal of Forecasting* **7**, 77-102 (1988).
136. E. P. Howrey, M. R. Donihue and S. H. Hymans, Merging monthly and quarterly forecasts: Experience with MQEM, *Journal of Forecasting* **10**, 255-268 (1991).
137. L. R. Klein and E. Sojo (1989), *Combinations of High and Low Frequency Data in Macroeconometric Models* in *Economics in Theory and Practice: An Eclectic Approach*, eds. L. R. Klein and J. Marquez (Kluwer Academic Publishing, Nijmegen, 1989), pp. 3-16.
138. M. Bańbura, D. Giannone, M. Modugno and L. Reichlin, *Now-Casting and the Real-Time Data Flow*, European Central Bank Working Paper 1564, July (2013).
139. B. Bok, D. Caratelli, D. Giannone, A. Sbordone, and A. Tambalotti, *Macroeconometric Nowcasting and Forecasting with Big Data*, Federal Reserve Bank of New York, Staff Report No. 830, November (2017).
140. J. Castle, D. F. Hendry and O. I. Kitov, *Forecasting and Nowcasting Macroeconomic Variables: A Methodological Overview*, Oxford University, Department of Economics Discussion Paper 674, September (2013).
141. F. Smets, A. Warne and R. Wouters, *Professional Forecasters and the Real-Time Forecasting Performance of an Estimated New Keynesian Model for the Euro Area*, ECB Discussion Paper 1571, August (2013).
142. F. Schorfheide and D. Song, Real-time forecasting with a mixed-frequency VAR, *Journal of Business and Economic Statistics* **33**, 366-380 (2015).
143. L. Hamill and N. Gilbert, *Agent-Based Modelling in Economics* (Wiley, New York, 2016).
144. J. D. Farmer and D. Foley, The economy needs agent-based modeling, *Nature* **460**, 685-686 (2009).
145. A. Haldane, *The Dappled World*, GLS Shackle Biennial Memorial Lecture, BIS, Basel, November (2016).
146. S. Ahn, G. Kaplan, B. Moll, T. Winberry and C. Wolf, *When Inequality Matters for Macro and Macro Matters for Inequality*, NBER Working Paper 23494, June (2017).
147. A. Pagan, *The Getting of Macroeconomic Wisdom in Advances in Macroeconomic Theory*, ed. J. Drèze, (Palgrave Macmillan, London, 2001), pp. 219-235.
148. O. J. Blanchard, The state of macro, *Annual Review of Economics* **1**, 209-228 (2009).

II. International Financial System

Mitigating the deadly embrace in financial cycles: Countercyclical buffers and loan-to-value limits[a]

Jaromir Benes, Douglas Laxton, and Joannes Mongardini

International Monetary Fund,
E-mails: jaromir.benes@gmail.com,
dlaxton@imf.org, jmongardini@imf.org

This paper presents a new version of MAPMOD (Mark II) to study the effectiveness of macroprudential regulations. We extend the original model by explicitly modeling the housing market. We show how household demand for housing, house prices, and bank mortgages are intertwined in what we call a *deadly embrace*. Without macroprudential policies, this deadly embrace naturally leads to housing boom and bust cycles, which can be very costly for the economy, as shown by the Global Financial Crisis of 2008-09.

Keywords: Lending booms; Credit crunch; Financial crisis; Financial cycle; Housing market; Countercyclical buffers; Loan-to-value limits; Macroprudential policies.

1.   Introduction

This paper assesses the effectiveness of countercyclical buffers (CCBs) and loan-to-value (LTV) limits for mitigating the risk and costs of financial crises. For this purpose, we use a version of the MAPMOD model augmented by an explicit housing sector.[b]

MAPMOD departs from the traditional loanable funds model. It assumes that bank lending is not constrained by loanable funds, but by the banks' own expectations about future profitability and banking regulations. In MAPMOD, the banking system may create purchasing power and facilitate efficient resource allocation when there are permanent improvements in the economy's growth potential. However, the possibility of excessively large and risky loans, not justified by growth prospects, also exists.[c] These risky loans can ultimately impair bank balance sheets and sow the seeds of a financial crisis. Banks respond to losses through higher spreads and sharp credit cutbacks, with adverse effects for the real economy. These features of MAPMOD capture key facts of financial cycles, like the correlations of bank credit with the business cycle and with asset prices[3-7].

---

[a] *IMF Working Papers* describe research in progress by the author(s) and are published to elicit comments and to encourage debate. The views expressed in IMF Working Papers are those of the author(s) and do not necessarily represent the views of the IMF, its Executive Board, or IMF management.

[b] A full technical description of the structure and equations of the model will be documented in a forthcoming paper entitled "MAPMOD Mark II: Adding Countercyclical Buffers and Loan-to-Value Limits."

[c] The financial accelerator of Bernanke, Gertler, and Gilchrist[1] and the leverage cycle of Geanakoplos[2], Mendoza[3] and Bianchi and Mendoza[4] embody a similar process.

MAPMOD has significant non-linearities in the banks' response toward regulatory capital and individual borrowers' creditworthiness. At an overall balance sheet level, the pricing of loans increases exponentially as banks get closer to their minimum capital-adequacy ratios (loan portfolio supply curve). Via this mechanism, banks remain compliant with minimum capital-adequacy ratios (CAR), and thus avoid regulatory sanctions or supervisory intervention. At an individual loan level, banks charge increasingly higher interest rate spreads the higher the LTV ratio in order to compensate for the greater risk of default (individual lending supply curve). The interactions of these non-linearities can produce financial cycles and crises in line with the historical record. The most recent case in point would be the Global Financial Crisis of 2008-09[6,8,9].

MAPMOD can account for good, as well as bad, credit expansions. As shown by Claessens, Ayhan and Terrones[11], credit expansions may be justified by lower uncertainty or by future productivity improvements. Under these circumstances, banks' increased leverage may prove to be consistent with future fundamentals. Other credit cycles, however, may be based on a misjudgment about uncertainty or by excessive optimism about future productivity, forcing banks eventually to unleash a costly deleveraging process on the economy. This is consistent with the evidence that the recessions that follow financial crises have been especially damaging in terms of lost output[12,13].

The MAPMOD Mark II model in this paper includes an explicit housing market, in which house prices are strongly correlated with banks' credit supply. This corresponds to the experience prior and during the Global Financial Crisis[6,14]. This *deadly embrace* between bank mortgages, household balance sheets, and house prices can be the source of financial cycles. A corollary is that the housing market is only partially constrained by LTV limits as the additional availability of credit itself boosts house prices, and thus raises LTV limits. Conversely, during a downturn, the LTV limit tightens as house prices fall, thus accentuating the financial cycle. This result is similar in nature to the credit cycles of Kiyotaki and Moore[15] and the leverage cycle of Geanakoplos[2], Mendoza[3], and Bianchi and Mendoza[4]. It differs, however, from the general equilibrium model developed by Goodhart and others[16,17] as house prices in the latter are not endogenously determined and thus there is no externality arising from the interaction between mortgages, household balance sheets, and house prices.

From a policy perspective, our simulation results require a rethinking of LTV limits that takes into account their intrinsic procyclicality. We conclude that LTV limits should be based on a historical moving average of house prices over several years, rather than just on current market values to reduce such intrinsic procyclicality. We also analyze the interaction between CCBs and LTV limits during the financial cycle. While CCBs alone can be effective in reducing banks' credit expansion in an upturn and easing the credit crunch in a downturn, our simulations show that they are not sufficient in limiting the *deadly embrace*, given that they do not limit credit specifically to the housing sector. If used in conjunction with LTV limits, the use of a historical moving average of house prices to calculate LTV limits would help to reinforce the countercyclical nature of CCBs.

The rest of the paper is structured as follows. Section 2 discusses the current toolbox of macroprudential regulations, the experience implementing these regulations so far, and the rationale for MAPMOD as an analytical foundation to analyze the impact of these regulations on the behavior of banks and the macroeconomy. Section 3 sets out a non-technical summary of MAPMOD and its extension to the housing market. We present a partial equilibrium analysis of banks, households, and the housing market. We then bring the pieces together in a consistent general equilibrium framework. Section 4 applies MAPMOD to two types of macroprudential policy, namely CCBs and LTV limits. Section 5 summarizes the policy conclusions.

2.   Macroprudential Regulations

The financial history of the last 8 centuries is replete with devastating financial crises, mostly emanating from large increases in financial leverage[9]. The latest example, the Global Financial Crisis of 2008-2009, saw the unwinding of a calamitous run-up in leverage by banks and households associated with the housing market[6,14]. As a result, the financial supervision community has acknowledged that microprudential regulations alone are insufficient to avoid a financial crisis. They need to be accompanied by appropriate macroprudential policies to avoid the build-up of systemic risk and to weaken the effects of asset price inflation on financial intermediation and the buildup of excessive leverage in the economy.

The Basel III regulations adopted in 2010 recognize for the first time the need to include a macroprudential overlay to the traditional microprudential regulations (Appendix I). Beyond the requirements for capital buffers, and leverage and liquidity ratios, Basel III regulations include CCBs between 0.0 and 2.5 percent of risk-weighted assets that raise capital requirements during an upswing of the business cycle and reduce them during a downturn. The rationale is to counteract procyclical-lending behavior, and hence to restrain a buildup of systemic risk that might end in a financial crisis. Basel III regulations are silent, however, about the implementation of CCBs and their cost to the economy, leaving it to the supervisory authorities to make a judgment about the appropriate timing for increasing or lowering such buffers, based on a credit-to-GDP gap measure. This measure, however, does not distinguish between good versus bad credit expansions (see below) and is irrelevant for countries with significant dollar lending, where exchange rate fluctuations can severely distort the credit-to-GDP gap measure.

One of the limitations of Basel III regulations is that they do not focus on specific, leverage-driven markets, like the housing market, that are most susceptible to an excessive build-up of systemic risk. Many of the recent financial crises have been associated with housing bubbles fueled by over-leveraged households. With hindsight, it is unlikely that CCBs alone would have been able to avoid the Global Financial Crisis, for example.

For this reason, financial supervision authorities and the IMF have looked at additional macroprudential policies[18,19]. For the housing market, three additional types of macroprudential regulations have been implemented: 1) sectoral capital surcharges through higher risk weights or loss-given-default (LGD) ratios;[d] 2) LTV limits; and 3) caps on debt-service to income ratios (DSTI), or loan to income ratios (LTI).

Use of such macroprudential regulations has mushroomed over the last few years in both advanced economies and emerging markets[19]. At end 2014, 23 countries used sectoral capital surcharges for the housing market, and 25 countries used LTV limits. An additional 15 countries had explicit caps on DSTI or LTI caps. The experience so far has been mixed. Cerruti, Claessens and Laeven[20] in a sample of 119 countries over the 2000-2013 period find that, while macroprudential policies can help manage financial cycles, they work less well in busts than in booms. This result is intuitive in that macroprudential regulations are generally procyclical and can therefore be counterproductive during a bust when bank credit should expand to offset the economic downturn.

Macroprudential regulations are often directed at restraining bank credit, especially to the housing market. They do not, however, take into account the tradeoffs between mitigating the risks of a financial crisis on the one side and the cost of lower financial intermediation on the other. In addition, given that these measures are generally procyclical, they can accentuate the credit crunch during busts. More generally, an analytical foundation for analyzing these tradeoffs has been lacking, with the notable exceptions of Goodhart and others[16,17], and Bianchi and Mendoza[4]. MAPMOD has been designed to help fill this analytical gap and to provide insights for the design of less procyclical macroprudential regulations.

3.   A Non-Technical Presentation of MAPMOD

3.1.   *MAPMOD, Mark I*

The starting point of the MAPMOD framework is the factual observation that, in contrast to the loanable funds model, banks do not wait for additional deposits before increasing their lending. Instead, they determine their lending to the economy based on their expectations of future profits, conditional on the economic outlook and their regulatory capital. They then fund their lending portfolio out of their existing deposit base, or by resorting to wholesale funding and debt instruments. Banks actively seek new opportunities for profitable lending independently of the size or growth of their deposit base—unless constrained by specific regulations.

This observation has significant repercussions for the role of banks in the economy. While banks in the loanable funds model provide passive intermediation between saving and investment, in MAPMOD they contribute directly to consumption and investment demand by providing the means to increase leverage in the economy on the expectation of future income and productivity growth. If banks' expectations materialize, the economy is better off and banks get paid back their loans. This we refer to as a good credit expansion.

---

[d] The LGD ratio is the share of the loan that is lost when a debtor defaults. The LGD ratios applied to different types of asset enter the calculation of risk-weighted assets. Thus, an increase in LGD ratios for a given loan portfolio would imply an increase in risk-weighted assets—and therefore an increase in required capital.

If, however, the economy does not produce the expected income and productivity growth, loans will turn non-performing, and banks will later need to cut bank on their lending through a process of deleveraging. We refer to this as a bad credit expansion. Ex-ante, however, banks (and other agents in the economy) do not know whether the economy is in a good or bad credit expansion. If banks are especially over-optimistic during an upswing, their lending behavior can turn a bad credit cycle into a full financial crisis.

MAPMOD can capture the distinction between good and bad credit expansion. The model comprises sectors for households, local producers, exporters, banks, the central bank, and the rest of the world. Borrowers use bank loans to finance consumption and investment expenditures, using their assets (physical capital, housing, stocks) as collateral. Ex post, defaults are a function of asset prices, which are driven by both common and idiosyncratic risks. Banks cannot fully diversify these risks, which therefore remain in part on their balance sheet.

Banks' behavior is driven by their assessment of the risk/return tradeoffs, and subject to regulatory constraints. In particular, a bank's ability to expand its balance sheet is limited by its own capital and regulations. The bank needs to ensure that its regulatory capital will be above the mandated minimum capital-adequacy ratio (CAR), regardless of the potential risks to its balance sheet. Hence, banks seek ex-ante to establish sufficient capital buffers — over and above the minimum CAR — to avoid regulatory sanctions or supervisory intervention ex-post. In the limit, enforcement may involve closure of the bank.

In MAPMOD, a bank makes decisions at two levels. First, it decides the optimal size of its loan portfolio, given its own expectations about future profitability and the risk absorption capacity of the bank's capital. In the real world, this is equivalent to the bank's annual budget cycle where bank management sets growth targets for the loan portfolio, subject to the desired capital buffers. Second, the bank assesses each potential borrower (and his/her assets) for creditworthiness. The parallel in the real world is for the loan to be assessed against the bank's risk matrix, and then approved by a credit risk committee.

Decisions at both levels are driven by non-linearities. A bank chooses its *optimal loan portfolio curve* as a function of lending spreads and minimum CARs. The closer the bank's capital is to the minimum required, the higher is the lending spread for additional loans. At the same time, the bank chooses its *individual lending supply curve* as a function of the lending spread and the LTV ratio for an individual loan applicant. The higher the LTV ratio, the wider the lending spread charged to individual customers. Both the *optimal loan portfolio curve* and the *individual lending supply curve* are shown in Fig. 1.

The bank's loan decisions critically depend on their expectations about the future. On the one hand, if a bank is overly conservative about the potential productivity improvements in the economy, it may lose market share against competitors. On the other hand, if a bank is overly optimistic about the future, it may experience a relatively larger increase in its loan portfolio during the upswing of the business cycle only to be faced later by a higher level of NPLs and a stronger requirement to deleverage during the downturn. If the whole banking sector is overly optimistic about the future, this induces a shift in the individual lending supply curves, and an underpricing of systemic risk in the banking sector

(Fig. 2). When banks eventually become aware of the extent of the risk on their balance sheets, they deleverage, causing a slowdown or contraction in economic activity.

The good versus bad credit cycle in MAPMOD can best be demonstrated through a series of simulations (Fig. 3). In these simulations, we assume that banks ex-ante expects a significant boost in productivity in the economy. As a result, they increase their lending at time 0. If the productivity boost is confirmed, the economy grows faster as a result and banks get repaid their loans over time (good credit expansion). If productivity, however, turns out lower than expected, banks will face higher NPLs (bad credit expansion). When the inevitable downturn arrives, banks are forced to deleverage to reestablish their optimal capital-adequacy ratio, and repair the capital losses associated with higher NPLs. In the worst-case scenario, where banks underprice the risk of their lending, the downturn can be severe and lead to a recession (bad credit expansion with overly optimistic banks).

3.2. *MAPMOD, Mark II*

In MAPMOD, Mark II, we extend the original model by introducing an explicit housing market. We use the modular features of the model to analyze partial equilibrium simulations for banks, households, and the housing market, before turning to general equilibrium results. This incremental approach sheds light on the intuition behind the model and simulation results.

The housing market is characterized by liquidity-constrained households that require financing to buy houses. A house is an asset that provides a stream of housing services to households. The value of a house to each household is the net present value of the future stream of housing services that it provides plus any capital gain/loss associated with future changes in house prices. We define the *fundamental house price* households are willing to pay to buy a house the price that is consistent with the expected income/productivity increases in the economy. If prices go above the *fundamental house price* reflecting excessive leverage, we refer to this as an *inflated house price*. The supply of houses for sale in the market is assumed to be fixed each period. House prices are determined by matching buyers and sellers in a recursive equilibrium with expected house prices taken as given. We abstract from many real-world complications such as neighborhood externalities, geographical location, square footage or other forms of heterogeneity.[e] Households with different and endogenously-determined down payments (and hence LTV

---

[e] We are aware that this is a strong assumption that does not match the real world. In fact, Mian and Sufi[14] provide ample evidence of entire neighborhoods in the United States being affected by foreclosures during the Global Financial Crisis. We plan to model a concept of neighborhood externality in future research.

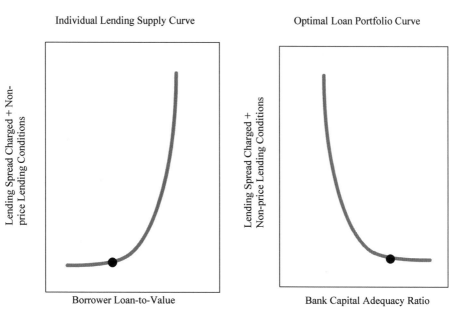

Fig. 1. Non-Linearities in Bank Lending Behavior.

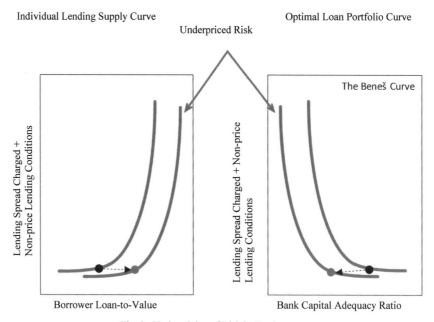

Fig. 2. Underpricing of Risk by Banks.

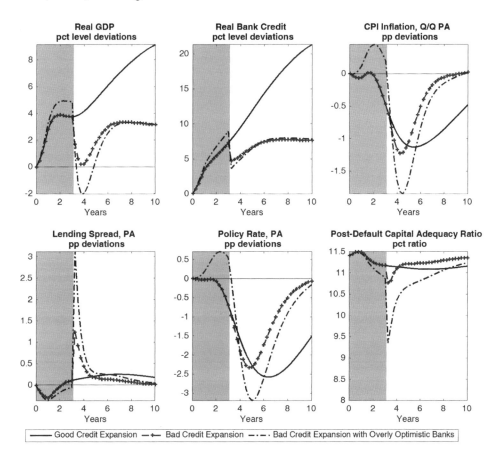

Fig. 3. Good vs. Bad Credit Cycles.

Source: Authors' simulations.

ratios) apply for long-term fixed-interest rate mortgages.[f] Each household faces the individual lending supply curve of the financing bank, defining combinations of the lending rate and loan volumes. The household's own economic conditions define its point on the curve (i.e. an intersection of credit supply and credit demand curves).

The probability of a household defaulting on the loan later into the lifetime of the loan is driven by a combination of the LTV and LTI ratios. These indicators therefore determine the riskiness of each borrower. Banks, aware of the market value of the house, are able to evaluate the probability of default for each mortgage and price it accordingly. They do not know ex-ante, however, whether any particular household will default on its loan. They only discover ex-post whether a borrower is able to repay. Cost of foreclosure is included

---

[f] In this paper, we consider only fixed-rate mortgages for simplicity. In future research, we plan to apply the same model to variable-rate mortgages, where the interest rate risk is shifted from banks to households.

in an LGD parameter, fixed at 0.25 in our simulations. So, if a borrower forecloses on a loan with outstanding balance of 100,000, the bank is only able to recover 75,000 in our baseline calibration.

Bank financing plays a critical role in the determination of house prices in the model. If banks provide a larger number of mortgages on an expectation of higher household income in the future, demand for housing will go up, thus inflating house prices. Conversely, if banks reduce their loan exposure to the housing market, demand for houses in the economy will be reduced, leading to a slump in house prices. House prices therefore move with the credit cycle in MAPMOD, Mark II, just as in the real world, as shown in the simulation in Fig. 4.

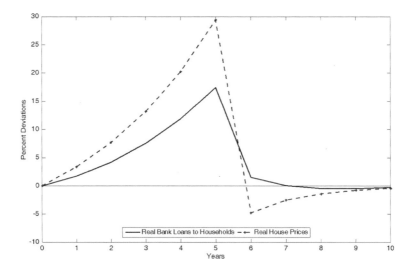

Fig. 4. Co-Movements in Bank Credit and House Prices.

Source: Authors' simulations.

Nonperforming loans and foreclosures in the housing market occur when households are faced with an idiosyncratic, or economy-wide, shock that affects their current LTV or LTI characteristics. Banks will seek to reduce the likelihood of losses by requiring a sufficiently high LTV ratio to cover the cost of foreclosure. But they will not be able to diversify away the systemic risk of a general fall in house prices in the economy. Securitization of mortgages in MAPMOD is not allowed. And even if banks were able to securitize mortgages, other agents in the economy would need to carry the systemic risk of a sharp fall in house prices. At the economy-wide level, the systemic risk associated with the housing market is therefore not diversifiable. The evidence from the Global Financial Crisis on securitization and credit default swaps confirms that this is the case, regardless of who holds mortgage-backed securities.

3.2.1. *Partial equilibrium analysis for banks*

In this section, we look at the equilibrium for a single bank in the model, while keeping the rest of the economy unchanged. In particular, a bank does not internalize the effects of its lending behavior on house prices in the economy and thus takes house prices as exogenous.

From a bank's perspective, the optimal choice is to lend to the housing sector as long as the expected return on an additional mortgage (conditional on the probability of default) is higher than the marginal cost of funds plus the marginal cost of maintaining the optimal capital adequacy ratio.[g] Value at risk is determined by the likelihood of default times the difference between the loan value and the recovery rate on the house price. As the LTV ratio rises, the bank will require higher spreads to approve a mortgage in order to offset the higher value at risk. This gives rise to the bank's own *individual lending supply curve* shown in Fig. 1.

On the demand side, households apply for mortgages based on their choice of housing and their endogenously-determined down payments as explained above. They therefore demand mortgages based on different LTV ratios that make them more or less likely to default on their mortgages. In turn, they may reduce the spread charged on their mortgage by raising their down payment (reducing their LTV ratio). A bank's optimal lending will therefore be where demand and supply for mortgages meet in the LTV/spread space (Fig. 5, Panel 1).

Missing from this partial equilibrium analysis is that, in a general equilibrium context, banks' own lending can affect house prices. As shown in Fig. 4, if all banks increase lending to the housing sector at the same time, house prices will start rising. This will increase the incentives for banks to lend to the housing sector as mortgage demand rises on expectations of higher future house prices. Their internal calculations of the value at risk will fall. Banks may therefore be willing to shift their lending supply curve, with a higher LTV ratio for a given spread. If all banks do the same, house prices will become inflated and thus systemic risk in the economy increases (Fig. 5, Panel 2). We will come back to this point in the general equilibrium analysis below.

3.2.2. *Partial equilibrium analysis for households*

Households buy houses for the expected capital gains and the housing services they provide. The higher the expected increase in house prices in the future, the higher will be the house price that households are willing to pay today and thus the greater the demand for housing. Households may therefore be willing to buy houses at *inflated prices*, because of the expected capital gain in a house-price bubble scenario.

In MAPMOD, Mark II, we assume that expectations of house prices are rational, based on the limited time horizon that households use to make decisions in an uncertain environment. In forming their expectations, households take the banks' lending behavior

---

[g] The marginal cost of maintaining the capital adequacy ratio can implicitly be thought of the opportunity cost of lending to other sectors of the economy on a risk adjusted basis. In future research, we plan to make this trade-off with other sectors of the economy explicit.

as given, and do not take into account the impact of a potential bank deleveraging scenario on future house prices.

Household demand for housing is thus linked to banks' willingness to lend in two ways. First, households need mortgages from banks because they are liquidity constrained. Without mortgages, households would not be able to finance the purchase of a house. Second, household expectations for future house prices depend on expectations of bank lending to the housing sector. We call this symbiotic relationship between household demand and bank lending the *deadly embrace* — it creates the housing boom and bust that we will see later in the general equilibrium context.

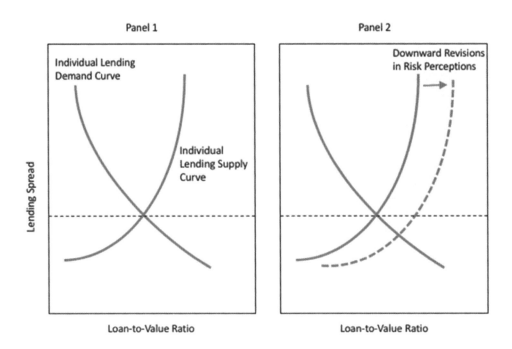

Fig. 5. Bank Lending Demand and Supply.

In a partial equilibrium context, the intersection between the fixed vertical supply curve of housing and the downward sloping demand curve will determine the equilibrium price for houses (Fig. 6, Panel 1). If banks increase lending to the housing sector, the expected future increase in house prices will rise (Fig. 6, Panel 2), implying an increase in current demand for housing and thus a higher *inflated equilibrium price*. This correlation between bank lending, house prices, and demand for housing illustrates the *deadly embrace* discussed above.

3.2.3. *Putting the pieces together: The general equilibrium story*

This *deadly embrace* becomes even more evident in a dynamic general equilibrium context. The interaction between bank lending behavior and household demand for housing has the potential to inflate house prices over time in a spiral unrelated to fundamental economic conditions. The bubble will ultimately burst when leverage in the economy reaches a point that is clearly excessive, and banks re-price the risk associated with housing market — perhaps at the behest of the regulators.

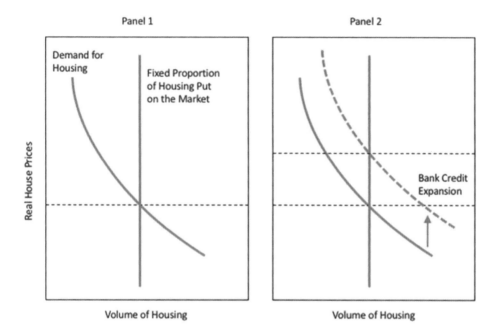

Fig. 6. Housing Demand and Supply.

The starting point for this housing bubble can originate from a positive shock to the economy or a lowering of risk standards by banks. Whichever the culprit, demand for housing or bank lending to the housing sector will start rising relative to the initial steady state. As a result, *inflated house prices* will encourage households to increase their demand for houses, and banks to lend more to the sector. This positive feedback mechanism will reinforce the upward pressure on house prices, demand for houses, and bank lending. This process represents a self-fulfilling housing bubble. The model simulations in Fig. 7 illustrate the process.

The bubble in these simulations would not be identified as such by standard financial soundness indicators. The increase in lending to the housing sector leads to a significant rise in real bank loans over the first five years of the simulations. This is accompanied by higher housing demand and thus an increase in real house prices over the same period. In turn, this increase in real house prices fuels private consumption through a wealth effect and thus growth in the economy. The increase in net lending is driven by what does not look like a more aggressive lending policy by the banks — indeed, the average LTV ratio for outstanding loans declines (although the LTV ratio on new loans rises). In addition, non-performing loans are declining, due to the large increase in new loans, which are by definition performing. Moreover, the capital adequacy of the banks is increasing through rising profitability. Banking supervisors would miss the increase in leverage in the economy if they looked just at these standard financial soundness indicators. The rapid increase in bank lending to the housing sector, and the consequent increase in prices, gives a more accurate warning signal. This is why the IMF is advocating the use of increases in mortgage credit and asset prices *jointly* as core indicators for the activation of LTV type measures[18].

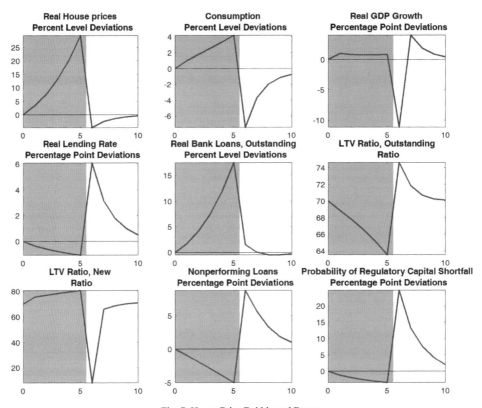

Fig. 7. House Price Bubble and Burst.

Source: Authors' simulations.

Once banks reassess their risk exposure to the housing sector, the impact on the economy can be severe. The reassessment in our simulations happens in year 5, when banks drastically cut their lending to the housing sector and hike their rate spreads. House prices collapse and new bank lending virtually stalls. This, in turn, leads to a severe recession, driven by the negative wealth effect on consumption of lower expected house prices in the future. Note also that standard financial soundness indicators jump, including NPLs and the average LTV ratios on outstanding loans. The losses from the jump in NPLs represent a decline in capital adequacy that will take time to restore through the process of deleveraging. Overall, these simulations show that the deadly embrace can be very costly for the economy.

4.   Macroprudential Policy to Mitigate the Deadly Embrace

Macroprudential policies that limit the *deadly embrace* between bank lending, house prices and household demand for housing would reduce economic instability. To the extent that neither banks nor households take into account the negative impact of their behavior on house prices, systemic risk slowly builds up in the economy during a housing bubble that can have devastating consequences for the economy when the bubble bursts. The existence of this externality provides an a priori case for appropriate regulatory controls.[h]

What specific controls would be effective? The answer would depend on specific circumstances for each economy. We focus on LTV limits and CCBs as ways to mitigate the risk of housing bubbles—but do not mean to imply that these are necessarily better than other options.

4.1.   *LTV limits*

In the simulations above, banks' underpricing of risk leads to an increase in LTV ratios for the same level of spreads. Such behavior has been widely documented prior to the Global Financial Crisis of 2008–2009.

The rationale for LTV limits would be twofold. First, if they are sufficiently low, they would prevent banks from excessive exposures to individual borrowers. Second, they create an equity buffer against defaults, since house prices could fall by the equivalent of the equity buffer before the value of the house is underwater, namely below the loan value. The cost of LTV limits is that they limit mortgage lending to households that do not have a sufficiently large down payment to meet the limit. First-time house buyers, normally younger households, would be particularly affected.

Our simulations show that LTV limits based on the current value of a house can dampen excessive lending behavior by the banks, but they are highly procyclical (Fig. 8). During the housing bubble, the LTV limit would reduce some of the increase in credit to the household sector compared with the no-policy scenario. However, as house prices rise,

---

[h] Bianchi and Mendoza[4] formally derive this externality as the difference between the decentralized equilibrium where agents do not internalize the impact of their actions on prices and a social planner optimization where the externality is taken into account. This leads the authors to argue for a state-contingent tax on borrowing as the optimal macroprudential policy. The authors, however, recognize the difficulty of implementing such a tax, given the uncertainty about the state of the economy.

the limit becomes less binding on lending to the marginal borrower as the value of the house increases. Conversely, once the housing bubble bursts, the decline in house prices makes the LTV limit ever more binding, implying that banks cannot restore their lending as quickly as under the no-policy scenario. This implies that the recession induced by the bursting of the housing bubble is more prolonged.

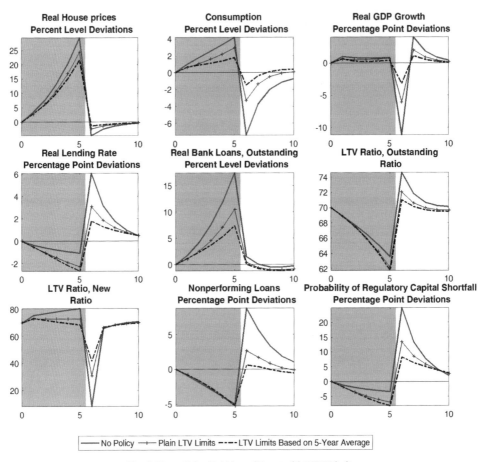

Fig. 8. House Price Bubble and Burst with LTV Limits.

Source: Authors' simulations.

The pro-cyclicality of the LTV limits could be substantially reduced by basing them on a moving average of house prices. In an alternative simulation, we base the LTV limit on the moving average of the last 5 years of house prices.[i] Using this moving average of

---

[i] This could easily be done in the United States where houses are subject to annual value assessments for the purpose of real estate taxes. In other countries, it may be more difficult for banks to have access to a time series of the price of the house being financed. However, this could be approximated

the value of the house significantly dampens the procyclicality of the LTV limits, reduces the swings in house prices, bank lending, and consumption. More importantly, it leads to a faster recovery in lending and thus in consumption and growth once the housing bubble bursts. In fact, in our simulations, the cumulative consumption gap under the 5-year moving average LTV limit is always higher after ten years than under the standard LTV limit or the no-policy scenario (Fig. 9).

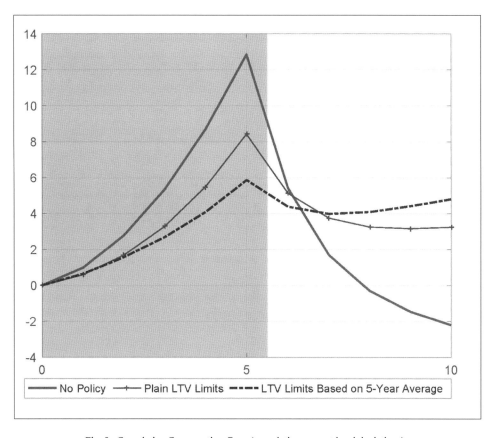

Fig. 9. Cumulative Consumption Gaps (cumulative percent level deviations).

Source: Authors' simulations.

4.2.   CCBs

CCBs can be another macroprudential policy to reduce the *deadly embrace*. If CCBs are raised during the upswing in house prices, banks would need to limit their lending in order to maintain the regulatory minimum capital buffer. Conversely, a reduction in CCBs after

by multiplying the current price of the house by the most relevant available index of house prices for the city or country where the house is located.

a housing bubble has burst would facilitate a recovery in credit, and make the post-bubble recession less severe. In our simulations, however, CCBs alone are ineffective at reducing bank lending during the upswing in real house prices, and they do little to dampen the positive impact on consumption and growth (Fig. 10). The boom-crash cycle is only slightly moderated.

One problem with CCBs from the viewpoint of the model is that they are not sector specific. Whereas the problem of instability originates in the housing sector, CCBs impinge on all sectors. As a result, systemic risk could still build up in the housing sector at the expense of lower intermediation in other sectors of the economy, which would be the worst of both worlds. CCBs alone are therefore not necessarily the solution to resolve the *deadly embrace*. This result also confirms the empirical evidence that CCBs are insufficient to avoid future financial crises stemming from housing bubbles[18,19]. This is why the IMF has been advocating additional "demand-side tools," such as LTV limits and DSTI caps.

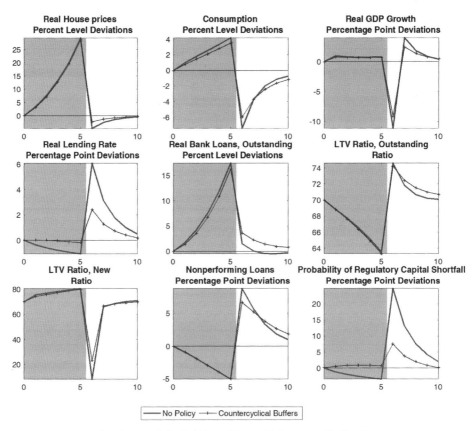

Fig. 10. House Price Bubble and Burst with Countercyclical Buffers.

Source: Authors' simulations.

4.3.   *A combination of LTV limits and CCBs*

The problem with LTV limits is their procyclicality. Even if they are accompanied with CCBs, they may constrain the banks' lending in a downturn, such that the relaxation of CCBs becomes ineffective in increasing banks' lending. In fact, banks may not expand lending to the housing sector, because of the constraint originating from falling house prices. As such, the release of CCBs after a housing bust may aid other sectors, but would not directly mitigate the impact of lower lending on house prices. If LTV limits are to be used with CCBs, they would again have to be based on a moving average of house prices, so as to reduce their procyclicality as shown in the simulations. The release of CCBs would aid only to the extent that capital buffers were close to the regulatory minimum CAR as in the simulations.

Overall, a combination of LTV limits on mortgages based on a moving average of house prices and CCBs is likely to mitigate (but not eliminate) the *deadly embrace*. Additional macroprudential policies may also be needed, including DSTI or LTI caps. However, it is also important to recognize that all these macroprudential policies come at a cost of reducing financial intermediation. They therefore dampen both good and bad credit cycles in the housing market.

5.   Policy Conclusions

This paper presented a new version of MAPMOD (Mark II) to study the effectiveness of macroprudential regulations. We extend the original MAPMOD by explicitly modeling the housing market. We show how lending to the housing market, house prices, and household demand for housing are intertwined in the model in what we call a *deadly embrace*. Without macroprudential policies, this naturally leads to housing boom and bust cycles. Moreover, leverage-driven cycles have historically been very costly for the economy, as shown most recently by the Global Financial Crisis of 2008–2009.

Macroprudential policies have a key role to play to limit this *deadly embrace*. The use of LTV limits for mortgages in this regard is ineffective, as these limits are highly procyclical, and hold back the recovery in a bust. LTV limits that are based on a moving average of historical house prices can considerably reduce their procyclicality. We considered a 5-year moving average, but the length of the moving average used should probably vary based on the specific circumstances of each housing market.

CCBs may not be an effective regulatory tool against credit cycles that affect the housing market in particular, as banks may respond to higher/lower regulatory capital buffers by reducing/increasing lending to other sectors of the economy.

A combination of LTV limits based on a moving average and CCBs may effectively loosen the *deadly embrace*. This is because such LTV limits would attenuate the housing market credit cycle, while CCBs would moderate the overall credit cycle. Other macroprudential policies, like DSTI and LTI caps, may also be useful in this respect, depending on the specifics of the financial landscape in each country. It is, however, important to recognize that all these macroprudential policies come at a cost of dampening both good and bad credit cycles. The cost of reduced financial intermediation should be taken into account when designing macroprudential policies.

6.   Appendix I — Basel III Regulations

This appendix summarizes the three pillars of the Basel III regulations, the liquidity standards and the phase-in arrangements approved by the Basel Committee on Banking Supervision of the Bank for International Settlements in 2010.[j] The main goal of the Basel III reforms is to strengthen microprudential regulation and supervision of the banks while adding a macroprudential overlay that includes capital buffers. In addition, Basel III regulations envisage higher capital buffers for global systemically important financial institutions (SIFIs) and domestic systemically important banks (DSIBs).

6.1.   *Pillar 1 — Capital and risk coverage*

Pillar 1 of the Basel III regulations covers capital adequacy requirements, risk coverage and a leverage ratio. On capital adequacy requirements, the microprudential regulations mandated an increase to 4.5 percent of common equity as a percentage of risk-weighted assets by end-2014. In addition, a capital conservation buffer of 2.5 percent of risk-weighted assets is expected to be phased in over 2016–2019, bringing the total common equity to 7.0 percent of risk-weighted assets by 2019. At that time, the overall capital adequacy requirement will be 10.5 percent of risk-weighted assets.

The macroprudential overlay to these microprudential regulations is in the form of CCBs on top of the capital adequacy requirements. CCBs can range between 0.0 and 2.5 percent and can be adjusted at the authorities' discretion when they deem that excessive credit growth is resulting in an *unacceptable buildup of systemic risk*. In other words, these buffers are expected to moderate excessive credit growth in boom cycles while mitigating the credit crunch during a downturn. Basel III regulations are silent, however, about the implementation of CCBs and their cost to the economy, leaving it to the supervisory authorities to make a judgment about the appropriate timing for increasing or lowering such buffers, based on a credit-to-GDP gap measure. This measure, however, does not distinguish between good versus bad credit expansions and is irrelevant for countries with significant dollar lending, where exchange rate fluctuations can severely distort the credit-to-GDP gap measure.

The Basel III regulations also envisage additional capital surcharges for SIFIs and DSIBs through a progressive common equity capital requirement of between 1.0 and 2.5 percent of risk-weighted assets. These surcharges are meant to protect the overall global and domestic financial system from a potential insolvency of a financial institution that could, by its systemic nature, affect the stability of the overall system.

Pillar 1 of the Basel III regulations also changes certain aspects of the risk calculations and coverage of assets. These include the capital treatment for complex securitizations, higher capital charges for trading derivatives and securitized assets in trading books, more

---

[j] See http://www.bis.org/bcbs/basel3.htm .

stringent requirements for counterparty credit risk, and a 2 percent risk weight for exposure to central counterparties (CCPs).

Finally, Pillar 1 also includes a leverage ratio to limit overall leverage of the financial institution. The leverage ratio, defined as tier 1 capital over total exposure, is required to be equal or above 3 percent. The leverage ratio is non-risk based and is calculated including off-balance sheet exposures.

6.2.   *Pillar 2 — Risk management and supervision*

Pillar 2 adds to the regulations on risk management and supervision already introduced in Basel II, including the Internal Capital Adequacy Assessment Process (ICAAP). Basel III regulations require firm-wide governance and risk management capturing the risk of off-balance sheet exposures and securitization, managing risk concentrations, and providing incentives for banks to better manage risk and returns over the long term. They also introduce sound compensation practices, valuation practices, stress testing, and updated accounting standards for financial instruments, corporate governance and supervisory colleges.

6.3.   *Pillar 3 — Market discipline*

Pillar 3 covers market discipline as it pertains to financial disclosures. The disclosure requirements include securitization exposures and sponsorship of off-balance sheet vehicles, enhanced disclosures on the detail of the components of regulatory capital and their reconciliation to the reported accounts. They also require a comprehensive explanation of how a bank calculates its regulatory capital.

6.4.   *Liquidity standards*

Basel III regulations introduced two liquidity ratios for the first time as part of the new global liquidity standards: the liquidity coverage ratio (LCR) and the net stable funding ratio (NSF). The LCR is defined as the ratio of high quality liquid assets to total net liquidity outflows over 30 days. The LCR floor is being introduced incrementally starting at 60 percent in 2015 and reaching 100 percent by 2019. In addition, the regulations include a net stable funding (NSF) ratio, defined as stable funding (customer deposits plus long-term wholesale funding) over long-term assets. The proposal is to introduce a minimum standard by 2018, although there is no agreement yet on what that standard will be.

Beyond these two ratios, Basel III regulations introduce new principles for sound liquidity risk management and supervision, based on the lessons learnt during the global financial crisis, and a liquidity framework to assist supervisors in identifying and analyzing liquidity risk trends at both the bank and system-wide level.

References

1. B. Bernanke, M. Gertler and S. Gilchrist, *The Financial Accelerator in a Quantitative Business Cycle Framework*, in *Handbook of Macroeconomics,* eds. J. B. Taylor and M. Woodford, Volume 1c (Elsevier Science, North-Holland, Amsterdam, 1999).
2. J. Geanakoplos, *The Leverage Cycle in NBER Macroeconomic Annual 24*, (University of Chicago Press, 2009), pp. 1–65.
3. E. G. Mendoza, Sudden stops, financial crises, and leverage, *American Economic Review* **100** (Dec), 1941-66 (2010).
4. J. Bianchi and E. G. Mendoza, *Optimal Time-Consistent Macroprudential Policy*, NBER Working Paper No. 19704 (2013).
5. M. Brei and L. Gambacorta, *The Leverage Ratio Over the Cycle*, BIS Working Paper No 471 (2014), http://www.bis.org/publ/work471.pdf .
6. A. Mian and A. Sufi, The great recession: Lessons from microeconomic data, *American Economic Review: Papers and Proceedings* **100** (May), 51-56 (2010).
7. T.-C. Wong, *Banking Procyclicality: Cross Country Evidence*, Ph.D. Dissertation, University of Hong Kong (2012), http://hub.hku.hk/handle/10722/161512
8. C. P. Kindleberger and R. Aliber, *Manias, Panics, and Crashes: A History of Financial Crises* (Hoboken, New Jersey: John Wiley & Sons, 2011).
9. M. Reinhart and K. Rogoff, *This Time is Different: Eight Centuries of Financial Folly* (Princeton University Press, 2009).
10. S. Claessens, M. A. Kose, and M. Terrones, What happens during recessions, crunches and busts?, *Economic Policy* **24**, 655-700 (2009).
11. S. Claessens, M. A. Kose and M. Terrones, *How do Business and Financial Cycles Interact?*, IMF Working Paper, 11/88, (2011) available at https://www.imf.org/external/pubs/ft/wp/2011/wp1188.pdf .
12. V. Cerra and S. C. Saxena, Growth dynamics: The myth of economic recovery, *American Economic Review* **98**(1), 439-57 (2008).
13. O. Jorda, M. Schularick, and A. M. Taylor, *When Credit Bites Back: Leverage, Business Cycles, and Crises*, Federal Reserve Bank of San Francisco Working Paper 2011–27, (2012).
14. A. Mian and A. Sufi, *House of Debt: How They (and You) Caused the Great Recession, and How We Can Prevent It from Happening Again* (The University of Chicago Press, Chicago, 2015).
15. N. Kiyotaki and J. H. Moore, Credit cycles, *Journal of Political Economy* **105** (Ch. 2), 211-248 (1997).
16. C. A. E. Goodhart, A. K. Kashyap, D. P. Tsomocos, and A. P. Vardoulakis, *Financial Regulation in General Equilibrium*, NBER Working Paper No. 17909 (2012).
17. C. A. E. Goodhart, A. K. Kashyap, D. P. Tsomocos, and A. P. Vardoulakis, An integrated framework for analyzing multiple financial regulations, *International Journal of Central Banking* **9** (S1), (2013).
18. International Monetary Fund, *Staff Guidance Note on Macroprudential Policy* (Washington, D.C., 2014a).
19. International Monetary Fund, *Staff Guidance Note on Macroprudential Policy – Detailed Guidance on Instruments* (Washington, D.C., 2014b) http://www.imf.org/external/np/pp/eng/2014/110614a.pdf.

20. E. Cerruti, S. Claessens and L. Laeven, *The Use and Effectiveness of Macroprudential Policies: New Evidence*, IMF Working Paper, 15/61, (2015) http://www.imf.org/external/pubs/ft/wp/2015/wp1561.pdf .

Spreads and bank ratings in the Euro area sovereign debt crises[a]

Heather D. Gibson

Bank of Greece
21 E Venizelos Ave, Athens, 10250, Greece

Stephen G. Hall

University of Leicester
University Road, Leicester LE1 7RH, United Kingdom

George S. Tavlas

Bank of Greece
21 E Venizelos Ave, Athens, 10250, Greece
Email: gtavlas@bankofgreece.gr

Since the inception of the Euro in 1999 there have been unprecedented movements in sovereign spreads. This has been particularly true since the beginning of the financial crises in 2008. This chapter summarizes the work in a series of papers which have examined the determinants of spreads between the 10-year benchmark government bond and the German 10-year sovereign for the main crises countries within the euro area; namely Greece, Italy, Spain, Portugal and Ireland. These studies have had a range of objectives. First, we sought to directly estimate the impact of the fundamentals. Second, we sought to determine the extent to which credit ratings assigned by the credit agencies were reflected in risk premia, given that credit ratings typically are constructed to reflect the present and prospective fundamentals of an economy. Third, we have explored the possibility of 'Doom Loops' between sovereign spreads and bank equity prices that is the idea that the two feed off each other in an irrational way. Finally, we argue that the market has been particularly harsh in its treatment of Greece during this episode. In this chapter we summarize this work and show how the separate pieces of work present a comprehensive picture of a serious overreaction on the part of markets and ratings agencies.

Keywords: euro area financial crisis, sovereign spreads, sovereign ratings, bank equity prices, panel data tests, Kalman filter, cointegration

1.   Introduction

The years following the inception of the euro in 1999 have seen some unprecedented movements of sovereign spreads of euro-area countries. In addition, there have been substantial downgrades in the ratings of sovereign debt which has been highly correlated with the movement in spreads. This development is especially striking since an aim of the common currency was to enhance stability among participating countries following the decade of the 1990s, which saw a number of currency crises (including in Europe in the early 1990s). These currency crises are now generally interpreted within the paradigm of third generation currency crises models, which emphasize the effects of market speculation and multiple equilibria, rather than fundamentals. Recently De Grauwe and Ji[1] have made

---

[a] We are grateful to Harris Dellas for valuable comments.

a theoretical argument to interpret the euro-area sovereign debt crises as a new manifestation of a speculative market attack on a sovereign, but in this case through yield spreads rather than through foreign exchange rates, since currency crises have essentially been precluded by the creation of the euro.[b]

In a series of papers we have examined the determinants of spreads between the 10-year benchmark government bond and the German 10-year sovereign for the main crises countries within the euro area; namely Greece, Italy, Spain, Portugal and Ireland. These studies have had a range of objectives. First, we sought to directly estimate the impact of the fundamentals. Second, we sought to determine the extent to which credit ratings assigned by the credit agencies were reflected in risk premia, given that credit ratings typically are constructed to reflect the present and prospective fundamentals of an economy. Third, we have explored the possibility of 'Doom Loops' between sovereign spreads and bank equity prices that is the idea that the two feed off each other in an irrational way. Finally, we argue that the market has been particularly harsh in its treatment of Greece during this episode.

In this chapter we summarize this work and show how the separate pieces of work present a comprehensive picture of a serious overreaction on the part of markets and ratings agencies.

The paper is organized as follows. After a review of some relevant literature (section 2), we begin by focusing on Greece (section 3). In addition to investigating the relationship between spreads and economic fundamentals, we investigate the relationship between spreads and (a) political uncertainty and (b) sovereign credit ratings. Both of those factors appear to have played an especially important role during the Greek financial crisis. As explained further below, political uncertainty in Greece underwent a sharp rise in 2008 and again in 2011 and early 2012; the latter period was marked by a political debate that had implications about whether Greece would remain in the euro area, thereby introducing currency risk into interest-rate spreads.[c] With regard to credit ratings, as mentioned above, a succession of sovereign downgrades created negative feedback loops among (a) spreads, (b) real economic activity, (c) debt sustainability, and (d) credit ratings. The impact of credit downgrades appears to have been pronounced in the case of Greece since the country began the crisis with a very high debt-to-GDP ratio. Consequently, credit downgrades and the ensuing rise in spreads had the potential to set-off unstable debt-dynamics, a potential that was, in fact, realized.

We go on in section 4 to widen our sample of countries to include all those affected at some point in time by the euro area sovereign debt crisis – in addition to Greece, we include Ireland, Italy, Portugal and Spain. We explore further the potential for feedback effects

---

[b] To the extent, however, that the increase in sovereign spreads during 2011 and 2012 in Greece, for example, possibly reflected expectations of a possible departure of that country from the euro area, currency risk may not have been completely eliminated.

[c] The political instability culminated in two national elections in the first half of 2012 – in May and June, respectively. The latter election led to the formation of a coalition government.

between spreads and ratings. We also include bank equity prices into the analysis, reflecting the feedbacks between banks and the sovereign, irrespective of whether the specific country crisis began with the sovereign (e.g. in the case of Greece) or the bank (e.g. Ireland, Italy).

2. Related Literature: Spreads, Sovereign Ratings, Bank Equity Prices and Fundamentals

A substantial empirical literature has already emerged examining the contributions of economic fundamentals to spreads both for the euro area as a whole and for individual euro area countries (e.g., Dötz and Fischer[2], Gibson, Hall and Tavlas[3,4], De Grauwe and Ji[1]; Aizenman, Hutchison, and Jinarak[5]; Beirne and Fratzscher[6]; Mink and de Haan[7], Ammer & Cai[8]; De Santis[9]; and Fontana and Scheicher[10]).

These studies have found that macroeconomic fundamentals played an important role in determining sovereign bond spreads or CDS spreads,[d] with determinants including indicators reflecting fiscal imbalances, current-account imbalances and growth.[e] Gerlach, Schulz and Wolff[11] assessed the impact of the size and structure of a country's banking sector on euro-area sovereign spreads, and found that the size of the banking sector is a positive determinant of a country's spread; as of early 2009, almost one percentage point of euro-area sovereign spreads could be explained by this factor.

However, the literature also finds that sovereign credit risk cannot be explained by the economic fundamentals alone. Thus, factors related to contagion — or, more generally, market psychology — are called upon to account for the unexplained portions of spreads. An earlier study by the present authors followed that approach (see Gibson, Hall and Tavlas[3]). In that study, we examined the macroeconomic determinants of spreads between the 10-year benchmark Greek government bond and the German 10-year sovereign. Our data sample was monthly and covered the period from January 2000 through September 2010. Thus, our data covered the pre-crisis period (i.e., the period prior to the fall of 2009) and the early part of the crisis period. Our results suggested that spreads were significantly below what would have been predicted by the fundamentals during the mid-2000s, but significantly above what had been predicted by the fundamentals for much of 2010.

We then examine the extent to which the determinants of Greek spreads changed over time. In this connection, we use the Kalman filter to estimate the underlying time-varying coefficients of those determinants. By doing so, we are able to measure the speed with which the impact of the determinants of spreads changed, as well as the timing of the changes that took place in the coefficients. As a preview of our results, we find that for a number of years after Greece's entry into the euro area, markets appeared to effectively discount the economic fundamentals in pricing Greek sovereign credit risk. With the

---

[d] Typically, the literature has found roles for other factors, including measures of international market volatility and capital flows into government bond markets, as drivers of sovereign risk.

[e] Gibson, Hall, and Tavlas[3] provide a more-thorough review of the literature.

collapse of Lehman Brothers in September 2008, and especially with the unexpected news about Greece's fiscal situation in the fall of 2009, the markets went through a process of learning as they increasingly priced credit (and, perhaps, currency) risk into Greek spreads, at times overpricing risk, thereby contributing to the self-reinforcing character of the crisis.

Aside from the fact that fundamentals do not provide a complete explanation for the movements in spreads, there is a substantial difference between the effects of macroeconomic variables on sovereign risk when the sample period excludes the crisis period and when it includes the crisis period. The precise dating of the start of the crisis period varies, however, depending upon whether the start of the period is considered to be the outbreak of the U.S. subprime crisis in the summer of 2007, the collapse of Lehman Brothers in September 2009, or the eruption of the Greek sovereign debt crisis in the fall of 2009. Bernoth, von Hagen and Schuknecht[12], treating the former (subprime) episode as the start of the crisis period, found that macroeconomic fundamentals were not significant determinants of spreads in the pre-crisis period but were significant if the sample is extended into the crisis period. Von Hagen, Schuknecht and Wolswijk[13] found that, while bond yield spreads in the euro area before and during the crisis can largely be explained by fundamentals, the market has penalized fiscal imbalances much more severely in the period after the collapse of Lehman Brothers than in the period before that episode. Similarly, Afonso, Argyrou and Kontonikas[14] found that euro-area bond spreads are well-explained by the macroeconomic fundamentals if account is taken of the onset of the global financial crisis in the summer of 2007, but spreads are not well-explained by the same fundamentals in the pre-crisis period.

An inference that can be drawn from the results of the above studies is that markets understated — or even overlooked — the role of some of the macroeconomic fundamentals in the determination of sovereign risk in the years leading up to the global financial crisis. In section 3, we investigate the reasons this may have been the case with regard to spreads on Greek sovereigns. In particular, we examine the relationship between macroeconomic fundamentals and Greek spreads, whether the fundamentals were important determinants of spreads prior to the outbreak of the Greek sovereign crisis, and, if not, whether and when they may have become significant determinants of spreads. In investigating the role of economic fundamentals, we control for potential independent influences stemming from political stability and ratings downgrades.

A further important characteristic of the crisis has been the emergence of strong feedback loops between the sovereign and banks. Thus, in section 4 of the paper, we widen our research to focus on bank equity prices. Prior to the outbreak of the 2007-2008 global financial crisis, the empirical literature on bank performance mainly focused on the determinants of bank profitability and bank stock returns. Among the factors that were found to influence bank performance were the following: (1) measures of market characteristics, including economies of scale, management efficiency, and bank size; (2) bank characteristics, including capital positions, loan-to-deposit ratios, and equity-to-total assets ratios; and (3) indicators of macroeconomic performance, including economic growth and the state of the business cycle. Recent studies that take into account the crisis period (beginning in 2007) include Yang and Tsatsaronis[15], Chan-Lau, Liu and Schmittmann[16] and Castrén, Fitzpatrick and Sydow[17].[f]

The effects of sovereign risk on bank performance have been less researched than the factors (i.e., bank characteristics and indicators of macroeconomic performance) mentioned above. The BIS[18] found that the rise in sovereign risk after 2009 pushed up the cost, and adversely affected the composition, of some euro area banks' funding, with the extent of the impact broadly related to the deterioration in the credit worthiness of the home sovereign. Demirgüç-Kunt, Detragiache and Merrouche[19] found that increases in bank CDS premia during the crisis were significantly related to deterioration in bank capital positions as well as public finances. Chan-Lau, Liu and Schmittmann[16] examined the impact of sovereign risk, measured as the arithmetic average of the five-year CDS spreads of Belgium, Greece, Ireland, Italy, Portugal, and Spain, on equity returns of euro-area (and other banks); the authors found that, for the period 2008-2010, equity returns in excess of a risk-free rate of return were driven mainly by the economic-growth outlook (as measured by the Purchasing Managers' Indices of both the euro area and the United States) and sovereign risk.

3.   A Focus on Greece

The unfolding of the Greek sovereign debt crisis beginning in late 2009 — and the euro-area crisis more generally — has called into question the extent to which the price of sovereign risk, as reflected in the interest rate spread on sovereigns, can be explained by macroeconomic fundamentals. In the run-up to Greece's entry into the euro area in 2001, the 10-year spread between Greek and German sovereigns fell precipitously, from about 600 basis points in the late 1990s to about 50 basis points at the time when Greece became a member of the single-currency area on January 1, 2001. Over the following years, 10-year spreads stabilized within a fairly narrow range of 20 to 50 basis points until the end of 2008, despite Greece's large and growing fiscal and external deficits (as we explain as follows). Then, in October of 2009, a newly-elected Greek government stunned the markets with news that the fiscal deficit for 2009 would likely turn out to be more than twice the outgoing government's projection of 6 percent of GDP[g].

That news set-off a relentless upward rise of spreads and a succession of ratings' downgrades of Greek sovereigns and Greek banks (which held large portfolios of sovereigns), resulting in what appeared to be self-reinforcing feedback loops between ratings and spreads. The increases in spreads contributed to a sharp contraction of real output, which impacted negatively on the debt-dynamics, a process which itself contributed to rating downgrades, further rises in spreads, and ultimately, an increase in political

---

[f] Chan-Lau, Liu and Schmittmann[16] provide a thorough review of the earlier literature on the determinants of banks' performance.
[g] The final figure would be 15.6 percent of GDP.

uncertainty.[h] This process took place despite an adjustment program agreed in May 2010 between the Greek government and official lenders — the International Monetary Fund, the European Commission, and the European Central Bank — a program that aimed to stabilize the debt dynamics. The self-reinforcing process came to a head in early 2012. By that time, it had become clear that the debt dynamics were unsustainable. In March 2012, the Greek government restructured its debt and agreed to a second adjustment program with official lenders. Prior to those actions, the 10-year spread had reached 4,000 basis points and, with an inversion of the yield curve (reflecting market expectations of a sovereign restructuring in the near term), the 2-year spread had peaked at 26,000 basis points.

3.1. *Data and stylized facts*

Typically, studies that deal with the macroeconomic determinants of sovereign risk focus on fundamentals that capture fiscal sustainability and external sustainability and/or competitiveness. Measures of fiscal sustainability include the fiscal balance and public debt. Measures of external sustainability and/or competitiveness include the current account balance, external debt, relative prices, trade openness and real growth (an important determinant of the sustainability of a country's external obligations). Where appropriate, variables are specified as ratios to GDP. Note that the foregoing variables tend to be interrelated. For example, an expanding fiscal deficit is often accompanied by an expanding external deficit and growing external debt, while a deterioration in competitiveness, as defined by movements in relative prices, tends to be accompanied by growing external and fiscal imbalances. In addition to variables representing macroeconomic fundamentals, in our previous study[3] we introduced a fiscal "news" variable in our specification of the determinants of Greek bond spreads on the supposition that unexpected (positive or negative) news — especially a series of unexpected developments — about fiscal fundamentals can drive market dynamics, particularly in the short term. We found that the accumulation of fiscal news had a significant impact on Greek sovereign spreads, a finding corroborated in a different context (both in terms of the definition of a news variable and in terms of countries considered) by Beetsma, Giuliodori, de Jong and Widijanto[20].

We now turn to a description of the variables used here. Our sample period runs from January 2000 to March 2012; the data frequency is monthly. Figure 1 shows the evolution of spreads during the period from January 2008 until March 2012.[i] (Prior to January 2008, both 2-year and 10-year spreads remained in a fairly narrow range of 20 to 50 basis points.) With the collapse of Lehman Brothers in September 2008, 2-year and 10-year spreads both began to rise. That rise became highly accentuated with the news about Greece's fiscal

---

[h] Between the end of 2008 and the end of 2012, real GDP contracted by about 20 percent. It continued to contract in 2013. To date, it has contracted by over one quarter.

[i] The literature has focused on two reference measures of sovereign risk — (1) spreads on government bond yields, and (2) CDS spreads. As Aizenman, Hutchison and Jinjarak[21] pointed out, however, recent studies suggest that both reference measures have common underlying determinants, rather than being entirely separate measures.

situation in the fall of 2009. By May 2010, the time of the first Greek adjustment program, 2-year spreads had reached around 850 basis points and 10-year spreads had reached 565 basis points. The agreement of Greece's adjustment program contributed to a narrowing of spreads until the fall of 2010, under the presumption in the markets that the debt-dynamics had stabilized. However, in late 2010 it became increasingly evident that the adjustment program had gone off-track. Markets began to speculate that Greece would need to restructure its debt; spreads accelerated sharply upward, with the acceleration of the 2-year spread far outpacing that of the 10-year spread.

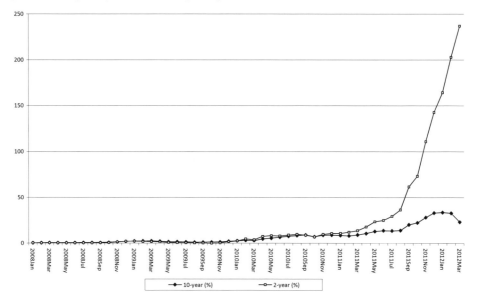

Fig.1. Greek Government Bond Yield Spreads (relative to Germany).

Source: ECB Statistical Data Warehouse.

The above story is reflected in the yield curves. Figure 2 shows the Greek sovereign yield curve at specific dates. The upper part of Fig. 2 shows the yield curve at four dates – 30 December 2005; 30 December 2008; 26 February 2010; and 30 April 2010. For the first three dates, the yield curve displays a normal upward slope, while steepening and shifting upward over time. By 30 April 2010, just prior to the agreement on the Greek adjustment program (2 May), the yield curve had become inverted, while shifting further upward; 10-year yields reached 9 percent and 2-year yields were almost 13 percent. The lower part of Fig. 2 shows the yield curve at three dates: 30 April 2010 (repeating the upper part of the figure for that date); 30 September 2011; and 29 February 2012. (Note the difference in the y-axes between the upper and lower parts of Fig. 2.) The inversion of the yield curve became more pronounced at short (2-years or less) maturities, reflecting increased market expectations of a debt restructuring.

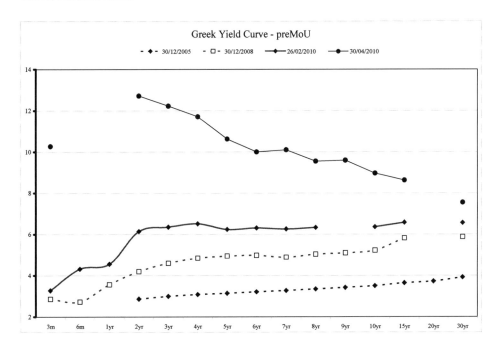

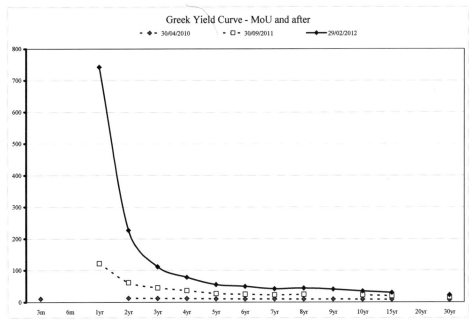

Fig. 2. The Greek Yield Curve at Selected Dates.

Source: Bloomberg.

To capture the effects of the fundamentals (economic and political) on spreads, we use the following variables. We include three measures of the fiscal situation.

(1) *The ratio of government debt to GDP.* The upper part of Fig. 3 shows the evolution of this variable. Greece entered the euro area with a debt ratio that was close to 100 per cent. By 2006 that ratio had risen to about 110 percent, where it remained until 2009. The sustainability of the debt-to-GDP ratio was clearly dependent on the sustainability of robust real GDP growth rates; between 2001 and 2007 real GDP rose at an average rate of almost 4 percent a year. The reversal of these high real growth rates, beginning in late 2008, led a sharp upward jump in the debt ratio in 2009; real growth moved into negative territory, and the debt dynamics became unsustainable.

(2) *The government fiscal balance relative to GDP.* The middle part of Fig. 3 shows the evolution of this variable. During much of the period from 2001 through *2006*, the deficit exceeded 5 percent of GDP, despite the high GDP growth rates. This outcome is explained by the fact that government spending was used to help generate economic growth.[j] By 2007, the deficit-to-GDP ratio began deteriorating, peaking at 15 ½ percent in 2009.

(3) *Fiscal news.* Since Greece's entry to the euro area in 2001, Greek fiscal data have been subjected to a number of revisions, sometimes several years after the *initial* (real-time) release of the data. These revisions have often involved upward revisions of the fiscal imbalances, generating negative surprises. In order to capture the news (or surprise) element that has figured prominently in the Greek experience, we also construct real-time fiscal data. In particular, using the European Commission spring and autumn forecasts, we create a series of forecast revisions. For example, the revision in the Spring 2001 forecasts is the 2001 deficit/GDP ratio in the Spring compared to the forecast for 2001 made in the Autumn of 2000. This procedure allows us to generate a series of revisions which, when cumulated over time, provides a cumulative fiscal news variable. As shown in the lower part of Fig. 3, the fiscal news variable deteriorated throughout 2000-2010, especially during the latter part of the period.

We use three variables to capture competitiveness.

(1) *Relative prices.* With Greece's nominal exchange rate fixed against the other euro-area countries, we use the Greek price level relative to that of Germany as a measure of the change in competitiveness. The top part of Fig. 4 displays this variable. As shown in the figure, Greece's competitiveness deteriorated markedly throughout the sample period.

---

[j] Between 2001 and 2009 the share of government spending in GDP rose by 9 percentage points, to 54 per cent.

Debt-to-GDP ratio

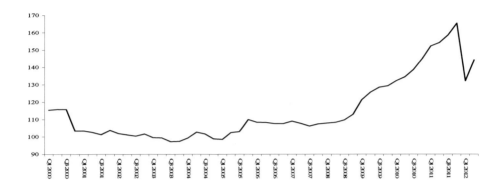

Fiscal balance to GDP ratio

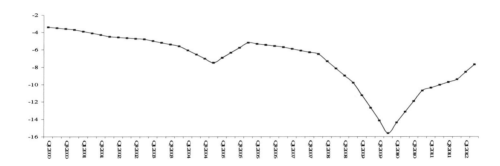

Fiscal news

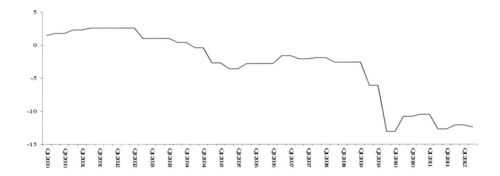

Fig. 3: Fiscal Indicators.

Source: Debt and general government balance, Datastream; Fiscal news, own calculations from EC forecasts.

Relative prices (ln HICP Greece – ln HICP Germany)

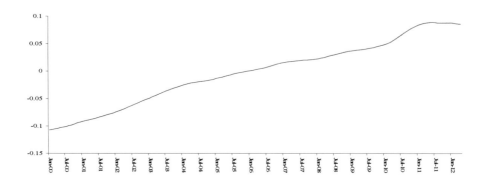

Brent oil price (US$ per barrel)

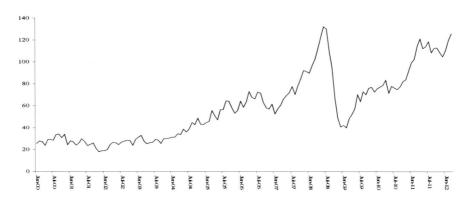

Current account balance (proportion of GDP)

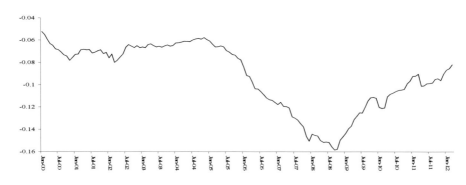

Fig. 4. Competitiveness Indicators.

Source: Datastream.

(2) *Oil prices.* The Greek economy is the most oil-dependent in the euro area. Consequently, changes in oil prices have substantial effects on Greece's current account balance. Our oil price variable is the US dollar price of a barrel of Brent crude, and is displayed in the middle part of Fig. 4.

(3) *Current-account balance.* As shown in the bottom part of Fig. 4, Greece entered the euro area with a current account deficit of about 7 per cent of GDP. In the years leading up to the outbreak of the Greek crisis, the deficit widened, peaking at 15 percent of GDP in 2008.

In addition to fundamentals dealing with the fiscal and external situations, we use the following variables.

(1) *Real GDP growth.* High real growth helps improve debt sustainability; therefore, higher growth would be expected to reduce spreads. Figure 5 displays the growth rate. As noted above, real growth averaged almost 4 percent per year during 2001-2007, before plunging in late 2008.

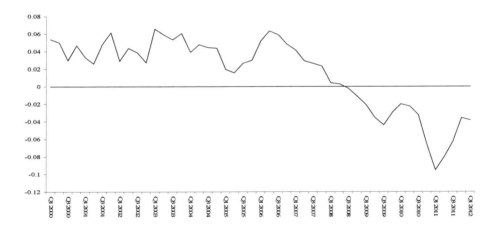

Fig. 5. Real GDP Growth.

Source: Bank of Greece.

(2) *Securities Markets Program (SMP).* In May 2010, the European Central Bank (ECB) embarked on a program under which the ECB purchased Greek sovereigns. The objective was to help reduce spreads. The SMP was implemented at various times during the period from May 2010 until January 2011. We use a dummy variable to capture the impact of the SMP.

(3) *Sovereign Downgrades.* We use the ratings assigned to Greek sovereigns by Moody's, S&P and Fitch. From March 2001 until the end of 2008, Greek sovereigns were rated A/A^+ by all three rating agencies. A series of downgrades began in early 2009, with the frequency of the downgrades accelerating in 2011. In February 2010, the Greek

sovereign was downgraded to selective default. These downgrades are displayed in Fig. 6. We assign values of 1-22 to different possible ratings (higher values represent a deterioration in ratings); changes in the ratings variable are based on which of the three agencies moved first. In this way, we capture what might be termed "important" rating downgrades or upgrades. However, ratings are dependent, in part, on the economic fundamentals. To deal with the issue of endogeneity, we regress our ratings variable against the economic fundamentals and use the residuals in our spreads' equations as a measure of the impact of ratings agencies, purged of economic fundamentals. The aim here is to examine the possible extent to which rating downwards may themselves have exerted on independent influence on spreads — over-and-above the influence of the fundamentals.

(4) *Political uncertainty.* We use the IFO World Economic Survey Index of Political Stability for Greece. Figure 6 shows the evolution of this index. A fall in the index signifies an increase in political uncertainty. The drop in the index in 2007-2008 reflects a series of domestic developments that seriously weakened the then-ruling Conservative Party. The further drop in the index in 2011 reflects the impact of the sovereign debt crisis.

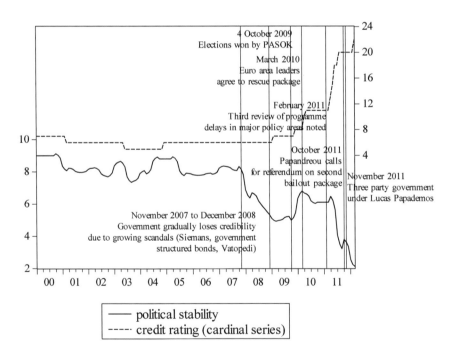

Fig. 6. Sovereign Ratings and Political Stability.

Source: CESifo Political stability index, Datastream; Sovereign ratings, Bloomberg.

The evolution of the aforementioned variables tells a coherent story. Upon entry into the euro area, Greece benefited from a low-interest rate environment, which contributed to high real growth rates. Nevertheless, the Greek economy walked a razor's edge between debt sustainability and the unsustainability of debt. Throughout the period 2001 to 2009, fiscal imbalances built up, despite the robust real growth rates and low interest rates, and competitiveness deteriorated. Until late 2009, however, spreads displayed little sensitivity to the warning alarms embedded in the fundamentals. Did the markets pay attention to any of the foregoing fundamentals? If so, which fundamentals? When did the markets begin to use the fundamentals to price risk into spreads? What roles did political uncertainty, SMP interventions, and rating downgrades play in the determination of spreads, over-and-above the role of the economic fundamentals? To answer these questions, we now turn to a formal analysis.

3.2. *Empirical results*

We begin by testing for cointegration among the above-listed variables for both the 10-year and the 2-year spread, assuming that the SMP dummy is exogenous. The results are reported in Table 1, for the 10-year spread and Table 2, for the 2-year spread. For the 10-year spreads there is strong evidence of up to six cointegrating vectors. As shown in Table 2 for the 2-year spread, there is evidence of at least five — and possibly six (using the trace statistic) — cointegrating relationships. Again, the hypothesis that spreads are exogenous is rejected. An implication of these results is that we can treat spreads as endogenous. We now proceed to an investigation of their determinants.

We begin with a simple static regression, which we interpret as the long-run determination of spreads. Given our above intuitive account of the evolution of the fundamentals and spreads, we do not expect this relationship to necessarily exhibit stable parameters and we are not especially concerned with the economic interpretation of each of fundamentals. Our objective here is simply to use the basic specification as a point of departure for a time-varying analysis. The results for the 10-year and 2-year spreads are reported in Table 3 and 4, respectively[k]. The main findings can be summarized as follows. For the 10-year spread equation, seven variables are correctly signed and significant: the debt-to-GDP ratio, fiscal news, real growth, oil prices, political uncertainty, the SMP program, and the residuals of an equation in which the economic fundamentals are used to determine ratings. The remaining four variables (the current account deficit-to-GDP ratio, relative prices, and fiscal deficit-to-GDP ratio) are either insignificant or incorrectly signed. This finding is not surprising; these three variables are measures of either the fiscal situation or competitiveness. Hence, they are collinear with other variables in the regression. For the 2-year spread equation, six variables are significant and correctly signed:

---

[k] In interpreting these results, note that both the current account balance and the fiscal balance (as percentages of nominal GDP) are treated in the following way. Declines in the current account and fiscal deficits should reduce spreads; hence, the signs on both variables are expected to be negative.

Table 1. Cointegration Tests: 10-Year Spread

Sample (adjusted): 2000M04 2012M03   144 observations
Lags interval (in first differences): 1 to 2
Endogenous variables included: 10-year spreads, current-account-to-GDP ratio, relative prices, general government balance, good fiscal news (squared), growth, oil prices, political stability, residuals from ratings regression. Exogenous variable: SMP

Hypothesized No. of CE(s)	Eigenvalue	Trace Statistic	0.05 Critical Value	Max-Eigen Statistic	0.05 Critical Value
None *	0.601	497.59	239.24	132.41	64.50
At most 1 *	0.518	365.18	197.37	105.12	58.43
At most 2 *	0.460	260.06	159.53	88.83	52.36
At most 3 *	0.293	171.23	125.62	50.02	46.23
At most 4 *	0.254	121.21	95.75	42.14	40.08
At most 5 *	0.226	79.06	69.82	36.80	33.88
At most 6	0.134	42.26	47.86	20.70	27.58
At most 7	0.087	21.56	29.80	13.17	21.13
At most 8	0.053	8.39	15.49	7.86	14.26
At most 9	0.004	0.53	3.841	0.53	3.84

Test for exogeneity of 10-year spreads
Cointegration restrictions: A(1,1)=0, A(1,2)=0, A(1,3)=0, A(1,4)=0, A(1,5)=0, A(1,6)=0
LR test for binding restrictions: Chi-square(6)=43.60   Probability=0.00
* denotes rejection of the hypothesis at the 0.05 level.

Table 2. Cointegration Tests: 2-Year Spread

Sample (adjusted): 2000M04 2012M03   144 observations
Lags interval (in first differences): 1 to 2
Endogenous variables included: 2-year spreads, current-account-to-GDP ratio, relative prices, general government balance, good fiscal news (squared), growth, oil prices, political stability, residuals from ratings regression. Exogenous variable: SMP

Hypothesized No. of CE(s)	Eigenvalue	Trace Statistic	0.05 Critical Value	Max-Eigen Statistic	0.05 Critical Value
None *	0.596	504.37	239.24	130.37	64.50
At most 1 *	0.552	373.99	197.37	115.67	58.43
At most 2 *	0.450	258.32	159.53	86.17	52.36
At most 3 *	0.306	172.15	125.62	52.57	46.23
At most 4 *	0.251	119.58	95.75	41.66	40.08
At most 5 [+]	0.193	77.93	69.82	30.80	33.88
At most 6	0.144	47.125	47.86	22.42	27.58
At most 7	0.103	24.70	29.80	15.67	21.13
At most 8	0.053	9.03	15.49	7.88	14.26
At most 9	0.008	1.15	3.84	1.15	3.84

Test for exogeneity of 10-year spreads
Cointegration restrictions: A(1,1)=0, A(1,2)=0, A(1,3)=0, A(1,4)=0, A(1,5)=0, A(1,6)=0
LR test for binding restrictions: Chi-square(6)=43.60   Probability=0.00
* denotes rejection of the hypothesis at the 0.05 level; [+] denotes rejection by the trace statistic at 0.05 level.

Table 3. 10-Year Spread — OLS Regression

Sample: 2000M01 2012M03   Observations: 147

	Coefficient	Std. Error	t-Statistic	Prob.
Constant	-6.411	3.29	-1.95	0.05
Current account to GDP	5.886	3.39	1.74	0.08
Relative prices	-14.754	6.39	-2.31	0.02
Government balance to GDP	0.277	0.05	5.89	0.00
Debt to GDP	0.136	0.02	6.51	0.00
Fiscal news	-0.038	0.01	-6.16	0.00
Growth	-149.108	38.27	-3.90	0.00
Oil prices	0.030	0.01	2.73	0.01
Political stability	-0.831	0.21	-3.92	0.00
SMP	-3.230	0.83	-3.89	0.00
Residuals from ratings equation	1.718	0.09	18.18	0.00

R-squared	0.922	Mean dependent var	2.913
Adjusted R-squared	0.916	S.D. dependent var	6.428
S.E. of regression	1.857	Akaike info criterion	4.148
Sum squared resid	469.232	Schwarz criterion	4.3726
Log likelihood	-293.893	Hannan-Quinn criter	4.239
F-statistic	161.176	Durbin-Watson stat	0.764
Prob(F-statistic)	0.000		

fiscal news, growth, oil prices, political uncertainty, the SMP program, and the residuals from the ratings equation.[1]

In interpreting these results, several points merit comments. First, ratings downgrades appear to have had a very important effect on spreads over-and-above the impact of the economic fundamentals. To explain, consider that for the 10-year spread regression, the adjusted R-squared without the residuals from the ratings equation is 0.733, with the residuals from the ratings equation the adjusted R-squared rises to 0.916. For the 2-year-spread equation, the adjusted R-squared without the ratings variable is 0.594; with the ratings variable the adjusted R-squared is 0.876. The clear implication of these findings is that ratings downgrades led to a self-perpetuating rise in spreads. Second, political uncertainty also appears to have contributed to the rise in spreads — higher stability reduces spreads. The decline in political stability beginning in 2007 and continuing in 2011 raised

---

[1] The impact of a one standard deviation increase in the explanatory variables on 2-year spreads is much greater than 10-year, reflecting the high levels to which 2-year spreads rose in the latter part of the sample.

spreads. Third, the SMP program appears to have reduced spreads during the short period for which it operated in Greece. In the case of the 10-year spread, SMP intervention reduced spreads by about 3 percentage points. For the 2-year spread, SMP intervention reduced spreads by about 33 percentage points. Fourth, the explanatory power of the equation for the 10-year spread is somewhat higher than the equation for the 2-year spread (0.916 for the former equation, 0.876 for the latter equation). Evidently, market psychology played a greater role in the evolution of the 2-year spread than the 10-year spread.

Table 4. 2-Year Spread — OLS Regression

Sample: 2000M01 - 2012M03   Observations: 147

	Coefficient	Std. Error	t-Statistic	Prob.
Constant	90.955	21.34	4.26	0.00
Current account to GDP	-6.290	21.98	-0.29	0.78
Relative prices	-161.857	41.43	-3.91	0.00
Government balance to GDP	1.77497	0.31	5.81	0.00
Debt to GDP	-0.283	0.14	-2.09	0.04
Fiscal news	-0.307	0.04	-7.74	0.00
Growth	-1943.101	248.33	-7.82	0.00
Oil prices	0.182	0.07	2.55	0.01
Political stability	-7.197	1.38	-5.23	0.00
SMP	-32.695	5.39	-6.07	0.00
Residuals from ratings equation	10.804	0.61	17.62	0.00

R-squared	0.876	Mean dependent var	8.813
Adjusted R-squared	0.867	S.D. dependent var	33.078
S.E. of regression	12.0528	Akaike info criterion	7.888
Sum squared resid	19756.59	Schwarz criterion	8.112
Log likelihood	-568.794	Hannan-Quinn criter.	7.979
F-statistic	96.366	Durbin-Watson stat	0.393
Prob(F-statistic)	0.000		

We now consider how precisely the effects of the fundamentals have changed over time.[m] To do so, we use the Kalman filter. The specific Kalman filter model we use is a time-varying parameter model (see Cuthbertson, Hall and Taylor[22]) that provides consistent estimates of the underlying time-varying coefficients. It is set up in the form of

---

[m] We have tested the above models for stability using recursive estimation and have found that both equations are highly unstable. Recursive estimation does not, however, provide consistent estimates of the underlying parameters if there is instability, as each recursion is based on the assumption of constant parameters

a state space model consisting of a measurement equation and a set of state equations which govern the evolution of the parameters. Our measurement equation is exactly the same specification as the two estimated models above. The state equations, for the parameters, specify that they follow a simple random walk, thus allowing them considerable freedom to change over time.

The time-varying parameter model, with the appropriate Kalman filter equations for the univariate case, following Harvey[23], is given by the following. Let

$$Y_t = \delta' z_t + \varepsilon_t \tag{1}$$

be the measurement equation, where y_t is a measured variable, z_t is the state vector of unobserved variables, δ is a vector of known parameters, which in this case are our explanatory variables, and $\varepsilon_t \sim NID(0, \Gamma_t)$. The state equation is then given as:

$$z_t = \Psi z_{t-1} + \psi_t \tag{2}$$

where Ψ are parameters and $\psi_t \sim NID(0, Q_t)$, Q_t is sometimes referred to as the hyperparameters. The appropriate Kalman filter prediction equations are then given by defining z^*_t as the best estimate of z_t based on information up to t, and P_t as the covariance matrix of the estimate z^*_t, and stating:

$$z^*_{t|t-1} = \Psi z^*_{t-1} \tag{3}$$

and

$$P_{t|t-1} = \Psi P_{t-1} \Psi' + Q_t . \tag{4}$$

Once the current observation on y_t becomes available, we can update these estimates using the following equations:

$$z^*_t = z^*_{t\backslash t-1} + P_{t\backslash t-1}\delta(Y_t - \delta' z^*_{t\backslash t-1})/(\delta' P_{t\backslash t-1}\delta + \Gamma_t) \tag{5}$$

and

$$P_t = P_{t\backslash t-1} - P_{t\backslash t-1}\delta\delta' P_{t\backslash t-1} /(\delta' P_{t\backslash t-1}\delta + \Gamma_t) . \tag{6}$$

Equations (1)-(6) then represent jointly the Kalman filter equations.

If we then define the one-step-ahead prediction errors as,

$$v_t = Y_t - \delta' z^*_{t|t-1} \tag{7}$$

then the concentrated log likelihood function can be shown to be proportional to

$$\log(l) = \sum_{t=k}^{T} \log(f_t) + N \log\left(\sum_{t=k}^{T} v^2_t / N f_t \right) \tag{8}$$

where $f_t = \delta' P_{t|t-1} \delta + \Gamma$ and N=T-k, where k is the number of periods needed to derive estimates of the state vector; that is, the likelihood function can be expressed as a function of the one-step-ahead prediction errors, suitably weighted.

We now turn to the results of the Kalman filter exercise. Were markets continuously focused on the same fundamentals throughout the sample period? Was the sensitivity of spreads to those fundamentals stable? In Figs. 7 and 8, we plot the coefficients from Kalman filter estimates of the regressions from 2006 onwards. Looking first at the 10-year spreads, several conclusions can be drawn. First, for the period before the international financial crisis, markets largely ignored all fundamentals. Second, for those variables which are correctly signed and significant (debt, fiscal news, growth, oil prices and political stability), there is evidence that markets began to price developments into yields and spreads as early as 2008 and more strongly from 2009. Third, those variables that have incorrect signs (the current account, the deficit-to-GDP ratio and, to a lesser extent, relative prices), move much later – in 2010 and 2011 – reflecting the large volatility of spreads which characterizes the latter part of the sample period. Fourth, the influence of political stability kicks in from early 2009 and then more strongly in 2011, as would be expected. Finally, the residuals from the ratings equations show a sharp increase from early 2011, reflecting the large number of downgrades that occurred along with the fact that they were multiple notch downgrades – in early 2011 Greece was BB+; by the end of the sample, she had been downgraded to Selective Default.

In the case of 2-year spreads (Fig. 8), the coefficients are more unstable. The current account actually has the correct sign (negative) until the latter part of the sample; the same pertains to the fiscal deficit. However, there is again evidence that the markets slowly wake up to fundamentals after the surprise news about Greece's fiscal situation in late 2009.

3.3.   *Conclusions for Greece*

In this section, in addition to the role played by economic fundamentals in determining sovereign spreads in Greece, we also focused on the contributions of political stability and sovereign credit ratings in the run-up to the restructuring of Greek debt (the so-called PSI – private-sector involvement).

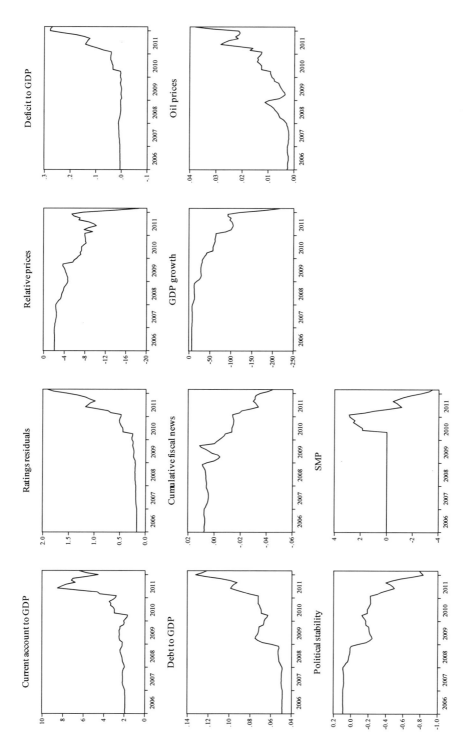

Fig. 7. Kalman Filter Estimates of Regression Coefficients: 10-Year Spreads.

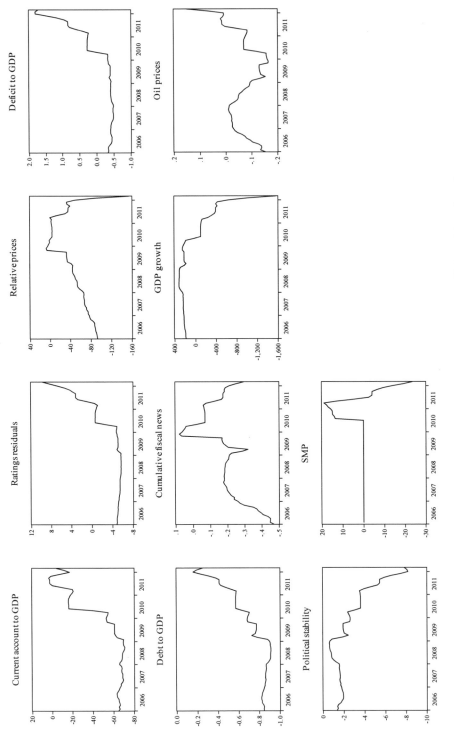

Fig. 8. Kalman Filter Estimates of Regression Coefficients: 2-Year Spreads.

Our results suggest that political uncertainty and sovereign credit ratings appear to have played a significant role in determining Greek spreads. Political uncertainty rose sharply in 2007-2008 and again in 2011-2012, during a period in which spreads also rose. Controlling for economic fundamentals, political stability appears to have played a significantly role in determining spreads, especially from 2009 onwards. With respect to sovereign spreads, we find evidence that supports our thesis of negative feedback loops between spreads, real economic activity, debt sustainability and credit ratings. Credit ratings, purged of economic fundamentals, appear to have played a significant role in determining spreads.

Our second contribution was to examine the extent to which the determinants of spreads change over time. Our results suggest that markets were not focused on the same fundamentals throughout the period. Indeed, before the collapse of Lehman Brothers, it appears that markets largely ignored economic fundamentals. The collapse of Lehman Brothers and the release of news concerning the fiscal situation in Greece caused markets to reassess their pricing of risk. Overall, the evidence points to markets slowly waking up to fundamentals, especially after the fiscal surprises in late 2009.

All this points strongly to the fact that markets were not rational during this period and this opens up the possibility of a self-reinforcing feedback loop between ratings and spreads. Ratings respond to a rise in spreads which then causes a further fall in the rating leading to further rises in spreads and so on. The evidence presented for Greece is consistent with the self-reinforcing feedback loop hypothesis.

4.   The Crises Countries

In this section, we explore further the potential for feedback loops between sovereign spreads and ratings by using a simultaneous system. Additionally, we extend the analysis to include other stressed countries, Ireland, Italy, Portugal and Spain. Using monthly data, we cover here the period from October 1998 through July 2014. Given the role of the banks in the crisis and the banks-sovereign nexus, we also include banks equity performance in our analysis.

A major characteristic of the euro-area financial crisis, especially in the stressed countries has been the strong linkages between banks' performance and sovereign stress[24] as downward revisions of markets' assessments of sovereigns impacted negatively on banks' financial conditions. Deteriorations in sovereign creditworthiness during the crisis affected banks' equity performance through several channels[18]: (i) the direct effects of banks' holdings of sovereign debt on banks' balance sheets and profitability; (ii) the reduction in the value of collateral available to banks to obtain wholesale funding and/or central-bank financing; and (iii) the reduced benefits from the implicit guarantee that, should the need arise, the state would step in to help honor banks' financial commitments.

The above linkages played-out in a number of advanced economies — both within and outside the euro area — during the global financial crisis that erupted in 2007-2008. However, European banks are particularly vulnerable to sovereign risk due to a number of factors. First, national banking systems tend to be especially large in the euro area. In 2012, for example, total bank assets as a share of euro-area GDP was almost 360 percent, compared with less than 80 percent in the United States[25]. Second, firms in the euro area are much more reliant on the banking system for finance than are U.S. firms; banks account for about three-quarters of total credit intermediation in the euro area, compared with about one-quarter in the United States. Third, domestic euro-area banks typically hold relatively-large shares of debt issued by their respective national governments in their portfolios, leaving banks' balance sheets vulnerable to doubts about sovereign solvency. In contrast, U.S. banks typically hold small amounts of local and state debt on their balance sheets; U.S. banks mainly hold U.S. government debt as their safe liquid assets[26]. Consequently, defaults by U.S. state and local governments have not involved financial-stability concerns for the U.S. financial system, in marked contrast to the concerns about euro-area financial stability raised by the restructuring of Greek sovereign debt in 2012.

4.1. *Data and empirical model*

To examine the links between sovereign stress indicators and banks' equity performance, we estimate a three-equation panel system in which bank equity prices, sovereign bond spreads and sovereign ratings are endogenous variables. This system framework allows us to fully explore the impact that sovereign stress can have on bank equity prices. As the sovereign becomes more stressed, sovereign spreads rise and ratings fall. This circumstance would be expected to impact on banks' market values. Market values fall as confidence in the ability of the state to meet potential obligations to banks – either direct obligations resulting from banks' holdings of sovereign assets, or indirect obligations through state guarantees – comes into question. Thus, in addition to bank-specific variables, we include sovereign spreads and sovereign ratings as determinants of banks' equity performance.

   We focus on the level of bank equity prices, and not equity returns. The reason is as follows. As mentioned above, if sovereign spreads rise and sovereign ratings fall, then we expect bank equity prices to fall. Initially, this fall in the level of equity prices will be associated with negative equity returns. If spreads and ratings stabilize at new levels (higher levels for spreads and lower levels for ratings), equity returns will go back to zero — that is, returns will improve from a negative number to a number that approaches (or equals) zero, even though spreads may remain high and ratings may remain low. This situation would give the (paradoxical) result that equity returns improve while sovereign stress indicators remain at extreme levels. Consequently, the appropriate relationship involves sovereign spreads, sovereign ratings and the level of equity prices (and not the rate of change of equity prices). A similar argument can be made with respect to the bank-specific variables. For example, if the capital ratio falls and then stabilizes at a lower level, we would expect the value of banks' equities to fall, and then to stabilize at a lower level. Returns would be highly negative, but would then go back to more-normal levels, even though the capital ratio remained low.

   This circumstance suggests that, in focusing on equity returns, previous studies have been mis-specifying the relationship since they have overlooked the effect on the level of equity prices. Equity returns move around zero throughout the period and the crisis period (beginning in 2007) is associated with a rise in volatility rather than a particular trend. By contrast, the level of the equity price index appears to be a more appropriate measure of bank health; that index exhibited a steady decline as sovereign spreads and sovereign ratings increased. (As we discuss below, our measure of sovereign ratings is constructed in such a way that a rise in our measure is associated with a downgrade of the sovereign.)

As noted, we focus on five stressed euro area countries – Spain, Greece, Ireland, Italy and Portugal. Figures 9 to 13 plot the three dependent variables for each country. The bank equity index is the FTSE index for the banking sector for each country.[n] Sovereign bond spreads are the yield on the 10-year benchmark bond in each country relative to that of Germany. Sovereign ratings are constructed as before.

Looking across Figs. 9 to 13 a number of stylized facts can be identified. First, bank equity prices, which had been rising relatively steeply in all five countries before the failure of Lehman Brothers (in September 2008), fell sharply thereafter. This decline was then following by a small recovery – the size of which is closely related to banks' involvement in the type of assets which sparked Lehman's failure – before the outbreak of the euro area sovereign debt crisis (in late 2009 and early 2010) sent bank equity prices falling again (in some countries, e.g., Greece and Ireland, bank equity prices remained at low levels through the end of our sample period). Second, spreads rose slightly in light of the turmoil associated with the failure of Lehman Brothers; it was not, however, until the sovereign crisis (beginning in late 2009 and 2010) that they underwent sharp rises. Third, sovereign ratings started deteriorating in 2009 in Ireland (associated with concerns about the fiscal cost of the banking crisis), Greece, and Portugal (concerns about the level of public debt in the former country and the total of public and private debt in the latter country) and, then, in 2011 in Spain (reflecting the fiscal consequences of the banking crisis following the collapse of the housing boom), and Italy (related to concerns about size of public debt). The final stylized fact is the close interconnection between movements in equity prices, spreads and ratings. Indeed, there appears to be a strong negative correlation between equity prices and sovereign spreads and, to a lesser extent, between sovereign ratings and banks' equity prices.

---

[n] Note, also, that the data are scaled to facilitate their presentation in a single figure. Thus, spreads are presented in basis points and sovereign ratings, which range between 1 and 22 in the original data, are multiplied by 10 for display in the figures.

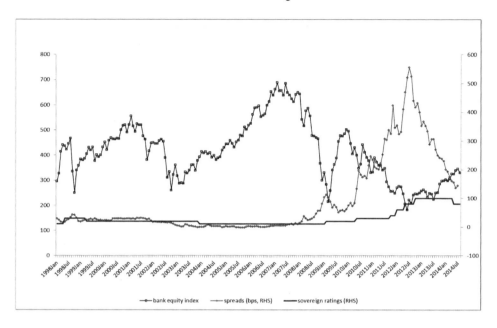

Fig. 9. Spain — Bank Equity Index, Sovereign Bond Spreads and Sovereign Ratings.

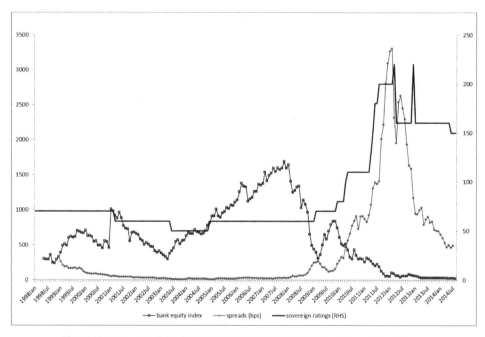

Fig. 10. Greece — Bank Equity Index, Sovereign Bond Spreads and Sovereign Ratings.

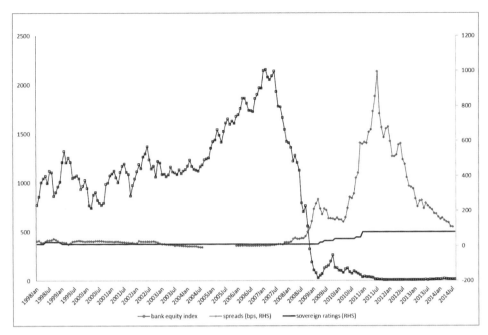

Fig. 11. Ireland — Bank Equity Index, Sovereign Bond Spreads and Sovereign Ratings.

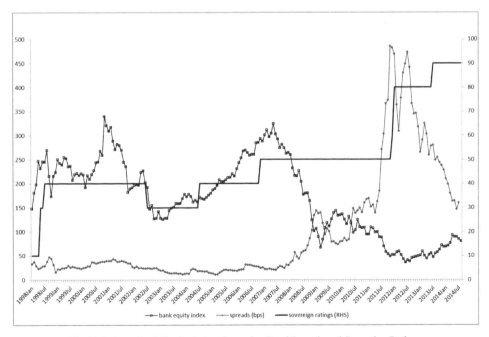

Fig. 12. Italy — Bank Equity Index, Sovereign Bond Spreads and Sovereign Ratings.

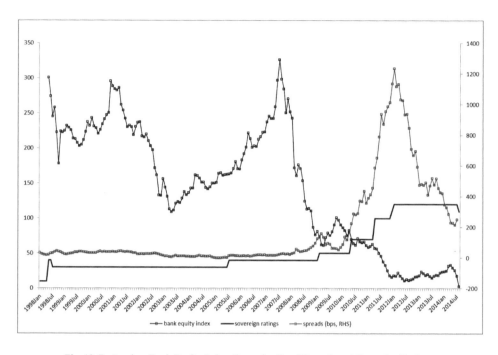

Fig. 13. Portugal — Bank Equity Index, Sovereign Bond Spreads and Sovereign Ratings.

These stylized facts motivate our three-equation system, which is estimated as a panel GMM system which is robust to autocorrelation and heteroskedasticity (HAC). We are interested in a three-equation dynamic simultaneous system for a group of N countries, estimated over T periods. Our baseline model can be expressed as:

$$S_{it} = \alpha_{0i} + \alpha_1 SR_{it} + \alpha_2 BE_{it} + \alpha_3 S_{it-1} + \sum_{k=1}^{K} \alpha_{3+k} X_{itk} + \varepsilon_{it} \qquad (9)$$

$$SR_{it} = \beta_{0i} + \beta_1 S_{it} + \beta_2 BE_{it} + \beta_3 SR_{it-1} + \sum_{k=1}^{K} \beta_{3+k} X_{itk} + \varpi_{it} \qquad (10)$$

$$BE_{it} = \chi_{0i} + \chi_1 S_{it} + \chi_2 SR_{it} + \chi_3 BE_{it-1} + \sum_{k=1}^{K} \chi_{3+k} X_{itk} + \upsilon_{it} \qquad (11)$$

where i=1...N, t=1...T and K is the number of exogenous regressors. S_{it} is the interest rate spread between country i and Germany, SR_{it} is the sovereign rating for country i, BE_{it} is the (log of the) equity price for commercial banks in country i and $\varepsilon_{it}, \omega_{it}$ and v are error terms and α_{0i} β_{0i} and χ_{0i} are fixed effects in each equation. We assume there are suitable exclusion restrictions on α β and χ to either exactly or over-identify the system. (This will be discussed further below.) The vector of exogenous variables is comprised of (1) bank-specific fundamentals, (2) macroeconomic fundamentals and (3) an index of political stability. As is clear from the above system, the initial model is fully simultaneous; each of the endogenous variables affects the other endogenous variables.

The bank-specific variables are constructed for each country based on data at the individual-bank level. In each case, individual country data are aggregated into a "country bank" and ratios calculated for this (fictitious) entity.[o] They cover various aspects of bank performance. Profitability is measured as pre-tax operating income as a percentage of total assets. Asset quality is calculated as loan loss reserves as a percentage of impaired loans. The capital adequacy of the banks is equity as a percentage of total assets. Finally, the liquidity condition of the banks is captured by the interbank ratio, that is, funds lent in the interbank market to other banks divided by funds borrowed; if the ratio takes the value of 100, then banks have a zero-net interbank exposure – they lend as much as they borrow. A value higher than 100 implies that the bank is a net lender to the interbank market and, vice versa, for a value lower than 100. For all four bank-specific variables, a rise in the ratio indicates a stronger financial situation; hence, we would anticipate that a rise in the ratio produces a rise in the bank equity indices. The macroeconomic fundamentals and index of political stability are as before.

It is important to consider the possibility that our 'exogenous' variables may not truly exogenous. In this paper, the general macroeconomic variables considered can be treated as exogenous. These variables move relatively slowly and smoothly over time, so that we would not expect, for example, any simultaneous feedback effects from spreads to GDP. A similar circumstance applies to some extent to the commercial-bank-specific variables. Nevertheless, some of these variables could react quickly enough to a bank's share price to raise possible doubts about exogeneity: the interbank ratio, for example, might be affected by a bank's equity price. Political stability could also raise concerns about exogeneity as there are obviously close links between sovereign spreads and political uncertainty. We decided, however, not to expand the system further because there are clear costs of doing so. We did experiment with instrumenting the political-stability variable within an unexpanded system, but this did not affect the final results in an important way.

Our data comprise an unbalanced panel covering, at its maximum, the period from October 1998 until July 2014, and the data are monthly; where they are quarterly or annual

---

[o] This is not the same as simply averaging the banks indicators, to give an example, to construct the ratio of non-performing loans to total loans we would take the absolute value of NPLs for each bank, sum them up, sum total loans across the banks, and then calculate the ratio of the two sums. This automatically takes into account the relative size of the banks and effectively calculates the ratio for top banks in the banking system.

(bank-specific data), we interpolate them to a monthly frequency. As the raw data are available at different frequencies, we had to decide whether to aggregate the data up to the lowest frequency (annual in this case) or to interpolate the data to the highest frequency (monthly). Since the objective of this study is to explain commercial bank equity prices, which are available on a monthly frequency, aggregating these data would have led to a substantial loss of information. By contrast, most of the data which are available at low frequencies — GDP, debt stocks, the fiscal deficit, etc. — tend to move quite smoothly and so interpolating these data to a monthly series is relatively straightforward and should not distort the results.

The identification of the system is done, as usual, on the basis of theory. First, we assume that the bank-specific variables only affect the bank equity price, and not the sovereign rating or spread. As mentioned, however, the general simultaneous system provides a channel through which bank equity prices affect both sovereign ratings and sovereign spreads. We further assume that the macroeconomic variables do not directly enter the bank equity equation. Again, however, we allow for a possible effect of sovereign ratings and spreads on bank equity prices via the simultaneous system. The identification of the sovereign ratings and the spread equation is more problematic as one might expect the same variables to enter each equation. Here, we make the identifying assumptions that GDP growth affects the spread and that the debt-to-GDP ratio affects ratings. We also include lagged dependent variables in all three equations. Given the identifying restrictions, we estimate the model in its most general form and then employ a general-to-specific methodology to nest the model down to a parsimonious one based on successively excluding insignificant variables and/or variables with incorrect signs.

4.2. *Results*

The results, following the nesting down process, are displayed in Table 5.[p] The following findings merit comment.

First, focusing on the equation for the bank equity index, two of the four bank-specific balance-sheet variables are significant and correctly signed; (1) a rise in reserves held to meet potential defaults on non-performing loans ensures that banks are healthier — a rise in the ratio reserves-to-non-performing loans is associated with a rise in the bank equity index; (2) higher profitability has a positive impact on the bank equity index.

Second, sovereign ratings play a substantial role in the determination of banks' equity, beyond the effects of the banking fundamentals. A deterioration in sovereign ratings (a rise in our ratings' index) causes the bank equity index to fall. This effect most likely reflects concerns about the ability of the country to meet the potential fiscal costs associated with

---

[p] It can be noted that we use all available observations for each of the estimations in Table 5. However, samples differ since the interbank ratio is available only from 2004 in 4 of the 5 countries. At the same time, the loan loss reserves to NPL ratio is only available in Greece from 2004. The system estimates, which do not contain the interbank ratio (since it was found to be insignificant), allow a larger sample to be used. It should also be noted that dropping the interbank ratio from Table 5 does not change qualitatively the results.

its explicit or implicit banking system support (deposit guarantee schemes, possible capital injections, etc.). Indeed, it appears that changes in sovereign ratings have larger effects on bank's equity prices than changes in the bank-specific variables. Abstracting from dynamics, our findings indicate that a one-notch sovereign downgrade results in a fall in bank equity prices of 10 percent. With the exception of Italy (which experienced a cumulative fall in sovereign ratings of only 4 notches), the other countries at the end of the period (mid-2014) were some 7–8 notches below their 2008 levels. Thus, sovereign rating downgrades explain a large amount of the sharp falls in bank equity indices displayed in Figs. 9–13, while bank-specific variables have much smaller effects. A 10 percent fall in the loan-loss-reserves-to-nonperforming-loans ratio causes a 3.6 percent fall in equity prices; a 10 percent fall in bank profitability causes equity prices to decline by almost 5 percent.

Third, there are also significant spillover effects of sovereign ratings on banks' equity prices. Specifically, there are direct effects through the two variables measuring sovereign ratings and the difference between bank rating and sovereign rating. Sovereign ratings are also affected by the sovereign spread so that there is also an indirect effect of spreads on bank equity prices through sovereign ratings. However, it should be noted that in the case of Spain and Italy, bank ratings deteriorated at a slower rate than the ratings of the sovereign. This behaviour implies that the differential between bank and sovereign rating had a positive effect on bank equity prices in these countries.

Fourth, if banks are downgraded at the same pace as the sovereign — that is, there is no change in the variable representing the difference between bank ratings and sovereign ratings — there is no effect on the bank equity prices apart from the effect of downgrades of the sovereign, which has a negative effect (with a coefficient of −0.13). However, if banks are downgraded at a faster pace than the sovereign — indicating more of a banking crisis rather than a sovereign crisis — the total effect of the two downgrades on bank equity prices is about three times larger than if sovereign downgrades occur at the same pace as bank downgrades; that is, the combined effect is −0.35 instead of −0.13.

Fifth, our results point to the importance of using levels of equity prices — rather than rates of return — in measuring banks' performance. The use of levels allows us to derive the determinants of long-run equity prices. Moreover, our focus on levels indicates that if sovereign ratings deteriorate, bank equity prices go down — and remain down — until sovereign ratings improve.

Sixth, sovereign spreads are determined mainly by economic fundamentals, as reflected in real growth and relative prices, and sovereign ratings, while sovereign ratings are determined primarily by the sovereign's debt ratio, political uncertainty, and the simultaneous effect of sovereign spreads. There are also strong dynamic effects at work in the equations for sovereign spreads and sovereign ratings.

We also investigated the possibility of non-linear effects of ratings on spreads by including a term in the squared value of ratings. The inclusion of this variable allows major downgrades to have a much larger effect on spreads than more minor ones. This effect did not prove to be significant (t-statistic of 0.7).

Table 5. Final Results of System Estimation after Nesting Down

		Coefficient	Std. Error	t-Statistic	Prob.
Spain – constant		−0.02	0.05	−0.4	0.66
Greece – constant		−0.14	0.1	−1.4	0.16
Ireland – constant		0.05	0.03	1.5	0.14
Italy – constant		−0.11	0.08	−1.4	0.15
Portugal – constant	Sovereign spread equation	−0.09	0.08	−1.1	0.26
Current account to GDP		−0.32	0.46	−0.7	0.48
Relative prices		1.01	0.46	2.2	0.02
Growth		−7.57	3.34	−2.3	0.02
Sovereign rating		0.03	0.02	1.8	0.08
Lagged spread		0.97	0.03	37.8	0.00
Spain – constant		−0.28	0.05	−5.1	0.00
Greece – constant		−0.40	0.08	−5.0	0.00
Ireland – constant		−0.22	0.05	−4.9	0.00
Italy – constant		−0.61	0.10	−5.8	0.00
Portugal – constant	Sovereign ratings equation	−0.21	0.05	−4.1	0.00
Relative prices		0.64	0.30	2.1	0.04
Debt-to-GDP		0.009	0.001	6.1	0.00
Spread		0.04	0.01	5.0	0.00
Lagged ratings		0.90	0.01	49.7	0.00
Spain – constant		5.14	0.20	21.2	0.00
Greece – constant		6.31	0.30	21.2	0.00
Ireland – constant		6.61	0.21	31.7	0.00
Italy – constant		4.88	0.17	28.2	0.00
Portugal – constant	Banks' equity price index	4.50	0.24	118.3	0.00
LLR/NPLs		0.004	0.0009	4.0	0.00
Profits/TA		0.87	0.08	10.5	0.00
Bank rating – sovereign rating		−0.21	0.04	−4.7	0.00
Sovereign rating		−0.10	0.02	−4.3	0.00

Overall sample October 1998 to July 2014, Total number of observations of 2455

To summarize, our findings indicate that a long-run recursive relationship between sovereigns and banks operated during the euro-area crisis. Specifically, for the five crisis countries considered shocks to sovereign spreads fed-through to sovereign ratings, which affected the equity performance of commercial banks. Indeed, our results suggest that during the euro-area crisis, a predominant part of the decline in banks' share prices reflected direct and indirect impacts from the sovereign sector. The combined effect of the average change in sovereign ratings across countries, along with the average change in the differential between bank and sovereign ratings, explains somewhat more than half of the actual fall in bank equity prices. In three of the program countries (Greece, Ireland and Portugal), this combined effect explains over 90 percent of the fall in bank equity prices. The cases of Spain and Italy, where bank ratings deteriorated by less than those of the sovereign between 2008 and 2014, highlight the need of further work examining the impact of banks on sovereigns, and not just the impact of sovereigns on bank equity prices as done in this study.

4.3.   *Conclusions for the crises countries*

During the course of 2014, several important actions were taken toward the creation of a banking union in the euro area.[q] These actions will go a long way in reducing the strength of the linkages between sovereigns and banks, linkages that played out during the recent crisis, deepening on the intensity of the crisis. Our results, however, suggest that a banking union may be a necessary, but not a sufficient, condition for financial stability. As long as domestic euro-area banks hold relatively-large shares of debt issued by their respective *national* sovereigns in their portfolios — and in the absence of a mechanism that ensures some form of debt mutualization — the potential will exist for a re-emergence of the interactions between sovereign spreads and sovereign ratings, on the one hand, and banks' performance, on the other.

Why might a debt-mutualization mechanism contribute to financial stability? After all, our empirical results indicate that rises in our measures of sovereign risk — sovereign ratings and sovereign spreads — lead to declines (both directly and indirectly) in banks' equity prices. Consequently, these results could be interpreted as the correct market reaction so that debt mutualization might not be necessary. The following points, however, need to be considered. First, the negative relationship we obtained between measures of sovereign risk and banks' equity prices was obtained inclusive of the period after the outbreak of the 2007-08 global financial crisis. Yet, as indicated in Figs. 9 through 13, during the period from the early 2000s until 2007 and 2008, bank equity prices rose for the five countries considered in this paper, while the two measures of sovereign risk were essentially unchanged. It was only after the crisis erupted that a significant negative relationship between banks' equity prices and sovereign risk emerged. In other words, market discipline occurred late in the day — this discipline was too late to prevent the outbreak of the crisis. Second, a debt-mutualization mechanism would undoubtedly involve features such as increased surveillance and stricter fiscal rules on members of the mechanism, enhancing discipline. For these reasons, we believe that debt mutualization would represent a significant step forward in crisis prevention.

---

[q] These include the establishment of a Single Supervisory Mechanism in November 2014 and a Single Resolution Mechanism on January 1, 2016.

5. Conclusions

This chapter has considered the behavior of financial markets during the sovereign debt crises for both Greece individually and for the five crises countries together. We offer strong evidence that the markets have had trouble in behaving rationally and that at times they have both failed to understand the nature of the crises and that they have probably acted to exaggerate the problem. It is clear that before the onset of the crises both ratings agencies and the markets more generally saw the Euro area as one homogeneous grouping and that all countries were perceived to be equally safe. The onset of the crises destroyed this view and threw the markets into disarray as they were forced to reappraise the situation. This then led to the development of the 'Doom Loop' scenario where markets and ratings agencies exaggerated the effect of the fundamental problems which were undoubtedly within the system.

References

1. P. DeGrauwe and Y. Ji, Self-fulfilling crises in the Eurozone: An empirical test, *Journal of International Money and Finance* **34**, 15–36 (2013).
2. N. Doetz and C. Fischer, *What Can EMU Countries' Sovereign Bond Spreads Tell Us About Market Perceptions of Default Probabilities During the Recent Financial Crisis?* Deutsche Bundesbank, Discussion Paper Series 1, Economic Studies, no. 11 (2010).
3. H. D. Gibson, S. G. Hall, and G. S. Tavlas, The Greek Financial Crisis: Growing imbalances and sovereign spreads, *Journal of International Money and Finance* **31**, 498–516 (2012).
4. H. D. Gibson, S. G. Hall and G. S. Tavlas, Fundamentally Wrong? Market Pricing of Sovereigns and the Greek Financial Crisis, *Journal of Macroeconomics* **39b**, 405–419 (2014).
5. J. Aizenman, M. Hutchison and Y. Jinjarak, What is the risk of European sovereign debt defaults? Fiscal space, CDS spreads and the market pricing of risk, *Journal of International Money and Finance* **34**, 37–49 (2013).
6. J. Beirne and M. Fratzscher, The pricing of sovereign risk and contagion during the European sovereign debt crisis, *Journal of International Money and Finance* **34**, 60–82 (2013).
7. M. Mink and J. de Haan, Contagion during the Greek sovereign debt crisis, *Journal of International Money and Finance* **34**, 102–113 (2013).
8. J. Ammer and F. Cai, *Sovereign CDS and Bond Pricing Dynamics in Emerging Markets: Does the Cheapest-To-Deliver Option Matter?* Federal Reserve System International Finance Discussion Papers No. 912 (Washington, DC, 2007).
9. R. A. De Santis, *The Euro Area Sovereign Debt Crisis: Safe Haven, Credit Rating Agencies and the Spread of the Fever from Greece, Ireland and Portugal*, European Central Bank Working Paper Series, no. 1419 (Frankfurt am Main, Germany, 2012).
10. A. Fontana and M. Schleicher, *An Analysis of Euro Area Sovereign CDS and Their Relation with Government Bonds*, European Central Bank Working Paper Series, no. 1271 (Frankfurt am Main, Germany, 2010).

11. S. Gerlach, A. Schulz, and G. B. Wolff, *Banking and Sovereign Risk in the Euro Area*, CEPR Discussion Paper, no. 7833 (2010).

12. K. Bernoth, J. von Hagen, and L. Schuknecht, Sovereign risk premiums in the European sovereign risk market, *Journal of International Money and Finance* **31**, 975–995 (2012).

13. J. von Hagen, L. Schuknecht, and G. Wolswijk, Government bond risk premiums in the EU revisited: The impact of the financial crisis, *European Journal of Political Economy* **27**(1), 36–43 (2011).

14. A. Afonso, M. G. Arghyrou, and A. Kontonikas, *The Determinants of Sovereign Bond Yield Spreads in the EMU*. University of Glasgow, Adam Smith Business School, Discussion Paper 2012–14 (2012).

15. J. Yang, J. and K. Tsasaronis, Bank stock returns, leverage and the business cycle, *BIS Quarterly Review*, March, 45–59 (2012).

16. J. A. Chan-Lau, E.X. Liu, and J. M. Schmittmann, Equity returns in the banking sector in the wake of the Great Recession and the European sovereign debt crisis, *Journal of Financial Stability* **16**, 164–172 (2015).

17. O. Castrén, T. Fitzpatrick, and M. Sydow, *What Drives EU Banks' Stock Returns? Bank Level Evidence Using the Dynamic Dividend-discount Model'*, ECB Working Paper, no. 677 (2006).

18. BIS, *The Impact of Sovereign Credit Risk on Bank Funding Conditions*, Committee on the Global Financial System, CGFS Papers, no. 43 (2011).

19. A. Demirgüç-Kunt, E. Detragiache, and O. Merrouche, Bank capital: Lessons from the financial crisis, *Journal of Money, Credit and Banking* **45**, 1147–64 (2013).

20. R. Beetsma, M. Giuliodori, F. de Jong, and D. Widijanto, Spread the news: The impact of news on the European sovereign bonds markets during the crisis, *Journal of International Money and Finance* **34**, 83–101 (2013).

21. A. Aizenman, M. Hutchison, and J. Lothian, The European sovereign debt crisis: background and perspectives, *Journal of International Money and Finance* **34**, 1–5 (2013).

22. K. Cuthbertson, S. G. Hall, and M. P. Taylor, *Applied Econometric Techniques*, (University of Michigan Press, Ann Arbor, 1992).

23. A. C. Harvey, *Applications of the Kalman Filter in Econometrics*, in *Advances in Econometrics: Fifth World Congress*, ed. T. F. Bewley Vol. 1 (Econometric Society Monograph No.13, Cambridge University Press, 1987).

24. J. Pisani-Ferry, *The Euro Crisis and its Aftermath* (Oxford University Press, Oxford, U.K, 2014).

25. J. Shambaugh, *The Euro's Three Crises,* Brookings Pap. Econ. Act. **44**(1), 157–231 (2012).

26. K. O' Rourke, and A. Taylor, 'Cross of Euros' *Journal of Economic Perspectives* **27**(3), 167–192 (2013).

Remarks on international financial stability[a]

Tiff Macklem

Dean, Rotman School of Management,
University of Toronto, Toronto, ON M5S 3E6
E-mail: macklem@rotman.utoronto.ca
www.rotman.utoronto.ca

1.   Introduction

My remarks today will focus on global financial reform, both what has been accomplished, and what remains to be accomplished. And particularly where global models could inform the debate. First, I will begin with a few personal comments about the value of models and the imperative of understanding our global interconnectedness.

2.   The Imperative of Models

I came to Ottawa to work at the Bank of Canada as a newly minted PhD 30 year ago motivated by the perhaps slightly naïve idea that theoretically rigorous, evidence-based research in economics and finance could inform public policy to the benefit of Canadians. Thirty years later, I believe this more than ever.

I spent the first 10 years of my career as a researcher at the Bank of Canada building models to understand how the Canadian economy works and advising the leadership of the Bank on issues like how to run what was then a very novel monetary policy regime called inflation targeting, the interaction between fiscal and monetary policy, and the effects of changes in oil prices. I had the privilege of working with some of you and drew on the work of many of you. Doug Laxton and I, in particular, worked together closely at the Bank of Canada.

Because Canada is such an open economy, we were very conscious of the need to model the international dimensions of the issues. Understanding developments in the rest of the world was essential to understanding the performance of the Canadian economy. But the limits of our imagination and computing power precluded us from building theoretically rigorous, empirically relevant and genuinely integrated international models of the global economy.

Since then the constraints of computing power have largely been lifted. And thanks to the pioneering contributions of Lawrence Klein and the many scholars that have built on his work, our imagination has expanded to be able to think and model the international dimensions of the issues in dynamic, stochastic settings. The models of the global

---

[a] Remarks given at luncheon speech at the Global Economic Modeling conference, June 12, 2015 at the Rotman School of Management, University of Toronto.

economy that are being presented, discussed and debated at this conference are truly breath-taking, and their ability to inform public policy to the benefit of citizens of the world is inspiring. This is the extraordinary legacy of Lawrence Klein. I am so very pleased to celebrate this legacy with you.

Thank you, Peter, for bringing us together to mark success, and to push us all to yet new breakthroughs and new insights.

3. The Global Financial Crisis

The global financial crisis both highlighted glaring weaknesses in our global models and underscored the interconnectedness of our world. The imperative of thinking through the issues in a global framework has never been more self-evident.

The policy response to the financial crisis only began to gain traction when we recognized this was a global crisis and we needed a global solution. The crisis was not simply a liquidity crisis in structured financial products, or a solvency crisis in a few troubled financial institutions. Rather it was a global systemic crisis. The global financial system was dangerously under-capitalized and vastly over-leveraged.

To my mind, the pivotal moment in the global crisis response came at the meeting of the G7 Finance Ministers and central bank Governors on October 10, 2008 in the Cash room of the US Treasury in Washington DC. You will all remember that four weeks earlier on September 15, Lehman had filed for bankruptcy. And in the four weeks that followed AIG had been bailed out, Washington Mutual closed, and Wachovia rescued. Across the Atlantic, HBOS and Bradford and Bigley had been rescued in the UK, Fortis was nationalized by the Dutch, Ireland had guaranteed all its banks, the German Hypo Real Estate Bank was rescued, and the Icelandic financial system had collapsed.

The G7 meeting on October 10 started very badly. The Europeans were extremely critical of the Americans for letting Lehman fail. There was much finger pointing and blame. But after some venting, a shared recognition began to forge in the meeting that the G7 had to act together. Separate actions by the G7 countries, no matter how courageous, would not stop the panic that was raging in financial markets.

What emerged from the meeting was the 5-point plan of action. It really had one overriding commitment. There would not be another Lehman. No systemically important financial institution in the G7 would be allowed to fail.

At the time I was not sure if this would just buy us another week or was a turning point. But in retrospect it was the pivotal moment in the crisis response. We were in the midst of a global systemic crisis. And it required a global system-wide response. Finally, we had the beginnings of one.

Recognizing that the economic fallout from the financial crisis was spreading well beyond the G7, George Bush convened the first ever G20 Leaders Summit in Washington six weeks later in November of 2008. That first G20 Leaders Summit focused on the imperative of coordinated fiscal stimulus to mitigate the global recession. The Summit also launched the reform of the financial system with agreement on a set of common reform principles.

4. Global Financial Reform

Five months later, at the London Summit in April 2009, the Leaders elaborated on those principles by committed to a sweeping and comprehensive reform agenda. Their fundamental objective was to build a resilient global financial system that would serve households and businesses in good times and in bad. To do this, the Leaders created the Financial Stability Board (FSB), and gave it four core tasks:

1. make banks safer;
2. end too-big-to-fail;
3. mitigate bank-like risks in the shadow banking sector, and
4. ensure continuously-functioning core financial markets.

Since the London Summit, a great deal has been accomplished. And the financial system is much safer as a result.

- Capital and liquidity buffers have been dramatically increased in Basle III, and banks have responded raising more than $700B of new capital globally.
- Additional lines of defense have been added, including a Canadian-style leverage limit and a countercyclical capital buffer.
- Globally systemic banks are subject to an additional capital surcharge and more intense supervision, and most FSB members have a framework in place for domestically systemic banks.
- Central counterparties for OTC derivatives should act as firewalls limiting contagion, and
- The most vulnerable shadow banking activities have either ceased or been reformed.

The tremendous progress that has been made has benefited from analysis using models that incorporate core features of banking, and capture the global connectedness of the financial system.

The Macroeconomic Assessment Group at the FSB, in particular, has produced research that has assessed the combined effects of various regulatory reforms and informed their calibration. The rigor of the analysis, which is based on a range of models, has also been helpful in undercutting exaggerated criticisms of the new capital and liquidity standards that have emanated from self-interested industry associations. Careful modelling by the Macro Assessment Group in coordination with the IMF has been essential to an informed and evidence-based debate.

Completion of the sweeping reforms that were launched at the London G20 Summit just over 6 years ago is now within reach. But two big issues remain.

1. Convincingly ending Too-Big-To-Fail

2. Assessing the systemic risks of large non-bank, non-insurer financial institutions. Or to put it more simply, determining if Blackrock is systemic, and if so, what to do about it.

Both of these issues would benefit from model-based research. As a way of encouraging this work, let me say a few words about both issues.

5.   Ending Too-Big-to-Fail

To end TBTF authorities need to be able to resolve globally systemic financial institutions without recourse to public money and without undue disruption to the wider financial system.

This is greatly complicated by two factors:

- A chapter 11-type process that is used in most other industries is way too slow for banks;
- Financial institutions and markets are global but regulation and resolution are national.

To overcome these obstacles, the FSB developed the *Key Attributes of Effective Resolution Regimes for Financial Institutions* and is proposing two final elements for agreement at the Antalya G20 Summit in November: A common international standard for Total Loss Absorbing Capacity (TLAC) for systemically important banks; and contractual arrangements for cross-border recognition of resolution actions.

Will this end TBTF?

To end TBTF, two conditions must be satisfied. First, home and host authorities and market participants must have confidence that systemically important banks have sufficient capacity to absorb losses both before and during resolution (i.e., the amount of Total Loss Absorbing Capacity – TLAC – is sufficient to resolve a failing bank from within without recourse to public money). Second, market participants must have confidence that home and host authorities have the powers, tools, capabilities and willingness to successfully execute an orderly resolution of a large cross-border bank that minimizes the broader impact on financial stability, ensures continuity of critical functions and avoids exposing taxpayers to loss.

Model-based research could contribute to advancing both these requirements.

Based on the analysis I have seen on the losses in past crises, the proposed quantum of TLAC appears appropriate in the range of 16-20% of RWAs and at least 2 times the Basle III leverage ratio. Further work by the FSB combined with the on-going market consultation and a QIS should further improve confidence in the quantum. Independent third-party model-based research on the quantum of TLAC required would be very helpful both in refining the ultimate calibration and in reinforcing the confidence of authorities and markets that the amount of TLAC will be sufficient in all but the most extreme of extreme situations, so the need for recourse to taxpayers should be truly very very remote.

There are also some important issues around where the TLAC should be located in a global bank. The FSB's proposal that material subsidiaries should have 75-90% of the TLAC requirement that would apply on stand-alone basis provides relatively modest opportunities for banks to allocate capital efficiently across jurisdictions. A model-based assessment of the costs of financial fragmentation would be very helpful in assessing the trade-off between the security to host jurisdictions in having local capital to absorb losses, and the system-wide efficiency benefits of allowing banks to allocate their capital globally.

6.   Is Blackrock Systemic?

Finally, let me turn to the systemic importance of non-bank, non-insurer financial institutions. Are Blackrock or Fidelity systemic, and if so, what do we do about it?

The FSB has recently published a proposed assessment methodology for identifying non-bank, non-insurer global systemically important financial institutions. So, called NBNI G-SIFIs. It's a catchy title. The proposed methodologies aim to identify NBNI financial entities whose distress or disorderly failure, because of their size, complexity and systemic interconnectedness would cause significant disruption to the wider financial system and economic activity at the global level.

The FSB has suggested 3 channels whereby the financial distress of NBNI financial entities could pose a threat to global financial stability: a counterparty exposure channel, an asset liquidation channel, and a critical function channel.

Blackrock and Fidelity are arguing they are not systemic. They stress asset managers are fundamentally different from banks and other financial institutions. They point out that fund managers take risks on behalf of clients. If the investments turn sour, it is not the fund management firm that takes the hit. It is the investor.

This is true enough, but given the size of these institutions, is there not a risk of crowded trades and the possibility that fire-sale prices could disrupt trading of funding in key markets, potentially provoking losses in other firms? The likelihood that this could cause significant disruption to the wider financial system and economic activity at the global level is the type of question that can only be assessed with a global model.

Model-based analysis of the potential for very large global asset managers to create systemic problems in global financial markets via the channels identified by the FSB would be very helpful in assessing the case for additional systemic regulatory requirements on such institutions, and weighing the benefits of these regulations against their efficiency cost.

7.   Conclusion

When I was directly engaged in building and using models to advise on economic and financial policies 20-30 years ago, we could only dream of global-scale models with the kind of asset and institutional detail necessary to examine the types of questions I have posed today. Thanks to the leadership of Lawrence Klein and the many who have built on his pioneering work, we can assess the implications of financial regulatory changes at the global level.

In the six years since the London G20 Summit, a great deal has been done to reform the financial system. A new breed of global models with the essential features of banking have been instrumental in assessing the macro implications of these reforms. This has been helpful in calibrating the regulatory changes, assessing their interaction and combined impact, and building a consensus around their importance.

The influence of DB pensions on the market valuation of the pension plan sponsor: For the FTSE 100 companies, size really does matter

Pete Richardson[a]

Senior Associate, Llewellyn Consulting,
London, United Kingdom
E-mail: pete.w.richardson@gmail.com

Luca Larcher

Doctoral student at the Department of Economics and Finance,
Queen Mary University London and Associate at Llewellyn Consulting
E-mail: l.larcher@qmul.ac.uk

This study examines the relationship between market valuations for the FTSE100 listed companies and their DB pension deficits and obligations over the period 2006 to 2012. A number of simple valuation models are estimated, relating the market valuations of each company to its non-pension book value and earnings and its corresponding pension liabilities, deficits and costs. In contrast to earlier U.S. studies, evidence is found of a well-defined and significant relationship between market valuations and DB pension deficits. Taken at face value, the influence of the pension deficit appears to be disproportionate, but this result is found to reflect the insufficiency of published data for pension deficits in representing the underlying structural factors, because of risk premia attached to the scale of disclosed pension obligations or inconsistencies and uncertainties in their measurement. Allowing for such risk premia suggests a more or less one-for-one relationship between market valuation and the pension deficit, but subject to an additional 20% risk premium attached to the values of disclosed pension liabilities. However, a more satisfactory one-for-one relationship is found by putting pension liability estimates on a consistent "risk free" basis, using standardized gilt rates in calculating their net present values. An important implication of these results is that the market values of companies with larger pension liabilities are likely to be penalized relative to smaller schemes having otherwise similar net pension asset positions.

Keywords: DB pensions, pension plan sponsor.

1. Introduction and Background

Driven by increasing concerns of affordability, reflecting secular changes in longevity trends, economic growth, investment returns, and other financial uncertainties, the past decade has seen a systematic shift in UK company pensions from defined benefit (DB) to

---

[a] The principle authors are *Pete Richardson*, Senior Associate at Llewellyn Consulting and *Luca Larcher*, doctoral student at the Department of Economics and Finance, Queen Mary University London and Associate at Llewellyn Consulting. The original version of this paper[1] was produced and published in collaboration with the Pension Insurance Corporation, which provided core financing for the project and advice on data issues, and Queen Mary University London. Special thanks also go to *Francis Breedon*, Professor of Economics and Finance at Queen Mary University London, for his expert advice and suggestions and Preston Llewellyn for his comments and editorial inputs. The views expressed in the study are those of the authors, who remain responsible for any errors or omissions.

defined contribution (DC) based schemes, and progressive changes to, and eventual closure of, existing DB schemes to new members.

DB pension liabilities and net assets nevertheless remain a large and potentially volatile component of company balance sheets. Indeed, in 2012 the DB pension net deficits and associated underlying pension benefit obligations of the FTSE 100 companies represented on average some 4.7% and 47.5% of their market capitalizations respectively. The figures were even larger during the recent period of recession and financial stagnation.

Since 2006, movements in pension net deficits have been influenced strongly by stock market movement through volatile equity prices and falling investment yields and interest rates, overlaid on the cost side by further secular increases in longevity, changes in inflation expectations and other pension related costs. At the same time, there is considerable variation in the scale of pension schemes and associated net asset positions across companies, with net deficits well in excess of 10% of market valuations for some companies, and pension benefit obligations well in excess of 100% for those with the largest schemes (Figs. 1 and 2).

The inherent uncertainties in companies' pension positions have led, in turn, to the development and utilization of a variety of products in an attempt to de-risk DB pension asset and liability positions. These range from financial instruments and insurance policies to hedge specific risks (such as interest rates, inflation rates and longevity), through to insurance buy-ins of specified liabilities and partial or outright buy-outs of the pension schemes.

This raises a number of important issues, from a number of perspectives:
• For companies, seeking to manage their pension schemes and make informed choices on the costs and benefits of reducing or de-risking their existing pension obligations for company values,
• For pension specialists, in the analysis of pension scheme performance, and in the choice and design of de-risking products for specific companies and scheme characteristics,
• For general market participants, in assessing the financial risks and investment opportunities associated with the performance of particular companies and their pension obligations.

Notwithstanding such wide-ranging interest, there have been relatively few systematic studies of the impact of DB pension deficits and related risks and obligations on the market valuation of companies.

A number of US studies have examined this issue in the context of the S&P 500 companies. These however, have been conducted against the background of a rather different regulatory system, particularly as regards the ability to settle pension obligations and the cost of doing so, as well as required pension disclosures, from that which obtains in the United Kingdom.[b]

---

[b] Two key US studies are those carried out at the Federal Reserve by Coronado and Sharpe[2] and Coronado, Mitchell, Sharpe and Nesbitt[3]. A key theme of both papers concerns the inadequacy of US reporting standards with respect to pension scheme disclosure, the implications for the US stock market, and the need for greater transparency.

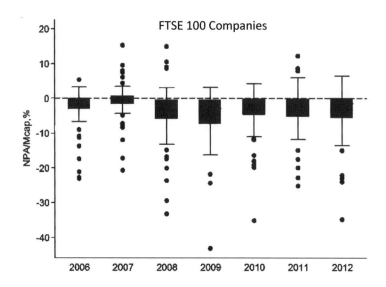

Fig. 1. DB Net Assets as a Share of Market Capitalization.

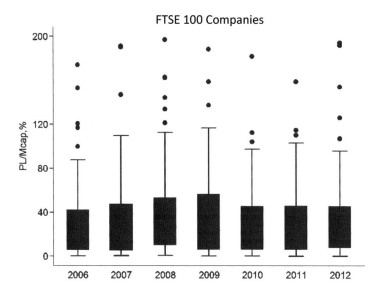

Fig. 2. DB Pension Liabilities as a Share of Market Capitalization.

Notes: The shaded grey areas indicate the inter-quartile range, with median values shown as a solid bar. Maximum and minimum values in the normal range are shown by the outer bars, whilst the dotted points represent minor outliers. A small number of major outliers which go beyond the scale of the graphs are not shown for some years. These include BA, BAE, BT, GKN, International Consolidate Airlines, Invensys and RBS.
Source: The DB Pensions Analytical Data Base.

In the United Kingdom, while there is an accumulation of anecdotal and case-study evidence on the effects of pension de-risking and buyout-related activities, there have been relatively few systematic studies of the possible influence across the range of UK company experiences. Some work has however been undertaken at the Bank of England, looking at pension deficits as a contributory factor to short-term stock market volatility; but as regards the effects on market valuation as a whole, UK evidence overall is relatively scant.[c]

This study seeks to address this situation by applying a basic stock market valuation model to the largest UK companies, as represented by their FTSE 100 composition, so as to assess the possible significance of the scale and net asset position of existing DB schemes for company market values over the period 2006 to 2012. This study also looks at major issues related to the valuation of pension risks, most importantly with respect to the market valuation of DB pension obligations, as well as possible influence of 'corridor adjustments' to the pension accounts.

2. The DB Pensions Analytical Data Base

An essential first requirement for this study was to construct a new research resource in the form of a DB pensions analytical data base (DBPADB). This data base, which covers the period January 2006 to March 2013, matches company financial- and DB-pension-related concepts taken from the company financial statements and pension notes with corresponding stock market performance and company valuation data. A number of sources, including the underlying assumptions and sensitivity analyses routinely provided in the pension notes of the majority of the FTSE 100 companies, were used in its construction.[d]

Published pension data sources are relatively heterogeneous in form and presentation, and differ considerably from company to company. To ensure that the data set was assembled on a consistent basis, a number of important procedural rules have been followed:

- The company sample is based on the specific composition of the FTSE 100 index for 2009. Companies affected by mergers and acquisitions or delisted over the sample period have therefore been included for those years in which the relevant accounts are available.

---

[c] See Trivedi and Young (2006), Bank of England Working Paper No. 289.
[d] The main data sources include Bloomberg company data sets, the published company accounts and pension notes included in annual financial statements and the Bank of England's historic information on market interest rates and gilts. Further specific details of the DBPADB are given in the Sources and Methods appendix.

- Multiple pension schemes have been aggregated, and all pension accounts expressed on a common sterling basis.

- The basic company, pension, and market valuation data have been aligned to a common period, typically attributed to the year to which they largely refer. For example, data for the accounting year closing in March 2013 have typically been attributed to 2012. Market valuations are based on those coinciding with the reporting dates of the accounts in question.

- A small number of companies have been excluded: those without DB schemes; those with activities, employees and pension schemes outside the EU and the US; and those with partial or inadequate pension data.

In the majority of cases, the pension notes provided sufficient information to recover robust estimates of the key assumptions underlying the net present value of pension obligations estimates. Where the relevant detail is insufficient, the sample average has been used.

Unless otherwise stated, the measure of pension net assets used throughout the study has been based on the strict economic definition, and therefore excludes any subsequent 'corridor' adjustments, although their significance has been examined as part of the study.

3. The Underlying Model

The starting point for the analysis is a simple valuation model based on the residual-income approach, as used by Coronado and Sharpe in their original US-based 2003 study, of the following form:

$$P = b0 + b1\ BVC + b2\ cor\ E + b3\ NPA + b4\ EPS + u \tag{1}$$

where the share price (P) is taken to be a function of: company book value (ex-pensions) (BVC); expected core earnings (coreE); pension net assets (NPA); and the pension-related counterpart to core earnings (EPS) – essentially derived from net periodic pension costs – all expressed per share.

Within this framework, two underlying valuation models were considered:

- The first is a 'transparent' model, in which market investors, when valuing a company, simply focus on the value of pension and non-pension net assets, rather than the associated flow of net financing pension accruals i.e. one in which b1, b3<1 and b4=0.
- The polar alternative, the 'opaque' model, is one where account is taken of the stream of pension related earnings and accruals, but no account is taken of the pension net asset position, that is, b3 = 0 and b4 >0.

The key finding of Coronado and Sharpe, who used data for the S&P 500 companies over the period 1993–2001, was that net pension assets were significant only when pension earnings were excluded from the equation. The data were therefore generally found to support the 'opaque' view, where expected pension earnings play a more significant role than pension net assets, in combination with the book value of assets and core company earnings. The authors take this as being specific criticism of the information content and transparency of the US pension accounts as permitted under the prevailing disclosure rules.

Similar results were found in the follow-up study, Coronado et al (2008), which extended the analysis to 2005. This study used a revised version of the model, in which the dependent variable is the market equity value of the company normalized by the book value of total assets, rather than by the share price, with all other relevant financial and pension-related regressors also normalized by the book value of total assets.

Essentially the model used in that extended study was of the following form:

$$MCAPA = (P*N/A) = b0 + b1\ BVCA + b2\ EA + b3\ NPAA + b4\ EPSA + u \qquad (2)$$

where MCAPA represents the current market value of the company; and BVCA, EA, NPAA and EPSA correspond to non-pension and pension book values and earnings, each scaled by total company assets (A).

Although observationally equivalent, there are strong prior reasons to consider that a non-normalized price model such as equation (1) is likely to be statistically unstable, in the sense that share prices and the regressors involved are all inherently volatile and non-stationary (trended and non-constant variance), and thereby prone to the various effects of heteroskedasticity, spurious correlations, and related estimation bias.

Econometrically, there are good reasons to believe that the normalized model is more likely to be stable, particularly during a period of high share price volatility which might otherwise mask the underlying economic relationship.

Since the sample for the current study, for the period 2006 to 2012, includes episodes of major share price volatility, all estimates are therefore based on the normalized model, equation (2).[e]

4. Evidence Based on the Published Data Set

Preliminary estimates of the corresponding market valuation models, based on the published data set, were made for three selected panels of companies. These include:

- **A 'full' sample**, comprising the unfiltered set of all companies for which the basic relevant information was available,
- **A 'deficits' subsample**, comprising all observations where pension net deficits were reported,

---

[e] Preliminary screening of the non-normalized data confirmed its general non-stationarity with high degrees of co-linearity. Corresponding tests on the model in normalized form confirmed general stability and stationarity of the variables involved.

- **A 'risk free'[f] subsample**, comprising those companies which provided sufficient information for the computation of 'risk free' pension liabilities and net assets.

The relevant model and parameter estimates obtained using the data sample, along with associated (robust) standard errors and conventional test statistics, are summarized in Table 1. All model estimates were obtained using the robust panel data estimation methods provided by the Stata package.[g]

All model estimates also included 7 annual time and 10 broad sector/industry-specific constant shift effects (not reported here), in order to pick up common influences related to the macroeconomic cycle and sectoral developments.

Results for two forms of the model are included:

(1) **The basic form** of equation (2), in which a single measure of DB pension net assets (NPAA) is used; and
(2) **A modified version,** in which a separate term in pension liabilities (PLA) is included as a test of the statistical sufficiency of the net assets variable in representing pension assets and liabilities.

The basic model (equations 1.1, 1.3, and 1.5).[h] While there are some variations in parameter estimates across different samples, some broad points of agreement emerge. In general, the basic model is supported by the data:

- The estimated correlation coefficients – at or above 0.5 – are reasonably high for a time series cross section study of this type, and the standard errors are reasonably low.
- The estimated coefficients for key variables, notwithstanding some variations, are fairly robust, have correct signs, and are mostly statistically significant.
- The estimated coefficients on company book values (BVCA) are all highly significant and in the plausible range of 0.45 to 1.0, and lowest for the 'risk free' sample.
- The estimated coefficients on net pension assets (NPAA) are all correctly signed, statistically significant, and notably greater than 1. This is consistent with the

---

[f] The term 'risk free' is used in a variety of senses in the economic and financial literature. In this paper it is used in a specific sense, explained fully in the following section.
[g] Stata is widely regarded as one of the most comprehensive statistical estimation packages available, with robust estimation techniques specially developed for time-series, cross-section and panel data analysis of this type (see http://www.stata.com).
[h] Results for the conditioning time and sectoral variables, which suggest some significant sectoral and cyclical differences, are not reported here.

Table 1. Valuation Model Estimates Using the Published Data Set

Dependant variable: Market value of company/total company assets, MCAPA = f (BVCA, EA, NPAA, NPPCA). Sample: 2006-2012. Companies as per notes.

Equation	1.1	1.2	1.3	1.4	1.5	1.6
Sample/equa tion notes	Net asset model Full sample N=581	Eq.1.1 with liability term Full sample N=581	Net asset model Deficits only N=471	Eq.1.3 with liability term Deficits only N=471	Net asset model 'risk free' sample N=543	Eq. 1.5 with liability term 'risk free' sample N=543
BVCA	0.8796*** (.22)	0.8340*** (.22)	1.0337*** (.28)	0.9889*** (.29)	0.4644** (.15)	0.4377** (.15)
EA	5.0030*** (1.01)	5.1116*** (1.02)	5.3788*** (1.17)	5.4940*** (1.17)	3.6975** (.80)	3.7924*** (.81)
NPAA	2.0347*** (.51)	1.0724** (.55)	2.1671*** (.56)	0.9421 (.70)	1.5990* (.49)	0.8469* (.54)
PLA		0.2153** (.09)		0.2145* (.11)		0.1765* (.08)
NPPCA	3.6317 (6.68)	0.6011 (7.09)	-2.2337 (7.13)	-4.9755 (7.56)	5.9406 (6.19)	3.2990 (6.53)
CON	0.4213** (.16)	0.4591 (.16)	.2349 (0.19)	0.2451 (.19)	-0.0048 (.14)	0.0232 (.14)
R2	.5266	.5309	0.5144	0.5182	0.5819	.5862
RMSE	.6187	.6165	.6314	0.6296	0.4799	0.4779

Notes: Year and sector fixed effects variables are also included in all equations but not reported here. Coefficient significance levels are indicated * $p<.05$ ** $p<.01$ *** $p<.001$ (equivalent to 90%, 98% and 99.8% confidence).
MCAPA= Market value of company/Total Assets
BVCA= Book Value of Company (ex Pensions)/Total Assets
EA= Company (non-pensions) Earnings/Total Assets
NPAA= Net DB Pension Assets/Total Assets
PLA= Pension Liabilities/Total Assets
NPPCA= Net Periodic DB Pension Costs/Total Assets

market ascribing a disproportionate weight to net pension assets relative to the book value of assets, and contrasts strongly with the US finding discussed earlier.[i]

• The estimated coefficients on company earnings (EA) are fairly robust, highly significant, and plausible – typically implying a £3.70 to £5.50 increase in

---

[i] Given that the focus of US research was on the inadequacy and lack of transparency in US company pension notes, a plausible explanation of this result is that superior EU pension reporting standards embodied in IAS19 and its precursors give the published pension accounts greater market credibility.

company value per £1 of additional earnings. These estimates are somewhat lower than those given by corresponding US studies.

- By contrast, the estimated coefficients on net periodic pension costs (NPPCA) are not well determined, but are of similar orders of magnitude and not significantly different from those for core earnings, implying that the market may give similar weight to both influences.
- The results for 'full' and 'deficits' samples are not significantly different, although the pension cost estimates for the 'deficits' sample are perverse and ill-defined.

At first sight a greater-than-unit coefficient estimate for net pension assets (NPAA) is somewhat puzzling, because it could be taken to imply that the market gives a disproportionately large weight to movements in pension deficits compared with changes in core book values (BVCA). Such a conclusion, however, would need to be carefully qualified when the corresponding estimates for equations 1.2, 1.4 and 1.6 are also considered.

5. Does Size Matter?

The modified model (equations 1.2, 1.4 and 1.6). The key finding here is that, by including a separate liabilities term, and giving different implicit weights to pension assets and liabilities, the coefficients on net pension assets fall to within a fairly narrow range around 1, with little effect on the coefficients of other significant variables. At the same time, the separate liability terms are all statistically significant and of the order of 0.2, i.e. around 20% of pension liabilities.

The broad conclusion here is that size matters. Thus, for two companies reporting identical levels of pension net assets in relation to total company assets, the company with the lower (higher) gross pension liabilities (also in relation to total assets) will tend to attract a higher (lower) market valuation. The implication is that reported pension liabilities are regarded by markets as being systematically undervalued and/or that a higher level of liabilities is viewed as representing a higher risk.[j]

The next section refines the analysis to consider alternative measures of 'risk free' liabilities and pension risks with a view to testing both these hypotheses.

6. Estimating 'Risk Free' and Reported Pension Liabilities

The consideration of 'risk free' valuation and pension risks necessitate closer scrutiny of the underlying data set, and greater focus on the detailed technical assumptions and sensitivity analyses contained within the pension notes.

---

[j] More generally the results imply that the published net pension assets measure is not a sufficient statistic for the overall company pension position.

Following the examination of data sources and sensitivity analysis using the net assets model, it was concluded that a number of company outliers should be excluded.[k] Typically these exclusions involved companies quoted on the London Stock Exchange but whose operations, employment and pension schemes are largely outside Europe and the United States; have particularly high and volatile market values (often they are in the mining, precious metals and raw material sectors); and have extremely low DB pension liabilities.[l] The resulting sample corresponds to the 'risk free' sample of companies used in Table 1.

Although there are a number of probable sources of systematic bias in pension liability estimates, the largest, and that for which the market is best equipped to account, relates to the discount rate assumptions embodied in the net present value estimates for pension obligations.[m]

While the IAS 19 accounting standards have been important in introducing additional pension disclosure requirements, and stipulating that liabilities and assets should be valued using market rates, there nonetheless remains some discretion in the choice of discount rates – both in the choice of a specific corporate bond rate, and in the adjustments used in making it appropriate for the maturity of the scheme's liabilities (which in turn depend on the proportion of pensioner and active members in the scheme). As a result, there is considerable variation in the discount rate assumptions used across companies and over time.

Accordingly, this study has sought to standardize the reported pension liability and net asset estimates by taking specific account of the differences between the discount rate assumptions used in calculating DB liabilities and the (usually lower) current market rates on government bonds (gilts) of similar maturity. To achieve this, associated measures of 'risk free' liabilities and associated pension net assets have been estimated, taking full account of the underlying technical assumptions and additional sensitivity analysis information reported in the standard pension notes, in particular those pertaining to interest rate sensitivity.[n]

A first step in the standardization process is to estimate the approximate duration (D) of pension obligations implicit in the reported present value of pension liabilities. These

---

[k] Data sensitivity analyses were carried out by sequentially trimming the sample for companies in the highest and lowest percentiles for pension net assets and market capitalization. The broad conclusion was that a very small number of companies with the highest and most volatile market capitalizations (most often reflecting commodity price volatility) exerted undue influence on parameter estimates.

[l] Typical examples are Fresnillo and Vedanta both of which are natural resource-based companies.

[m] Other differences, for example those related to pension increases and longevity, may be equally important but are less easily allowed for by the market.

[n] For a further discussion of the choice of discount rates see the Box: IAS19 and the choice of rates for discounting Defined Benefit pension obligations and the references therein.

The current provisions of the IAS19 guidelines require that pension obligations be discounted using the yield on high-quality corporate bonds, or government debt when there is no deep market in high-quality corporate bonds. Most companies interpret this provision as a recommendation for the use of AA rated corporate bond yields of currency and duration matching those of the pension obligations. As a result, there can be considerable variability in discount rate assumptions across companies according to the chosen bond rate. There is nonetheless a long standing academic debate about the choice of discount rate for such an exercise, summarized most recently by Napier[4].

Financial theory suggests that the determination of the pension obligation is a two steps process. The first is the proper estimation, where the schedule of future pension payments is computed using a range of actuarial assumptions which depend upon the specific situation of each DB scheme and the demographics of its participants. In the second step, once the future cash outflows of the pension fund have been estimated, they need to be discounted to compute the net present value of the projected benefit obligation (PBO) which the sponsoring company has to fund and disclose in its financial statements. The discount rate used in such an exercise should be determined considering the risk of these future payments from the sponsor's standpoint. From such a perspective however, the future benefit payments are certain, at least with regard to credit risk. The only way in which a sponsor can escape such payments is to file for bankruptcy or negotiate a reduction of pension benefits with the scheme's participants (in effect a salary cut). Hence it seems clear that the appropriate discount rate should reflect only the time value of money and no credit risk at all. A similar point is made by various researchers considering the US framework, including Brown and Pennacchi[5] and Brown and Wilcox[6].

In the UK, the choice of a discount rate based on AA rated corporate bonds is also not without controversy. In a recent discussion paper, the UK Accounting Standards Board (2009) suggests that the pension obligation should be discounted at a (credit) risk free rate[a], as does the report authored by the Pensions Institute[8] Moreover, both the UK Pensions Regulator and the UK Pension Protection Fund (PPF) use government bond yields rather than corporate bond rates in discounting defined benefit obligations, for example in the PPF Purple Books[e] and in calculating the levy that each sponsor has to pay to fund the PPF's guarantee.

Consistent with this literature, the present study supports the view that the correct rate to discount pension obligations should not incorporate any credit risk and uses yields on UK government bonds as a proxy for the risk-free rate to compute alternative "risk free" measures of pension obligations. This method of standardisation essentially involves identifying the approximate duration of pension obligations by scheme, matching these with rates for gilts of the same period and duration and re-estimating the corresponding net present values of pension obligations. Specific details of the computations involved are described in more detail in the Sources and Methods annex to this report.

Box 1. IAS19 and the Choice of Rates for Discounting Defined Benefit Pension Obligations

[a] See Pro-Active Accounting Activities in Europe[7], the financial reporting of pensions, UK Accounting Standards Board, January 2008.
[b] See The Purple Book[9], DB Pensions Universe Risk Profile, published annually by the UK Pensions Regulator and the UK Pensions Protection Fund.

are estimated on the basis of the discount rate sensitivity estimates given by individual company pension notes using the following expression:[o]

$$D = - (dPL/PL) *(1+r)/dr \qquad (3)$$

where D represents the estimated duration; and dPL/PL the proportionate change in the present value of DB liabilities reported in the pension notes for a given change (dr) in the discount rate (r), as used in calculating the present value for a given company and year.[p]

---

[o] Effectively the estimated duration D is backed out of the interest rate sensitivity calculation using the derivate rule for the net present value of liabilities of duration D.
[p] Where multiple schemes exist, duration estimates were based on the sensitivities reported for the largest representative scheme.

In practice, sufficient information was available to calculate implicit durations for over two-thirds of the sample. Estimates ranged from 12 to 25 years, with a sample average and median of around 18 ½ years.

For companies where discount rate sensitivities are not reported in the pension notes, the sample average duration was used.[q] Corresponding 'risk free' adjustments to pension liability estimates were then made using gilt rates, matched to the timing of the company accounts and the duration of the defined benefit obligations (DBO), using the following expression:[r]

$$FVPL = PL*[1 - D*(g-r)/(1 + r)] \qquad (4)$$

where the 'risk free' pension liability estimate (FVPL) is the reported net present value of pension liabilities (PL) rescaled by 1 minus the duration (D) times the difference between gilt (g) and published (r) discount rates as a ratio of the published discount factor (1 + r).

These adjustments typically result in a much higher level of liabilities, but with considerable variation over time and companies, depending on the risk premia assigned by the market to the chosen corporate bonds over gilts, for each company and at each given point in time.

Averaged across companies, these adjustments added approximately 20 to 25% to the levels of liabilities and pension net asset positions.[s] As illustrated in Figs. 3, 4, and 5, the effects measured at the aggregate level are quite substantial, particularly at the time of the financial crisis in 2008 and to a lesser extent in 2011 – reflecting not only the fall in market values, but also the larger disconnects between corporate bond and gilt rates.

7. 'Risk Free' Estimates versus the Published Data Set

To test the relative explanatory power of the published versus 'risk free' pension estimates, Table 2 presents a series of summary model estimates designed to illustrate different features, all based on the same data sample. Four key results emerge:

- Although most parameter estimates are little affected by the choice of net asset and liability estimates, 'risk free' net assets appear to provide a more satisfactory explanation, with uniformly-higher goodness of fit and greater plausibility.

- Equations using the 'risk free' measures (comparing equation 2.1 to 2.4), exhibit more plausible net asset coefficients (of the order of 0.9 to 1.0), without the inclusion of a separate liabilities term, which is also statistically insignificant and close to zero in equation 2.4.

---

[q] Further experimentation suggested that subsequent estimates were relatively robust to variations in this assumption in the range of 15 to 20 years.
[r] Equation 4 essentially applies the sensitivity rule on which equation 3 is based.
[s] Such an adjustment effectively eliminates all but a few reported pension net asset surpluses in the sample.

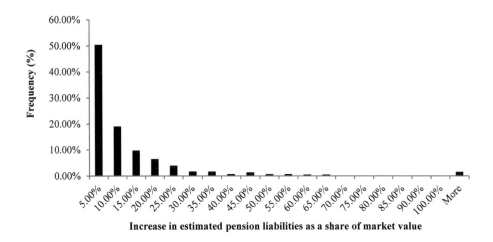

Increase in estimated pension liabilities as a share of market value

Fig. 3. The Impact of 'Risk Free' Adjustments on Pension Liabilities as a Percent of Market Value.

Notes: Fig. 3 reports the frequency distribution of percentage revisions to pension liabilities made through fair valuation adjustments as described in the main text.
Source: The DB Pensions Analytic Data Base.

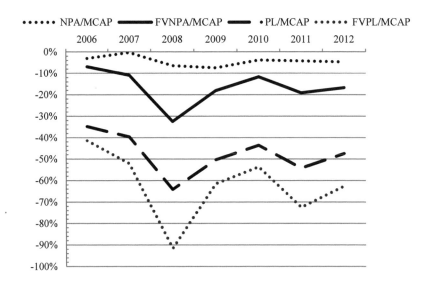

Fig. 4. The Effects of 'Risk Free' Adjustments on Pension Net Assets and Liabilities as Percentage of Market Value.

Notes: The dashed lines correspond to the 'risk free' adjusted values of pension net assets and liabilities.
Source: DB Pensions Analytical Data Base.

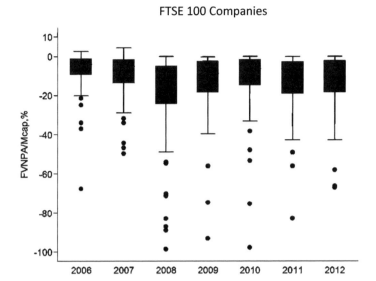

Fig. 5. Estimated 'Risk Free' DB Net Assets as a Share of Market Capitalization.

Notes: See the notes for Figs. 1 and 2.
Source: DB Pensions Analytical Data Base.

- Testing for the significance of the differences between published and 'risk free' net pension assets, the published data add nothing to the basic 'risk free' model (2.3), with the corresponding measure (FVdif) close to zero and insignificant as in equation 2.5.

- Following up earlier observations about the apparent insignificance of periodic pension costs, equation 2.6 confirms that they can be readily combined within a single company earnings term (E) without loss of significance or impact on other parameter estimates. Indeed equation 2.6 provides the simplest and most parsimonious representation of the 'risk free' model, achieving the lowest overall standard error, and without loss of explanatory power.

To examine further the robustness of the basic 'risk free' model and to address possible concerns that the results could be biased by outliers with respect to the scale of pension liabilities in relation to market values (those having so-called 'super-sized' pension obligations), additional estimates were made using sequential tests with smaller samples of company pension data, as reported in Table 3. These estimates were made by sequentially removing data points ordered by the ratio of pension liabilities to market capitalization (R).

Table 2. Summary of Results for the 'Risk Free' vs. Published Data-Based Model Estimates

Dependent variable: Market value of company/total company assets, MCAPA = f (BVCA, EA, FVNPAA, NPPCA). Sample: 2006-2012. Companies as per notes.

Equation	2.1	2.2	2.3	2.4	2.5	2.6
Sample/ equation notes	Net asset model FV sample N=543	Eq.2.1 with liabilities term N=543	FV Net asset model N=543	Eq.2.3 with liabilities term N=543	Eq.2.3 with valuation test N=543	Eq.2.3 with total earnings term N=543
BVCA	0.4644*** (.15)	0.4377*** (.15)	0.4310** (.15)	0.4376** (.15)	0.4295*** (.15)	0.4296** (.15)
EA	3.6975*** (.80)	3.7923*** (.81)	3.7853*** (.80)	3.7647*** (.80)	3.7872*** (.80)	
E						3.7692*** (.80)
NPAA	1.5990*** (.49)	0.8469* (.54)				
FVNPAA			0.9276*** (0.22)	1.1742** (.47)	0.9457*** (.29)	0.9054*** (.19)
FVdiff				-0.0596 (.47)		
PLA		0.1765* (.08)				
FVPLA				-0.0690 (.43)		
NPPCA	5.9406 (6.19)	3.2991 (6.52)	2.5567 (6.27)	2.6723 (6.39)	2.5894 (6.3)	
CON	-0.0048 (.14)	0.0232	0.0027 (.14)	-0.0043 (.14)	0.0002 (.14)	0.0225 (.10)
R2	0.5819	0.5862	0.5897	0.5899	0.5897	0.5896
RMSE	.4799	0.4779	0.4754	.4758	0.4759	0.4750

Notes: Year and sector fixed effects variables are also included in all equations but not reported here. Coefficient significance levels are indicated * p<.05 ** p<.01 *** p<.001 (equivalent to 90%, 98% and 99.8% confidence).
MCAPA= Market value of company/Total Assets
BVCA= Book Value of Company (ex Pensions)/Total Assets
EA= Company (non-pensions) Earnings/Total Assets
E= Total Company Earnings/Total Assets
NPAA= Net DB Pension Net Assets/Total Assets
FVNPA= 'Risk free' DB Pension Net Assets/Total Assets
FVdiff= FVNPA-NPAA
PLA =Pension Liabilities/Total Assets
FVPLA='Risk free' Pension Liabilities/Total Assets
NPPCA=Net Periodic DB Pension Costs/Total Assets

An overall conclusion is that market valuations over the estimation period appear to have been most consistent with the 'risk free' representation of DB pension liabilities and net assets, as opposed to the actual reported data. It seems unlikely, however, that many investors would make such formal calculations of the inconsistencies in assumptions and market discount rates: more likely is that they would simply apply a rule of thumb, for example by adding roughly 20% to reported pension liabilities.

Table 3. Testing the Sensitivity of the 'Risk Free' Model (Eq. 2.3) to Changes in Sample Composition.

Dependent variable: Market value of company/total company assets, MCAPA = f (BVCA, EA, FVNPAA, NPPCA). Sample: 2006-2012. Companies as per notes.

Equation	3.1	3.2	3.3	3.4
Sample/ equation notes	Full sample N=543	Excluding R>3 N=532	Excluding R>2 N=500	Excluding R>1 N=486
BVCA	0.4310** (.15)	0.4136** (.15)	0.4225** (.15)	0.4080** (.15)
EA	3.7853*** (0.80)	3.7256*** (0.80)	3.6554*** (0.80)	3.6311 (0.80)
FVNPAA	0.9276*** (0.22)	0.8965*** (0.23)	0.9199** (0.37)	0.8356** (0.38)
NPPCA	2.5567 (6.27)	0.8633 (6.51)	0.0111 (7.7)	-0.8326 (7.81)
CON	0.0027 (.14)	0.8295*** (.11)	0.8667*** (.12)	0.8645 (.12)
R2	0.5897	.5901	.5892	0.5828
RMSE	0.4754	.4760	.4845	0.4897

Notes: Year and sector fixed effects variables are also included in all equations but not reported here. Coefficient significance levels are indicated * $p<.05$ ** $p<.01$ *** $p<.001$ (equivalent to 90%, 98% and 99.8% confidence).
MCAPA= Market value of company/Total Assets
BVCA= Book Value of Company (ex-Pensions)/Total Assets
EA= Company (non-pensions) Earnings/Total Assets
FVNPAA= 'Risk free' estimate of Net DB Pension Assets/Total Assets
NPPCA= Net Periodic DB Pension Costs/Total Assets
R = -PL/MCAP= Ratio of DB Pension Liabilities to market capitalization

In Table 3, the estimation sample was sequentially reduced by excluding individual observations according to the ratio of company pension liabilities to market capitalization (R), as follows:

	R>3	R>2	R>1
BA/ICA Group	X	X	X
BT Group	X	X	X
GKN	X	X	X
Invensys	X	X	X
BAE Systems		X	X
RBS		X	X
Aviva		X	X
RSA Insurance Group			X
Rexam			X
Marks & Spencer Group			X
National Grid			X
Barclays			X
Lloyds			X
TUI Travel			X
Rolls Royce Holdings			X
IMI			X

Note: The mean value of R over the estimation sample period is 0.47, with a standard deviation of 0.8.

8. Allowing for Generic Risks

An alternative to the 'risk free' calculations would be to assess the risks associated with the specific characteristics and structure of each of the pension schemes. To do this comprehensively would be highly demanding, and go beyond the scope and information set of this study. However, taking it forward on a broad generic basis, the study has constructed composite risk indicators designed to embody rules of thumb for selected risks, as follows:

- Longevity risks +5% of gross pension liabilities,
- Discount risk The effect of a 1% shift in rates on pension liabilities,[t]
- Equity risks - 20% of equity assets.

Although arguably broad-brush and somewhat arbitrary, such a composite risk measure does at least reflect, in a consistent quantified manner, some of the main concerns of pension specialists in assessing the uncertainties attached to specific schemes.

---

[t] The discount risk is calculated using the same method used to evaluate 'risk free' liabilities, allowing also for an average 10% holdings in bonds.

As illustrated in Fig. 6, the resulting risk indicator is relatively smooth at the aggregate level, compared with the corresponding degrees of 'risk free' adjustments, rising significantly in 2008 and relatively stable thereafter. There is nonetheless considerable variation at the company level, rising to 100% or more for those companies with greatest exposure (Fig. 7).

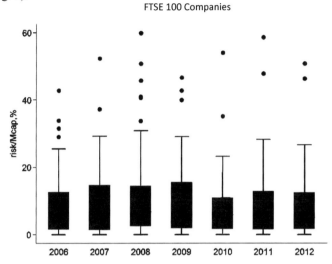

Fig 6. Generic Risk Variables as a Share of Market Capitalization.

Notes: See the notes for Figs. 1 and 2.
Source: DB Pensions Analytic Data Base

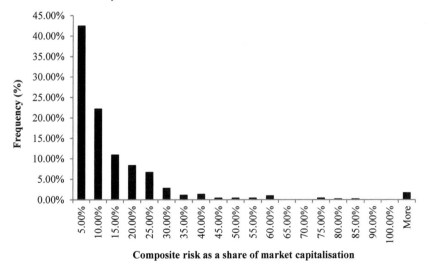

Fig. 7. Distribution of Composite Risk within the 'Risk Free' Sample.

Notes: This figure reports the frequency distribution of the composite risk variable as described in the main text.
Source: DB Pensions Analytical Data Base.

Table 4a and 4b report a variety of model estimates using the composite risk variable in conjunction with published and 'risk free' data, all based on the same 'risk free' sample of companies. On this basis, a number of points emerge:

- First, the composite risk variable (Risk A) is found to be significant, with a plausible and correctly-signed parameter of 0.9 where the published net assets data are used (compare 4.1 with 4.2), performing much the same role as liabilities in reducing the net asset term to a plausible value of 0.8.
- It is also plausible in the unrestricted form of the model (4.3 and 4.4), but its statistical significance and those of the separate assets and liabilities are greatly reduced.
- Overall, equation 4.2 with reported net assets and the risk variable is the most acceptable representation.

In the 'risk free' models, by contrast, the risk variable performs relatively poorly (4.5 to 4.8). Its influence is small and insignificant in the basic 'risk free' specification (4.6) and, though plausible, remains insignificant in the unrestricted form of the model (4.7 and 4.8). Overall, the basic 'risk free' models (4.4 and also 2.6) still appear to provide the most satisfactory statistical explanations.

9. How Important Are Corridor Adjustments?

The measure of DB pension net assets used throughout the study is based on the strict economic definition, and therefore excludes any subsequent 'corridor' adjustments. The rationale for doing so is that the market ought to be sufficiently sophisticated to use all the information available to 'see through' any accounting adjustments that are made to 'smooth the data'.

'Corridor accounting' allows exceptional gains and losses from pensions schemes to be deferred, (or 'smoothed'), over a period of years. Concerns have been expressed in some quarters about the call for a halt in the practice as announced in the pension scheme accountancy standards for 2013 (IAS 19). According to some analysts, the changes will bring about greater financial cost to schemes and changes to investment decisions, such as increasing the move to lower-risk portfolios and incentivizing more de-risking within the pensions industry.

Accordingly, to explore this issue further, additional tests were run using both the original full sample and the 'risk free' model, incorporating some allowance for corridor smoothing in the form of a variable equivalent to the corridor adjustment in those cases when they are made, and zero otherwise.

The corresponding results are reported in Table 5. Admittedly, the test is of relatively low power, affecting fewer than 10% of observations, but the broad outcome is that the effects of corridor adjustment appear to be insignificant and possibly negative. To this extent they support the view that the market essentially sees through any corridor smoothing. [u]

Table 4a. Testing Alternative Models against a Generic Risk Measure (RiskA) (Equation 4.1-4.4)

Dependent variable: Market value of company/total company assets. Sample: 2006-2012. Companies as per notes.

Equation	4.1	4.2	4.3	4.4
Sample/ equation notes	Net asset model N=543	Eq. 4.1 with risk term N=543	Unrestricted basic model N=543	Eq. 4.3 with risk term N=543
BVCA	0.4644*** (.15)	0.4216** (.15)	0.4377*** (.15)	0.4231** (.15)
EA	3.6975*** (.80)	3.7955*** (.81)	3.7924*** (0.81)	3.7981** (.81)
NPAA	1.5990*** (.49)	0.8033 (.57)	0.8469* (.54)	0.7854 (.56)
FVNPAA				
PAA				
PLA			0.1765* (.08)	0.0317 (.13)
FVPLA				
RiskA		-0.8958* (.43)		-0.7641 (.79)
NPPCA	5.9406 (6.19)	3.3157 (6.39)	3.2990 (6.53)	3.2277 (6.42)
CON	-0.0048 (.14)	0.1334 (.14)	0.0232 (.14)	0.1181 (.16)
R2	.5819	0.5869	.5862	0.5870
RMSE	.4799	.4775	.4779	0.4779

Notes: Year and sector fixed effects variables are also included in all equations but not reported here. Coefficient significance levels are indicated * p<.05 ** p<.01 *** p<.001 (equivalent to 90%, 98% and 99.8% confidence). RiskA = Generic pension risk variable/Total Assets

---

[u] In principle a negative effect would imply that corridor adjustments are not only discounted but may have a perverse effect.

Table 4b. Testing Alternative Models against a Generic Risk Measure (RiskA) (Equation 4.5-4.8)

Dependent variable: Market value of company/total company assets. Sample: 2006-2012. Companies as per notes.

Equation	4.5	4.6	4.7	4.8
Sample/ equation notes	FV net asset model N=543	Eq. 4.5 with risk term N=543	Unrestricted FV model N=543	Eq. 4.7 with risk term N=543
BVCA	0.4310** (.15)	0.4296** (.15)	0.4376** (.15)	0.4301** (.15)
EA	3.7853*** (.80)	3.7879*** (.80)	3.7647*** (.80)	3.7688*** (.80)
NPAA	0.9276** (0.22)	0.9006** (0.43).		
FVNPAA	0.9276** (0.22)	0.9006** (0.43).	1.1742** (.47)	1.1571** (.48)
PAA				
PLA				
FVPLA			-0.0690 (.13)	-0.1413 (.13)
RiskA		-0.0463 (.72)		-0.4722 (.82)
NPPCA	2.5567 (6.27)	2.5379 (6.39)	2.6723 (6.39)	2.6020 (6.36)
CON	0.0027 (.14)	.0094 (.15)	-0.0043 (.14)	.0573 (.16)
R2	0.5897	.5897	.5899	.5902
RMSE	0.4754	.4759	.4758	.4761

Notes: Year and sector fixed effects variables are also included in all equations but not reported here. Coefficient significance levels are indicated * $p<.05$ ** $p<.01$ *** $p<.001$ (equivalent to 90%, 98% and 99.8% confidence). RiskA = Generic pension risk variable/Total Assets

Table 5. Testing the Significance of Corridor Adjustment Effects

Dependent variable: Market value of company/total company assets. Sample: 2006-2012. Companies as per notes.

Equation	5.1	5.2	5.3	5.4	5.5	5.6
Sample/ equation notes	Net asset model Full sample N=581	Eq. 5.1 with Corridor test N=581	Net asset model 'risk free' sample N=543	Eq. 5.3 with Corridor test N=543	'Risk free' model N=543	Eq. 5.5 with Corridor test N=543
BVCA	0.8707*** (.22)	0.8836*** (.22)	0.4644** (.15)	0.4682** (.15)	0.4310** (.15)	0.4344** (.15)
EA	4.9979*** (1.02)	4.9799*** (1.02)	3.6975** (.80)	3.6630*** (.80)	3.7853** (0.80)	3.7551*** (0.80)
NPAA	2.0320*** (0.51)	2.0152*** (0.51)	1.5990** (0.50)	1.5676** (.49)		
FVNPAA					0.9276*** (0.22)	0.9022*** (0.22)
DIFNPA		-1.7586 (1.66)		-2.4728 (1.73)		-2.0017 (1.40)
NPPCA	3.6368 (6.68)	2.8302 (6.99)	5.9406 (6.19)	4.7265 (6.51)	2.5567 (6.27)	1.7270 (6.41)
CON	0.4216* (.17)	0.4140 (.16)	-0.0048 (.14)	-0.0744 (.16)	.0027 (.14)	-0.0544 (.16)
R2	.5243	0.5272	0.5819	0.5838	.5897	.5910
RMSE	.6215	0.6189	0.4799	0.4793	.4754	.4752

Notes: Year and sector fixed effects variables are also included in all equations but not reported here. Coefficient significance levels are indicated * $p<.05$ ** $p<.01$ *** $p<.001$ (equivalent to 90%, 98% and 99.8% confidence). DIFNPA = Corridor adjustment to NPA/Total Assets; zero where corridor is not used.

10. Summary Conclusions

Overall this study provides reasonably robust empirical support for the simple company valuation approach when applied to UK FTSE 100 companies over the recent past, with evidence of statistically-significant influences coming from core (non-pension) company book values, company earnings, and pension liabilities and deficits.

In contrast to comparable US studies, the UK market appears to ascribe quite large and significant weight to pension liabilities and deficits in the overall valuation process as reflected in share prices and market capitalization.

Given that the focus of US research has been on the inadequacy and lack of transparency in US company pension notes, a plausible explanation of this result is that superior EU pension reporting standards embodied in IAS19 and its precursors give the published pension accounts greater market credibility.

Taken at face value, the preliminary evidence based on the published data suggests that a relatively large weight (160%) is given to net pension deficits, and that this weight is somewhat greater than that given to non-pension company book values. This implies that overall company values are reduced by about £160 per £100 of pension deficit.

On the face of it this presents a puzzle. This apparent puzzle, however, can be explained by making further allowance for systematic bias or risks associated with the measurement and scale of pension estimates as a simple proportion of gross liabilities or by more sophisticated means.

In the former case, making allowance for the scale of pension liabilities suggests a more plausible weight for pension deficits (of around 85%), but an additional deadweight loss equivalent to around 17% of total pension liabilities.

Looking more closely at sources of bias and systematic risk associated with estimated pension liabilities, the one which the market may be best able to allow for – and the largest – relates to the differences between corporate bond rates used in their estimation and the market rate for gilts. Making such an allowance, in the form of ''risk free' adjustments' to the present values of pension liabilities and net asset positions, is found to have substantial effects on the scale of liabilities (increased by 20% on average) and deficits, most notably in the recession period (Fig. 4 and comparing Figs. 5 and 1). Indeed, in such a case, few if any FTSE 100 company pensions are likely to have been in surplus since 2008.

Empirically, models that incorporate such 'risk free' adjustments are found to be generally more satisfactory in terms of plausibility and explanatory power, and appear to be unaffected by changes in company sample, e.g. the removal of those with 'supersized' pension schemes. The weight given to 'risk free' pensions is found to be reasonably close to 90%, but in this case size also matters, to the extent that it affects the scale of the 'risk free' adjustments to liabilities and deficits.

Where unadjusted published data are used, there is also evidence of the market giving systematic weight to the range of other risk influences, for example those associated with longevity, interest rates, and equity risks. However, these prove to be marginally outperformed by the simple 'fair valuation' model.[v]

The overall conclusion is that, whether through valuation adjustments, specific risk assessment, or crude rules of thumb, both the size of the pension deficit itself and the scale of the associated pension obligations, really do matter to markets when assessing company value.

---

[v] A secondary conclusion drawn from the same analysis is that the market appears to "see through" so called "corridor adjustments" to pension valuations by giving no significant weight to such distortions, although this result is based on a rather small set of observations.

Whether the same overall conclusions apply also to the wider set of companies, for example to the FTSE 350, is an interesting question that warrants investigation, because it would encompass a much wider range of schemes and experiences, as well as offering the scope to explore a more refined set of risk factors.

The data requirements for such a study would pose considerable further challenges, reflecting the much wider range of pension accounting and reporting practices amongst the FTSE 350 companies.

Appendix: Sources and Methods

This appendix describes the main sources and methods underlying the data set used in the DB pensions study – the DB Pensions Analytical Data Base (DBPADB) – along with associated formulae and assumptions used in estimating the various concepts used.

The data set currently covers a range of company financial and DB pensions related variables for the FTSE 100 companies, based on its 2009 composition.

A.1 *Data sources*

The data are drawn from 3 main sources:

1) The bulk of the DB pension-related information comes from the pension notes annex to the annual financial statements of each company.
2) Corresponding annual time series for broad company accounting concepts and performance variables come from Bloomberg data services, verified against the corresponding company financial statements. Daily share price and exchange rate information come from Bloomberg's high frequency data sets.
3) Additional time series data for market related information such as interest rates and more specifically the yields on UK government bonds (gilts) come from the on-line historical data sets maintained by the Macro Financial Analysis Division of the Bank of England.

A.2 *Sample period, accounting years, and company coverage*

The estimation sample period relates to company and pensions performance over the period from 2006 to 2012, as reported in the annual financial statements for those years. Not all companies publish or report the relevant accounts at the same point in time or for the same accounting period. While the accounts for most FTSE100 companies are calendar-year based, a small minority relate to the financial year closing at end-March, while a handful of others variously report accounts to end-January, June, July, and September. Thus, the data set ranges from January 2006 to March 2013, depending on the company.

For the purposes of the study the data for individual companies have been aligned so that all variables (standard accounts, pension related, share prices, interest and exchange rates) refer to precisely the same accounting period, namely that coinciding with the published financial statement and pensions notes. In terms of data file organization, data for companies closing their accounts in January or March year (t+1) were attributed to year t, although this has no implications for the results.

The companies included in the main sample used in model estimation are based on the 2009 composition of the FTSE 100 companies subject to specific exclusions relating to:

- Companies without DB pension schemes,
- Companies whose operations and pension schemes are primarily outside of the UK, the European Union and the United States,
- Companies whose financial statements and pension notes are incomplete or absent.

A.3 *Data notes*

The following notes describe a number of key assumptions and the basis of specific estimates included.

A.3.1 *Currencies, exchange rates and variable scaling*

All data are expressed in UK sterling terms. Where company accounts are in other currencies e.g. \$US or €, they were converted to sterling terms using the rates prevailing at the balance sheet closing date. Since in estimation all variables are expressed as ratios to Total Company Assets, the results are unaffected by the specific choice of conversion rates.

A.3.2 *Multiple schemes*

Where companies have multiple DB schemes, pensions data have been aggregated across schemes, and pension-specific technical assumptions, where relevant, are based on those reported for the dominant (largest) scheme.

A.3.3 *Mergers, acquisitions and delisting*

Changes in company structure and coverage through mergers and acquisitions over the sample period are treated pragmatically, the overriding aim being to maintain consistency between financial and pension accounts at a given point in time: for example, British Airways (BA) is included separately prior to the International Consolidated Airlines merger. Companies which have been delisted as a result of foreign mergers are included in the sample for those years where they were listed on the London exchange: for example, International Power PLC is included up to its acquisition by GDF Suez, which is listed on the Paris exchange.

A.3.4 *The definition of net pension assets*

Throughout the study the definition of net pension assets corresponds to the reported gross economic surplus (or deficit) disregarding any deferred taxes, corridor adjustments, or irrecoverable surplus/minimum funding liabilities. In some cases, this measure may therefore differ from that shown on the overall company balance sheet, which may include numerous non-economic adjustments.

A.3.5 *The estimation of 'risk free' pension liabilities, net assets and related estimates*

The measures of 'risk free' liabilities and net pension assets used in the study rely on a number of technical assumptions based on additional sensitivity analysis information reported in the standard pension notes, in particular those pertaining to interest rate sensitivity.

A.3.6 *The duration of pension obligations*

A first step is to derive an estimate of the duration of pension obligations (D) implicit in the reported present value of pension liabilities (PL). These were calculated on the basis of the discount rate sensitivity estimates given by individual company pension notes using the following expression:

$$D = - (dPL/PL) *(1+r)/dr \qquad (A.1)$$

where D is, for a given company and year, the estimated duration and dPL/PL the proportionate change in the present value of DBO liabilities reported in the pension notes for a given change (dr) in the discount rate (r) used in calculating the present value (based on high quality corporate bond rates). In cases of multiple schemes, duration estimates were based on the sensitivities reported for the largest representative scheme.

Sufficient information was available to calculate implicit durations for over two-thirds of the FTSE 100 sample, providing duration estimates ranging from 12 to 25 years, with a sample average and median of around 18 ½ years. For companies where discount rate sensitivities were not reported in the pension notes, the sample average duration was used in subsequent estimates. Experimentation suggested that subsequent estimates were relatively robust to variations in this assumption in the range of 15 to 20 years.

A.3.7 *'Risk free' liabilities*

The main factor taken into account in calculating 'risk free' pension liabilities is the difference between the discount rate (AA corporate bond) assumptions used in the calculation of DBO liabilities, as reported in the pension notes, and the usually-lower market rates on government bonds (gilts) of similar maturity. Effectively corresponding 'risk free' estimates were made using gilt rates, matched to the timing of the company accounts and the duration of the DBO, based on the following expression:

$$FVPL = PL*[1 - D*(g-r)/(1 + r)] \qquad (A.2)$$

where the 'risk free' pension liability estimate (FVPL) is the reported net present value of pension liabilities (PL) rescaled by 1 minus the difference between gilt (g) and published (r) discount rates as a ratio of the published discount factor (1 + r), times the estimated duration (D). These adjustments typically resulted in a higher level of liabilities, but with considerable variation over time and companies, depending on the risk premia assigned by the market to the chosen corporate bonds over gilts, at a given point in time. Averaged across companies and time, such 'risk free' adjustments added approximately 20% to 25% to the levels of pension liabilities.

Corresponding risk free of pension net assets were then recomputed as the difference between the 'risk free' of scheme assets (PA), reported in the pension notes and estimated 'risk free' of liabilities (FVPL), thus:

$$FVNPA = PA + FVPL. \qquad (A.3)$$

On average this adjustment added approximately 25% of the reported value of pension liabilities to net pension asset positions, effectively eliminating all but a few reported net surpluses.

A.3.8 Risk variables

In addition to the size of pension liabilities and net pension assets, a number of individual and composite variables were calculated to represent the possible influence of other risk factors, on the basis of the following rules of thumb:

1) Longevity extension - 5% of gross liabilities
2) Discount rate - the effect of a 1% shift in discount rates on liabilities
3) Asset and bond risk - 20% of equity assets less 10% of bond holdings
4) Composite risk - the sum of longevity, discount rate and asset risks

References

1. P. Richardson and L. Larcher, *The Influence of DB Pensions on The Market Valuation of The Pension Plan Sponsor: For the FTSE 100 Companies, Size Really Does Matter* (Llewellyn Consulting, London, 2014).
2. J. L. Coronado and S. A. Sharpe, Did pension plan accounting contribute to a stock market bubble?, *Brookings Papers on Economic Activity* **1**, 323–271 (2003).
3. J. Coronado, O. S. Mitchell, S. A. Sharpe, and S. Blake Nesbitt, Footnotes aren't enough: The impact of pension accounting on stock values, *Journal of Pension Economics and Finance* **7**(03), 257–276 (2008).
4. C. J. Napier, The logic of pension accounting, *Accounting and Business Research* **39**(3), and *International Accounting Policy Forum*, 231–249 (2009).
5. J. R. Brown and G. G. Pennacchi, *Discounting Pension Liabilities: Funding Versus Value*. NBER Working Paper No. 21276 (National Bureau of Economic Research, London, 2015).
6. J. R. Brown and D. Wilcox, Discounting state and local pension liabilities, *American Economic Review* **99**(2), 538–42 (2009).
7. DRSC, EFRAG, ASB (UK), CNC, FSR and OIC, *Pro-Active Accounting Activities in Europe* (2008).

8. D. P. Blake, Z. Khorasanee, J. Pickles and D. Tyrrall, *An Unreal Number: How Company Pension Accounting Fosters an Illusion of Certainty* (The Pensions Institute and The Cass Business School, City of London, 2008).

9. UK Pensions Regulator and the UK Pensions Protection Fund. *The Purple Book, DB Pensions Universe Risk Profile, Annual reports* (UK Pensions Regulator and the UK Pensions Protection Fund, London).

III. Trade and Development

What makes China grow?

Lawrence J. Lau[a]

The Chinese University of Hong Kong,
13/F, Cheng Yu Tung Building, 12 Chak Cheung Street,
Shatin, New Territories, Hong Kong
E-mail: Lawrence@lawrencejlau.hk

China has made tremendous progress in its economic development since it began its economic reform and opened to the world in 1978. It is currently the fastest growing economy in the world—averaging 9.6% per annum over the past 37 years (even though it has begun to slow down, to around 6.5% year-on-year growth). It is, however, historically unprecedented for an economy to grow at such a high rate over such a long period of time. Why has China been able to do so? What makes China grow? Will China be able to continue to grow at such a high rate in the future? The Chinese economic fundamentals, the Chinese initial conditions in 1978, as well as the economic reform policies and measures adopted and implemented by China are examined and analyzed. Long-term development of the Chinese economy is also assessed and long-term forecasts are generated and reported.

Keywords: *The Chinese economy, economic reform.*

1.   Professor Lawrence R. Klein and China

It is my honor and privilege to participate in this Conference in Memory of Professor Lawrence R. Klein. Professor Klein was an intellectual giant. He was a pioneering econometrician, having constructed the first econometric model of the United States, the Klein Model I, and followed it with a succession of increasingly larger and more sophisticated econometric models, including the Wharton Econometric Model. He not only founded Project LINK, a global project linking national econometric models together for joint prediction and simulation, as one country's exports must be the imports of other countries, with Robert Aaron Gordon, Bert G. Hickman and Rudolf R. Rhomberg, but also acted as the patriarch of the extended Project LINK family. To me personally, he was a selfless mentor, an exemplary role model, and a most respected and dear friend.

In the late 1960s, through the introduction of Professor Bert Hickman, my colleague at Stanford, Professor Klein invited me to construct the first econometric model of China and contribute it as one of the national models in Project LINK. Thus, began my long association with Professor Klein and Project LINK. Professor Hickman and I also

---

[a] Ralph and Claire Landau Professor of Economics, The Chinese University of Hong Kong, and Kwoh-Ting Li Professor in Economic Development, Emeritus, Stanford University. This paper was presented at Global Economic Modeling: A Conference in Honor of Lawrence Klein, held at the Institute for International Business, Rotman School of Management, University of Toronto, Toronto, Canada, on 11th June 2015. The author is grateful to Ayesha Macpherson Lau for her valuable comments but remains solely responsible for any errors. All opinions expressed herein are the author's own and do not necessarily reflect the views of any of the organizations with which the author is affiliated.

constructed aggregated and disaggregated trade matrix models that were used in the linkage of the national econometric models. In 1979, Professor Klein invited me to join the first delegation of the American Economic Association to the People's Republic of China, led by him and hosted by the Chinese Academy of Social Sciences. This was the first time I visited China as an adult. We were received by Vice-Premier GU Mu. Professor Klein then followed up with organizing the "The Summer Palace Workshop on Econometrics" in 1980, with one hundred participants drawn from all over China. This was the first introduction of econometrics in China. In addition to Professor Klein, there were six faculty members in the Workshop—Professors Theodore Anderson, Albert Ando, Gregory Chow, Cheng Hsiao, Vincent Su and me. We were received by Vice-Premier YAO Yilin. Our Workshop eventually led to the establishment of the Institute of Quantitative and Technical Economics at the Chinese Academy of Social Sciences. Later, Professor Klein also served as an Adviser to the State Planning Commission of the People's Republic of China for one U.S. Dollar a year.

In 2010, at the Thirtieth Anniversary Celebration of the Summer Palace Workshop on Econometrics, Professor Klein, who was not able to attend but sent a pre-recorded videotape, laid down the challenge: Can the highly successful Chinese economic growth since its economic reform and opening in 1978 be explained? What are the factors common to all economies that have been able to grow successfully? And what are the factors unique to the Chinese economy due to its own history and circumstances? This study is an attempt to provide a preliminary answer[b].

2. Introduction

China has made tremendous progress in its economic development since it began its economic reform and opened to the world in 1978. It is currently the fastest growing economy in the world—averaging 9.6% per annum compounded over the past 37 years. It is historically unprecedented for an economy to grow at such a high rate over such a long period of time. Between 1978 and 2015, Chinese real GDP grew more than thirtyfold, from US346 billion to US$10.4 trillion (in 2015 prices), to become the second largest economy in the world, after the U.S. (see Fig. 1, in which the levels and the rates of growth of Chinese real GDP are presented). By comparison, the U.S. real GDP of approximately US$17.9 trillion was a little less than 1.7 times the Chinese real GDP in 2015. However, the Chinese economy has recently begun to slow down, to an average annual rate of growth of around 6.5%, in a process of transition to a "New Normal". In 2016, the Chinese economy grew 6.7% in real terms.

---

[b] See also Perkins[1]. For a different perspective, from the point of view of a foreign entrepreneur in China, see Beardson[2].

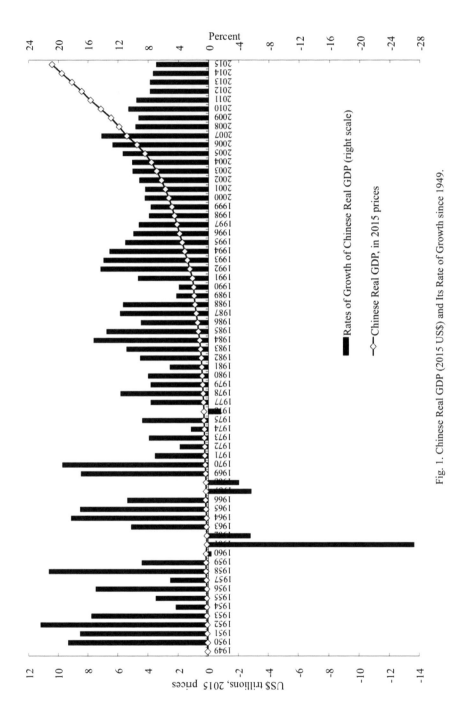

Fig. 1. Chinese Real GDP (2015 US$) and Its Rate of Growth since 1949.

Why has China been able to grow at such a high rate and for such a long period of time? What makes China grow? Will China be able to continue to grow at such a high rate in the future? Of course, the adoption and implementation of the correct economic policies and measures by the Chinese Government, led by the Chinese Communist Party, and their uninterrupted continuity since 1978, are important reasons for China's highly successful record of economic growth. However, we shall also examine the Chinese economic fundamentals as well as the Chinese initial conditions in 1978 to analyze why the adopted and implemented economic reform policies and measures were so effective in China.

During this same period, China also had to face many domestic and international challenges and several financial crises, such as the East Asian currency crisis of 1997–1998, the bursting of the internet bubble in 2000, the global financial crisis of 2007–2009 as well as the European sovereign debt crisis. China was able to survive all of these crises relatively unscathed, even maintaining a healthy rate of real economic growth. The Chinese Government leaders have demonstrated their ability to confront these challenges and solve difficult problems. The Chinese economy has recently begun a process of transition to a "New Normal", with a lower average annual rate of growth of between 6.5 percent and 7 percent, a cleaner environment, and a greater contribution from innovation than from the growth of tangible inputs.

In Table 1, the performance of the Chinese economy before and after its economic reform began in 1978 is compared. It is clear that the Chinese economy has done significantly better in almost every dimension—real GDP, real consumption, exports and imports—under the economic reform, on both an aggregate and a per capita basis. The only economic indicator that has performed worse is the rate of inflation, which rose from 0.6% per annum in the pre-reform period to 5.1% per annum in the post-reform period.

Table 1. Key Performance Indicators before and after Chinese Economic Reform of 1978

	Growth rates Percent per annum	
	Pre-Reform Period 1952-1978	Post-Reform Period 1978-2015
Real GDP	6.1	9.6
Real GDP per Capita	4.0	8.5
Real Consumption	5.0	9.2
Real Consumption per Capita	2.9	8.2
Exports	10.0	15.9
Imports	9.1	14.6
Inflation Rates (GDP deflator)	0.6	5.1

However, despite its rapid economic growth in the aggregate, in terms of the level of its real GDP per capita, China is still very much a developing economy because of its large population. China is the most populous country in the world. In 1978, the Chinese real

GDP per capita was US$360 (in 2015 prices), less than 1.2 percent of the then U.S. real GDP per capita of US$30,886. Between 1978 and 2015, Chinese real GDP per capita grew more than 21 times, to US$7,584, still less than one-seventh of U.S. GDP per capita of US$55,759 (see Fig. 2, in which the levels and the rates of growth of Chinese real GDP per capita are presented).

While many problems have arisen in the Chinese economy within the past decade — for example, increasing income disparity at both the inter-regional and intra-regional levels, uneven access to basic education and health care, environmental degradation, inadequate infrastructure and corruption — it is fair to say that every Chinese citizen has benefitted from the economic reform and opening to the world since 1978, albeit to varying degrees, and few want to return to the central planning days.

Chinese international trade in goods and services has also grown very rapidly since the beginning of its economic reform in 1978, and the rate of growth accelerated after Chinese accession to the World Trade Organization (WTO) in 2001. Chinese total international trade grew from US$20.3 billion in 1978 to US$4.67 trillion in 2015, making China the second largest trading nation in the world, just after the U.S. with its total international trade of US$5.21 trillion. (See Fig. 3, in which the black lines and black columns represent the levels and rates of growth of Chinese international trade respectively, and the open-square lines and grey columns represent the levels and rates of growth of U.S. international trade respectively). While China is the largest exporting nation in terms of goods and services (US$2.56 trillion in 2015), followed by the U.S. (US$2.22 trillion), the U.S. is the largest importing nation in terms of goods and services (US$2.76 trillion), followed by China (US$2.11 trillion). China is also the largest exporting nation in terms of goods alone, followed by the U.S. The U.S. is the largest exporting as well as importing nation in terms of services, followed by respectively the United Kingdom and Germany.

3.   China in the Global Economy

The most important development in the global economy during the past thirty-seven years is the reform and opening of the Chinese economy and its participation in the world. As a result, the center of gravity of the global economy, in terms of both GDP and international trade, has been gradually shifting from North America and Western Europe to East Asia, and within East Asia from Japan to China. In 1970, the United States and Western Europe together accounted for almost 60% of world GDP. By comparison, East Asia (defined as the 10 Association of Southeast Asian Nations (ASEAN) — Brunei, Cambodia, Indonesia, Laos, Malaysia, Myanmar, Philippines, Singapore, Thailand, and Vietnam — + 3 (China including Hong Kong, Macau and Taiwan, Japan and the Republic of Korea)) accounted for approximately 10% of world GDP. (Hong Kong, the Republic of Korea, Singapore and Taiwan are also known collectively as the East Asian "Newly Industrialized Economies (NIEs)".) By 2014, the share of the United States and Western Europe in world GDP has declined to approximately 40%, whereas the share of East Asia has risen to around 25% (see Fig. 4 and Fig. 5). The Japanese share of world GDP declined from a peak of almost

18% in the mid-1990s to 5.6% in 2015 while the Chinese share of world GDP rose from 3.1% in 1970 and less than 4% in 2000 to over 14.8% in 2015 (see Fig. 6).

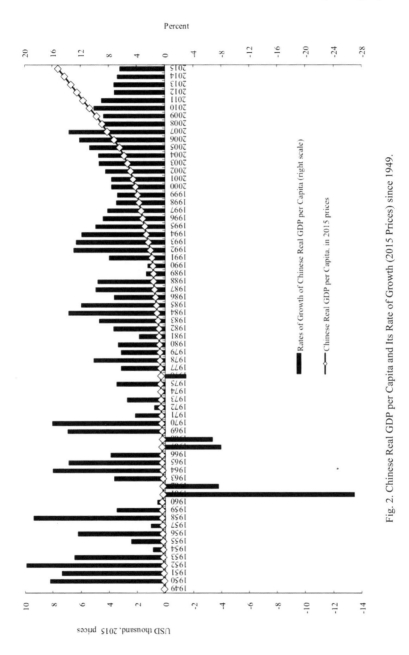

Fig. 2. Chinese Real GDP per Capita and Its Rate of Growth (2015 Prices) since 1949.

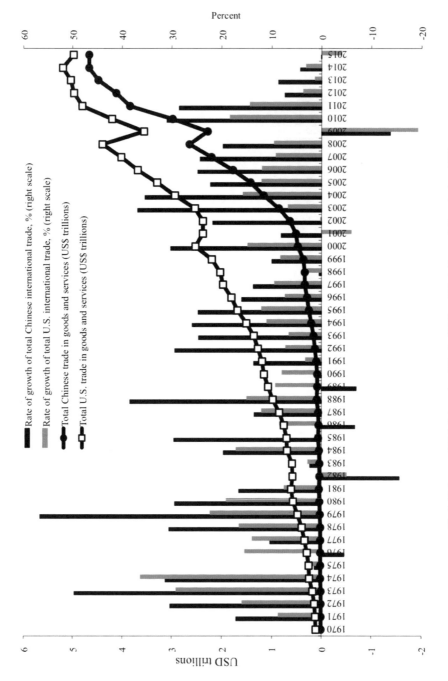

Fig 3. Chinese and U.S. International Trade (US$) and Their Rates of Growth since 1970.

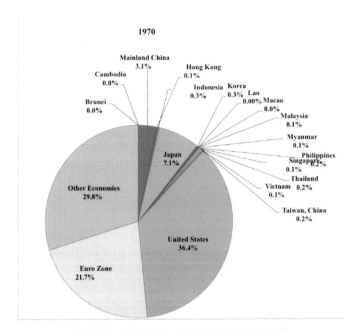

Fig. 4. The Distribution of World GDP, 1970, US$.

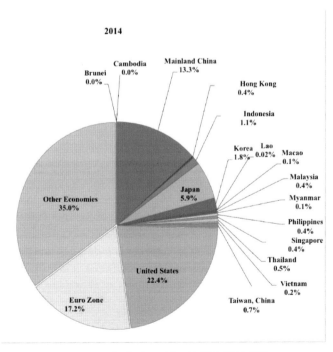

Fig. 5. The Distribution of World GDP, 2014, US$.

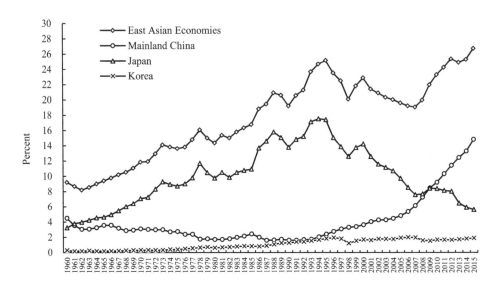

Fig. 6. The Shares of East Asia, China, Japan and South Korea in World GDP, 1960–Present.

A similar shift has occurred in the distribution of world trade. In 1970, the United States and Western Europe together accounted for almost 60% of world trade in goods and services. By comparison, East Asia accounted for 9.5% of world trade. By 2014, the share of United States and Western Europe in world trade has declined to 41% whereas the share of East Asia has risen to almost 28% (see Figs. 7 and 8).

The Chinese share of world trade rose from 0.6% in 1970 to 12.2% in 2015 (see Fig. 9). The growth in Chinese international trade may be attributed in part to the reform of the Chinese exchange rate system in the early 1990s, accompanied by a significant devaluation, to Chinese accession to the World Trade Organization in 2001, and to the expiration of the Multi-Fibre Agreement governing world trade in textiles. China has also become either the most important or the second most important trading partner of almost all of the economies in the Asia-Pacific region (see Table 2).

Contrary to the public impression, the ratio of Chinese exports of goods and services to GDP is actually relatively low compared with other economies (see Fig. 10). Among large economies, only Japan and the U.S. have a lower share of exports in GDP than China. This is a reflection of the fact that China is a large continental economy, with relatively abundant diversified natural resources and a huge domestic market. Most of the other East Asian economies (except Japan) are either export-oriented or were export-oriented when they began their processes of economic development. Their exports to GDP ratios have been and continue to be much higher than that of the Chinese economy. The same is true of the ratio of Chinese imports of goods and services to GDP (see Fig. 11) and for the same reasons.

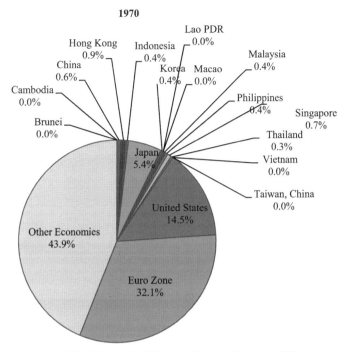

Fig. 7. The Distribution of Total International Trade in Goods and Services, 1970.

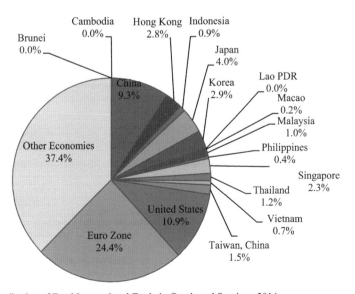

Fig. 8. The Distribution of Total International Trade in Goods and Services, 2014.

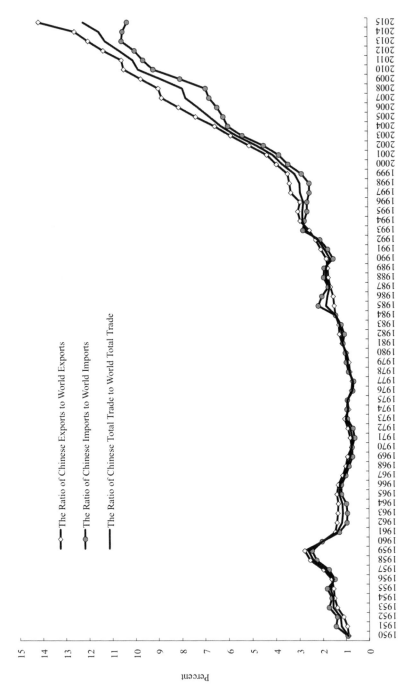

Fig. 9. The Chinese Share of Total World Trade, 1950–Present.

Table 2. The Ranks of China as Trading Partner of Asia-Pacific Countries/Regions and Vice Versa, 2014

Country/Region	Chinese rank as trading partner of country/region	Rank of country/region as trading partner of China
Australia	1	9
Brunei	3	107
Cambodia	2	87
Hong Kong	1	4
Indonesia	1	20
Japan	1	5
Korea	1	6
Laos	2	90
Macau	1	84
Malaysia	1	10
Myanmar	1	36
New Zealand	1	45
Philippines	2	27
Singapore	1	15
Taiwan	1	7
Thailand	1	17
United States	2	2
Vietnam	1	13

In Fig. 12, Chinese exports and imports as a share of its GDP over time are presented. It is clear that these shares peaked in 2006 and have been declining steadily since then. Moreover, the Chinese trade surplus as a percent of its GDP has also begun to decline as well. This trend is expected to continue in the future.

China has also opened its economy to inbound foreign direct investment (FDI). China imported from abroad capital goods as well as advanced technology that enhanced its domestic production capacity. Foreign direct investment also enabled the surplus resources of the Chinese economy, principally labor, to be productively employed.

As a result of the accumulated trade surpluses and, to a lesser extent, the net capital inflows since the mid-1990s, the Chinese official foreign exchange reserves have also risen steadily, reaching a peak of approximately US$4 trillion in mid-2014, and becoming the largest official foreign exchange reserves held by any central bank in the world (see Fig. 13).

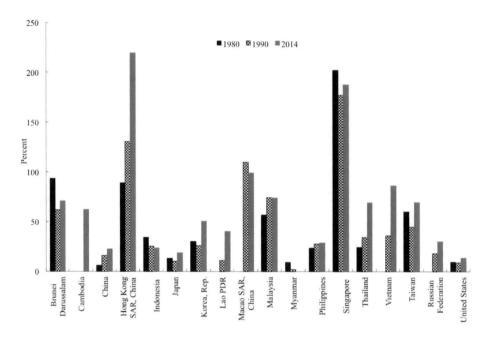

Fig 10. Exports of Goods and Services as a Share of GDP in Selected Economies.

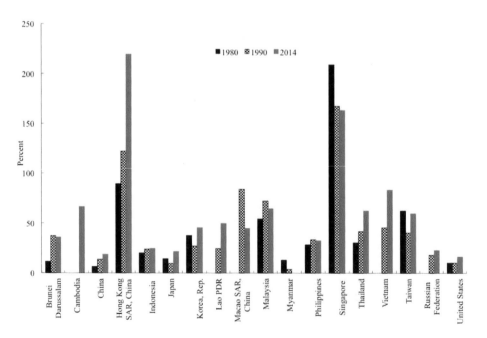

Fig. 11. Imports of Goods and Services as a Percent of GDP: Selected Economies.

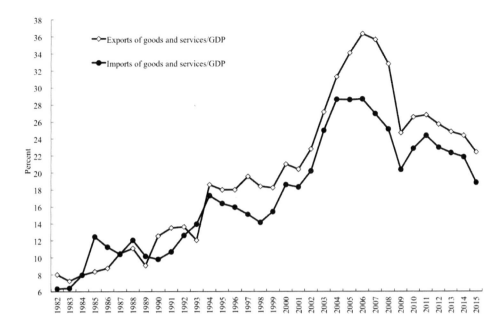

Fig. 12. Exports and Imports of Goods and Services as a Percent of Chinese GDP, 1982–2015.

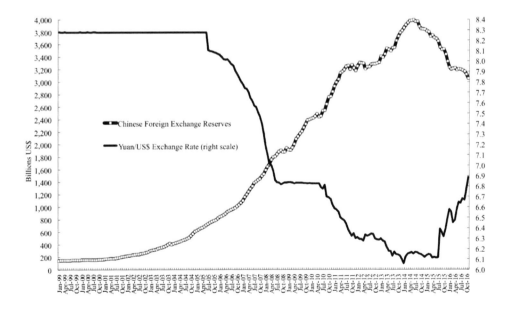

Fig. 13. Chinese Foreign Exchange Reserves and the Yuan/US$ Exchange Rate.

In the meantime, the exchange rate of the Chinese currency, the Renminbi or Yuan, vis-a-vis the U.S. Dollar, has also undergone huge changes during the past 37 years (see Fig. 14). In 1978, US$1 is worth less than 2 Yuan. In order to maximize the benefits of the policy of economic reform and opening, the Chinese Government began to devalue the Renminbi significantly with respect to the US$ in 1980, to a more competitive and sustainable level. For a few years in the early 1990s, China maintained dual exchange rates: an official rate and an "adjustment" rate determined in a market restricted to Chinese exporters and importers with import licenses. At the time, foreign exchange certificates (FECs) were also used by foreign visitors to China instead of the Renminbi. China implemented full current accounts convertibility in 1994. In both nominal and real terms, the Renminbi has been appreciating relative to the U.S. Dollar since 1994, but especially after 2005 (see Fig. 15), until the past couple of years.

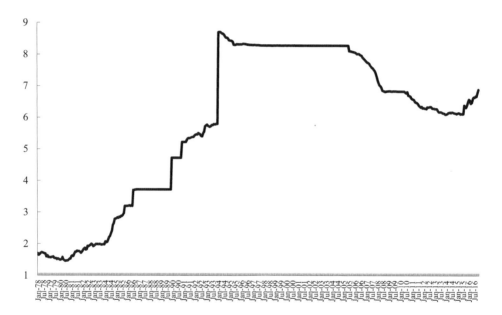

Fig. 14. Nominal Exchange Rate of the Renminbi, Yuan/US$, 1978–Present.

Since 2010, the Renminbi has been increasingly used as an invoicing and settlement currency for cross-border transactions, especially those involving Chinese enterprises as transacting parties. The proportion of Chinese international trade settled in Renminbi has grown rapidly, from almost nothing in the first quarter of 2010 to 32.5% of the total value of Chinese international trade in goods in the third quarter of 2015, equivalent to US$334 billion (see Fig. 16). However, the proportion has since declined to just over 20%, with an approximate total value of US$800 billion of Chinese international trade settled in Renminbi annually.

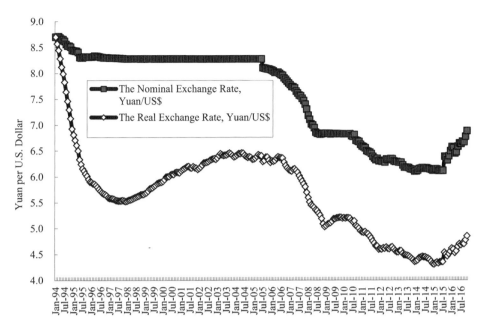

Fig. 15. The Nominal and Real Yuan/US$ Exchange Rates.

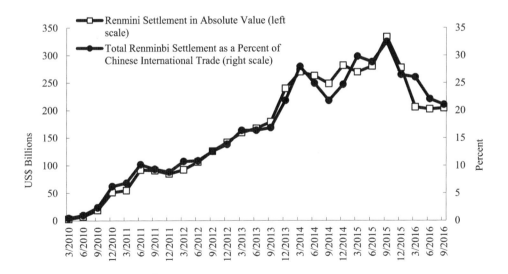

Fig. 16. Renminbi Settlement of Chinese Cross-Border Trade, Billion US$ and Percent.

The Renminbi is also used for foreign direct investment and portfolio investment both inbound and outbound, but its use can be further expanded. The central banks and monetary authorities of many countries and regions have entered into swap agreements with the People's Bank of China, the central bank of China, which facilitate the use of Renminbi as an invoicing, clearing and settlement currency. In Figs. 17 and 18, the share of each currency used in world trade settlement and the share of the issuing country or region in world trade are compared in 2010 and in November 2016 respectively. In 2010, the Renminbi was not even within the top twenty currencies used in world trade settlement. By November 2016, it became the fifth most used currency in world trade settlement. However, even though China accounted for approximately 11% of world trade, the Renminbi accounted for only 2% of world trade settlement in November 2016; and while the U.S. had a similar share of world trade as China, the U. S. Dollar accounted for 41.1% of world trade settlement in November 2016. By comparison, Japan accounted for 3.8% of world trade and its currency, the Yen, accounted for 3.4% of world trade settlement in November 2016. There is still plenty of room for the expansion of the use of Renminbi for cross-border trade settlement in the future. If the Japanese experience is any guide, the use of the Renminbi for world trade settlement should triple or even quadruple over the next few years.

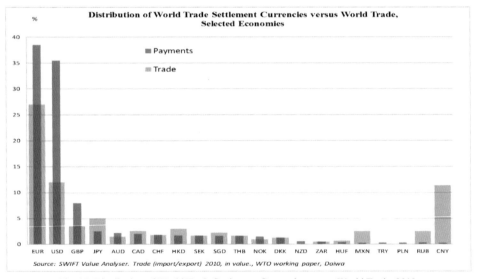

Fig. 17. Distribution of World Trade Settlement Currencies versus World Trade, 2010.

The exchange rate of the Renminbi relative to the U.S. Dollar is likely to hold steady over the next few years. This should facilitate the further expansion of the use of the Renminbi for the invoicing, clearing and settlement of international transactions. Capital account convertibility is expected to be achieved for the Renminbi before 2020. It can occur sooner if short-term capital flows, both outbound and inbound, can be appropriately regulated or "discouraged", for example, with the imposition of a "Tobin tax"[c] on capital account inflows and outflows.

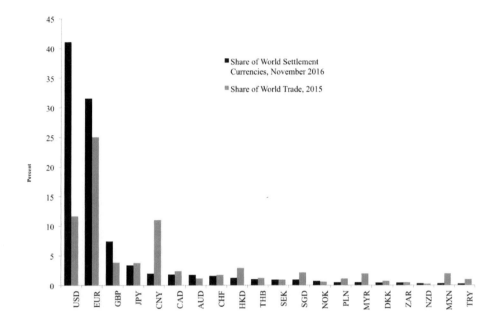

Fig. 18. Distribution of World Trade Settlement Currencies versus World Trade, November 2016.

One reason the Chinese economy has been able to survive the successive financial crises, beginning with the 1997–1998 East Asian currency crisis, followed by the global financial crisis of 2007–2009, the European sovereign debt crisis, as well as the successive quantitative easing on the part of the U.S. Federal Reserve Board (QEI, II and III), the Bank of Japan and the European Central Bank (ECB), relatively unscathed is its relative insulation from the financial disturbances in the world economy through its maintenance of controls on both inflows and outflows of capital. Moreover, China did not have to depend on foreign capital because of its own high domestic saving rates. Potential contagion from abroad has therefore been minimized.

4.   The Chinese Economic Fundamentals

The long-term economic growth of a country depends on the rates of growth of its primary inputs — capital (tangible or physical) and labor — and on technical progress (or equivalently, the growth of total factor productivity) — that is, the ability to increase output without increasing inputs. The rate of growth of tangible or physical capital depends on the rate of investment on structure, equipment and basic infrastructure, which in turn

---

[c] This is a financial transaction tax, first proposed by Professor James Tobin[3], Nobel Laureate in Economic Sciences, which can be applied to currency conversion transactions.

depends on the availability of national savings. The rate of technical progress depends on investment in intangible capital (including human capital and research and development (R&D) capital).

The most important source of Chinese economic growth over the past 37 years has been the growth of inputs, principally the growth of tangible capital (structure, equipment, and basic infrastructure), and not technical progress. Thus, past Chinese economic growth was mainly due to "working harder, not working smarter". The growth of tangible capital accounts for the bulk, approximately 75% of the measured economic growth in China. This experience is not unlike those of other East Asian economies such as South Korea and Taiwan and even Japan as well as that of the United States at a similarly early stage of economic development. The growth of inputs, principally tangible capital, has always been found to be the most important source of growth at an early stage of development. This is especially true of economies with initially abundant supplies of surplus labor.

Chinese economic growth since 1978 has been underpinned by a consistently high domestic investment rate, enabled by a national savings rate on the order of 30% and above except for a brief start-up period in the early 1950s (see Fig. 19). Since the early 1990s, the Chinese national saving rate has stayed around 40% and has at times approached or even exceeded 50% in more recent years. This means, among other things, that the Chinese economy can finance all of its domestic investment needs from its own domestic savings alone, thus assuring a high rate of growth of the tangible capital stock without having to depend on the fickler foreign capital inflows (including foreign direct investment, foreign portfolio investment, foreign aid, or foreign loans). In particular, it does not need to borrow abroad and bear the potential risks of a large, short-term and often interruptible, foreign-currency denominated debt. Hence the Chinese economy is also more immune from external disturbances than other economies. In addition, since new resources are made available each year from new savings, enabling new investments to be made, the necessity of restructuring, redeploying or privatizing existing fixed assets is greatly diminished (thus making it more possible to avoid potentially politically divisive issues and the creation of "losers"). A high national savings rate also allows the normally more efficient non-state sector greater room and greater scope for development and expansion as there is less likelihood of "crowding out".

The national saving rate in China will remain high in the foreseeable future even though it is expected to decline gradually, in part, because the household or labor share of GDP is relatively low, below 50% (the household disposable income was approximately 43% of GDP in 2014), and that the Chinese enterprises, especially the state-owned enterprises, distribute little or no cash dividends, reinvesting almost all of their profits.

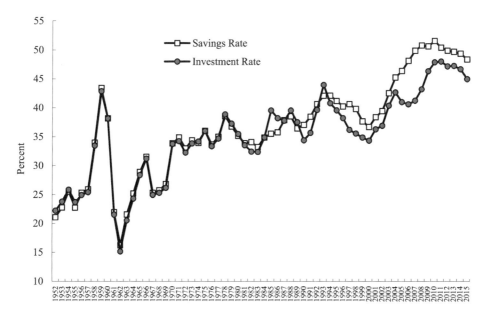

Fig. 19. Chinese National Saving and Gross Domestic Investment as Percents of GDP.

However, tangible capital input-driven economic growth has its limitations, because as the stock of tangible capital relative to labor increases, the marginal productivity of tangible capital will begin to decline and will eventually reach a point when additional tangible capital is no longer productive. This is a point made by Professor Paul Krugman[d].

China, like Japan, Taiwan, and South Korea in their respective early stages of economic development, has an unlimited supply of surplus labor—there is therefore no shortage of and no upward pressure on the real wage rate of unskilled, entry-level labor. This means the Chinese economy can continue to grow without being constrained by the supply of labor or by rising real wage rates of unskilled, entry-level labor over an extended period of time. Investment in tangible or physical capital such as structure, equipment and physical infrastructure is very productive under conditions of surplus labor. As long as there is sufficient complementary domestic physical capital, the surplus labor can be gainfully employed and enable the real output of the economy to grow rapidly. This is exactly what the late Professor W. Arthur Lewis[4], Nobel Laureate in Economic Sciences, said in his celebrated paper on surplus labor sixty years ago[e].

The distribution of Chinese GDP by originating sectors in 2015 was approximately: Primary (agriculture), 9.0%; Secondary (manufacturing, mining and construction), 40.5%; and Tertiary (services), 50.5% (see Fig. 20). (Note that mining is normally included in the primary sector in most other economies.)

---

[d] Krugman[5] drew on the work of Kim and Lau[6]. See also Kim and Lau[7], Lau and Park[8] and Lau and Park[9].

[e] For an alternate model of the development of a dual economy, see Jorgenson[10].

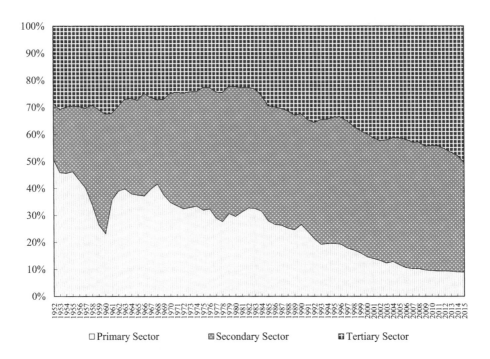

☐ Primary Sector   ▨ Secondary Sector   ▣ Tertiary Sector

Fig. 20. The Distribution of Chinese GDP by Originating Sector since 1952.

By comparison, in 2015, the distribution of employment by sector was: Primary 28.3%, Secondary 29.3%, and Tertiary 43.4% (see Fig. 21). The agricultural sector employs 28.3% of the Chinese labor force but produces only 9% of the Chinese GDP in 2015. Thus, labor can be productively transferred to the other two sectors where labor productivities and wage rates are higher as long as complementary capital and demand are available. Hence, as long as the percentage of labor force employed in the primary sector significantly exceeds the percentage of GDP originating from the primary sector, there will be little or no upward pressure on the real wage rate of unskilled, entry-level labor in the secondary and tertiary sectors. Surplus labor will continue to exist in the Chinese economy.

Even with increases in the levels of minimum wage rates in the different provinces, regions and municipalities, the real wage rate of unskilled, entry-level labor for the country as a whole has basically remained stable and is expected to be stable for a long time because of the continuing existence of significant surplus labor in the Chinese economy. However, there is upward pressure on the real wage rates of skilled and experienced labor, which is actually in short supply, especially as Chinese enterprises move up the value-added chain. But given the trend of rapid expansion of Chinese tertiary education in recent years, with more than 6 million new graduates projected annually, the increase in the real wage rate of even skilled labor is likely to be relatively limited going forward.

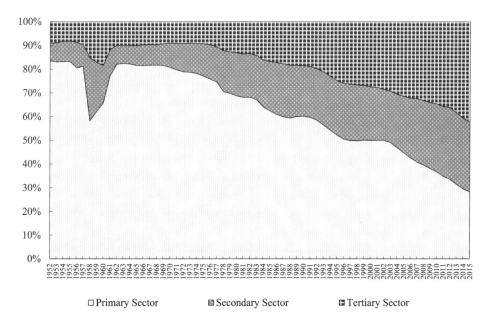

Fig. 21. The Distribution of Chinese Employment by Sector since 1952.

China has a long tradition of emphasis on education and learning (human capital) and will be increasing its investment in human capital. The enrollment rate of tertiary education has been rising rapidly and stands at approximately 30 percent today. It is expected to rise further over the next decades as private tertiary educational institutions become more numerous in response to demand and facilitated by government policy. China has also begun to increase its expenditure on Research and Development (R&D), with the goal of increasing it from the 2.1% in 2015 to 2.5% of GDP by 2020. However, relative to many other economies, China lags behind in investment in both human capital and R&D capital. (This deficit and gap will be further discussed in Section 13.)

The size of the Chinese economy is a natural advantage. The huge domestic market of 1.34 billion consumers with pent-up demand for housing and transportation and other consumer goods and services (e.g., education and health care) enables the realization of significant economies of scale in production. The huge domestic market also greatly enhances the rate of return on investment in intangible capital (e.g., R&D capital and goodwill, including brand building) by allowing the fixed costs of the R&D for a new product or process or advertising and promotion in brand building to be more easily amortized and recovered. For intangible capital, once the initial fixed costs are recovered, any additional revenue is almost all pure profit. Brand-building enables the owners of brand names to have much more pricing power and higher profit margins than enterprises that do only OEM (original equipment manufacturing) business. The huge domestic market also facilitates active Chinese participation in the setting of product and technology standards, for example, in fourth-generation (4-G) standards for telecommunication, and sharing the economic benefits of such standard-setting.

An economy with significant economies of scale will grow faster than an economy with constant returns to scale given the same rates of growth of the measured inputs. The degree of returns to scale at the economy-wide level is not precisely known. The assumption used by Edward F. Denison[11] for the degree of returns to scale for the U.S. is 1.1, that is, if all inputs are doubled, output will be increased by 1.1 times. On the assumption that this also holds for the Chinese economy, it implies that Chinese economic growth will be 10% higher each year than an economy with the same rates of growth of capital and labor inputs but without the economies of scale. Of course, the effects of economies of scale are sometimes confounded with those of technical progress or growth of total factor productivity (there is an identification problem)[f]. However, if there were economies of scale at all, they should be manifested in the Chinese economy.

Suppose the annual rates of growth of the inputs in the economy are 7%. Under constant returns to scale, the economy will grow at 7% per annum. However, under increasing returns to scale of degree 1.1, the economy will grow at 7.7% per annum. In 10 years, the economy with economies of scale will be 7% larger than the one without; in 20 years, 14%; and in 40 years, 31%, a significant difference. Thus, the existence of economies of scale can make a huge difference in the level of GDP in a few decades. Moreover, economies of scale can increase the rates of return to investment and may lead to higher investment rates than otherwise.

Another important and favorable implication of a large domestic economy is the relatively low degree of external dependence and hence vulnerability. Large continental economies, such as China, Russia and the United States, are likely to be self-sufficient in many of the resources because of their large size and geographically diversified location. These economies are also mostly driven by their internal demands, and not by international trade. For example, exports have never been very important to the U.S. economy, and the U.S. economy has never been dependent on international trade, except perhaps in the 19th Century. The Chinese economy is similar — China has adequate supplies of most natural resources domestically (with the possible exception of oil). Chinese economic growth in the future decades will be mostly driven by internal demand rather than exports.

The powerful advantage of a large economy can be seen by an examination of Figs. 22, 23, and 24 on the rates of growth of exports, imports and real GDP of selected Asian economies (with the solid black line representing China). The figures show that even though Chinese exports and imports fluctuate like those of all the other selected Asian economies, the rate of growth of Chinese real GDP has remained relatively stable compared to those of the other economies. It is relatively immune to external economic disturbances.

---

[f] See Boskin and Lau[12] for a method of identifying both the degree of returns to scale and the rate of technical progress by analyzing the pooled time-series data of several economies simultaneously.

In addition to a high national savings rate, a large pool of surplus labor, rising investment in intangible capital (human capital and R&D capital), and the large size of its economy, China also has the advantage of relative backwardness, which has enabled the Chinese economy to learn from the experiences of successes and failures of other economies; to leap-frog and by-pass stages of development (e.g., the telex machine, the VHS video-tape player, the fixed landline telephone are all mostly unknown in China); and to have creation without destruction (e.g., online virtual bookstores like Amazon.com do not have to destroy brick and mortar bookstores which do not exist in the first place; internet shopping takes away business from brick and mortar malls).

However, while good economic fundamentals are necessary for a sustained high rate of growth of an economy, they are by no means sufficient. In the thirty years between 1949, the year of the founding of the People's Republic of China, and 1978, the first year of the Chinese economic reform and opening to the world, China also had (1) a high domestic saving rate; (2) an unlimited supply of surplus labor; and (3) a large domestic economy. But the Chinese economy did not experience a sustained high rate of growth during that period. Similarly, the former Soviet Union also had a high rate of tangible capital accumulation as well as a large domestic economy, but did not experience a sustained high rate of economic growth either.

5.   The Inherent Economic Inefficiency of Central Planning

Why didn't China and the former Soviet Union experience sustained high-rate economic growth despite favorable economic fundamentals? The short answer is that both the Chinese economy before its economic reform of 1978 and that of the former Soviet Union operated under central planning, with its inherent economic inefficiencies. From 1953, when China adopted its First Five-Year Plan, to the end of the last Century, the Chinese economy operated under a series of mandatory central plans. Similarly, the former Soviet Union and the East European countries operated under central planning until 1989.

A principal characteristic of a centrally planned economy is the administrative allocation, rather than market allocation, of scarce resources. What goods and services to produce? How much to produce? Where to produce them? What raw materials and parts should be used to produce them? From which enterprises should the raw materials and parts be bought? To which enterprises should the outputs be sold? All of these decisions are made by the central planners and embodied in the mandatory central plan. Enterprises do not have any autonomy in these decisions. The prices of goods and services are also completely determined in the central plan. They do not necessarily reflect relative scarcities in the economy, and do not play any role in the equilibration of market supply and demand. The prices are only used for accounting purposes.

Why is there inherent economic inefficiency in a centrally planned economy? We begin by defining what economists mean by efficiency. A production allocation or plan for an economy is said to be efficient if for given aggregate quantities of inputs (the tangible capital stock and labor), no output of any good or service can be increased without decreasing the output of another good or service. In other words, there is no slack: the

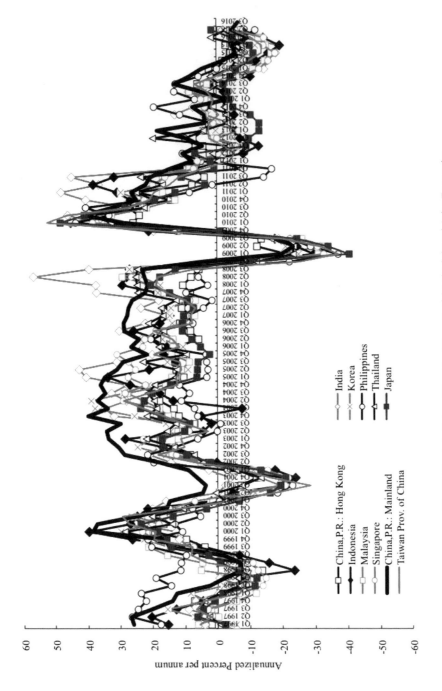

Fig. 22. Quarterly Rates of Growth of Exports of Goods: Selected Asian Economies.

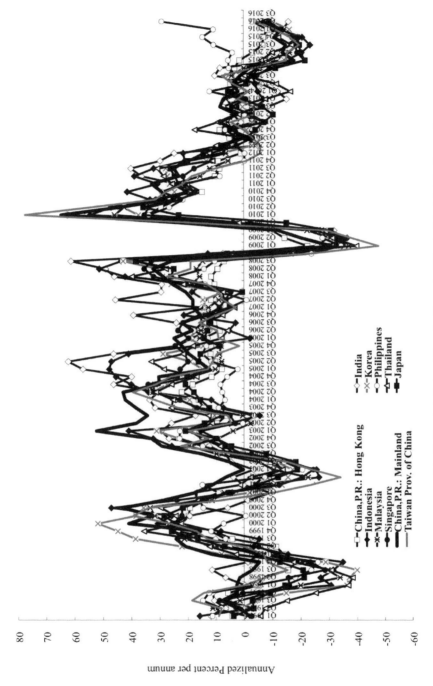

Fig. 23. Quarterly Rates of Growth of Imports of Goods: Selected Asian Economies.

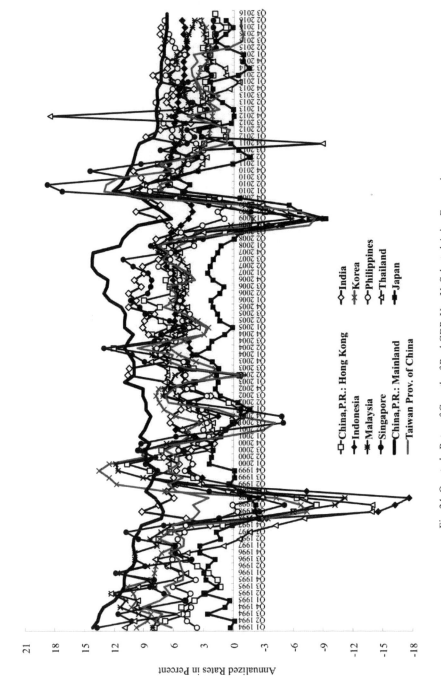

Fig. 24. Quarterly Rates of Growth of Real GDP, Y-o-Y: Selected Asian Economies.

economy is operating on the frontier of its set of production possibilities. A production allocation or plan is said to be inefficient if it is possible to increase the output of any good or service without decreasing the output of any other good or service. In other words, the economy is operating in the interior of its set of production possibilities.

It is important to understand and distinguish between the two different ways in which the real output of an economy can be increased: either through an outward movement of the frontier of the set of production possibilities, or through a movement from the interior of the set of production possibilities set to its frontier. The first way can only occur either through an increase in the inputs, tangible and intangible, or from the adoption of a more efficient technology imported from abroad. The second way can occur even in the absence of any increase in the inputs or technology transfer. It can be regarded as a pure increase in domestic economic efficiency, resulting in an increase in actual output, but without an increase in potential output. In Fig. 25, the expansion of the old production possibilities set (shaded in light gray) to include the area shaded in darker gray, is accompanied by the movement of the old production possibilities frontier (the line with black diamonds ♦) to the new (the line with black squares ■). The movement from the old production point to the inner frontier line represents a movement from the interior of the old production possibilities set to the old frontier.

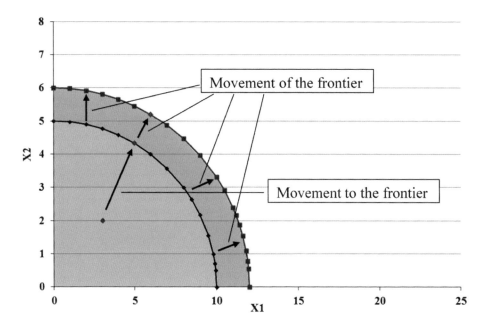

Fig. 25. Movement of the Production Possibilities Frontier versus Movement to the Frontier

But for various reasons — incomplete information, failure to optimize and the lack of incentive — a centrally planned economy always operates in the interior of its set of production possibilities. Thus, output can always be increased by simply moving to the frontier from the interior of the set of production possibilities, without any increase in inputs. The existence of this inherent inefficiency therefore also implies the existence of surplus potential output. In order to understand why there always exists inefficiency and hence surplus potential output in a centrally planned economy, we consider the following simple example drawn from agriculture.

There are two farm households, A and B. Each has a hectare of land. Both cotton and rice are needed by the economy. The central planner's problem is to decide — which household should grow cotton and which household should grow rice, as well as how much of each crop to grow. First of all, there may be a problem of insufficient or incorrect information. The central planner may not know which plot is more suitable for growing cotton and which plot is more suitable for growing rice. Moreover, the central planner may not know whether Farmer A can grow cotton better than Farmer B or vice versa. If the central planner makes any mistake in the assignment of production responsibilities, a simple exchange of the assignment can increase aggregate output without having to increase any input.

Second, even with full, complete and accurate information, it is still possible for the central planner to fail to optimize. The optimization problem may be too large or too complex; or the problem may not be well-behaved (for example, there may be non-convexities); or the problem may have multiple possible distinct solutions.

Third, there is also the problem of a lack of incentives on the part of the farmers to become more efficient—to try to move to their respective production possibilities frontiers. Under a centrally planned system, the farmers are generally wary of exceeding the assigned production targets even if they are in principle able to do so. To them, if they manage to produce outputs that exceed the assigned production targets, not only would their income not increase, so that the extra efforts would have been in vain, but also the assigned production targets for the following year might be raised, making it more difficult for them to fulfill their then obligations. (This is sometimes referred to as the "ratchet" effect.) Thus, under a centrally planned system, the best strategy for the farmers is to each try to produce the respective assigned target output and not to exceed it.

However, if there is a way to provide the necessary incentives to the farmers, then without increasing the aggregate inputs assigned under the central plan, aggregate output can also be increased. For example, the farmers can be given the autonomy to grow anything on their plots once they have fulfilled their obligations under the central plan, and to retain the resulting profits and to bear the resulting losses, if any; or they can also be allowed to exchange their assigned responsibilities with each other. The combined outputs of the two farmers will be higher than before without any increase in the aggregate inputs.

On the eve of the beginning of its reform and opening in 1978, the Chinese economy still operated under a mandatory central plan, and therefore had significant surplus potential output or slack. The countries of the former Soviet Union and Eastern Europe were all centrally planned economies on the eves of their economic transitions and thus also had similarly significant surplus potential outputs. If the surplus potential outputs can be fully exploited and realized, the real rates of growth of these economies can become very high, even without any significant growth in their aggregate inputs, at least in the near term. With growth in aggregate inputs, the economies should be able to grow even faster.

We may therefore conclude that for an economy under central planning, there always exists inefficiency and hence surplus potential output. Moreover, the surplus potential output should and can be realized with the introduction of economic reforms granting autonomy to the producers and providing incentives for them through the free markets, even without an increase in the aggregate inputs.

6.   The Benefits of an Open Economy

What are the benefits of an open economy? The "Theory of Comparative Advantage" tells us that free and voluntary trade between two trading partner countries always benefit both (although the distribution of the gains between them and within them may not be uniform). Exporters and importers will tend to benefit, whereas import-competing industries and their workers may lose. An economy may also benefit from the ability to import and augment resources not sufficiently available domestically using its export revenues or relying on foreign direct investment, foreign portfolio investment, foreign loans and foreign aid. Technology transfer is another way in which an economy can benefit, resulting in an expansion of its set of production possibilities (equivalently the outward shifting of its production possibility frontier).

Figure 26 makes it clear how opening the economy to the rest of the world always improves aggregate social welfare. For an economy without international trade, the consumers can only consume what can be produced domestically. The consumption possibilities set is therefore the same as the production possibilities set (the area shaded in gray). With international trade, the consumption possibilities set becomes the entire area of the triangle bounded by the international price line (gray line) tangent to the production possibilities set and the vertical and horizontal axes, which properly contains the old consumption possibilities set in the absence of trade. Since every consumption plan (combination of good 1 and good 2) in the old consumption possibilities set is attainable with trade, but not every consumption plan in the new consumption possibilities set is attainable in the old consumption possibilities set, aggregate social welfare must be higher with trade, because more consumption choices are available. As shown in Fig 26, without trade, the economy operates at the old production point which is the same as the old consumption point. With trade, the economy operates at the new production point but through exports and imports achieves the new consumption point, with the same quantity of good 1 as and a higher quantity of good 2 than the old consumption point. Aggregate social welfare must have increased.

Even if the international relative price is the same as the domestic relative price in the absence of international trade, so that the optimal combination of the goods to be produced remains the same with or without international trade, given the possibility of exports and imports, every point on the international relative price line is a possible domestic consumption plan. The domestic consumption point can be different from the domestic production point, and since the set of consumption possibilities has expanded, the resulting aggregate social welfare must also be higher with international trade. Thus, it is possible for aggregate social welfare to increase even if the production possibilities set remains the same as the economy opens to the world.

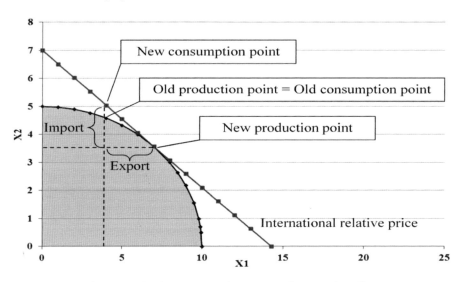

Fig. 26. Opening the Economy Enhances Domestic Economic Welfare.

It may be thought that with the inherent economic inefficiency of a centrally planned economy, its real rate of growth must be very high as it makes its transition from a centrally planned to a market economy. Similarly, one should expect aggregate social welfare to rise as an autarkic economy opens to the world. However, empirically, this turns out not to be true in general, except for the few rare cases such as the Chinese economy.

7.   The Transition from a Closed Centrally Planned to an Open Market Economy

In the former Soviet Union and the formerly socialist Eastern European countries, the transition from a closed centrally planned economy to an open market economy beginning in the late 1980s was both difficult and painful. Many of these countries experienced negative real rates of growth for approximately a full decade, from 1989 to 1999 (see Fig. 27) and suffered from extremely high rates of domestic inflation (see Fig. 28). Real GDPs per capita in these formerly centrally planned economies took even longer to recover to the same levels of 1989, the year in which central planning was first abandoned (see Fig. 29). For example, the real GDP per capita of Russia (solid gray line) did not recover to its 1989 level until 2007.

    In contrast, the transition from a closed centrally planned economy to an open market economy in China beginning in 1978 was smooth and highly successful (see Figs. 1 and 3).

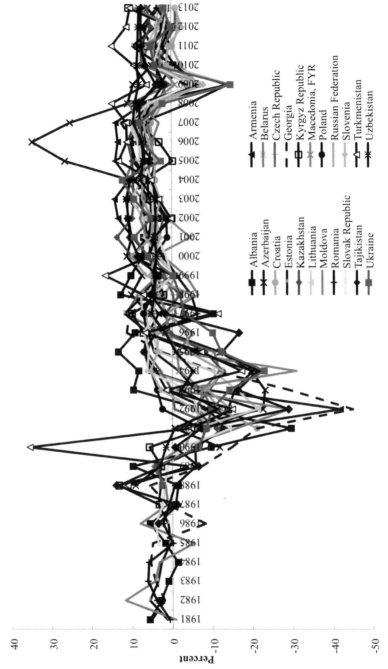

Fig. 27. The Rates of Growth of the Real GDP of Former Soviet Union and Formerly Socialist Eastern European Countries.

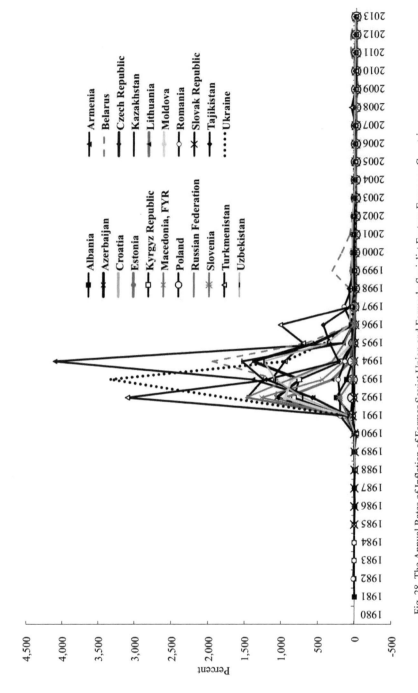

Fig. 28. The Annual Rates of Inflation of Former Soviet Union and Formerly Socialist Eastern European Countries.

Note: Georgia is omitted because some of its data are off the scale of the figure.

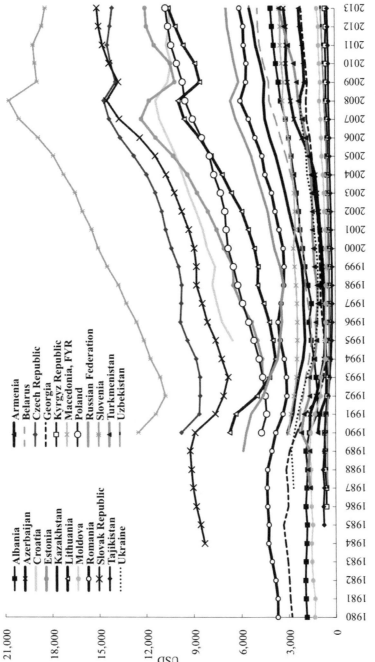

Fig. 29. The GDP per Capita of Former Soviet Union and Formerly Socialist Eastern European Countries (2005 US$).

Both Chinese real GDP and real GDP per capita have grown rapidly and continuously beginning in 1978. There was not even a single year of decline in either aggregate or per capita real GDP as in the other formerly centrally planned economies.

8.   Reform without Losers — The Chinese Strategy for Economic Reform

We have identified two factors that contributed to Chinese economic success since 1978: favorable economic fundamentals and the prior existence of surplus potential output. But these factors were also common to other transition economies such as those of some of the former Soviet Union and the formerly socialist Eastern European countries. What Section 7 has shown is that for a previously centrally planned economy, even though there might have been good economic fundamentals and prior economic inefficiency (and hence surplus potential output), introduction of producer autonomy and the free market and opening to the world may not be sufficient to ensure a successful economic transition and a high rate of real economic growth. Only China was able to do so.

Why was the Chinese economic reform and opening to the world so successful? Why was China able to achieve a smooth and successful transition from a closed centrally planned economy to an open market economy while some of the other countries attempting similar transitions failed so miserably? It turns out that the choice of strategy for the economic transition matters. In the former Soviet Union and the formerly socialist Eastern European countries, the strategy adopted for the transition was the so-called "shock therapy" or "big bang" strategy — that is, a strategy that calls for the immediate and full abolition of the mandatory central plan, relying completely and solely on the newly introduced and still relatively primitive free markets, which lacked the necessary facilitating and supporting institutions. In China, instead of dismantling the mandatory central plan all at once, the Chinese Government adopted the "Dual-Track" approach: introducing "conditional" autonomy and free markets in goods and services on the margin while continuing to enforce the existing central plan. "Conditional" autonomy means that for a household, a village, a commune, a township, or an enterprise, as long as it has already fulfilled its assigned obligations under the mandatory central plan, it is free to engage in any other economic activity and sell the resulting goods and services produced on the free markets at market-determined prices if it wishes to do so.

There were therefore in the Chinese economy simultaneously a "Plan Track" and a "Market Track", which operated in parallel but separately from each other. As everyone — a commune, a township, a village, an enterprise, a household or even an individual--had the option of staying with the pre-reform arrangements under the mandatory central plan, with identical rights and obligations as before (both prices and quantities), no one would be worse off under the "Dual-Track" approach. Thus, there could not be any "losers"; and in addition, everyone had the opportunity to "win". All the "vested interests" were "grandfathered", as they did not have to suffer any losses. This "Dual-Track" approach as implemented in China can be shown to be not only Pareto-improving, that is, making everyone better off (hence creating no losers), but also would enable the economy to achieve full economic efficiency (see Lau, Qian and Roland[13]).

All economic reforms are supposed to generate a net increase in aggregate social welfare, if not in real GDP, of the entire economy. Economic reform requires government leadership; it cannot occur autonomously, otherwise it would have occurred on its own already. However, most economic reforms create both winners and losers in the economy. While it is true that in the aggregate, the gains from economic reform should outweigh the losses, it is often difficult, if not impossible, to redistribute the gains so that no one is worse off. And the redistribution, if any, has to be implemented by a government with the authority, the power and the will.

The key to the success of the "Dual-Track" approach is that the production targets in the mandatory central plan are entirely fixed and must be fulfilled at the fixed plan prices before autonomy and participation in the free markets are allowed. Thus, profits and losses (taxes and subsidies) of enterprises under the central plan remain the same before and after the introduction of the "Dual-Track" approach. Differences between plan and free market prices of plan-assigned inputs and consumption goods constitute feasible lump sum transfers among enterprises and households. The government, by continuing to enforce the plan, ensures that this de facto redistribution built into the plan continues to take place. Thus, the continued planned consumer goods deliveries enable the maintenance of the pre-reform standard of living for all people as a floor. Since no one has to lose and everyone could win, opposition to the economic reform was minimized, support for the reform was maximized, and social stability was preserved. Such a win-win strategy for economic reform has the best chance of success.

As a result of the "Dual-Track" approach, the Chinese economic reform proceeded smoothly and did not result in economic chaos or contraction as in the former Soviet Union and the formerly socialist Eastern European countries. The Chinese economy was able to continue to grow rapidly in the midst of its transition from a closed centrally planned economy to an open market economy. Ultimately, in the late 1990s, the centrally planned part of the Chinese economy, which had been contracting relative to the market part of the economy, became sufficiently insignificant so that the mandatory features of the central plan could be gradually phased out. The transition to an open market economy in goods and services (but not yet in factors) was thus completed[g].

The feasibility of the dual-track approach depended critically on the continued enforcement of the rights and obligations under the existing central plan, which in turn depended on whether the central government had sufficient authority, credibility, power and will to do so. Credibility of state enforcement, and expectations thereof, affect the behavior of enterprises and households, and hence their degree of compliance with the central plan (post-reform). The governments of the former Soviet Union and the formerly socialist East European countries all became relatively weak around 1989, and did not really possess the ability to continue to enforce the pre-existing central plans. And after the former Soviet Union evolved into the Commonwealth of Independent States, what used to be domestic trade became international trade overnight, which became even more

---

[g] See also the discussion in Naughton[14] and Naughton[15].

difficult for the successor governments to control and operate. It was therefore almost impossible for these countries to avoid the creation of losers.

The Chinese Government, in the implementation of its economic reform, tried to minimize as much as possible the creation of losers and the impact of the reform on the existing economic system and the vested interests. At the same time, it also tried to allow new value and new winners to be created on the margin. Examples of reform measures that preserve pre-existing vested interests include the introduction of the "household responsibility system" in agriculture, the township and village enterprises in the rural areas, the special economic zones, the "processing and assembly" trade, the reforms of the foreign exchange system and the national taxation system. Related to the principle of "reform without losers" is the idea of treating existing people and new people differently even though they may be in identical situations. "New People, New Way; Old People, Old Way"[h] is the Chinese contribution to the method of implementing new economic reform. It embodies the idea of "grandfathering" — whatever rights and privileges (and obligations) a person had before the reform, he or she would have the option of retaining the same afterwards and thus would not have to lose anything. In a way, the two-tiered wage structure used in some enterprises and industries (e.g., the airline industry) in developed market economies also reflects the same underlying considerations — "grandfathering" — minimizes opposition to any reform by vested interests.

9. The Monopsonistic Labor Market in China

Before the economic reform of 1978, the Chinese Government was the sole employer for workers in China and could set the wage rates for all workers in the urban areas. As the sole employer, the Chinese government exercised its monopsonistic power and pursued a low-wage policy, resulting in a low share of labor in GDP. The low-wage policy was designed to increase national savings so that the needed investments can be financed. The objective of the low-wage policy was similar to the "price scissors" policy of maintaining a large gap between industrial prices and agricultural prices adopted by the former Soviet Union.

Even after the economic reform of 1978, the Chinese central government, together with all the local governments, its affiliated units, and the state-owned enterprises, has remained the largest employer in China and continued to exercise its monopsonistic power to keep the wage rates low. Even in 2010, Chinese private employers still accounted for less than half of the total Chinese employment of workers. The low wage rate paid by the largest employer have kept the wage rates paid by the other employers low (see Fig. 30).

This low-wage policy has had two effects: first, it has kept both the labor share (and the household share) of GDP low; and secondly, it has created large profits for state-owned as well as private enterprises. The low household share of GDP has in turn resulted in a lower Chinese household consumption to GDP ratio, currently around 40 percent, than in most other economies with a comparable real GDP per capita, because the Chinese

---

[h] In Chinese, "Xinren Xinbanfa, Jiuren Jiubanfa (新人新办法, 旧人旧办法)".

households have less disposable income to spend. The saving rate of Chinese households out of their disposable income may be estimated at approximately 30%, comparable to ethnic Chinese households in the economies of Hong Kong and Taiwan. The large profits of the enterprises, both state-owned and private, have resulted in a higher national saving rate in China than in most other economies, because the enterprises, especially the state-owned enterprises, declare little cash dividends and save and re-invest almost 100% of their profits. It has been recently reported that the wages and salaries of civil servants will be raised by almost 60%. This is great news. It will not only lead to a significant increase in the consumption of their households but also to a general increase in wages and salaries across the board.

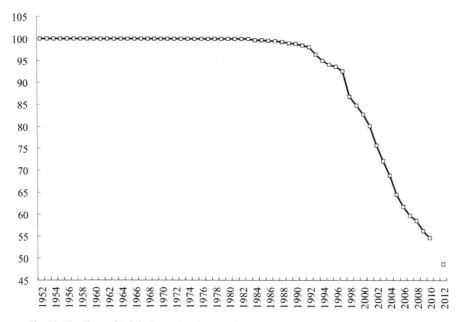

Fig. 30. The Share of Public Sector Employment in Total Non-Agricultural Employment in China.

10. The "Wild Geese Flying Pattern" — The Further Advantage of China's Size

Professor Kaname Akamatsu[16] was the first to introduce the metaphor of the "wild-geese-flying pattern" of East Asian economic development, which suggests that industrialization will spread from economy to economy within East Asia as the initially fast-growing economies, beginning with Japan, run out of surplus labor and face labor shortages, rising real wage rates, and quota restrictions on their exports, and need to relocate some of its industries to lower-cost economies. The fastest-growing economy will thus slow down and a lower-cost economy will take over as the fastest-growing economy.

Thus, East Asian industrialization spread from Japan to first Hong Kong in the mid-1950s, and then Taiwan in the late 1950s, and then South Korea and Singapore in the mid-1960s, and then Southeast Asia (Thailand, Malaysia, Indonesia) in the 1970s, and then to Guangdong, Shanghai, Jiangsu and Zhejiang in China as China undertook economic reform and opened to the world beginning in 1978. During this industrial migration, the large trading firms such as Mitsubishi, Mitsui, Marubeni and Sumitomo of Japan and Li and Fung of Hong Kong played an important role as financiers, intermediaries, quality assurers, and managers of logistics and supply chains.

However, this metaphor actually applies not only to East Asia but also to China itself because of its large size. Within China, industrialization first started in the coastal regions and then would migrate and spread to other regions in the interior—to Chongqing, Henan, Hunan, Jiangxi, Shaanxi and Sichuan—as real wage rates rose on the coast. As the coastal regions began to slow down in their economic growth, the regions in the central and western regions of China would take their turns as the fastest growing regions in China. China as a whole will therefore be able to maintain a relatively high rate of growth for many more years to come.

11. China as a Surplus Economy

With a high domestic investment rate of over 40% of its GDP, China in the early 2000s has begun to evolve into not only a surplus labor economy but also a surplus capital economy. The high domestic investment rate, enabled by a high national saving rate, has resulted in massively excess manufacturing capacities almost everywhere — in coal, steel, cement, glass, ship-building, aluminum, solar panels, etc. The average capacity utilization rate in many manufacturing industries is around 70%. Given the excess manufacturing capacities, Chinese real GDP going forward is actually not supply-constrained but aggregate demand-determined. As long as there is aggregate demand, there will be sufficient supply forthcoming to meet the demand. However, the growth of exports and fixed investment in manufacturing and residential housing can no longer be the principal drivers of the growth of Chinese aggregate demand.

How did the surplus economy come about? It came about because of massively excess fixed investment in manufacturing and in residential housing. Fixed investment in manufacturing was undertaken by both state-owned and private enterprises without regard to its potential rate of return, often supported by local government officials eager to increase local real GDP and employment. Fixed investment in residential housing was undertaken by developers at the local level, often also with the support of local governments.

Since the performance of Chinese local government officials are judged by key performance indicators which include the growth of the local GDP and employment, they have a strong incentive to do whatever is possible during their term of office to increase both. Beginning in the early 2000s, the local government officials began to realize that they could make use of the land under their control to finance the development of local manufacturing industries, such as steel, cement and glass as well as residential housing. In order to protect the local manufacturing industries that were established with their support, the local governments imposed, illegally, effective bans on the use of competitive manufactured products of non-local origin within their respective jurisdictions. Moreover, since a local government official is usually promoted to a different locality at the end of his or her term, he or she is not too concerned with the longer-term viability of these fixed investments in manufacturing, leaving them for the successor to deal with. Private enterprises also participated in making fixed investment in manufacturing and in residential real estate development, either with the support of local government officials or with loans made possible by a loose credit culture. Furthermore, many residential real estate developments are financed by pre-sales of units yet to be constructed rather than by construction loans from commercial banks.

Thus, as long as there is growth in Chinese aggregate demand, the Chinese economy should be able to continue to grow at an average annual rate of between 6.5 percent and 7 percent for the next five to ten years, more or less independently of what happens in the rest of the world. The growth of Chinese aggregate demand will come principally from domestic demand, consisting of public infrastructural investment, public goods consumption, and household consumption. Public infrastructural investment will consist of high-speed railroads, urban mass-transit systems (China and the world cannot afford "a car in every garage"); facilities for the support of universal free or low-cost internet access in urban areas; and affordable housing through urban slum clearance and renewal. Other public infrastructural projects can include the construction of sea water desalination plants as an alternative source of fresh water supply in the coastal areas in northern China and storage facilities for a national strategic petroleum reserve. Continually rising urbanization can not only increase the demand for public infrastructure and housing, but also promote the growth of the service sector, on both the supply and the demand sides. Public goods consumption (including the necessary related investments) can consist of education, health care, care for the elderly, and environment control, preservation and restoration — securing cleaner air, water and soil. Household consumption, especially from the fast expanding and rising middle class, has actually been growing quite rapidly since the first quarter of 2009. The rates of growth of real retail sales have been running at approximately one and a half times the rates of growth of real GDP. However, it will be a long time before Chinese household consumption can become the principal driver of Chinese economic growth. The share of disposable household income in Chinese GDP was approximately 43% in 2014. Even if the household saving rate declines to zero, household consumption cannot possibly exceed 50% of GDP, compared to between 65% and 70% for developed economies.

Both public infrastructural investment and public goods consumption require the leadership and support of the central and local governments. While expenditures on public goods consumption, including the necessary related investments, will count as GDP, much of the benefits of these expenditures may not be pecuniary, for example, cleaner air, water and soil, better education, better national health, etc., and may not be fully reflected in the conventional measurement of GDP. However, the increase in general social welfare as a result of these expenditures is definitely real. Moreover, increasing public goods consumption is an effective method of redistribution in kind. For example, since everyone breathes the same air, if the air is cleaner, both the wealthy and the poor benefit equally; and better access to health care may benefit the lower-income households more. Expansion of public goods consumption can thus also reduce the real income disparity.

In order to reduce the further growth of excess manufacturing capacity, one must reduce the moral hazard in borrowing and hence in investing. Vigorous enforcement of loan collection and bankruptcy laws and prosecution of bribery and financial fraud will help to reduce moral hazard. However, a change in the set of "key performance indicators" for the local government officials may also be necessary, so that the production and supply of public consumption goods such as the environmental enhancement (air, water and soil quality), education, health care, elderly care, and long-term economic viability and sustainability are also taken into account in addition to short-term growth in real GDP and employment.

12. The Importance of Expectations

Expectations of the future are important determinants of enterprise and household behavior, which in turn determines whether an economy grows or stagnates. Expectations often have the ability to be "self-fulfilling". If everyone believes that the economy will do well and act accordingly, by investing and consuming, the economy will indeed turn out to do well, and vice versa. The Chinese central government has the proven credibility to change expectations through its plans and actions.

In 1989, there was the June 4 incident, as a result of which economic growth ground to a virtual halt in the years that followed. However, in early 1992, Mr. Deng Xiaoping undertook his famous southern tour, urging people everywhere to take advantage of the opportunity to invest, which changed expectations in the entire country overnight. Enterprises started investing and households started consuming. As a result, 1992, 1993 and 1994 were boom years. In 1997, at the height of the East Asian currency crisis, Premier Zhu Rongji held the Renminbi/US$ exchange rate steady amidst the external chaos, and thus managed to maintain the confidence of the investors and consumers about China's economic future, and succeeded in keeping the economy growing. In 2008, after the collapse of Lehman Brothers, the export orders received by Chinese enterprises declined by 50 percent overnight, because of the frozen banking sector in the U.S. and other developed economies, creating widespread panic. Barely six weeks later, Premier Wen Jiabao launched the 4 trillion Yuan economic stimulus program, which once again helped to hold the confidence of Chinese enterprises and households in their economic future and changed their expectations. The Chinese economy has continued growing since.

In all of these cases, the Chinese government was able to turn around the very negative expectations about the future of the Chinese economy into positive ones, and in so doing greatly reduced the uncertainty pertaining to the future and increased general business confidence. These changes in turn fueled investment booms that resulted in the subsequent economic growth. Expectations will continue to play an important role in the Chinese economy. A strong central government with the power to mobilize aggregate demand can credibly change expectations in a positive direction to keep the economy growing.

13. The On-Going Economic Challenges

Despite its record of great success during the past thirty-six years, the Chinese economy still faces many significant on-going challenges: the rapidly aging population, corruption, rising income disparity, environmental degradation, excess manufacturing capacity, excess supply of residential real estate, shadow banking, local government debt, the deficit in human capital and the innovation gap, to name only a few. However, a hard landing of the Chinese economy seems unlikely. The principal challenge facing the Chinese economic policy makers is not so much the growth of real GDP but employment. In 2013, 13 million new jobs were created. In 2014, 10 million new jobs were created. The employment target is achievable because the service sector (50.5% by GDP and 43.4% by employment) is now larger and growing faster than the manufacturing sector (40.5% by GDP and 29.3% by employment). An expansion of the service-sector GDP creates 30% more employment than an expansion of the manufacturing-sector GDP by the same amount and requires much less fixed investment. Space does not allow a discussion of all of the economic challenges. We shall focus on the two challenges that have the most significant implications for long-term economic growth — the deficit in human capital and the innovation gap.

First, we examine the Chinese deficit in human capital relative to other economies. One indicator of the level of human capital in an economy is the average number of years of schooling per person in the working-age population. In Fig. 31, the average number of years of schooling of the working-age population is compared across selected economies. By this measure, the United States and Japan are clearly the global leaders. South Korea has been catching up fast. Most of the other East Asian economies also have quite rapidly increasing levels of human capital but it will take a while before they can catch up with the levels of human capital in the developed economies. China, Indonesia and Thailand have lagged behind in terms of human capital, but China has been expanding its tertiary education sector rapidly and can be expected to catch up to the levels of the developed economies by 2020 or so.

Second, we examine the innovation gap between China and the developed economies. Investment in R&D capital is important for promoting innovation (technical progress). China has also begun to invest more heavily in R&D in recent years — its R&D expenditure has been rising rapidly, both in absolute value, and as a percentage of GDP; but it still lags behind the developed economies as well as the newly industrialized economies of East Asia. (The Chinese R&D Expenditure/GDP ratio is targeted to reach 2.5% in 2020, equal to the historical average for the U.S.) The Republic of Korea currently leads the world with the percentage of its GDP expended on R&D exceeding 4%, followed by Japan, with an average ratio of 3% over the past quarter of a century (see Fig. 32).[i]

---

[i] The discussion on R&D is based on Lau and Xiong[17] as well as their unpublished research.

One indicator of the potential for innovation, or national innovative capacity, is the number of patents created each year. In Fig. 33, the number of patents granted in the United States each year to the nationals of different countries, including the U.S. itself, over time is presented. The U.S. is the undisputed champion over the past forty years, with 140,969 patents granted in 2015, followed by Japan, with 52,409. (Since these are patents granted in the U.S., the U.S. may have a home advantage; however, for all the other countries and regions, the comparison across them should be fair.) The number of patents granted to Chinese applicants in the United States each year has increased from the single-digit levels prior to the mid-1980s to 8,166 in 2015. The number of domestic patents granted to domestic applicants in China reached 263,436 in 2015, exceeding those of Japan (225,571 in 2013 and 146,749 in 2014). China aims to increase the stock of Chinese patents in force held by Chinese nationals from 4 per 10,000 inhabitants in 2013 to 14 per 10,000 inhabitants by 2020. However, it is not clear whether these patents are all comparable in quality to those approved in the U.S.

The stock of R&D capital may be defined as the cumulative past real expenditure on R&D less depreciation of 10% per year. It should quite properly be treated as capital since R&D efforts generally take years to yield any results. Since China has had both a much lower R&D expenditure to GDP ratio and a much lower GDP than the United States and other developed economies in the past, it will take more than a couple of decades before the Chinese R&D capital stock can catch up to the level of U.S. R&D capital stock. In 2013, Chinese R&D capital stock was only US$ 727 billion (in 2013 prices) compared to the United States' US$ 3.7 trillion. On per capita terms, China would be even further behind.

The stock of R&D capital can be shown to have a direct causal relationship to the number of patents granted. (See Fig. 34, in which the annual number of U.S. patents granted is plotted against the R&D capital stock of that year for each economy). Fig. 34 shows clearly that the higher the stock of R&D capital of an economy, the higher is the number of patents granted to it by the U.S. It will take at least a couple of decades before the level of Chinese R&D capital stock can catch up to that of the U.S. and hence to the number of U.S. patents granted each year.

However, successful innovation also depends on the existence of competition and free entry to markets. Monopolies are generally not very good in innovation and not very good in making full use of their own discoveries and inventions. China must create and maintain a competitive market environment with free entry and exit so as to encourage innovation in addition to investing in human capital and R&D capital. Moreover, in order to encourage innovation, China also needs to protect intellectual property rights vigorously, a direction in which it has been moving.

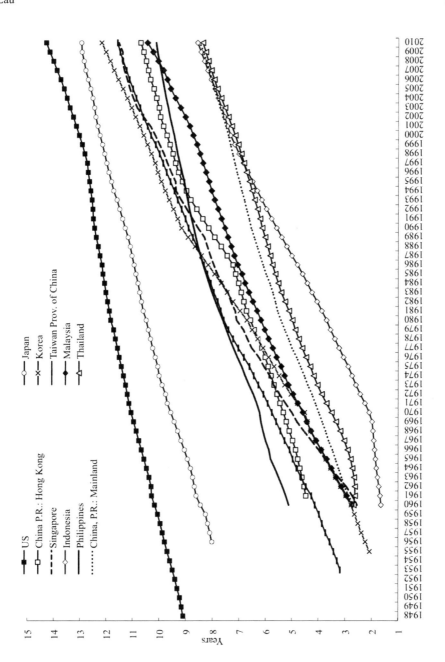

Fig. 31. Average Number of Years of Schooling of the Working-Age Population, Selected Economies (1945–Present).

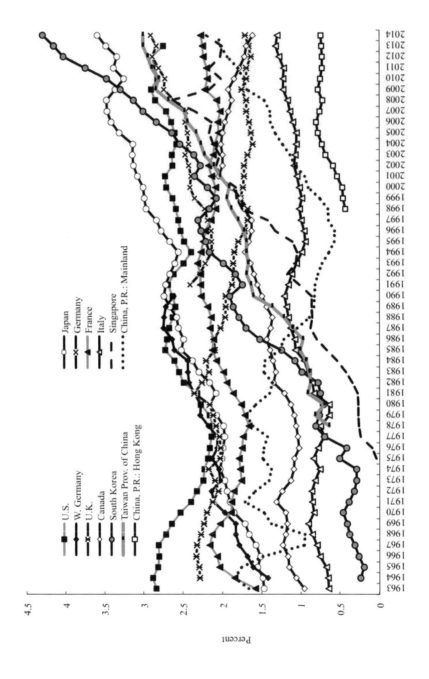

Fig. 32. R&D Expenditures as a Ratio of GDP: G-7 Countries, 4 East Asian NIES & China.

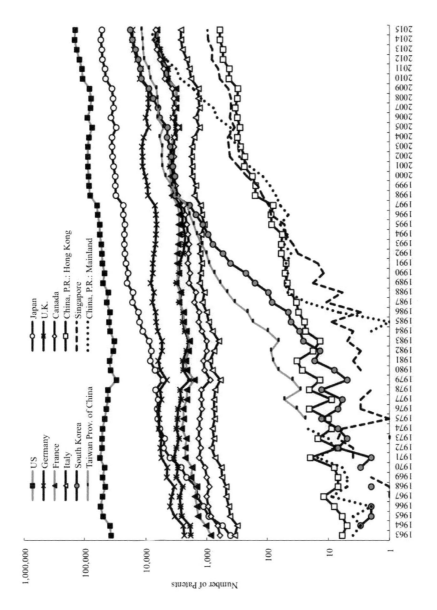

Fig. 33. Patents Granted in the United States: G-7 Countries, 4 East Asian NIEs & China.

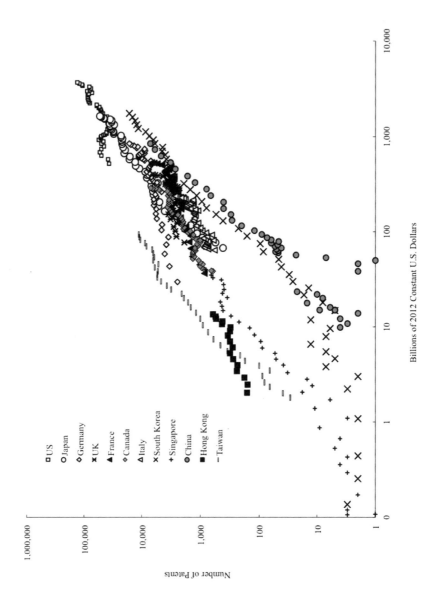

Fig. 34. Patents Granted in the United States and R&D Capital Stocks, Selected Economies.

14. The Long-Term Economic Outlook

Going forward, will the Chinese economy continue to grow at close to 10 percent per annum in the future? The short answer is no, for many reasons. The target rate of growth under the "New Normal" is between 6.5 percent and 7 percent per annum. However, it is important to realize that because the Chinese economy is now much bigger — a 7-percent rate of growth today will generate an absolute increase in real GDP equivalent to what a 14-percent rate of growth would have done ten years ago. On the supply side, the Chinese economy will still have strong economic fundamentals — a high domestic saving rate, abundant labor, and a huge domestic market that enables the realization of economies of scale — for a couple of decades. Moreover, advances in the information and communication technology have enhanced the positive effects of economies of scale even further. On the demand side, Chinese economic growth will be driven by the growth of its own internal demand, consisting of public infrastructural investment, public goods consumption as well as household consumption, rather than the growth of exports, or fixed investment in the manufacturing sector, or high-priced residential real estate.

In the medium term, say three to five years from now, economic stimulus is unlikely to be inflationary because of the excess manufacturing capacities already in place, especially if the economic stimulus is carefully targeted. In the longer term, there is still a great deal of room for Chinese GDP to grow. There is still significant surplus labor. Both the tangible capital and the intangible capital per unit labor in China are still relatively low compared to the developed economies.   Moreover, there is substantial scope for improvement in human capital and R&D capital. China has also been gradually changing from its role as the world's factory to the world's new growth market. It is already the world's largest exporting country and is on its way to becoming the largest importing country in goods and services combined in a couple of years.

It is projected that the Chinese and the U.S. economies will grow at average annual real rates of approximately 6.6% and 3.0% respectively between 2015 and 2030 (see Fig. 35). Chinese real GDP is thus projected to catch up to U.S. real GDP in approximately 15 years' time — around 2030, at which time both Chinese and U.S. real GDP will be around US$28 trillion (in 2015 prices). This is almost three times the Chinese GDP and approximately one and a half times the U.S. GDP in 2015. By then, China and the U.S. will each account for approximately 15% of world GDP. One may consider that the projected rates of economic growth for China and the U.S. may be a little on the optimistic side. However, the year in which the two GDPs become approximately the same will not be too far off.

By 2030, the Chinese real GDP per capita is projected to reach 19,000 (in 2015 prices), which would still be less than a quarter of the projected then U.S. real GDP per capita of US$77,000. It will take around more than 40 years from now, till 2060, for China to catch up to the United States in terms of real GDP per capita. By that time, Chinese GDP is likely to be more than three times the U.S. GDP, and will account for perhaps 30 percent of world GDP (depending on the rates of growth of other economies, especially the developing economies of today), the same percentage of world GDP that China had in the early 19th Century, according to an estimate made by Professor Angus Maddison[19].

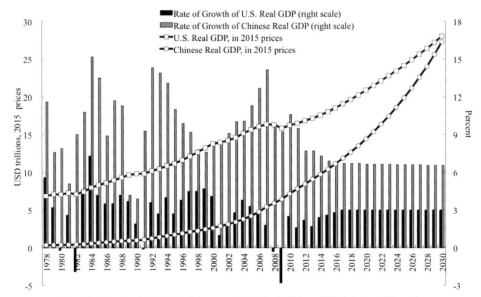

Fig. 35. Actual and Projected Chinese and U.S. Real GDPs and Their Rates of Growth.

15. Concluding Remarks

The highly successful experience of Chinese economic growth over the past 37 years (as well as those of other East Asian economies) strongly reaffirm the fundamental importance of having and maintaining a high investment rate, enabled by a high national savings rate, and surplus labor. In addition, the size of the Chinese domestic economy is a favorable factor allowing the ready realization of economies of scale and reducing vulnerability to external disturbances. However, these favorable factors alone were not sufficient, as the Chinese economy did not experience sustained economic growth between 1949 and 1978.

Economic reform and opening to the world in 1978 allowed the realization of the surplus potential output, helped to enhance and assure the efficiency of the Chinese economy and facilitated technology transfer from abroad. It is the unique achievement of China that in its transition from a closed centrally planned economy to an open market economy, it was able to use a "Dual-Track" rather than the "Big-Bang" approach, which ensured the success of reform without creating losers. Such a strategy maximized support, minimized opposition and preserved social stability. It led to win-win for all. Moreover, the "Dual-Track" approach also enabled the economy to achieve full economic efficiency. As a result, the Chinese economic transition was smooth, stable, successful and sustainable.

Chinese economic growth during the past 37 years can also be attributed to the growth of tangible inputs — tangible capital and labor, and in particular, tangible capital — rather than the growth in intangible capital or technical progress, just as the past economic growth of other East Asian economies at a similar stage of economic development. The speed of Chinese economic growth can be sustained longer than in other East Asian economies principally because of the size of the Chinese economy and its surplus labor and more recently its surplus capital.

Continuing economic growth going forward will depend mostly on the growth of internal demand (infrastructural investment, public goods consumption and household consumption) and not on exports and not on fixed investment in manufacturing capacity in the existing industries or residential real estate. China is a large continental country like the United States and will similarly develop into a largely internal-demand driven economy. International trade and international investment will not have a decisive impact on the Chinese economy in the future. Eventually, Chinese exports as a percent of its GDP should be relatively low, in the teens. Chinese economic growth will be marginally, but not critically, affected by a large decline in its exports, as demonstrated by its experience in the past several years as well as during the 1997-1998 East Asian currency crisis. Thus, it will be able to survive even prolonged economic recessions or stagnation in the European and U.S. economies.

Given the huge excess capacities in the Chinese manufacturing industries, in the time frame of the next five to ten years, Chinese real GDP, as mentioned above, will not be supply-constrained but will be primarily determined by aggregate demand. China should have no problem achieving a rate of real economic growth of between 6.5 percent and 7 percent. Thus, the goal of doubling real GDP per capita by 2020, declared in 2013, should be readily achievable. The "New Normal" is neither a "boom" of close to double-digit rates of growth, nor a "bust" of negative or low single-digit real rates of growth. There will be both sufficient supply and demand in the Chinese economy to support continuing growth.

Beyond that, on the basis of its strong economic fundamentals, China should also be able to continue to grow at about the same average annual rate for the following decade, more or less independently of what happens in the rest of the world. In the longer run, Chinese economic growth will make a transition from being driven by the growth in tangible inputs to the growth in intangible inputs and innovation.

Is the Chinese economy a miracle or a bubble? A bubble is a transitory and unsustainable phenomenon that is ready to self-destruct any time. But the Chinese economy has been growing at a sustained high real rate of almost 10% per annum for the past 37 years, and is expected to continue to grow between 6.5 percent and 7 percent per annum for another couple of decades. It cannot therefore possibly be a bubble. And the model of Chinese economic development has also been adopted and emulated, at least in part, by Vietnam, another economy in the process of transitioning from a centrally planned to a market economic system, with some degree of success. It is also a model for other potential transition economies such as Cuba, Laos and North Korea. As the Chinese economic development experience can be replicated and reproduced elsewhere, it cannot be considered a miracle either. What is not replicable is its economies of scale. The only economy that has the potential of benefitting from economies of scale to the same degree as China is India.

References

D. H. Perkins, *The Economic Transformation of* China, (World Scientific Publishing Company, Singapore, 2015).

T. Beardson, *Stumbling Giant: The Threats to China's Future*, (Yale University Press, New Haven, 2013).

J. Tobin, *The New Economics One Decade Older*, Eliot Janeway Lecture, Princeton (Princeton University Press, New Jersey, 1974).

W. A. Lewis, Economic development with unlimited supplies of labour, *Manchester School of Economic and Social Studies* 22, 139-191 (1954).

P. Krugman, The myth of Asia's miracle, *Foreign Affairs*, November/December, (1994).

J.-I. Kim and L. J. Lau, The sources of economic growth of the East Asian newly industrialized countries, *Journal of the Japanese and International Economies* 8(3), 235-271 (1994).

J.-I. Kim and L. J. Lau, The role of human capital in the economic growth of the East Asian newly industrialised countries, *Asia-Pacific Economic Review* 1(3), 3-22 (1995).

L. J. Lau and J.-S Park, *Sources of East Asian Economic Growth Revisited*, Working Paper, Department of Economics, Stanford University, Stanford, CA, December (2002).

L. J. Lau and J.-S Park, *Sources of East Asian Economic Growth Revisited*, Working Paper, Department of Economics, The Chinese University of Hong Kong, July (2007).

W. A. Lewis, Economic development with unlimited supplies of labour, *Manchester School of Economic and Social Studies* 22, 139-191 (1954).

D. W. Jorgenson, The development of a dual economy, *The Economic Journal* 71(282), 309-334 (1961).

E. F. Denison, *The Sources of Economic Growth in the United States and the Alternatives Before Us* (Committee for Economic Development, New York, 1961).

M. J. Boskin, and L. J. Lau, International and intertemporal comparison of productive efficiency: An application of the meta-production function approach to the Group-of-Five (G-5) countries, *Economic Studies Quarterly* 43(4), 298-312 (1992).

L. J. Lau, Y. Qian and G. Roland, Reform without losers: An interpretation of China's dual-track approach to transition, *The Journal of Political Economy* 108(1), 120-143 (2000).

B. Naughton, *Growing Out of The Plan: Chinese Economic Reform, 1978-1993*, (Cambridge University Press, Cambridge, 1995).

B. Naughton, *The Chinese Economy: Transitions and Growth*, (The MIT Press, Cambridge, MA, 2007).

K. Akamatsu, A historical pattern of economic growth in developing countries, *Journal of Developing Economies*, 1(1), 3-25 (1962).

L. J. Lau and Y. Xiong, *Are There Laws of Innovation: Part I, Introduction*, Working Paper No. 39, (The Institute of Global Economics and Finance, The Chinese University of Hong Kong, 2015).

A. Maddison, *The World Economy: Vol. 1: A Millennial Perspective and Vol. 2: Historical Statistics*, (Development Centre of the Organization for Economic Co-operation and Development, Paris, 2006).

Global value chains and changing trade elasticities

Byron Gangnes

Department of Economics and UHERO, University of Hawaii
Honolulu, HI 96822, USA
E-mail: gangnes@hawaii.edu
www.economics.hawaii.edu

Ari Van Assche

Department of International Business, HEC Montréal
Montréal, Québec, H3T 2A7 CANADA
E-mail: ari.van-assche@hec.ca
www.hec.ca

The trade collapse of 2008-2009 and the anemic trade growth since then raise the question of whether trade elasticities may be undergoing fundamental structural change. A potential source of such change is the spread of global value chains (GVCs), which have brought a marked increase in the use of intermediate goods and changes in the nature of trade competition. We review the recent literature on the impact of GVCs on measured trade elasticities and the ways in which their emergence may affect how we estimate and interpret trade responsiveness. We then draw out a few implications of recent research for global modeling.

Keywords: elasticities, global value chain, modelling

1.   Introduction

Global economic modelling depends on satisfactorily describing the flows of international trade in goods and services. Estimating trade equations therefore has a long history in macroeconometric modelling. Of particular interest has been the responsiveness of trade volumes to income and relative prices, the so-called trade elasticities.

Recent developments in the global economy have led modelers to question whether trade elasticities may be undergoing fundamental structural change. A first eye opener was the Great Trade Collapse in the wake of the global recession in 2008-2009. Compared to previous economic downturns, the drop in trade was unprecedentedly sudden, severe and synchronized, with world trade declining more than 30 percent in the first quarter of 2009 relative to a year earlier[1]. This led to the question of whether the unusually large trade response reflected a structural increase in the responsiveness of trade to income in comparison to previous periods[2].

There is substantial evidence that trade did indeed become more sensitive to income growth at the close of the 20th century. Cheung and Guichard[3] find that the long-run income elasticity of world trade almost doubled from 1.3 in the period 1975-1986 to 2.5 in the 1986-2008 period. Escaith et al.[4] find a similar increase in the income elasticity of trade in the 1990s, but suggest that it had stabilized by the early 2000s. Ceglowski[5] finds evidence of the same pattern in a study of U.S. aggregate imports.

More recent events raise the possibility that income elasticities may once again have shifted, this time in the downward direction. After an initial bounce from the 2008-2009 recession, world trade growth has been unusually anemic, a development often referred to as the Great Trade Slowdown. For the first time in nearly half a century, global trade has grown more slowly than GDP. In 2011-2014, the value of merchandise exports expanded at an annual rate of just 3.3 percent, less than half the average of roughly 7 percent for the 1985-2007 period. This has led to an intense debate among scholars over whether income elasticities have started to come down, and what might be the cause (for a fairly comprehensive discussion, see the collection of papers in Hoekman[6]).

Trade modelers have raised similar questions about price elasticities, following recent episodes where large depreciations appeared to have had little impact on exports. And there is some recent suggestive evidence of a downward trend in price elasticity. Ahmed et al.[7] find that the responsiveness of manufacturing exports to changes in the real effective exchange rate has declined from an absolute elasticity of 1.1 in the first part of the 1996-2012 period to 0.6 by the end of the period. While this is by no means a settled fact (see, for example, the contrasting view of Leigh et al.[8]), a decline in the price sensitivity of trade would have important implications for exchange rate adjustment and related issues.

In the ongoing discussion about changing trade elasticities, global value chains (GVCs) are the elephant in the room. A key simplifying assumption implicit in workhorse trade models is that products have clear national identities, that is, their entire production process is concentrated within the borders of the home country. In this traditional view, each country produces differentiated products that compete against the products of other countries in destination markets. In this case, the quantity of exports demanded can be expressed as a function of demand in the destination market, own prices, and prices of competing products.

This national view of production, however, is disconnected from today's reality. Thanks to reduced communication and transportation costs, many companies have long abandoned the practice of producing goods in a single country. Through offshoring, they have sliced up their supply chains and dispersed their production activities across many countries, leading to GVCs. A consequence of the emergence of GVCs is that countries increasingly specialize in adding value at a particular stage of production rather than producing entire finished products[9]. Making final products requires them to connect with foreign value chain partners both upstream and downstream. Upstream, countries increasingly rely on foreign inputs for their exports. Johnson and Noguera[10] provides evidence that the share of foreign value added embodied in a country's exports increased for virtually all countries between 1970 and 2008. Downstream, countries increasingly export intermediate goods that are used by foreign companies to make their respective exports. As a result, a significant portion of a country's exports is now ultimately consumed in a country other than where they were first exported.

The spread of GVCs, the increasing role of intermediate goods, and the changing nature of trade competition may have important implications for both income and price elasticities of trade. In this chapter, we review the recent literature on the impact of GVCs on measured trade elasticities and the ways in which their emergence may affect how we estimate and interpret trade responsiveness. We will then draw out a few implications of recent research for global modeling.

2.   The Standard Trade Model

As we noted above, the traditional empirical model of trade rests on the idea of a national production paradigm, where exports are wholly produced within one country and then compete with those of other countries on international markets. The demand for a country's exports is therefore typically modeled as a function of income in the rest of the world, home export prices, and foreign prices measured in domestic currency. Following Goldstein and Khan[11,a],

$$X_t^d = g(Y_t^* e_t, PX_t, P_t^* e_t) \qquad (1)$$

where X_t^d is export demand at time t, Y_t^* is a measure of foreign income, PX_t is the home export price, P_t^* is the price of competing foreign goods, and e_t is the effective exchange rate in domestic currency per unit of foreign currency.

Equation (1) is consistent with consumer choice over domestic and foreign goods, which are assumed to be imperfectly substitutable[12], as is well supported by the data. Note that in this two-region formulation, the domestic country's exports to the rest of the world are also the rest of the world's imports from the domestic country, so the trade flow can equivalently be interpreted as a foreign import demand equation.

Under homogeneity, export demand is a function of real income abroad and relative export prices,

$$X_t^d = g\left(\frac{Y_t^*}{P_t^*}, \frac{PX_t}{P_t^* e_t}\right). \qquad (2)$$

Empirical versions of equation (2) have most often been estimated in log-linear (double log) form[13],

$$log X_t^d = \alpha + \beta \cdot log\left(\frac{Y_t^*}{P_t^*}\right) + \gamma \cdot log\left(\frac{PX_t}{P_t^* e_t}\right) + \varepsilon_t \qquad (3)$$

where β is the income elasticity of export demand and γ the relative price elasticity.

Empirical trade equations based on (2) and (3) have dominated trade modeling over the years. Examples extend back to the earliest days of applied econometric modeling, with income and relative price forms at least as early as Adler[14], Hinshaw[15], and Chang[16,b]. The log-linear form (3) can be found as early as Chang[16].

---

[a] This model has been used so often in the literature that Goldstein and Khan[11] refer to it as the "standard export model."
[b] The canonical survey of trade elasticities is Goldstein and Khan[11]. Marquez[17] provides a chronological listing of trade elasticity estimates for studies between 1941 and 2001. He cautions that his list may not be comprehensive. Hillberry and Hummels[18] review a number of more recent papers, including research that applies cross-sectional and panel methods, with an eye to their use in computable general equilibrium models.

The standard trade model has played an enduring role in international macroeconomics and in macroeconometric modeling. Trade elasticities play a central role in discussions of exchange rate and balance of payment adjustment. Estimated trade equations represent important channels for external conditions to impact domestic economies and to condition policy responses, and in multi-country models, such as the Project LINK model pioneered by Lawrence Klein and others, they serve as a key linkage between national economies[19]. The precise form of trade equations has evolved over time, with early macro models (e.g. Klein-Goldberger[20]) often adopting forms relating trade demand to income alone, without consideration of relative price effects. In part this may reflect the Keynesian preoccupation with the income determination of demand, but it may also reflect limited trade price data available at the time. Models including relative price terms have been standard for many years and continue to play a role in both econometric and CGE trade models.

Despite its longevity, there are well-known limitations to the modeling approach in (2) and (3) and in its common application, including omission of trade determinants such as immigration, adjustment costs, trade regime changes, and supply-side developments.[c] Theory-based or ad hoc modifications have sometimes been made to address these issues (see for example, Marquez[17], Gagnon[21], and Garcia-Herrero[22]). When used as a single equation to determine trade volumes, the model ignores supply-side interactions. Effectively, this assumes infinite supply elasticities, something that is clearly not supported by the literature (Goldstein and Khan[11], pp. 1087-88). Of particular relevance for the current discussion, derived as it is from consumer demand theory, the standard trade model is not well suited for describing trade in intermediate goods[d].

The model in log-linear form (3) implies constant trade elasticities. In fact, by now there is compelling evidence that this is not the case and that elasticities can change significantly over time. Marquez[17] is largely devoted to this question and what theory and practice can tell us about it. A recent google search turned up 2950 pages with "structural breaks" and "trade elasticity" or a similar term. The apparent shifts of the past two decades that were described above are but the most recent examples.

Past attempts to deal with parameter instability have including applying more flexible functional forms, including other variables that may influence trade (see above), the introduction of dummy variables for known events or to capture unexplained shifts, estimation over shortened time periods (which amounts to the same thing), use of greater disaggregation, and so on (e.g., Patel et al.,[27]). The hypothesis in question here is whether

---

[c] Econometric concerns such as Orcutt's[23] critique of bias in estimates of price elasticities or more recent concerns about nonstationarity and spurious regressions can typically be overcome by using appropriate empirical methodology.

[d] A limited number of models focused on intermediate goods have been developed over the years. These models derive the demand for imported intermediates as the result of a profit maximizing (alternatively cost minimizing) choice between imports and domestic inputs. Goldstein and Khan[11] cite Burgess[24] and Kohli[25]; Marquez[17] cites Kohli[26].

the recent evolution of measured trade elasticities may be linked directly to the emergence and changes in the manner of production associated with GVCs.

3.   Global Value Chains

The introduction of GVCs fundamentally alters the nature and determinants of trade patterns. It has been widely documented that production chains for goods and services are not concentrated within single countries, but are now increasingly fragmented, with corporations dispersing activities across multiple countries and companies[28]. As a consequence, countries increasingly specialize in the production and exports of slivers of the value chain, not of entire goods[9]. Furthermore, countries increasingly connect with foreign value chain partners to make final goods and services. As a result, trade in intermediate inputs now accounts for roughly two-thirds of all international trade[29].

Countries can connect with foreign value chain partners in two directions to produce goods and services: upstream and downstream. Upstream, they can import intermediate goods from their foreign value chain partners which they then use for the production and export of their own goods. This is called *backward participation*. Downstream, countries can export intermediate goods to their foreign value chain partners which use them to make their own respective exports, i.e. *forward participation*.

A new TiVA dataset compiled by the OECD and the WTO allows us to gain insights into the extent of a country's backward and forward participation in GVCs[30]. By combining input-output data for multiple countries with trade statistics, the dataset allows a country's gross exports to be decomposed into two parts: (1) *domestic value added* which is generated in the exporting country and (2) *foreign value added* which comes from outside the exporting country. As is shown in Fig. 1, foreign value added captures a country's backward participation in GVCs.

Domestic value added can be further decomposed into two subparts: *domestic value added consumed in the destination country* and *domestic value added embodied in a foreign country's exports*. The latter term captures a country's forward participation in GVCs. In the remainder of this section, we will use the TiVA dataset to document trends in countries' integration in GVCs.

3.1.   *Backward participation*

Starting with Hummels et al.[31], scholars have used the foreign value added share embodied in gross exports as an indicator of a country's backward participation in GVCs, since it indicates how heavily a country relies on imported inputs to produce its exports (see also Johnson and Noguera[29]). As Fig. 2 shows, foreign value added is responsible for a significant and growing share of G-20 countries exports around the world. Between 1995 and 2011, the average share of foreign value added in gross exports for the G20 countries grew from 16 percent to 23 percent. This share varies across countries in a predictable fashion. It is substantially smaller for large economies such as the United States, since they have a large pool of intermediate inputs to draw on, and for countries with substantial natural resources such as Saudi Arabia, since mining activities require fewer intermediate goods in the production process. It is also smaller for countries that are located far from big markets and suppliers, such as Indonesia, since it is relatively more expensive for them to import inputs.

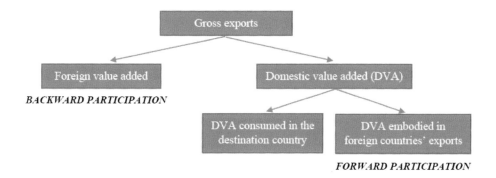

Fig. 1. Decomposition of Gross Exports.

The foreign value added share embodied in gross exports varies not only across countries, but also across industries[30]. Fig. 3 depicts the foreign value added share embodied in gross exports for various Canadian industries in 2011. It exceeds 35 percent in the durable goods industries *Transport equipment* (motor vehicles, airplanes), *Electrical and optical equipment* (computers, telecommunication devices) and *Basic metals and fabricated metal products*. In contrast, it is less than 10 percent in the services sectors *Electricity, gas and water supply*, *Community, social and personal services,* and *Total business sector services,* as well as in *Mining and quarrying*.

As we will see later, the variation across industries is important, because it implies that the composition of a country's exports may vary substantially when expressed in gross versus value added terms, and that this discrepancy can become larger as countries alter their backward participation in GVCs. Durable goods account for a larger share of G20 non-oil exports when expressed in gross terms than in value-added terms, and that discrepancy has increased over time. In 2011, durable goods exports accounted for 38 percent of G20 non-fuel gross exports, but only 34 percent of G20 non-fuel value added exports.[e]

3.2. *Forward participation*

Countries also export intermediate goods to foreign value chain partners, who use them to produce their respective exports. For example, a Canadian aerospace company may export an intermediate good to Seattle, which Boeing then uses to produce and sell planes all

---

[e] In this calculation, durable manufacturing goods includes *Basic metals and fabricated metal products* (C27T28), *Machinery and equipment* (C29), *Electrical and optical equipment* (C30T33), *Transport equipment* (C34T35). Non-mineral fuel exports are total exports minus *Mining and quarrying* (C10T14).

around the world. As we noted earlier, to capture a country's *forward participation* in GVCs, the TiVA dataset allows a further decomposition of a country's domestic value added into two subcategories: (1) domestic value added consumed in the destination country; and (2) domestic value added embodied in foreign countries' exports. The latter term captures a country's forward participation in GVCs.

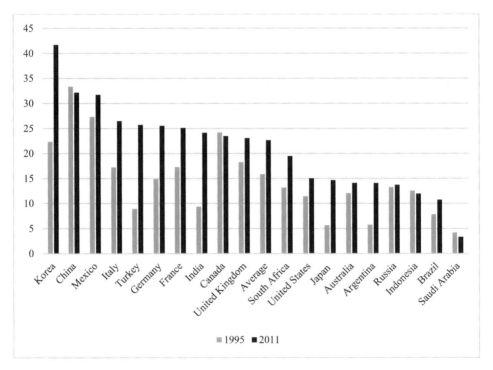

Fig. 2. Share of Foreign Value Added in Gross Exports, G-20 Countries, 1995 and 2011.

Source: Authors' calculations using the OECD-WTO TiVA database.

Fig. 4 shows that the majority of G-20 countries have increased their forward participation in GVCs over the past few decades. Between 1995 and 2011, the average share of domestic value added embodied in foreign exports grew from 17.2 percent to 24.3 percent. Here again, the share varies across countries. It is larger for countries with substantial natural resources such as Saudi Arabia and Russia, since natural resources tend to be an important input embodied in foreign countries' exports. It tends to be lower for countries such as China and Mexico that specialize in the final assembly of manufacturing exports.

A country's forward participation in GVCs means that its exports are not necessarily determined by demand conditions in the destination country, but rather in the country where they are ultimately consumed[32]. Table 1 uses the example of Canadian exports to demonstrate the importance of taking this distinction into account. In gross terms, 66.7

percent of Canada's exports were destined for the United States in 2011. If we only consider the domestic value added that is embodied in Canada's gross exports (value added trade), the share of Canada's exports to the United States drops to 65.5 percent. If we then consider where Canada's domestic value added is ultimately consumed, the share of Canadian exports to the United States drops to 58.1 percent. The relative shares for other Canadian export destinations vary, depending on the nature of trade between Canada and each destination market. Note that the differences would be more dramatic for an exporting country more heavily specialized in intermediate goods trade.

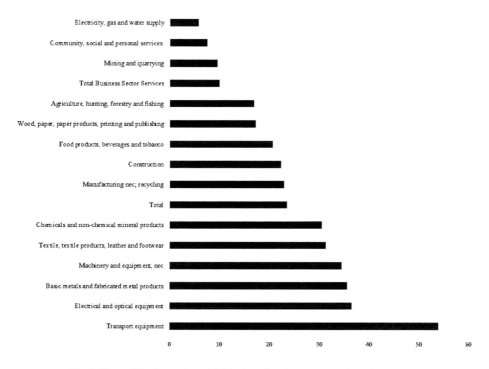

Fig. 3. Share of Foreign Value Added in Canadian Gross Exports, by Industry, 2011.

Source: Authors' calculations using the OECD-WTO TiVA database.

3.3.   *Total participation*

Combining the numbers for backward and forward participation allows us to obtain an estimate of the importance of GVCs in a country's total trade. Fig. 5 shows that for the G20 countries the share of gross exports that takes place within GVCs has doubled from a bit more than 33 percent in 1995 to 46 percent in 2011. Clearly GVC production arrangements have become a key element of G-20 countries' exports over the past several decades.

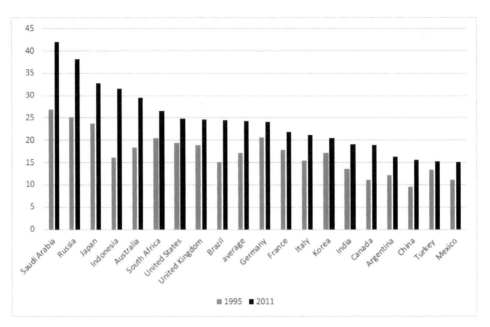

Fig. 4. Domestic Value Added Embodied in Foreign Exports as Share of Gross Exports, G-20 Countries, 1995 and 2011.

Source: Authors' calculation using the OECD-WTO TiVA database.

Table 1. Share of Canada's Exports by Destination Country, 1995 and 2011

	Gross exports		Domestic value added content of gross exports		Domestic value added in foreign final demand	
	1995	2011	1995	2011	1995	2011
United States	70.9	66.7	68.1	65.5	63.5	58.1
EU-15	8.3	8.4	9.2	8.9	10.4	10.1
China	1.1	4.9	1.2	5.1	0.9	4.4
Japan	5.7	3.0	6.4	3.2	7.4	3.9
Mexico	0.8	2.5	0.9	2.2	1.0	2.5

Source: Authors' calculation using the OECD-WTO TiVA database.

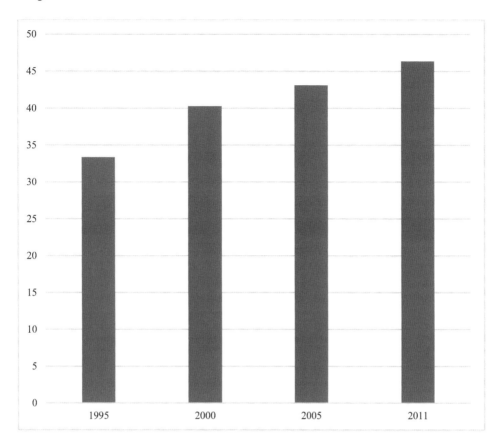

Fig. 5. GVC Trade as a Share of G20 Countries' Gross Exports Value, 1995–2011.

Source: Authors' calculations using the OECD-WTO TiVA database.

4. Implications for Trade Elasticities

Countries' growing integration in GVCs has potentially important implications for trade elasticities. Below we consider the impacts on price and income elasticities of the backward and forward participation in GVCs.

4.1. *Price elasticity*

The price elasticity of exports summarizes the effect of a change in the relative price of domestic and foreign goods on export volume. Traditionally the focus has been on the manner in which relative price change (often associated with currency appreciation or depreciation) alters the competitiveness of domestic and foreign producers on final demand. A country's participation in GVCs can alter the elasticity of its exports to relative price change in a number of ways[7,33].

We have seen in Fig. 2 that G-20 countries increasingly rely on imported inputs to produce exports. Recent studies argue that this has important implications for the sensitivity of a country's exports to exchange rate fluctuations[33]. If a portion of the exporter's intermediate inputs are imported, and these costs are not denominated in the exporter's domestic currency, then an exporter's marginal cost of production will only be partly exposed to exchange rate fluctuations. All else equal, we should therefore expect that exports of a country with a higher proportion of foreign value added will have a lower responsiveness to an exchange rate fluctuation.

The price elasticity of a country's exports should also depend on its degree of forward participation in global value chains. A currency fluctuation not only affects the competitiveness of domestic value added that is sold to foreign consumers, but also the domestic value added embodied in foreign countries' exports. For example, a depreciation of the Canadian dollar increases the competitiveness of Canadian aerospace components embodied in Boeing's planes. The effect on the price elasticity is complex. On the one hand, a depreciation may make downstream foreign producers (like Boeing) more competitive in third markets which could boost the responsiveness of a country's intermediate good exports to a currency fluctuation. On the other hand, the rising competitiveness of foreign downstream producers may dampen the export demand for their domestic competitors in the destination market.[f] For example, a rise in competitiveness of Boeing can dampen the rise in export demand for Canadian-based Bombardier planes.

Efforts have been made to calculate more accurate measures of the real effective exchange rate (REER) that take into account backward and forward participation in GVCs. Bayoumi et al.[35] develop a measure of competitiveness based on the IMF REER, but which adjusts component price indices using new bilateral trade weights that reflect value-added trade. They find that competitiveness losses of emerging economies that rely heavily on imported inputs are significantly larger when value-added weights are used. Bems and Johnson[36] devise a new method for calculating a country's "value added real effective exchange rate" by modifying both the price and trade-weight components. Similar to Bayoumi et al.[35], they constructed new bilateral trade weights that reflect value-added trade rather than gross trade. They then replaced consumer prices with the GDP deflator to better reflect the value-added component of trade competitiveness. They find that this approach can yield very different paths for relative price change than traditional gross REER measures, as well as for measures of the degree of openness.

To our knowledge, there are very few papers that provide direct evidence of the effect of GVCs on price elasticities. Ahmed et al.[7] find that the rise of participation in global value chains explains on average 40 percent of the recent fall in the elasticity, and that correction of the REER for participation in global value chains does not present the same decreasing pattern in elasticity. Athukorala and Khan[37] find that while the price elasticity

---

[f]Athukorala and Khan[37] describe other channels through which GVCs may affect the responsiveness of trade to relative price changes. On the one hand, the ability to outsource itself could make it easier for firms to move production in response to relative price changes. However, trade responsiveness could be limited by potentially high costs of setting up international production arrangements and limited substitutability of inputs sited in different locales.

of import demand for final goods is large (greater than 2 in the long run), that of intermediate goods is not significantly different from zero. Arndt and Huemer[33] find that the real exchange rate has greater explanatory power for non-manufacturing US imports from Mexico than it does for manufacturing imports, where GVC arrangements are common; in the case of autos, the effect of real exchange rate change disappears altogether.

4.2. *Income elasticity*

The emergence of GVCs also has implications for the responsiveness of trade to changes in national income. Certainly, the coincidence of rapid GVC trade growth before the Great Recession and the documented rise of income elasticities suggests it may be a primary candidate for structural change in the trade-income relationship. Several existing studies find that the inclusion of proxies for GVC prevalence can in some cases reduce income elasticity estimates and/or eliminate structural breaks[4,5,38].

There are two primary ways by which a country's backward participation in a GVC may affect its income elasticity. First, it may increase the sensitivity of its exports to foreign income movements by making its export bundle more concentrated in durable goods industries (a *composition effect*). Second, it may increase the income elasticity due to features inherent to the GVC production structure (*supply chain effects*).

Countries that increase their reliance on imported inputs for their exports can see an increase in their income elasticity due to a composition effect. Durable goods tend to have a higher sensitivity to income shocks than do non-durables goods (see, among others, Ceglowski[5] and Aziz and Li[39]). In economic downturns, for example, households and companies disproportionately delay purchases of durable and capital goods as they await clearer evidence that the economic climate is improving. If GVC trade growth is primarily centered in durable goods industries (see section 3), this will raise the weight of higher-income-elasticity goods in trade, potentially leading to an increase in the aggregate income elasticity.

Bems et al.[40] use a global input-output table to show that the asymmetric expansion of GVCs in durable goods sectors has raised the weight of durable goods in world trade compared to their weight in world GDP. By 2008, durable goods had grown to nearly 40% of trade, but amounted to only 10% of final demand. Building on this stylized fact, Engel and Wang[40] set up a two-country, two-sector model in which durable goods are tradable while nondurables are nontradable. They show that since durables expenditures are several times more volatile than GDP and international trade is highly concentrated in these durable goods, trade should also experience larger swings than GDP. This has also been used to explain the severity of the trade collapse during the Great Recession. Bems et al.[40] and Eaton et al.[42] estimate that the composition effect accounted for 70 to 80 percent of the global decline in the trade-to-GDP ratio during the crisis.

In Gangnes et al.[43], we find evidence that China's growing backward integration into GVCs has led to a rise in the durable goods share of gross exports, and that this has led in turn to a higher measured income elasticity. To capture China's backward integration into GVCs, we exploit data from China's Customs Statistics for the years 1992-2011 that distinguish between trade under two distinct customs regimes: the processing trade regime and the ordinary trade regime. Under processing trade, firms enjoy duty-free importation of inputs that are used in production, but face restrictions on selling in the domestic market. As a result, firms use it almost exclusively if they rely heavily on imported inputs and export their products, that is, if they are integrated into GVCs. Under ordinary trade, firms face duties on imported inputs but can sell their output locally. Firms that export under the ordinary trade regime, therefore, have more extensive domestic value chains.

We first show that the share of processing trade (that is, GVC trade) in China's exports increased rapidly in the 1990s before stabilizing in the early 2000s. Second, we demonstrate that GVCs have primarily emerged in durable goods sectors, therefore altering the composition of Chinese exports. As the data in Table 2 indicate, in 2011 processing trade accounted for 84% of durable goods exports, but only 16% of non-durable goods exports. The rapid growth of durable goods processing trade raised the share of durable goods in total trade from 42% in 1995 to 69% by 2011.

Using panel data that varies across industries, customs regimes and years, we next estimate a standard export-demand model that relates trade volume to foreign income and relative prices (real exchange rates), with interaction terms for durable-nondurable goods and for processing versus other trade.[g] Consistent with the literature, we find that Chinese exports of durables have substantially higher income elasticities than those of non-durable goods exports. The income elasticity for durables is nearly four times higher than for non-durables (see Table 3, column 2). For non-durables, the elasticity on real GDP growth is 1.123; for durables it is $1.123 + 3.052 = 4.175$.

In addition to the role of GVCs in shifting the composition of trade toward higher-income durable goods, there may also be characteristics of the GVC structure itself that make exports relying heavily on imported inputs inherently more responsive to income movements, what we term *supply chain effects*. Suppose for example that the organization of GVCs allows companies to more rapidly ramp production up or down in the wake of a foreign demand fluctuation. In this case, it may be that — within a given industry — the income elasticity of demand is larger for GVC trade than for non-GVC trade.

Ma and Van Assche[46] find preliminary evidence that GVC trade was more sensitive to demand fluctuations than non-GVC trade during the Great Recession of 2008-2009. As is shown in Table 4, within HS 8-digit industries the share of processing exports in total exports declined between the first quarter of 2008 and the first quarter of 2009.

---

[g] Our model is estimated in growth rates to avoid spurious regression, and it includes lagged terms of left and right-hand side variables, a proxy for productivity growth, and industry or industry-regime fixed effects. Because the model is estimated in growth rates, the fixed effects will capture secular trade growth.

Table 2. China's Exports, by Sector, Various Years

	HS Codes	Share of total exports		Annualized growth rate	Processing exports share	
		1995	2011	1995-2011	1995	2011
DURABLES						
Machinery, electrical	84-85	18.6	44.3	22.4	8.3	64.2
Misc. Manufacturing	90-97	9.6	9.2	15.6	3.7	8.9
Metals	72-83	8.1	7.0	14.9	8.0	2.2
Transportation	86-89	2.7	5.6	21.4	3.6	7.5
Stone and glass	68-71	3.0	2.5	14.7	2.0	1.6
Total durables	68-97	42.0	68.7	19.5	55.6	84.3
NON-DURABLES						
Textiles	50-63	24.2	12.7	11.3	20.9	4.9
Non-manufacturing	01-27	13.8	5.0	8.7	3.8	2.3
Chemicals	28-38	5.7	4.8	14.6	1.7	1.5
Plastics and rubbers	39-40	2.9	3.1	16.5	4.0	3.6
Footwear and headgear	64-67	5.5	2.8	11.1	8.1	1.7
Wood and wood products	44-49	2.2	1.5	13.2	1.2	1.0
Raw hides, skins, leathers & furs	41-43	3.8	1.5	9.2	4.7	0.7
Total non-durables	01-67	68.7	31.3	11.5	44.4	15.7
Total		100.0	100.0	16.0	49.6	46.9

Source: Gangnes et al.[43]

Table 3. Estimated Income Elasticities (impact), 1995–2009

Dependent variable:	(1)	(2)	(3)
Real GDP growth	1.831***	1.123***	1.072**
Durable goods		3.052**	3.608**
Processing trade			0.096

Source: Gangnes et al.[43], page 484. The coefficients on real exchange rates, productivity, one-year time lags, cross-interaction terms and fixed effects are not shown. Significance: ***1% level, **5% level, * 10% level.

Table 4. China's Processing Exports as a Share of Total Exports (HS 8-digit level)

Variables	Number of observations	Mean	Standard error
Share of processing exports in total exports, 08Q1	4760	0.31	0.004
Share of processing exports in total exports, 09Q1	4760	0.29	0.004
Difference	9520	0.020***	0.003

Source: Ma and Van Assche[46]. Significance: *** 1% level, ** 5% level, * 10% level.

Further analysis by Gangnes et al.[43] suggests that this effect may have been particular to the Great Recession. Referring back to Table 3, the addition of a processing trade interaction term to our panel analysis permits us to test whether processing trade has a higher income elasticity over and above the difference that can be explained by industry composition. The evidence in column 3 suggests that it does not. Once we adjust for the industrial composition of trade, the results fail to show that GVC trade has a higher income elasticity than trade taking place outside GVCs.[h]

What about the impact of forward participation in GVCs? Here, attention has been given to the role of inventory dynamics. The management of inputs by GVC firms may be one driver that amplifies the volatility of GVC trade to income movements[44,45]. The logic for such a *bullwhip effect* is the following: businesses typically face errors in their sales forecasts against which they hedge by accumulating buffer stocks of inventories. When a downstream firm is confronted with an unexpected drop in demand, it may attempt to smooth production by running down its inventories and suspending new purchases of imported inputs, leading to potentially large declines in exports by upstream firms. This

---

[h] Cross interaction effects of processing on durables and real GDP, not shown here, also failed to show a positive effect.

disproportionate falloff in trade in inputs may lead to a higher sensitivity of GVC trade to foreign income shocks compared with regular trade.

A number of scholars have found evidence of bullwhip effects in international trade during the Great Recession of 2008-2009. Alessandria et al.[44] find that in the U.S. auto industry two-thirds of the decline in imports was due to firms running down their inventory stocks. Altomonte et al.[45] use French firm-level data to show that imports of intermediate goods during the crisis overreacted to the final demand shock as firms ran down their inventory stocks. Ma and Van Assche[46] find that China's processing imports across industries contracted more severely than processing exports in the first quarter of 2009 compared with a year earlier (see Fig. 6).

Further analysis by Gangnes et al.[47] suggests that this effect too may have been particular to the Great Recession. We find no evidence that foreign demand shocks are amplified as they move from processing exports to processing imports during the period 1988-2009. This may be because severe economic downturns such as the Great Recession create greater than usual demand uncertainty, which can create exceptionally large bullwhip effects in industries that do not normally see bullwhip effect behavior.

5.   GVCS and the Recent Trade Slowdown

As we noted in the introduction, after a period of apparent rise in income elasticities, the anemic pace of trade growth in recent years has led some scholars to look to GVCs as a potential source for an elasticity falloff. In the context of our discussion above, a lower measured income elasticity could emerge if there has been shift away from the high share of durable goods that has emerged in the GVC era (a compositional effect), either for structural or cyclical reasons. A lower income elasticity could also emerge if there has been a general retreat from GVC production arrangements in the post-crisis world and if, contrary to our results for China, GVC trade is inherently more sensitive to income shocks than normal trade (supply side effects).

In Gangnes et al.[48], we evaluate the recent trade slowdown in light of GVC-trade linkages, trying to tease out some insights from the limited experience to date. Looking first at composition effects, we find little evidence of a decline in the importance of durable goods trade in the recent period. Instead, we find that after accounting for a decline in low-elasticity mineral exports, the share of durable goods in world exports has remained roughly stable both in the past few years and in the period extending back to 2000. It does not appear that there has been a fundamental shift in the composition of non-mineral exports away from durables.[i]

---

[i] This indication that the durable/non-durable composition has remained relatively stable stands in contrast to the evidence from Boz et al.[49] that the composition of final demand has shifted away from import-intensive goods. According to Bussiere et al.[50], the latter include investment goods that have relatively high durable good shares.

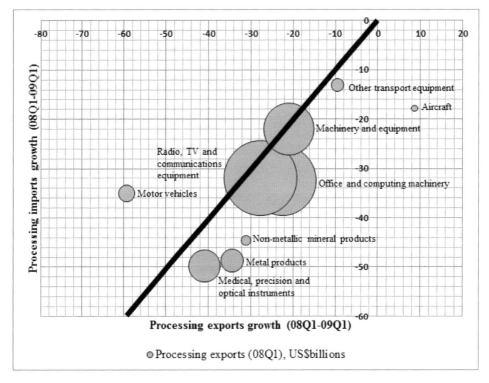

Fig. 6. Bullwhip Effect in Chinese Processing Trade, 2008Q1–2009Q1.

Source: Ma and Van Assche[46].

Might the lower apparent sensitivity of trade to income reflect a pullback from GVC production arrangements? Some have argued that such a process of "reshoring" may be occurring as firms reconsider exposures and expenses associated with far-flung value chains, or because of changing regional cost conditions[49,51]. Again, a disproportionate retreat from GVCs is not evident in the data. The share of intermediate goods in both non-mineral exports and durable goods exports has remained stable over the past decade, contrary to what one would expect if a disproportionate pullback from GVC arrangements were to blame for the drop in income elasticities.[j]

What then might explain the anemic growth of trade relative to income in the post-crisis period? The main competing hypothesis is that it is primarily cyclical, the result of temporarily weak demand for those categories of goods that have the highest import propensities, consumer durable goods and investment goods, because of the disappointing pace of economic recovery. Among other explanations are a rise in protectionism and post-crisis constraints on trade finance. (See the various contributions in Hoekman[6].) One

---

[j] It could be the case that measured elasticities have fallen because of a slowdown in the rate of adoption of new GVC production arrangements, which may have temporarily raised the growth rate of gross trade in recent decades.

particularly interesting structural explanation is the potential effect on trade of heightened uncertainty in the post-recession era, which may have negatively affected overall trade. Taglioni and Zavacka[52] show that there is a strong negative relationship between uncertainty and trade, and that this relationship is non-linear. When uncertainty is low, a marginal increase in uncertainty has little impact on trade. If it surpasses a threshold, however, it can lead to a significant decline in trade, both within and outside of GVCs. The heightened uncertainty is of course not likely to stay around forever. Each of these competing explanations, if true, would suggest that the trade slowdown is more likely temporary, rather than an indication of a permanently lower rate of trade growth.

6. Lessons for Modelers

We have focused in this chapter on the implications of GVCs for the measured responsiveness of trade to changes in income and relative prices. This may be of interest in its own right, but of course it has broader importance for macroeconomists. How trade responds to income has implications for how macro shocks in one country are transmitted abroad and how the domestic economy itself is affected by home-grown developments or policies that affect aggregate demand. Price elasticities are central to understanding exchange rate adjustment, and they play a role in assessing the impact of changes in competitiveness.

By now we know that aggregate trade elasticities can shift markedly and that the rise of global value chains may explain at least a part of the recent changes. At the same time, the staying power of the standard trade model suggests that in some form it will continue to play a central role in macroeconometric modeling.[k] Because production arrangements will continue to evolve, this presents a challenge for international economists. What's a modeler to do?

The most promising avenue is the ongoing development of new datasets that distinguish between gross trade and trade in value added. These data get at the heart of the problem posed by modern complex global production systems. For now, the data series are too short to be used in time-series econometrics, but they may still be useful as a tool for identifying trade flows where caution is particularly important. And as time series become longer, they will permit a much more satisfactory—and it is hoped more stable— identification of trade determinants.

In the meantime, there are some things that we can do. One is to match carefully the specification of trade equations to the nature of the flow being modeled. If trade is dominated by intermediate goods, then it makes little sense to try to "explain" the flow as a function of final demand and relative consumer prices. As we have shown for the case of China, a key part of the recent story has been the shift in the composition of trade toward durable goods, so attention to an appropriate level of disaggregation is important. Neither of these issues is new to trade modeling, although they are often ignored. Finally, there is

---

[k] Indeed, as Marquez[17] has noted, the simple constant-elasticity log-linear trade model often has greater explanatory power than more flexible functional forms.

some evidence that incorporating proxies for GVC development may help to achieve more stable estimates of traditional trade equations.

References

1. R. Baldwin, *The Great Trade Collapse*. (London: Centre for Economic Policy Research; 2009.)
2. C. Freund, *The Trade Response to Global Downturns: Historical* Evidence, World Bank Policy Research Working Paper 5015 (Washington, D.C., 2009).
3. C. Cheung and S. Guichard. Understanding the World Trade Collapse, OECD Working Paper No. 729 (Paris, 2009).
4. C. Escaith, N. Lindenberg, and S. Miroudot, *International Supply Chains and Trade Elasticity in Times of Global Crisis*, WTO Staff Working Paper ERSD-2010-08. (Washington, D.C., 2010).
5. J. Ceglowski, Has trade become more responsive to income? Assessing the evidence for US imports, *Open Economies Review* **25**, 225-241 (2014).
6. B. Hoekman (ed.), *The Global Trade Slowdown: A New Normal?* (VoxEU ebook, CEPR Press, 2015).
7. S. Ahmed, M. Appendino and M. Ruta, Depreciations without Exports? *Global Value Chains and the Exchange Rate Elasticity of Exports*, World Bank Trade and Competitiveness Global Practice Group working paper 7390 (August, 2015).
8. D. Leigh, W. Lian, M. Poplawski-Ribeiro and V. Tsyrennikov, *Exchange Rates and Trade Flows: Disconnected?* in *World Economic Outlook*, IMF (October 2015).
9. G. Grossman, and E. Rossi-Hansberg, Trading tasks: A simple theory of offshoring, *American Economic Review* **98**(5), 1978-97 (2008).
10. R. C. Johnson and G. Noguera, *A Portrait of Trade in Value Added over Four Decades* (Darmouth College, unpublished paper, 2014).
11. M. Goldstein and M. S. Khan, *Income and Price Effects in Foreign Trade* in *Handbook of International Economics*, eds. R.W. Jones and P. B. Kenen. Vol II, (Elsevier, 1985).
12. P. S. Armington, A theory of demand for products distinguished by place of production, *IMF Staff Papers* **16**(1), 159-178 (1969).
13. H. Houthhakker and S. P. Magee, Income and price elasticities in world trade, The *Review of Economics and Statistics* **51**(2), 111-125 (1969).
14. J. H. Adler, United States import demand during the interwar period, *The American Economic Review* **35**(3), 418-430 (1945).
15. R. Hinshaw, American prosperity and the British balance-of-payments problem, *The Review of Economics and Statistics* **27**(1), 1-9 (1945).
16. T. Chang, International comparison of demand for imports, *The Review of Economic Studies* **13**(2), 53-67 (1946).
17. J. Marquez, *Estimating Trade Elasticities, Advanced Studies in Theoretical and Applied Econometrics* (Kluwer Academic Publishers, Boston, 2002).
18. R. Hillberry and D. Hummels, *Trade Elasticity Parameters for a Computable General Equilibrium Model* in *Handbook of Computable General Equilibrium Modeling*, (Elsevier, 2013), pp. 1213-1269.
19. B. G. Hickman, *Project LINK and Multi-Country Modelling* in *A History of Macroeconometric Model-Building*, eds. R. G. Bodkin, L. R. Klein, K. Marwah (Edward Elgar, England, 1991). pp. 482–506.

20. L. R. Klein, A. Goldberger, and S. Arthur, *An Econometric Model for the United States, 1929–1952* (North-Holland, Amsterdam, 1955).

21. J. Gagnon, Adjustment costs and international trade dynamics, *Journal of International Economics* **26**, 327-44 (1989).

22. A. Garcia-Herrero and T. Koivu, *Can the Chinese Surplus be Reduced Through Exchange Rate Policy?* Bank of Finland, BOFI, Institute for Economies in Transition Discussion Paper 6 (2007).

23. G. H. Orcutt, Measurement of price elasticities in international trade, *The Review of Economics and Statistics*, 117-132 (1950).

24. D. F. Burgess, Production theory and the derived demand for imports, *Journal of International Economics* **4**, 103-117 (1974).

25. U. R. Kohli, Relative price effects and the demand for imports, *Canadian Journal of Economics* **15**(2), 202-219 (1982).

26. U. R. Kohli, *Technology, Duality, and Foreign Trade* (University of Michigan Press, Ann Arbor, 1991).

27. N. Patel, Z. Wang, and S.-J. Wei, *Global Value Chains and Effective Exchange Rates at the Country-Sector Level*, National Bureau of Economic Research Working Paper No. w20236 (2014).

28. R. C. Feenstra, Integration of trade and disintegration of production in the global economy, *The Journal of Economic Perspectives* **12**(4), 31-50 (1998).

29. R. C. Johnson and G. Noguera, Accounting for intermediates: Production sharing and trade in value added, *Journal of International Economics* **86**(2), 224-236 (2012).

30. K. De Backer and S. Miroudot, *Mapping Global Value Chains*, ECB Working Paper No. 1677 (Frankfurt am Main, 2014).

31. D. Hummels, J. Ishii and K. M. Yi, The nature and growth of vertical specialization in world trade, *Journal of International Economics* **54**(1), 75-96 (2001).

32. A. Ma and A. Van Assche, Is East Asia's economic fate chained to the West? *Transnational Corporations Review* **5**(3), 1-17 (2013).

33. S. W. Arndt and A. Huemer, Trade, production networks and the exchange rate, The *Journal of Economic Asymmetries* **4**(1), 11-39 (2007).

34. R. Bems, R. C. Johnson and K. M. Yi, The great trade collapse, *Annual Review of Economics* **5**(1), 375-400 (2013).

35. T. Bayoumi, M. Saito and J. Turunen. *Measuring Competitiveness: Trade in Goods or Tasks?* IMF Working Paper WP/13/100 (2013).

36. R. Bems and R. C. Johnson, *Demand for Value Added and Value-Added Exchange Rates*, IMF Working Paper WP/15/199 (2015).

37. P. Athukorala and F. Khan, Global production sharing and the measurement of price elasticity in international trade, *Economics Letters* **139**, 27-30 (2016).

38. C. Cheung and S. Guichard, *Understanding the World Trade Collapse*, OECD Working Paper No. 729 (Paris, 2009).

39. J. Aziz and C. Li, China's changing trade elasticities, *China & World Economy* **16**, 1-2 (2008).

40. R. Bems, R. C. Johnson and K.-M. Yi, Demand spillovers and the collapse of trade in the global recession, *IMF Economic Review* **58**(2), 295-326 (2010).

41. C. Engel and J. Wang, International trade in durable goods: Understanding volatility, cyclicality and elasticities, *Journal of International Economics* **83**(1), 37-52 (2011).

42. J. Eaton, S. Kortum, B. Neiman, and J. Romalis, *Trade and the Global Recession*, NBER Working Paper No. 16666 (National Bureau of Economic Research, Cambridge MA, 2011).

43. B. Gangnes, A. Ma and A. Van Assche, Global value chains and trade elasticities, *Economics Letters* **124**(3), 482-486 (2014).

44. G. Alessandria, J. Kaboski and V. Midrigan, The great trade collapse of 2008-2009: An inventory adjustment? *IMF Economic Review* **58**, 254-294 (2010).

45. C. Altomonte, F. Di Mauro, G. I. Ottaviano, A. Rungi and V. Vicard, *Global Value Chains during the Great Trade Collapse: A Bullwhip Effect?* ECB Working Paper No. 1412 (Frankfurt am Main, 2012).

46. A. Ma and A. Van Assche, *Global Production Networks in the Post-Crisis Era Chapter 21 in Managing Openness: Trade and Outward-Oriented Growth after the Crisis*, eds. M. Haddad and B. Shepherd (World Bank, Washington, D.C., 2011), pp. 275-286.

47. B. Gangnes, A. Ma and A. Van Assche, *Global Value Chains and the Transmission of Business Cycle Shocks*, Asian Development Bank Economics Working Paper Series No. 29, June (2012).

48. B. Gangnes, A. Ma, and A. Van Assche, *Global Value Chains and the Trade-Income Relationship: Implications for the Recent Trade Slowdown* in *The Global Trade Slowdown: A New Normal?* ed. B. Hoekman, VoxEU ebook, (CEPR Press, 2015).

49. E. Boz, M. Bussière and C. Marsilli, *Recent Slowdown in Global Trade: Cyclical or Structural?* VoxEU.org 12, November (2014).

50. M. Bussière, G. Callegari, F. Ghironi, G. Sestieri and N. Yamano, Estimating trade elasticities: Demand composition and the trade collapse of 2008-2009, *American Economic Journal: Macroeconomics* **5**(3), 118-151 (2013).

51. Canadian Trade Commissioner, *Is Global Value Chain-Driven Trade on the Wane?* December, (2014).

52. D. Taglioni and V. Zavacka, *Innocent Bystanders: How Foreign Uncertainty Shocks Harm Exporters*, ECB Working Paper No. 1530, (Frankfurt am Main, 2013).

IV.   New Dimensions

Is technological progress behind growing income inequality?

Zsolt Darvas[a]

Department of Mathematical Economics and Economic Analysis
Bruegel and Corvinus University of Budapest
Rue de la Charité 33, B-1210 Brussels, Belgium
E-mail: zsolt.darvas@uni-corvinus.hu

Income inequality might be boosted by skill-biased technical change, which shifts production to technology that favours skilled over unskilled workers and thereby might increase the wages of skilled relative to unskilled workers. Robotisation and globalisation might also increase income inequality, due to the reduced number of jobs and reduced wages of certain less skilled workers. However, we cast doubt on the hypothesis that technology-driven developments were a major factor behind rising inequality in the United States and some other advanced countries. Despite many similarities in labour market developments, the skill premium and income inequality evolved differently in the United States and the European Union. We show that the United States was an outlier to the cross-country relationship between the unemployment rate of tertiary-educated workers and their pay rises, and also an outlier to the relationship between the share of tertiary-educated workers and their wages relative to lower-educated peers. Therefore, even though our analysis suggests that technological change tends to favour those with greater skills, it is hard to see how this has contributed to rising income inequality. Other factors, such as redistribution, social protection and education policies or the regulation of certain professions may be more relevant.

1. Introduction

Income inequality has increased in a number of developed countries. One possible explanation for widening inequalities is the skill-biased technological progress, which may reward skilled workers more in comparison with unskilled workers. Those with higher skills, such as IT developers, are able to generate a great deal more output thanks to new technologies, and so they receive the proportionate remuneration. In contrast, those with lower skills, such as waiters, cannot generate much more value using new technologies and therefore do not receive extra compensation. Thereby, technological development might increase income inequality.

In addition, robots are replacing certain types of human labor altogether. Some jobs are more easily robotized than others, but certain low-skilled or routine tasks are the most easily automated. These workers risk finding themselves out of employment, which might further increase income inequality.

Globalization may amplify the impacts of technological change on income inequality. The immigration of low-skilled workers, a widespread phenomenon in many developed countries, may dampen the wages of local low-skilled workers by increasing the labor

[a] The MasterCard Center for Inclusive Growth supported most of the research underlying this chapter, which was summarised in Darvas and Wolff[1]. I thank Guntram B. Wolff for a great research cooperation and Uuriintuya Batsaikhan, Pia Hüttl and Jaume Martí Romero for excellent research assistance.

supply. Furthermore, offshoring production to low-wage emerging countries, as well imports of goods from these emerging economies, may supplant local jobs and further dampen the wages of local low-skilled workers and thereby boost income inequality.

In this chapter we assess whether technological progress can explain growing income inequality in the United States and some other advanced countries. We first highlight that income inequality evolved differently in the United States and the European Union, despite similarities in labor market developments. Next, we assess the relevance of skill-biased technological change for wage developments in a number of advanced countries. We then briefly summarize the literature on the risk of robotization of jobs and draw policy conclusions. The final section summarizes our key findings.

2.   Divergent Income Inequality Developments in the US and Europe

European countries are different from most countries in terms of how income inequality has developed. Unfortunately, income inequality indicators are not available from official statistical sources for the EU as a whole[b]. Therefore, Darvas[2] estimated the EU the Gini coefficient of income inequality from 1989 to 2015 (Box 1).

The EU-wide distribution of income using country-specific data can be estimated the same way as the global distribution of income is estimated from country-specific data. A number of academic works have estimated the global distribution of income. Seminal works include Bourguignon and Morrisson[3], Bhalla[4], Milanovic[5], and Sala-i-Martin[6], which works use quantile data. In contrast, Chotikapanich, Valenzuela and Rao[7] assume that within-country distributions follow the log-normal distribution (with different parameters in different countries) and use only the country-specific Gini coefficient and mean income to estimate the parameters of this distribution. Darvas[2] analysed the accuracy of various methods in the particular cases of four countries: The United States, Australia, Canada and Turkey. The national statistical offices of all four countries make both territorial (ie state-level) and country-wide income distribution data available. Thus, using data from the 50 US states and Washington DC, the 8 Australian states and territories, 10 Canadian provinces and 12 Turkish regions, one can calculate exactly how accurate the various methods are in estimating the country-wide Gini coefficient. One can also assess the accuracy of various methods using quantile data from Eurostat for European countries. Darvas[2] finds that many methods work quite well if the right level of detail is used about quantile income shares. In the end, however, he finds that methods based on two-parameter distributions are among the most accurate. Moreover, the method based on two-parameter distributions is simpler, easier to implement and relies on a more internationally-comparable dataset of national income distributions than other approaches used in the literature to calculate the global distribution of income. Therefore, Darvas[2] uses the method based on two-parameter distributions to estimate the combined distribution of income of the 28 countries which are currently members of the European Union, for the period 1989-2015.

Box 1. Estimating EU-Wide Income Inequality Indicators

---

[b] While Eurostat, the European Union's statistical office, publishes Gini coefficients for 28 EU members and for various groups of countries within the EU, these Gini coefficients are population-weighted averages of country-specific Gini coefficients, which are not the Gini coefficients that correspond to the combined income distribution of the countries. See Darvas[2] for more details.

Figure 1 shows a marked difference between the United States and the European Union in inequality over time. In the US, income inequality declined in the 1960s and remained broadly unchanged in the 1970s. Since then, however, there has been a steady increase in income inequality, both before redistribution (so-called 'market' inequality) and after taxes and transfers ('net' inequality).

There was a sharp increase in EU-wide inequality from 1989-93, reflecting a large increase in inequality among the first 15 EU member states and among the 13 countries that joined the EU from 2004 onward. The central and eastern European countries in the latter group suffered from massive output declines because of their transitions from socialist to market-based economies during this time, which widened the income gap between their citizens and those of western European countries, pushing up aggregate EU-wide income inequality.

Nevertheless, the most notable feature of Fig. 1 is the steady and remarkable decline in net income inequality in the 28 current EU countries from 1995 to 2008. This development differentiates the EU not just from the US, but also from most other countries.

The decline in EU-wide net income inequality stopped in 2008 and income inequality has remained broadly stable since then. Therefore, the recent global and European financial and economic crises might have played a role in halting the 15-year long trend of declining net income inequality in the EU.

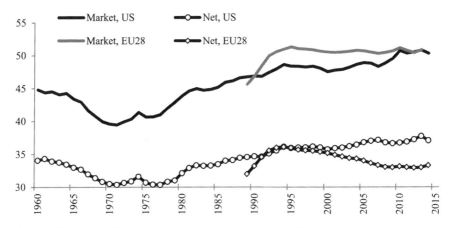

Fig. 1. Gini Coefficient of Market (before taxes and transfers) and Net (after taxes and transfers) Income Inequality: Comparing the EU as a Whole with the US, 1960–2014.

Note: A Gini index of zero represents perfect equality (i.e. incomes are perfectly evenly distributed) and a Gini index of 100 indicates perfect inequality (all incomes are owned by one person).

Source: US data: The Standardized World Income Inequality Database (SWIID) from Solt[8]; EU28 data: Darvas[2], which is based on the individual country data from Solt[8]; thereby the US and EU28 data reported in this figure are comparable.

Another notable development to be noted from Fig. 1 relates to the differences between market and net measures of income inequality. In the EU, market inequality jumped to a Gini coefficient level of about 51 in the early 1990s and has remained broadly stable since then. The EU's social redistribution systems played a key role in achieving the declining trend of net income inequality between 1995 and 2008. In the US, both market and net income inequality rose in the past four decades. Social redistribution in the US therefore has not played such an important role in containing the rise in net inequality. Interestingly, market inequality in the US increased to practically the same level as the EU in 2010-2014, yet net inequality is much lower in the EU, underlining the importance of redistribution.

Unfortunately, missing data does not allow calculation of the EU28-wide Gini index before 1989. In order to show inequality over an even longer term for some EU countries, Fig. 2 reports Gini coefficients for the five largest EU countries compared to Brazil, China, Japan and the US. While there were some fluctuations, the Gini coefficient tended to be lower in France and Germany than in other countries. Italy, Spain and the UK are less equal than France and Germany, yet they are much more equal than the Brazil, China and the US.

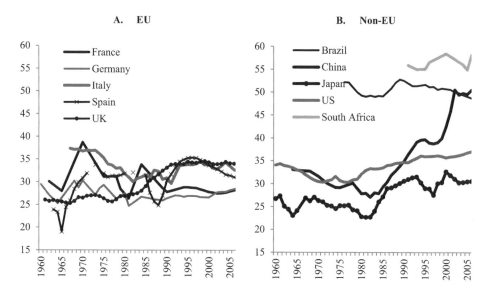

Fig. 2. Gini Coefficient of Net Income Inequality (after taxes and transfers), Selected Countries, 1960–2014.

Note: A Gini index of zero represents perfect equality (i.e. incomes are perfectly evenly distributed) and a Gini index of 100 indicates perfect inequality (all incomes are owned by one person).
Source: The Standardized World Income Inequality Database (SWIID) of Solt[8].

While the EU as a whole, and individual EU countries, tend to be characterized by lower income inequality than the US and most emerging/developing countries, there is are significant differences between EU countries, as Figure 3 shows for the five largest EU countries. Fig. 3 maps the inequality levels of EU countries between 2010-2014. Mediterranean countries, Baltic countries and the United Kingdom exhibit relatively high Gini coefficients, while Nordic countries and 'core' continental EU countries are characterized by lower income inequality levels.

⬤	< 26
⬤	26—28
⬤	28—31
⬤	31—33
⬤	33—36

Fig. 3. Gini Coefficient of Net Disposable Income in the EU, Average of 2000–2014.

Note: Gini coefficient is after taxes and social transfers; darker shaded countries show higher inequality.
Source: The Standardized World Income Inequality Database (SWIID) of Solt[8].

3.   Long-Term Structural Changes to Labor Markets: The EU and US Are Similar

Despite differing developments in net income inequality, there is a striking similarity between the EU and the US in terms of a major long-term change in the labor market: the decline in jobs with low education requirements and the increase in jobs with high education requirements. This development has major implications for social mobility.

While the categorization of jobs according to education requirements differs somewhat between the EU and the US, Fig. 4 and Fig. 5 show notable similarity.

The number of jobs for people with higher education has increased significantly and steadily in both the EU and the US, starting at least after 1992 (since when there is available EU data). The number of such jobs has practically doubled in two decades. It is really noteworthy that during the global and European financial and economic crises of the past few years, employment of highly-educated workers continued to increase in the EU, even in countries suffering from large increases in unemployment, such as Cyprus, Italy, Ireland, Lithuania, Portugal and Spain. In three other hard-hit countries, Estonia, Latvia and Greece, the employment of the highly educated remained broadly stable. In the US, there was just a slight decline in the number of jobs requiring high-level educational attainment in 2009, since the increasing trend has resumed[c].

Jobs requiring medium-level qualifications also increased significantly after 1992 in both the EU and the US, but the growth of such jobs stopped in the EU in 2008 and after some decline, only a slow job growth has resumed in the US.

On the other hand, the number of jobs in the EU for people with lower qualification levels declined between 1992 and 2007[d] and dropped massively during the crisis. In the US, the number of such jobs was more or less stable from 1993 to 2007, after which there was a major decline.

Therefore, the recent global and European crises have amplified the difference between the availability of jobs requiring high and low levels of education, even though the divergence started at least 25 years ago.

Using data from the United States, Bitler and Hoynes[9] report that lower income earners experience much greater income variability than higher earners. Furthermore, this disproportionate effect of recessions on low earners was greater in the great recession of 2008-2009 compared to the previous 1980s recession. The vulnerability of low-skilled workers likely applies in the EU too.

The long-term decline in the number of jobs for low-educated workers, and the consequent vulnerability of those workers, underline the importance of upward social mobility. More and more children and young people need to attain higher levels of education, including those who were born to parents with low educational achievements.

Developments in China have been different, reflecting its different level of economic and social development (Fig. 6). In 1997, almost 100 million jobs were filled by illiterate people, declining to close to zero by 2014. The number of jobs for workers with only primary education also declined considerably from 246 million to 143 million between 1997 and 2014, possibly related to urbanization and the decline in agricultural jobs. On the

---

[c]An important aspect of the steady increase in jobs with tertiary-educated workers is under-employment: that is working in jobs that typically do not require a university degree. By analysing under-employment in the United States following the Great Recession, Abel and Deitz[10] conclude that recent under-employed college graduates were not forced into low-skilled service jobs, but into jobs that appeared to be more oriented toward knowledge and skills when compared to the distribution of jobs held by young workers without a college degree. Moreover, they also find that under-employment is a temporary phase for many young graduates when they enter the labour market, because it often takes time for new graduates to find jobs suited to their education level.

[d] There were a few exceptions to this trend, like in Spain and Ireland, where the pre-crisis housing bubbles were associated with the creation of low-skilled jobs in the construction sector. However, the excess creation of such jobs proved to be unsustainable.

other hand, only 20 million jobs, less than 3 percent of total jobs, were occupied by people with college and higher degrees in 1997. The number of such jobs increased tremendously

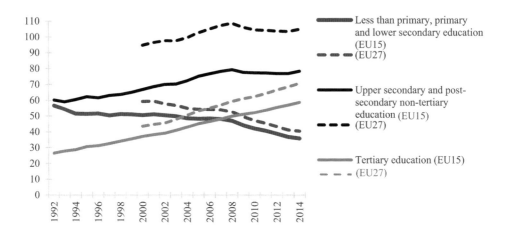

Fig. 4. Employment by Educational Attainment in the EU, 1992–2014 (millions of jobs)

Note: The solid line shows the aggregate of EU15 countries (EU members before 2004), which is available from 1992. The same-colour dashed line indicates the aggregate for 27 EU member states, which is available from 2000.

Source: Eurostat 'Employment by sex, occupation and educational attainment level (1 000) [lfsa_egised]' dataset.

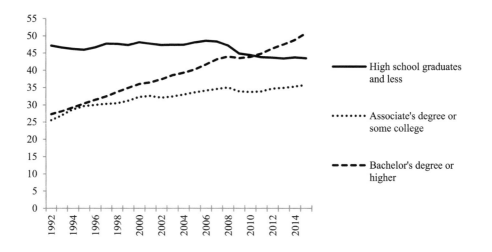

Fig. 5. Employment by Educational Attainment in the US, 1992–2015 (millions of jobs).

Note: Annual averages for employed persons 25 years and over.
Source: US Census Bureau. http://data.bls.gov/pdq/SurveyOutputServlet.

to 112 million by 2014, reaching a share of 15 percent of all jobs. Among workers with college and higher education, the number of university graduates increased from 10 million in 2001 to 46 million in 2014. The number of jobs requiring junior and senior school qualifications also went up. It has to be noted, moreover, that the number of illiterate and semi-literate workers declined sharply from 90 million in 1997 to 14 million in 2014.

On the other hand, it is notable that the total number of jobs in China increased only by 11 percent from 1997 to 2014, which corresponds to 0.6 percent per year job creation, while average GDP growth during the same period was 9.5 percent.

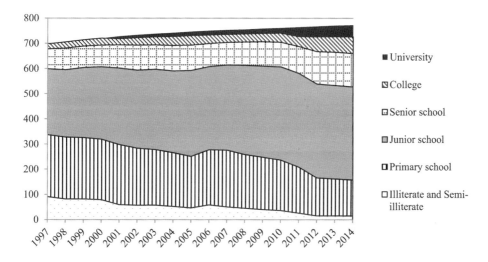

Fig. 6. Employment by Educational Attainment in China, 1997–2014 (millions of jobs).

Note: Data for employment of university graduates and above only available from 2001 onwards. China has 9 years of publicly funded compulsory education, which consists of 6 years of primary school and 3 years of junior school. After 9 years of primary and junior school, there is 3 years of senior school. After senior school graduation (equivalent to US high school education and EU upper-secondary education) people enter either college (equivalent to US and EU specialized and vocational education) or university (equivalent to US bachelor's degree or higher and EU tertiary education).
Source: National Bureau of Statistics of China.

4. Technological Change and the Skill Premium

Recent economic research studying the impact of technology on the labor market emphasized the role played by skill-biased technical change, the idea that technical changes shifts production to technology that favors skilled over unskilled workers (see Katz and Autor[11], and Violante[12], for surveys of the literature). By increasing the productivity of skilled workers, and thereby the demand for such workers, skill-biased technical change may explain rising wage inequality.

The skill premium and/or returns from schooling refer to the gain that a worker gets by investing in higher education. It is calculated as the ratio of wages of the high-skilled workers to the wages of low-skilled workers. Autor (2014) notes the dramatic rise in the skill premium in the US and argues that this contributes substantially to the rise in income inequality. Figure 7 shows that the median weekly earnings of high-skilled workers continually increased during the 1980s and 1990s, whereas the weekly earnings of those with primary and high school education experienced a decline. Since about 2000, however, the increase in the skill premium has stopped.

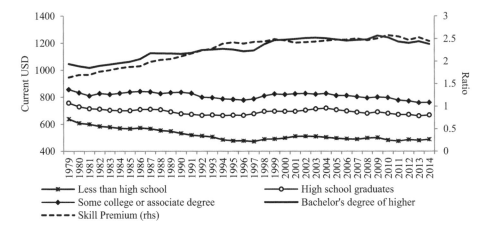

Fig. 7. Median Weekly Earnings by Education (left hand scale) and the Skill Premium (right hand scale) in the US, 1979–2013.

Note: The sample is not longitudinal (i.e. not following the same people through time) and thereby compositional changes (e.g. the arrival of new workers with a lower wage) influence the median value. In Figure 9 we show the average real wage growth according to skill level, which is not a longitudinal sample either. Figure 9 suggests that there was some real wage increase even for low-skilled workers (though such an average statistic is also influenced by compositional changes). Still, Figure 9 confirms that the skill premium has increased in the United States.
Source: US Bureau of Labor Statistics.

Autor[13] attributes the sharp increase in the skill premium in the US to:

• The decline in non-college employment in production, administrative and clerical work;
• The sharp rise in low-skilled labour supply and competition from the developing world;
• The decline in the bargaining power of labour unions and reductions in top marginal tax rates.

However, the question remains of whether, in such analyses, education can be used interchangeably with skills, i.e. if we can credibly state that education translates into skill and thus has an impact on wages. The OECD Program for International Assessment of Adult Competences (PIAAC) provides an internationally compatible database of adult cognitive skills and skills needed in the workplace, namely literacy, numeracy and problem-solving. The results of the survey indicate that cognitive skills differ greatly depending on educational attainment. Figure 8 compares the mean numeracy score of adults with lower than high school education to the scores of those who have obtained tertiary education. Workers with tertiary education have higher numeracy scores in all countries, particularly in the US where the mean score difference is greatest at 82 points between those with less than high school education and those with college education. France ranks second with a 78 point gap.

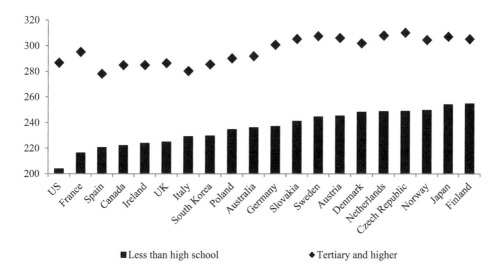

Fig. 8. Mean Score on the Numeracy Test by Educational Attainment, 2013.

Source: OECD PIAAC survey, 2013.

However, over time, the skill premium has not increased everywhere. As Figure 9 shows, in the United States, the wages of high-skilled workers increased much more than the wages of low-skilled workers from 1995 to 2009. While such a development can also be observed in China and to a much lesser extent in Germany, exactly the opposite has happened in France, Italy, Spain, the United Kingdom, Sweden and Japan, where the wages of high-skilled workers declined relative to the wages of the low-skilled, while in Korea wages increased broadly at the same rate in all three skill categories. Consequently, there are major differences in the level of skill premium. While it is around 2.5 in the US and China, the EU average skill premium is around 1.6, albeit with significant differences between EU countries (Fig. 10). Turkey and Brazil have the highest skill premiums among the countries considered.

One possible reason for the differences in the way skill premiums have developed is the supply of higher-educated workers. The supply of such people in a given year is composed of those who obtained their degrees earlier, those who obtained their degrees in the current year, the net immigration of people with university degrees, minus those who left the labor force because of retirement or any other reason. It is not easy to obtain data for each of these components, but we report two relevant indicators: the annual number of

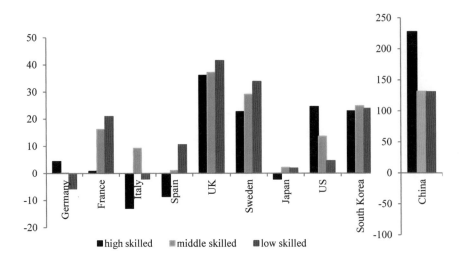

Fig. 9. Percent Change in Wage per Hour Worked from 1995–2009 (deflated by the consumer price index).

Note: Definition of skills follows 1997 ISCED level, where LOW encompasses primary education or first stage of basic education and lower secondary or second stage of basic education; MEDIUM is (Upper) secondary education and post-secondary non-tertiary education; HIGH is first stage of tertiary education and second stage of tertiary education.
Source: World input output database, July 2014 release.

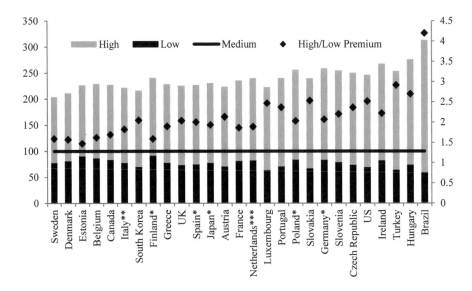

Fig. 10. Relative Earnings of Workers by Educational Attainment (earnings of medium-educated workers = 100), 2013.

Note: Adults with income from employment, medium education refers to upper secondary education and equals 100. (*) Data for 2012. (**) Data for 2011. (***) Data for 2010.
Source: OECD Education at a glance, 2015.

new graduates (representing the annual 'home production' of workers with university degrees) and the unemployment rate among people with tertiary education (which indicates the tensions in the labor market).

The number of new graduates has increased steadily in the EU and in the US (Fig. 11). Interestingly, the total percent increase from 1998 to 2014 was very similar: 85 percent in the US and 90 percent in the EU. In our view, this slight difference in the number of new graduates cannot explain the major differences in the EU and US skill premium trends. On the other hand, there was a huge increase of new graduates in China, where the skill premium increased dramatically.

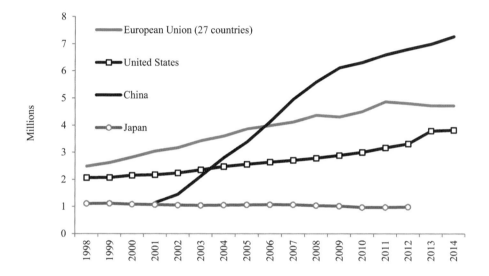

Fig. 11. Number of New Tertiary Education Graduates per Year, Millions, 1998–2014.

Note: Tertiary education is classified as ISCED 5 and above/bachelor's degree and above. EU27 for 1998-2012, EU28 for 2013-2014.
Source: Eurostat, OECD and Chinese Ministry of Education.

Moreover, the unemployment rate among people with tertiary education should be a useful indicator, reflecting the tightness of the labor market. Figure 12 shows that there is a statistically significant association between the unemployment rate among people with tertiary education and the change in the skill premium: a lower unemployment rate is associated with a higher increase in the skill premium, as expected. But the increase in the skill premium in the United States was much faster than the regression relationship would have implied. Figure 12 therefore suggests that the supply-demand conditions were not the key determinants of the major skill premium increase in the United States, and that there were other reasons.

Therefore, relative to the EU and China, the data does not support the claim that a reduced supply of university graduates relative to demand has been one of the main reasons for the increased skill premium in the United States.

In terms of the wage skill premium, Hanushek et al[14] find that on average one standard deviation increase in numeracy score is associated with an 18 percent increase in wages. In Sweden, the Czech Republic and Norway the returns range from 13-15 percent, while in the US, Ireland and Germany the wage returns to skill average 24-28 percent, thus showing significant differences between countries.

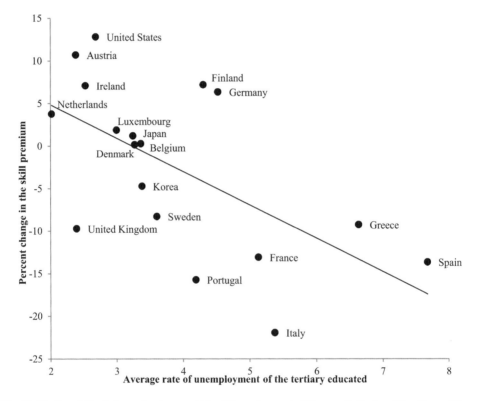

Fig. 12. The Correlation between the Average Rate of Unemployment of Those with Tertiary Education and the Change in the Skill Premium, 1998–2009.

Source: Eurostat, OECD. Skill premium is calculated from World Input-Output database.

Felgueroso et al[15] document the reasons for the falling wage skill premium in Spain in two periods: from the mid-1980s and from the mid-1990s to 2010. The authors conclude that despite the significant increases in the number of graduates with tertiary education, Spain recorded a falling wage skill premium starting from the beginning of 1990s. Over-education and a continuous mismatch between education and occupation explain the falling returns on education among high skilled workers. Structural changes to the Spanish labor market with a marked increase in temporary employment also contributed to the falling premium. Temporary contracts have affected workers of all ages and educational levels, in particular the middle skilled, which affects their employment and wages in later stages of their careers.

We note that the United States is also an outlier in terms of the relationship between the share of tertiary-educated workers and the tertiary education premium: in OECD countries where the share of tertiary-educated workers is high, the tertiary education premium tends to be relatively low (Fig. 13). But the United States and Ireland are exceptions to this trend and the relatively high share of tertiary-educated workers is associated with a relatively high tertiary education premium. On the other hand, Italy, where income inequality is relatively high, is an outlier on the other side: the very low share of tertiary-educated workers is associated with a rather low tertiary education premium.

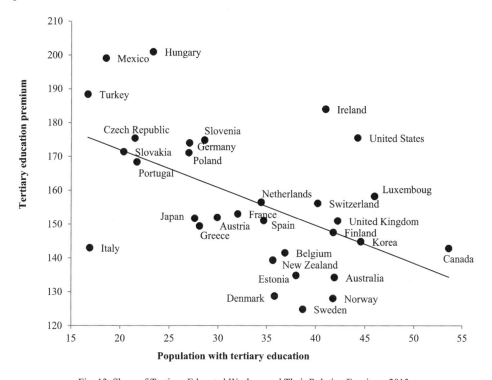

Fig. 13. Share of Tertiary-Educated Workers and Their Relative Earnings, 2013.

Note: Workers with medium education= 100. Data for Netherlands: 2010; France and Italy: 2011; Australia, Canada, Finland, Japan, Poland, Spain: 2012.
Source: OECD, Education at a glance 2015.

Finally, we report data on the composition of the top 1 percent of income earners. If technological development were the key driver of the skill premium, then we would expect many high-tech sector workers to be in the top 1 percent. This is not really the case for the

US: many of the top earners are lawyers, doctors and financial service employees, and very rarely ICT sector workers (Fig. 14). Rothwell[16] argues that these high-earning sectors enjoy high levels of protection in the US and thereby enjoy unjustified rents relative to their skills.

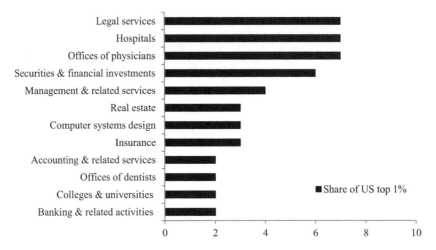

Fig. 14. Industries with the Most Top 1% Earners in the United States.

Source: Rothwell (2016).

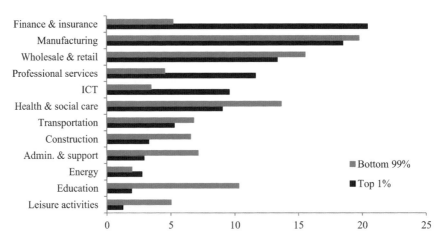

Fig. 15. Industries with the Most Top 1% Earners in the European Union.

Note: Employees in the public administration are not available for all countries and are therefore removed from the sample for cross-country comparison. Germany is excluded from the average since its industry classification is different.
Source: Denk[17].

Europe is different from the US in terms of the composition of the top 1 percent. As calculated by Denk[17], after finance and insurance, manufacturing is the second industry with about 18 percent of the top 1 percent of earners, and ICT also ranks prominently. In Germany, manufacturing sector employees account for 34 percent of the top 1 percent of earners. Therefore, in Europe a larger share of technology-intensive sector workers is privileged to be in the top 1 percent, compared to the US.

To sum up, our comparison of countries suggests that even though technological change tends to favor those with greater skills, it is hard to see in the data how it has contributed to rising skill premia and consequent income inequalities. Most likely, other factors were more important, such as redistribution and education policies or regulation of certain professions. This result is in line with the findings of Anderson and Maibom[18], who argue that political changes can explain the movements of the United States toward higher efficiency and lower equity during recent decades.

5. Technological Change and the Risk of 'Robotization'

Autor, Levy and Murnane[19] argue that technology can replace human labor in routine tasks, whether manual or cognitive, but (as yet) cannot replace human labor in non-routine tasks. Combining these two strands, Goos and Manning[20] argue for the UK that the impact of technology leads to rising relative demand in well-paid skilled jobs, which typically require non-routine cognitive skills, and rising relative demand in low-paid least-skilled jobs, that typically require non-routine manual skills. At the same time, demand for 'middling' jobs, that have typically required routine manual and cognitive skills, will fall. The authors call this process 'job polarization'.

Acemoglu and Autor[21] found similar results for the US and concluded that technological change increased the demand for skilled labor. Technology was incorporated into the subset of core job tasks previously performed by middle-skill workers, causing substantial change. When differentiating employment growth by occupation, one can see similar developments also in Europe (Fig. 16). The number of high-education jobs such as managers, engineers and health professionals, is growing, while the number of middle-education jobs (clerks, machine operators, assemblers) is declining. By contrast, the number of low-education service occupations, such as shop workers, which are non-standard and difficult to replace by automatization, is growing.

Looking ahead, a second wave of robotization is on its way, in which intelligent robots will more and more be capable to carrying out high skill level jobs. In recent years, a series of studies has revived the debate about robotization taking over jobs. Frey and Osborn[22] in particular sparked a debate by claiming that 47 percent of US jobs are at risk of being automated. Bowles[23] redid these calculations for the European labor market, and found that on average, 54 percent of EU jobs are at risk of computerization.

By contrast, Arntz et al[24] argue that one of the major limitations of Frey and Osborn is that they view occupations rather than tasks as being threatened by automation. They therefore focus on the task-content of jobs, and find that in the US only 9 percent of jobs (as opposed to 47 percent) are potentially automatable. Figure 17 shows their results by country. Breaking down the risk according to educational attainment (Fig. 18), one can see that low-educated workers will likely bear the brunt of technological change related adjustment costs.

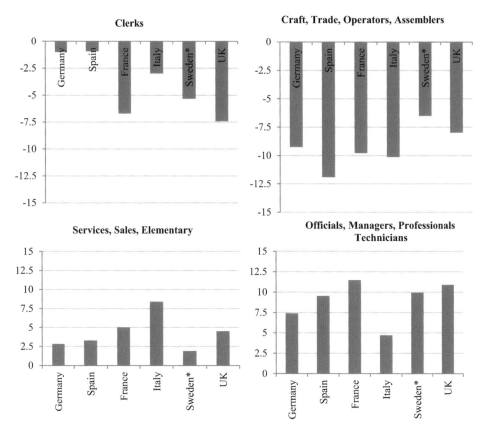

Fig. 16. Employment Growth, 1995–2015, by Occupation.

Note: Top left panel: Clerks include office clerks (e.g. secretaries and keyboard-operating clerks, library, mail and related clerks, etc.) and customer services clerks (e.g. cashiers, tellers, client information clerks). Top right panel: Craft and related trades workers include extraction, building trades, metal, machinery, precision, handicraft, craft printing, food processing, wood treaters textile and related trades workers, while operators and assemblers include stationary-plant operators, machine operators and assemblers, drivers and mobile plant operators. Bottom left panel: Professions included are service workers and shop and market sales workers, agriculture, fishery and related laborers, and laborers in mining, construction, manufacturing and transport. Bottom-right panel: Professions include legislators, senior officials, managers and various professionals and technicians (including physical, mathematical, engineering science, life science, health, teaching, business, finance, legal, social science and other professionals, police inspectors and detectives). See the complete classification here: http://ec.europa.eu/eurostat/documents/1012329/6070763/ISCO88.pdf/192120ae-49cb-4f24-bfbc-06f054471e3b.

Source: Eurostat. *data for Sweden started only in 1997.

What these estimates imply for policy is clear: if we believe that technology will start to be able to cope with non-routine cognitive tasks then we must equip the next generation of workers with skills that benefit from technology rather than being threatened by it. Such skills are likely to emphasize social and creative intelligence, which suggests that appropriate shifts in education policy are surely required in order to meet the challenge of automation.

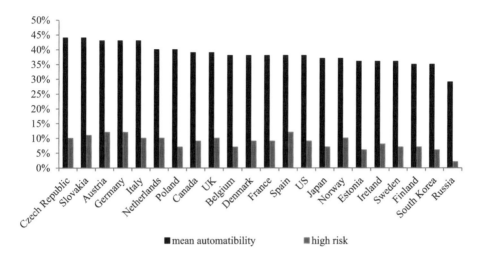

Fig. 17. Potential for Automation of Jobs, OECD Countries.

Source: Arntz et al (2016) based on the Survey of Adult Skills.

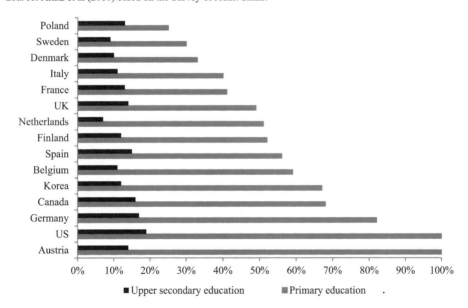

Fig. 18. Share of People with at Risk of Automation of Their Jobs by Educational Level and Country.

Source: Arntz et al (2016) based on the Survey of Adult Skills.

6.   Summary

In this chapter we cast doubt on the hypothesis that technology-driven developments were a major factor behind rising inequality in the United States and some other advanced countries. We find that both the European Union and the United States are characterized by strikingly similar labor market developments: there has been a decline in the number of jobs for workers with low levels of educational attainment over the past 25 years, while there has been a tremendous increase in jobs for workers with tertiary education. Both in the US and the EU, only jobs for tertiary educated workers expanded after the global financial and economic crisis erupted in 2008, even in several countries that were hit hard by crisis. While underemployment, when a worker takes a job for which they are over-qualified, is a prevailing phenomenon, it tends to be temporary.

If a greater share of jobs is only open to tertiary-educated workers, it could contribute to increasing inequality, if tertiary-educated workers earn ever more, relative to lower educated colleagues. Data shows that this has been the case in the United States and China, and to a much more limited extent in Germany. However, exactly the opposite has happened in many other countries during the past two decades, including the United Kingdom, Italy, Spain, France, Sweden and Japan. In these countries the skill premium has actually fallen.

The divergent wage developments for tertiary-educated workers cannot be explained by the supply of workers. First, we find that the number of new graduates increased at the same rate at both sides of the Atlantic, which is a good indicator of supply, even though labor migration and demographic developments also influence labor supply. Second, a negative statistical relationship can be established between the unemployment rate of tertiary-educated workers and their pay rises, but the United States is an outlier: the wage growth of tertiary-educated workers was faster than what their unemployment rate would have implied. Third, we also establish a negative statistical relationship between the share of tertiary-educated workers and their wages relative to lower-educated peers, but the United States is again an outlier: its relatively high share of tertiary-educated workers is associated with a relatively high skill premium.

These developments highlight that something special was going on in the United States, which contributed to the rising rate of compensation of tertiary-educated workers, which in turn boosted income inequality. Technological progress cannot really be the main explanation, since technology also impacts Europe, but most European economies saw a relative wage decline of tertiary-educated workers. Moreover, we also show that income inequality has actually declined in the union of the current 28 EU members from 1994-2008, after which it remained relatively stable.

Instead, the explanation for the rising skill premium in the United States may be related to public policies and the protection of certain occupations. In the United States, a rather small fraction of the top one percent of earners comes from high-tech industries such as ICT and manufacturing. The bulk of top earners are lawyers, doctors, dentists and financial sector professionals. Some of these industries enjoy a relatively high level of protection, while the impact of technological change on their productivity may still be comparatively modest. Europe tells a different story. In many European countries, a much higher share of the top one percent of earners than in the United States is in the manufacturing sector.

Public policies, such as redistribution, education and labor market policies, may also play a role. Redistribution from the rich to the poor is at a much lower level in the United States than in Europe. Certainly, the national redistribution system could be made more effective in a number of European countries, but overall redistribution and social protection is much stronger in the EU.

Therefore, even though our analysis suggests that technological change tends to favor those with greater skills, it is hard to see how this has contributed to rising inequality. Other factors such as redistribution and education policies or the regulation of certain professions may be more relevant.

In any case, a new machine age is in the making, and ever more jobs will be replaced by automation. If technology is able to begin dealing with non-routine cognitive tasks, then the next generation of workers must be equipped with skills that benefit from technology rather than being threatened by it. Such skills are likely to emphasize social and creative intelligence. Appropriate shifts in education policy are therefore surely required in order to meet the challenge of technological development.

References

1. Z. Darvas, and G. B. Wolff, *An Anatomy of Inclusive Growth in Europe*, Bruegel Blueprint 26, (2016) http://bruegel.org/2016/10/an-anatomy-of-inclusive-growth-in-europe/.

2. Z. Darvas, *Some Are More Equal Than Others: New Estimates of Global and Regional Inequality*, Bruegel Working Paper 2016/08, http://bruegel.org/2016/11/some-are-more-equal-than-others-new-estimates-of-global-and-regional-inequality/

3. F. Bourguignon and C. Morrisson, Inequality among world citizens: 1820-1992, *American Economic Review* **92**(4), 727-744 (2002).

4. S. S. Bhalla, *Imagine There is No Country*, Peterson Institute for International Economics, (Washington DC, 2002), http://bookstore.iie.com/book-store/348.html .

5. B. Milanovic, True world income distribution, 1988 and 1993: First calculation based on household surveys alone, *The Economic Journal* **112**(476), 51-92 (2002), http://onlinelibrary.wiley.com/doi/10.1111/1468-0297.0j673/abstract.

6. X. Sala-i-Martin, The world distribution of income: Falling poverty and... convergence, period, *The Quarterly Journal of Economics* **CXXI**(2), 351-397 (2006).

7. D. Chotikapanich, R. Valenzuela and D. S. Prasada Rao, Global and regional inequality in the distribution of income: Estimation with limited and incomplete data, *Empirical Economics* **XXII**, 533-546 (1997).

8. F. Solt, The standardized world income inequality database, *Social Science Quarterly* 97, SWIID Version 5.1, (2016), dataset available at http://fsolt.org/swiid/

9. M. Bitler and H. Hoynes, Heterogeneity in the impact of economic cycles and the great recession: Effects within and across the income distribution, *The American Economic Review* **105**(5), 154-160 (2015).

10. J. R. Abel and R. Deitz. *Underemployment in the Early Careers of College Graduates Following the Great Recession*, NBER Working Paper 22654, (2016), http://www.nber.org/papers/w22654.

11. L. F. Katz and D. H. Autor, *Changes in the Wage Structure and Earnings Inequality*, in *Handbook of Labor Economics* Vol 3, eds. O. Ashenfelter and D. Card (North Holland, 1999), http://economics.mit.edu/files/11684.

12. G. L. Violante, *Skill-biased Technical Change,* in *The New Palgrave Dictionary of Economics*, Second Edition, eds. S. Durlauf and L. Blume, (Palgrave Macmillan, 2008), http://www.dictionaryofeconomics.com/article?id=pde2008_S000493.

13. D. Autor, Skills, education, and the rise of earnings inequality among the other 99 percent, *Science* **344**(6186), 843-851 (2014).

14. E. Hanushek, G. Schwerdt, and S. Wiederhold, Wößmann, Ludger, Returns to skills around the world: Evidence from PIAAC, *European Economic Review* **73**, 103-130 (2015).

15. F. Felgueroso, M. Hidalgo, and S. Jiménez-Martín, *Explaining the Fall of the Skill Wage Premium in Spain,* FEDEA Working Papers 2010-19, (2010).

16. J. Rothwell, *Make Elites Compete: Why The 1% Earn So Much and What to Do About It?*, Brookings Long Memos, No. 19-20, (2015).

17. O. Denk, *Who Are the Top 1% Earners in Europe?* OECD Economic Department Working Papers, No. 1274. (OECD, Paris, 2015).

18. T. Anderson and J. Maibom, *The Trade-Off Between Efficiency and Equity*, 29 May, VOX — CEPRs Policy Portal, (2016).

19. D. H. Autor, F. Levy, and R. J. Murnane, The skill content of recent technological change: an empirical investigation, *Quarterly Journal of Economics*, 118, 1279-1333 (2003).

20. M. Goos and A. Manning, Lousy and lovely jobs: The rising polarization of work in Britain, *The Review of Economics and Statistics* **89**(1), 118-33 (2007).

21. D. Acemoglu and D. Autor, Skills, tasks and technologies: Implications for employment and earnings, *Handbook of Labor Economics* **4**(B), 1043-1171 (2011).

22. C. B. Frey and M. A. Osborne, *The Future of Employment: How Susceptible Are Jobs to Computerisation?* mimeo (University of Oxford, 2013).

23. J. Bowles, *The Computerization of European Jobs*, Bruegel blog, (2014), http://bruegel.org/2014/07/the-computerisation-of-european-jobs/.

24. M. Arntz, T. Gregory, and U. Zierahn, *The Risk of Automation for Jobs in OECD Countries: A Comparative Analysis*, OECD Social, Employment and Migration Working Papers, No. 189, (OECD, Paris, 2016).

Deepened structural modeling: The case of energy

Stefan P. Schleicher[a]

Wegener Center for Climate and Global Change at the University of Graz
Brandhofgasse 5
8010 Graz, Austria
stefan.schleicher@uni-graz.at

Conventional economic analysis of energy systems is just not sufficient or even misleading in understanding the implications of the emerging energy innovations and the challenges for the design of energy and climate policies. We stress that it is essential to move from the usual black-box approach of energy modeling to deepened structural specifications which are based on the full value chain of an energy system. We explain this argument by looking at conventional approaches to energy modeling, in particular in the context of econometrics. We then demonstrate by using data for China, the United States, and the European Union, how an appropriate energy data analysis can provide insights into the structure of energy systems. Finally, we explain in a nutshell the building blocks of a deepened structural modeling approach which enables to tackle the new challenges; radical technological innovations, a very long time horizon, and the accompanying new designs for business and regulation.

Keywords: energy modeling, deepened structural modeling, energy policy, climate policy

1.   Introduction

Energy is getting for many reasons increasing attention both in the design of domestic and global policies. Above all, it is the prospect of radical innovations. We can see already now a new generation of buildings that hardly needs any energy from outside and a next generation that will be able to collect more energy than they need for themselves. We can observe the evolution of our transport systems to integrated mobility concepts with fully electric vehicles both for road and railway traffic and an integration of all modes of transport. Self-driving cars might provide storage services for the electric grid and reflect the shift in business models from selling ownership to providing mobility services. Production of goods is exhibiting new materials, e.g. polymers that are already now substituting energy intensive steel and aluminum, new processes that are characterized by additive manufacturing or 3D printing, and increasing use of robotics. Renewable energy has become to an extent competitive that was unthinkable a few years ago and in most developing countries has become the cheapest source for electricity.

And then there are new global policy commitments. In the context of climate change it is the Paris Agreement (UNFCCC, 2015) with the ambition to keep the global temperature increase below 2°C, which would require a complete phase out of fossil energy

---

[a] I am deeply indebted to Lawrence R. Klein, who as a teacher and mentor introduced me into understanding economic structures both in the tradition of econometrics and the challenges that have shaped our economies over the past decades.

sources by the end of this century (Deep Decarbonization Pathways Project, 2015, World Economic Forum, 2016)). Similarly, the Sustainable Development Goals (United Nations, 2015), the 2030 Agenda for Sustainable Development, are intimately linked to a fundamentally new design of our energy systems.

This paper proposes that conventional economic analysis of energy systems is just not sufficient or even misleading in understanding the implications of the emerging energy innovations and the challenges for the design of energy and climate policies. We stress that it is essential to move from the usual black-box approach of energy modeling to deepened structural specifications which are based on the full value chain of an energy system. Therefore, the cascade of transformation of primary energy together with the application technologies for fulfilling the ultimate purpose of any energy system, namely the thermal, mechanical and specific electric functionalities or services, needs to be addressed. This can be accomplished by deepened structural modeling approaches.

We explain this argument by looking at conventional approaches to energy modeling, in particular in the context of econometrics. We then demonstrate by using data for China, the United States, and the European Union, how an appropriate energy data analysis can provide insights into the structure of energy systems. Finally, we explain in a nutshell the building blocks of a deepened structural modeling approach which enables to tackle the new challenges; radical technological innovations, a very long time horizon, and the accompanying new designs for business and regulation.

2.   Conventional Econometric Methods in Energy Modeling

Econometric methods have a long tradition in accompanying the modeling energy systems. We evaluate econometric practices with respect to their adequacy in dealing with long-term transformations of energy systems.

2.1.   *Simple causal specifications*

Mainstream approaches to determining the demand for an energy flow e typically postulate the relationship

$$e = e(q, p, w, z) \tag{1}$$

with the causal variables q for an economic activity, p for a (real) energy price, w for other variables (e.g. a weather variable) and z for an autonomous technical change.

Assuming a sample of time series, a general econometric specification of this relationship might be the following linear relationship

$$a(L)e_t = b(L)q_t + c(L)p_t + d(L)w_t + z \cdot t + u_t \tag{2}$$

which adds lag distributions, a linear trend component and a stochastic error term u. The variables are typically transformed into logarithms, thus obtaining elasticities for the estimated parameters.

This modeling approach faces a number of limits. The number of parameters to be estimated, in particular those for the lag distributions, require a long sample range which in turn may violate the underlying model specification of an invariant structure. Furthermore, this model specification is not able to deal with interfuel substitution, i.e. switching the energy mix.

These limits lead to extended model specifications which include on the one hand additional data by using also cross-section information (panel data) and on the other hand additional restrictions on the parameters of the general specification (2).

Demand for energy obviously needs to be considered in the context of an energy mix which in turn stimulates research for explaining the causalities for the composition of the bundle of energy consumed by households or needed in the production of goods. For modeling this interfuel substitution basically two approaches have emerged.

The Almost Ideal Demand Systems (AIDS) results from a consumer demand model that partition total expenditures (i.e. for energy) for a bundle of goods (i.e. different fuels) according to the prices of the individual goods (i.e. fuel prices). A production-based approach explains energy as the output of several factors (i.e. fuels). A further extension includes non-energy inputs, as the capital, labor and materials in a KLEM model. In a so-called translog specification the main drivers for these models are relative energy and relative factor prices.

The econometric implementation of these modeling approaches suffers most often from rather unreliable time series on factor prices and energy prices, a deficiency that is echoed in the rather weak significance of estimated direct and cross price elasticities.

2.2.   *Modeling integration, co-integration and Granger causality*

A very different modeling paradigm has emerged over the last three decades in the context of non-stationary stochastic processes. Accordingly, economic variables as GDP and energy are investigated with respect to their individual long-term behavior (typically exponential trends before the economic crisis that started in 2008) and thus classified by what is called the degree of integration. In a next step, joint relationships of variables are investigated under the heading of co-integration. Finally, statements are made, if one variable improves the prediction of another variable and this is termed Granger causality.

It seems to be fair to say that these modeling approaches just reflect the application of econometric methodology that has become available to energy data without reflecting if this methodology is adequate to the issues to be dealt with. The exponential trends of the past seem to be gone, a fixed long-term relationship, even of a stochastic type, is rather not desirably if we postulate this for an energy flow and an economic activity. Finally, predictability should not be prematurely mixed with causality in the sense of cause and impact.

2.3.   *Some conclusions for long-term transformation analyses*

In view of the usability of econometric models for obtaining a better understanding of the long-term transformation options in an energy system, the conclusions are rather sobering.

Almost all econometric specifications include market driven behavioral assumptions, visible in the role of energy prices in the model specifications. The specifications are therefore hardly able to deal with non-price determined mechanisms that are representative in particular in the context of innovation policies. The estimated elasticities for prices and activities have very limited credibility because of the inherent conflict between the required long time series from a statistical point of view and the accompanying structural changes that violate the statistical model assumption of structural invariance. Most econometric analyses of the energy system just ignore this issue by not reporting the sensitivity of their estimates with respect to variations in the sample size and in the specifications.

Other deficiencies are even more fundamental, as the almost complete absence of details in the energy cascade, in particular the central role of functionalities that are provided by the interaction of energy flows and corresponding stock variables. This extended view of an energy system emerges, however, as a prerequisite for understanding the subtleties of long-term transformation processes.

3.　Data Analysis for Investigating the Drivers of Energy Use and Emissions

Energy systems typically reflect decisions about technologies and ongoing economic activities. In the context of climate policy, the link to greenhouse gas emissions has become a new focus. A useful data analytic approach to investigate the underlying structural properties of energy systems is the following identity which relates greenhouse gases to emissions intensities of energy, energy intensity of production, and finally production itself:

$$g = g^e \cdot e^q \cdot q \tag{3}$$

with

g　emissions of greenhouse gases
e　energy
q　production (e.g. GDP)
g^e　emissions intensity of energy (g/e)
e^q　energy intensity of production (e/q)

We rewrite Eq. (3) by

$$g = g^q \cdot q \tag{4}$$

with

g^q total emissions intensity of production (g/q)

The energy intensity is a measure for energy efficiency. The emissions intensity reflects the carbon intensity of the energy mix, i.e. the composition of fossil fuels and the share of renewables and nuclear. These relationships hold for any type and scale of economic activity. If we are considering national scales, economic activity might be measured by gross domestic product (GDP) in volume terms. These relationships can be visualized in graphs that reveal a lot about the drivers of greenhouse gas emissions.

We start with evidence for the European Union in Fig. 1. The left chart indicates that the total intensity of emissions has declined between 1990 and 2015 by 49 percent which results from a 35 percent reduction of the energy intensity and a 14 percent reduction of the emissions intensity. The right chart adds to the reducing impact of the total intensity the expanding impact of economic activity measured by GDP, which grew between 1990 and 2015 by 25 percent. Adding to the positive GDP growth the negative total intensity impact explains the decline of emissions of 24 percent over 1990. Obviously, the main driver for emission reduction in the European Union is the improvement of energy intensity, which is mainly due to the vast potential for improving the energy efficiency in the new Member States.

Fig. 2 provides a similar analysis for the United States. The left chart reveals that the 43 percent decline of the total intensity results from a 37 percent improvement of energy intensity but only a 6 percent contribution of emissions intensity because of the rather modest impact of renewables so far. The right chart adds to the total intensity the impact of the substantial 48 percent GDP growth, thus causing a 5 percent increase of emissions.

China exhibits, as can be seen from Fig. 3, a completely different emissions path. Total intensity has declined by 69 percent because of a 58 percent reduction of energy intensity and a 11 percent reduction of emissions intensity. Outstanding, however, is the almost triplication of GDP by 298 percent. This explains the 229 percent increase of China's emissions over the past 26 years. The remarkable big improvement of energy efficiency in China is despite heavy investments into renewables still not matched by a similar improvement in the emissions intensity.

4. Deepened Structural Specifications for Modeling Energy Systems

The considerable structural differences that have emerged from this data analysis for the three biggest users of energy und emitters of greenhouse gases call for more detailed explanations. We claim that this just can't be done with conventional approaches as indicated in the context of econometric models. We propose therefore, what is coined a deepened structural modeling approach that is composed of a set of integrated modeling layers.

4.1. *The physical layer: Energy flows and functionalities*

A deepened structural specification of the energy sector considers its full value chain from primary energy via transformation technologies to final energy consumption and via application technologies to the functionalities of an energy system. It is these functionalities which are the ultimate purpose of any energy system which deserve being explicitly considered as they are providing thermal, mechanical and specific electric (as lighting and electronics) services that are relevant for our well-being. Thus, in a nutshell the physical layer of an energy system is described by the following relationships.

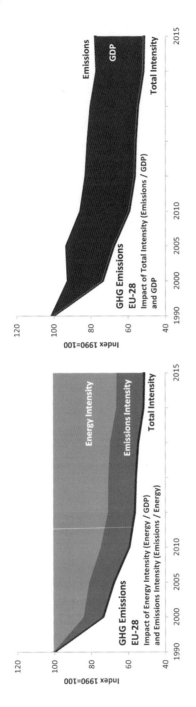

Fig. 1. Greenhouse Gas Emissions of EU-28 — Impact of Technologies and Economic Activity (own calculations based on Eurostat data).

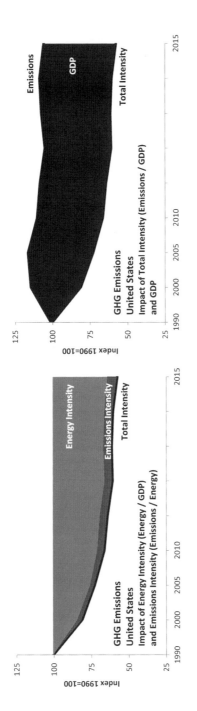

Fig. 2. Greenhouse Gas Emissions of United States — Impact of Technologies and Economic Activity (own calculations based on Eurostat data).

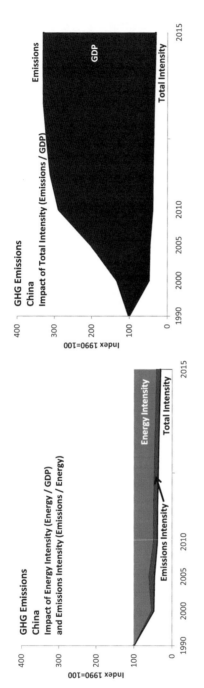

Fig. 3. Greenhouse Gas Emissions of China — Impact of Technologies and Economic Activity (own calculations based on Eurostat data).

The demand for energy relates energetic functionalities via their energy intensities to energy flows:

$$e = T^F(K^F) \cdot F \tag{5}$$

with

    F energetic functionalities (thermal, mechanical, specific electric)

    T^F energy intensity of functionalities (e/F)

    K^F capital stock relevant for energy intensity of functionalities

The energy mix is split into a fossil and a non-fossil component:

$$e^{foss} = e \cdot s^{foss} \tag{6}$$

$$e^{n\text{-}foss} = e \cdot (1 - s^{foss}) \tag{7}$$

with

    e^{foss} fossil energy

    $e^{n\text{-}foss}$ non-fossil energy

    s^{foss} share of fossil energy in total energy (e^{foss}/e)

Emissions of greenhouse gases are determined by the volume of fossil energy and the related emissions intensity:

$$g = g^{foss} \cdot e^{foss} \tag{8}$$

with

    g emissions of greenhouse gases

    g^{foss} emissions intensity of fossil energy (g/e^{foss})

All variables of this layer are measures in physical units as joules, watthours or kilograms of oil equivalents for energy and tons of CO_2 equivalents for greenhouse gas emissions.

A number of benefits emerge from this deepened structural specification of the physical energy system. The full scope of the energy value chain reveals the mostly overlooked but decisive role of functionalities, the high relevance of capital stocks for the related energy intensities, and the importance of the energy mix for greenhouse gases.

4.2. *The economic layer: Linking the physical energy layer with the economic system*

The physical energy system interacts with the economic system via the consumption of energy flows and investments for transformation and application technologies.

Expenditures for energy consumption of energy are determined by the volume of physical energy flows and the related energy price:

$$c^e = p^e \cdot e \tag{9}$$

with

    c^e consumption expenses of energy
    p^e price of energy

Investments in the capital stock of the energy system result from changes in this stock and replacement requirements:

$$i^e = \Delta K^F + r^F \tag{10}$$

with

    i^e investment expenses for the capital stock in the energy system
    K^F capital stock relevant for energy intensity of functionalities
    r^F replacement requirements for this capital stock

The economic system can be split into the sectors for energy and non-energy goods.

The supply of energy goods results from domestic production and imports and the related supply from domestic consumption and exports:

$$s^e = q^e + m^e \tag{11}$$

$$d^e = c^e + x^e \tag{12}$$

Similarly, the supply of non-energy goods results from domestic and foreign sources and the related demand reflects in addition investments for the stocks in the energy sector:

$$s^n = q^n + m^n \tag{13}$$

$$d^n = c^n + i^n + i^e + x^n \tag{14}$$

The notation for the energy sector with superscripts e and the non-energy sector with superscripts n describes

    s total supply
    d total demand
    m imports
    x imports

This representation of the economic sector deliberately from any further behavioral specifications that determine, e.g., for the non-energy sector consumption, investment and imports.

4.3. *The institutional layer: Coordination and incentives by market and non-market mechanisms*

Another defining feature of this deepened structural approach to modeling energy system is the deliberate separation of the specification of structures and the role of institutions that generate these structures. By the notion of institutions we summarize all kinds of mechanisms which contribute to the coordination of economic activities, including the related incentives. We proceed now by taking into account the possibility of causalities based on economic activities and prices

Activity-based interactions may relate in the non-energy sector consumption, investment and imports to activity variables as GDP. In an econometric specification these relationships are parameterized by income elasticities. The related issue is the stability and validity of these parameters beyond a sample period. Similarly, in the energy sector the demand for functionalities could be specified by economic activity but with the same caveats.

Price-based interactions deserve even more caution since the econometric evidence over the past decades is rather fragile and only with strong prior restrictions, e.g. from neoclassical demand theory, the direct and cross price elasticities postulated can be quantified.

The next step in completing a modeling design is mechanisms for coordination. Although markets seem to be the preferred coordination mechanism for economic activities this is not necessarily supported by evidence if we are dealing with the energy sector. Even if we stick to market mechanisms, it is useful to distinguish between a Keynesian type and a neoclassical type of market coordination. A Keynesian type market coordination would assume that supply basically adjusts to demand, thus giving less attention to potential supply restrictions. A neoclassical type market coordination emphasizes the role of prices for equilibrating demand and supply, thus considering at least some supply restrictions.

The energy sector typically reflects many economic decisions that are not based on markets but incentives from the non-market agenda, in which also vested interests may be of stronger relevance. Most decisions in the energy sector are determined by the relevant infra-structure or the capital stocks that determine the available application and transformation technologies. This is the existing stock of buildings and machinery, the network of roads and railways, and past investments for generating and providing energy. Most decisions in the energy sector are determined by the relevant infra-structure or the capital stocks that determine the available application and transformation technologies.

All these aspects considered so far with respect to non-market based coordination and incentives have implications for the design of models. Again, the recommendation emerges to deepen the structural specifications in order to improve the handling of these issues.

5.   Deepened Structural Energy Modeling Will Serve Other Economic Modeling Tasks

The challenges to modeling energy systems are obvious. First it is the expected radical innovations that will fundamentally change the existing physical structures of supply and demand of energy and the related business models. Second it is the long time horizon that needs to be addressed which is way beyond what usually is considered the long-run in conventional economic analysis. Third it is the need to address the full value chain from primary resources to the ultimately relevant functionalities of an energy system.

These insights point to similar challenges that emerge in almost all other economic modeling exercises (Schleicher, 2016). In the context of macroeconomic modeling we are facing very similar issues: a better metric for well-being needs to be decoupled from gross domestic product and for this the concept of functionalities can be further developed; the upcoming innovations need to be better understood with respect to impacts from basic research to new business models and for this a careful analysis of the complete value chain offers a suitable tool; finally the conventional institutional designs for coordination and incentives need to be reconsidered as to their adequacy, in particular those that are market based. Most of these issues can be very well tackled by deepened structural modeling approaches for which we are gaining already promising results in the context of modeling the transformation of the energy sectors.

References

1. UNFCCC, *The Paris Agreement*. 2015, http:// www.unfccc.int.
2. Deep Decarbonization Pathways Project, *Pathways to Deep Decarbonization 2015 Report*, 2015, SDSN - IDDRI.
3. World Economic Forum, *Five Reasons We Should All Be Climate Optimists*. 2016, http://www.weforum.org.
4. United Nations, *Transforming Our World: The 2030 Agenda for Sustainable Development*, 2015.
5. S. P. Schleicher, *Deepening the Scope of the "Economic" Model: Functionalities, Structures, Mechanisms and Institutions* in *Dynamic Approaches to Global Economic Challenges*, (eds.) B. Bednar-Friedl, and J. Kleinert (Springer, Heidelberg, 2016).

Policymaking in the age of sustainable development[a]

Sudip Ranjan Basu, Ph.D.

Economic Affairs Officer, United Nations
Economic and Social Commission for Asia and the Pacific
E-mail: basu@un.org

The growing development challenges and policy uncertainties over the past decades have transformed the global discourse from focusing on economic growth to developing an action-oriented framework that supports sustainable development. The present paper highlights that a multivariate latent variable methodology can be used to formulate development needs and policies and the requirements of institutions that would enhance the efficiency of long-term policy planning. It argues that by linking institutions and policies with development outcomes, policymakers can calibrate a set of strategies to strengthen policy coherence at multiple levels. The examples in the paper indicate that policymakers need to focus more on strategic interventions to achieve greater coherence in an integrated approach. Global economic modelling is essential to move forward with a Klein-type analysis to estimate interlinkages among the various dimensions of sustainable development for conducting policy analysis and simulation.

Keywords: Klein-type analysis; economic growth; sustainable development; principal component method.

1.   Introduction

Nobel Prize winning economist Lawrence R. Klein, who completed his PhD thesis under Paul Samuelson, recalled that being guided by this Nobel Laureate in Economics was "an unforgettable experience." Similarly, I must humbly admit that being supervised by Klein for my Ph.D. thesis was "an *extraordinarily* unforgettable experience!" I will always be grateful to Klein for inviting me to join him at the University of Pennsylvania to collaborate on research with his colleagues, students and associates to develop and refine modelling and measurement frameworks to enhance our understanding of global economic policies. Perhaps, the most enriching lesson during my almost decade-long interaction with him is the importance of maintaining professionalism and providing the correct information to engage with policymakers for creating a society to share prosperity for all. This chapter aims to showcase some of these aspects of my research collaboration with Klein that

---

[a] The earlier version of this paper was presented at the Global Economic Modeling: A Conference in Honor of Lawrence Klein, which was held at the Rotman School of Management, University of Toronto, 11-13 June 2015. I would like to express my sincere thanks to Peter Pauly for his insightful suggestions on the previous draft. Thanks are due to Pingfan Hong, Byron Gangnes, Stephen Hall and other participants for their comments. I would like to extend my thanks to Gayatrika Gupta, Alan Cooper and Erin Bell for their valuable suggestions. The views expressed in this paper are those of the author and do not necessarily reflect the views of the United Nations Secretariat or its officials or member States. Any errors in this paper are those of the author.

advanced the thinking in global economic modelling, especially in the context of the current discourse on sustainable development.

In the foreword contributed by Klein for the United Nations publication *Developing Countries in International Trade 2005, Trade and Development Index*[1], Klein wrote that "real per capita gross world product is not the only key concept... although it has served economists well, in increasingly refined calculations, but it behooves economic analysts *to move on to other dimensions* for judging world economic health".[b] In particular, the observation implies that quality change is extremely important in measuring *estimates* of inflation, output growth, and related socioeconomic variables. However, the measurement of quality of growth is a *problem* of great interest in its own right if one is attempting to determine economic, social, environmental or political/institutional characteristics at the national level, which is often referred to in the policymaking arena as key pillars of sustainable development[2].

Here, I take a look at the current debate among policymakers vis-à-vis striking the right balance between economic, social and environmental dimensions in achieving sustainable development rather than merely economic growth. In exploring the linkages between economic growth and welfare that can lead to sustainable development, a Klein-type analysis would emphasize two key elements: (1) benchmarking and diagnosis; and (2) "link" policy to development outcomes[3-6].

Under the first criteria, I believe that current policy narratives and analyses should take into consideration the following issues in framing national planning and development strategies:

- Policy question and national objective;
- Conceptualization of the framework;
- Data, statistical information and measurement technique;
- Policies and institutions;
- Differential level of development outcomes within and across countries.

As for the second criteria, the global policy discussion needs to focus on two essential parameters:

- International economic policy coordination;
- Impact analysis on national economic output, and analysing the nature and quality of economic growth.

It's a well-known fact that economic policy changes are often triggered by low levels of economic output and quantity of employment. Klein[7] argued that "we need a non-profit institution like the government, which can provide a comprehensive, minimum program of

---

[b] The report provided me with a unique opportunity to interact with Klein, and his associates around the world, in many cases through Project LINK, to attain an informed understanding of global policymaking.

social security in order to reduce the propensity to save. This program must cover the entire population, and it must cover all those contingencies which cause people to save on a large scale for the future". In other words, at the national level, to overcome low output levels, governments need to initiate economic reform processes and better understand structural policies so as to achieve higher levels of economic and employment growth[c] Economic policy can only accelerate the quantity of economic growth towards a better quality of economic growth if coherent policy instruments are aligned with the policy targets[d]. Governments should adopt multiple policy combinations together and implement them in a way that creates space to overcome the structural bottlenecks and ensure effective use of available resources.

Since the 1990s, we have noticed the following patterns in the economic growth story:

- Impressive but *uneven* development progress globally, in particular growing challenges in achieving *health and environmental targets;*
- Convergence but *gaps* between developed and developing countries, including least developed countries, in particular, continues in terms of socioeconomic progress, and for several large economies, within-country disparities, it is as large as cross-country disparities, especially for *disadvantaged and vulnerable* population groups;
- Integration but *lack* of cross-sectoral policy coherence across regions, especially through the lens of sustainability, in laying the foundations for stability, dignity and opportunity for all.

I vividly remember a conversation with A.L. Nagar, one of the stalwarts of modern econometric theories, in the winter of 1998 as a graduate student at the Jawaharlal Nehru University in New Delhi, about his academic association with Klein in preparing a research project related to the measurement of quality of life and modified concept of the United Nations-led human development paradigm. Nagar encouraged me get hold of *The Brookings Model: Some Further Results,* which was edited by Klein in 1969. After reading some of the chapters of the book, including the chapter that Nagar[10] wrote, I was convinced of the importance of building economic models for policy analysis and simulation and, then use them for attaining insights to policy coordination and coherence.

During my research collaboration with Nagar and Klein in the 2000s to estimate progress in quality of life around the world with a new set of methodologies and

---

[c]As Stiglitz[8] noted "technically, reform can mean any change, or at least any change perceived by those perpetrating it to be an improvement on the status quo".

[d] Tinbergen[9] advocated three different types of policy changes depending on the degree of underlying policy structure. These are: (a) quantitative policy constitutes a quantitative change in given instruments of policy, such as changes in tax rates; (b) qualitative policy changes for changing economic structure, keeping the foundation intact, such as a change in the type of taxes implemented; and (c) economic reform as an instrument to changes in foundations, which he defined as changes in more fundamental features of social organizations are the most far-reaching types of policy.

measurement techniques, I attempted to produce a series of research papers that could support policymakers in their efforts to meaningfully intervene and make changes at various levels[11-15].

Our research indicated several interesting global stylized facts among them are:

- A large number of countries in the developing regions, especially least developed countries, often suffer from fluctuating economic growth, limited structural transformation and climate-change vulnerabilities.
- Rising income and social inequalities in major developing countries have a negative impact on global poverty reduction efforts.
- The growing scale and size of sociopolitical tensions regularly hinder opportunities for women and youth to enjoy the fruits of economic growth and gives rise to feelings of social injustice.
- A large group of policymakers struggle to address economic growth and distributional challenges within the national development plans.
- National policymaking has focused on the right to development as one of the central elements for promoting compassion in pursuit of a sustainable future for our children.[e]

I will illustrate two examples of differences within countries and polarization among countries in addressing challenges to sustainable development. This observation can be illustrated by comparing two results. First, as Fig. 1 shows, there is a difference in presenting gross domestic product (GDP) growth with and without adjustments by income inequality, as captured by the Gini Index[18] by averaging the global GDP growth over the past decades.

This concept of inequality adjusted income is important because of its negative impact on economic growth outcomes, as seen by discounting levels of real economic growth achievement by a factor proportional to the extent of inequality[f]. It is indeed acknowledged universally that during the 1990s and 2000s, the regions around the world increasingly experienced varying degrees of income and social inequality[20-22].

As Fig. 2 shows, that while the developing region is catching up with the developed region, the level of development of least developed countries still does not converge with the developed countries. The gap between the least developed countries and developed countries has only grown significantly since 1980, both in terms of GDP per capita and human development.[g]

---

[e] See Sengupta[16] on the issue of conceptual aspects of the right to development. See also Sengupta and Basu[17] on the measurement issues of the right to development.

[f] Sen[19] proposed a measure of welfare-based national income that incorporates efficiency and equity as well as a conventional measure of national income. The measure is defined as $W=\mu\,(1\text{-}G)$, where μ is the mean income of the society, and G is the Gini coefficient of the income distribute.

[g] More information and methodology of the Human Development Index (HDI) can be found in the statistical annex of the *United Nations Human Development Report 2014*[23]. The index is based on three key dimensions: a long and healthy life, being knowledgeable and have a decent standard of living.

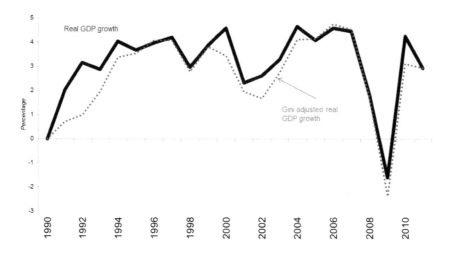

Fig. 1. Trends in Global Gross Domestic Product Growth: Quantity versus Quality.

Notes: 148 countries data, with and without Gini index adjusted GDP growth rates.
Source: GDP growth based on the United Nations and Gini Index based on various data sources.

In this context, it's noteworthy to mention that in 2015, United Nations General Assembly adopted the 2030 Agenda for Sustainable Development, which recognized that achievement of the Agenda would be challenging unless the global community addresses the issue of inequality as enshrined in Goal 10 "reduce inequality within and among countries"[h].

Following my research interactions with Klein, I want to focus on two issues in the chapter that I believe have made a scientific contribution to advancing thinking of policymakers and researchers. In this context, there is a clear need to broadly describe the frameworks that I developed jointly with Klein and Nagar and illustrate some of key issues of measurements associated with it. In this chapter, I propose to compare (i) sustainable development performance in China and India and (ii) cross-country experience in linking policy variability to development outcomes.

2.   Conceptual and Measurement Framework

The theory of economic growth, based on measurement of GDP, originated in the writings of classical economists, such as Smith[26] and Ricardo[27], in the eighteenth century. After the *Great Depression* in the 1930s, the development of Keynesian-type macroeconomic

---

[h] The UN report[24] is available at https://sustainabledevelopment.un.org/post2015/transforming ourworld

principles changed the thinking about the functioning of the market economy and policymaking in the real world. In particular, Keynesianism showed how the steady state of the economy was influenced by the equilibrium values of output and employment through macroeconomic policies[i]. Subsequently, theories, such as that of the Solow-Swan macroeconomic analysis, failed to fully explain some of these basic facts about economic growth in developing countries, and their different levels of performance.

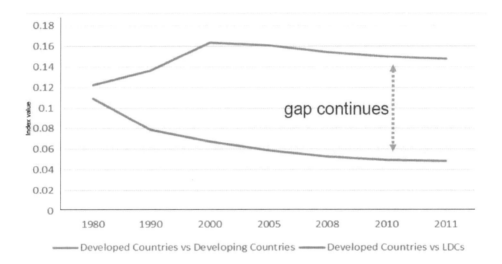

Fig. 2. Trends in Global Development Polarization.

Notes: Polarization index is based on Basu[25]. The Human Development Index (HDI) convergence in developing vs. developed countries and developed countries vs. least developed countries (LDCs) based on the Gini Index. *Source*: Shashoua and Basu[22].

This has led to a new set of growth theories that have endogenized the process of technological progress in which the model is extended in two ways: (a) endows a crucial role to human capital and (b) devotes a share of national product to investment in education[29-31]. In particular, over the years, economists have come to a consensus that the GDP per capita based measure to show the differential level of performance is rather weak and provides only a partial picture of a country's sustainable development. In recent writings of several economists including Sen and Stiglitz, it has been underscored that GDP remains an *inadequate metric* to gauge well-being and sustainability of development. [j]

In this chapter, I use the term sustainability as follows: whether these levels of well-being can be sustained over time depends or whether stocks of capital that matter for our lives (*human, social, physical, environmental*) are passed on to future generations. In the words of Klein[33]: "in familiar summaries of the world economic situation, we have become

---

[i] Klein[7] provided a detailed account of Keynes[28] economic ideas and policy implications.
[j] For further analysis of the concepts and framework, please see Stiglitz, Sen and Fitoussi[32].

accustomed to examining gross world product (GWP) as an appropriate average of the gross domestic product (GDP) of the individual economies. GWP or *GDP are not the only measures* that we need to consult in order to gain an immediate description of the world economic situation." In particular, policymakers have found that the trade-offs between growth-enhancing and social welfare-driven economic policies could lead to different types of incentives and development outcomes (Basu, Fan and Zhang, 2007)[34].

2.1. *Conceptual framework*

To go beyond GDP obsession, there has been a large move forward among economists and observers to introduce the concept of well-being and/or the quality of life as a much more robust measurement for informing strategic policymaking. In particular, human well-being and/or quality of life is defined in terms of both economic resources, such as income, and with non-economic aspects of peoples' lives. Furthermore, institutional strengthening is one of the critical elements in translating economic growth into a higher socioeconomic well-being, which, in turn, ensures society to embark on a more sustainable development path. Initially with Nagar[35], and then jointly with Klein[36], I proposed a new composite measure of well-being and/or quality of life by incorporating different dimensions of the socioeconomic, environmental and institutional characteristics that foster a stable and conducive policy-environment for inclusive economic growth and sustainable development.

At the conceptual level, policymaking entails that the government seeks to enlarge the "capabilities" of the individuals in the society. With efforts geared towards economic cooperation and policy coordination increasing around the world, there has been rising concern of exclusion from the social safety net, and more generally about the ethos and philosophy of the *human well-being and/or quality of life* that should form the cornerstone of policymaking. The evidence suggests that that many of the developing countries have registered an increase in economic growth (of GDP per capita) but have failed to make progress in terms of social and environmental indicators, such as literacy, infant mortality and carbon dioxide (CO_2) emissions. Hence, the focus now is definitely shifting towards a more qualitative nature of economic growth and sustainable development. According to Sen[37], the realization of human *capabilities*, which enlarge the range of human choices, is essential for a broader notion and measure of economic well-being and/or the quality of life and human development. Within this principle, policymaking is then regarded as one of the essential elements for transitioning from economic growth into a sustainable process.

The notion of well-being and/or quality of life as it relates to sustainable development was initiated during an expert group meeting organized by the United Nations in 1954[38]. The expert group then recommended that in addition to real per capita national income, quantitative measures in the fields of health education, employment, and housing should be used for assessing the standard of living. So, real national income was to be supplemented by a further set of indices, reflecting various constituents and determinants of aggregate development.[k] In 1990, the consultation organized by the United Nations, the variables of production and distribution of commodities and the expansion and use of human capabilities were added to the measuring of human well-being. Thus, the Human Development Index was born.[l] The information cited above refers to some of the key academic studies and United Nations-led policy initiatives that have looked beyond the GDP per capita level to attain a more comprehensive yardstick for sustainable development.

I contend that to implement a forward-looking plan for undertaking holistic policymaking the following conditions should be considered: (a) the initial level of social and environmental endowment; (b) differences in countries economic growth; and (c) policymaking capacity.

I believe that policymakers need to change their mindset for short-term adaptability to policy shocks and from measuring only economic production. There has to be a clear shift in emphasis to measuring people's well-being. It's apparent that over the past century, the economic profession has invested heavily in discussing and understanding the theoretical and empirical aspects of economic growth performance and its fluctuations. The literature on well-being and/or quality of life is much more subdued but has picked up starting in the early 2000s (see Fig. 3). This figure illustrates that over the past decades, academia and United Nations organizations have made important contributions towards building a better understanding of the process of economic growth and development research. The evidence here suggests that economic growth has been the primary focus of research conducted by academic institutions and think-tanks, especially since the 1980s when research on "economic growth" increased substantially. In the aftermath of World War II, the implications of economic growth[43-47] on the real sector were identified through several transmission mechanisms[48] in developing countries. In parallel, research on various aspects of sustainable development, such as inequality[49,50], quality of life[39], human well-being/development[41], trade[51] and economic performance[51], has been increasing. In 2000, the adoption of the United Nations Millennium Declaration (2000) prompted policymakers to focus on eight time-bound and quantified targets, known as the Millennium Development Goals, to be achieved by 2015. This has led to renewed interest among researchers and stakeholders to focus on development outcomes, especially with respect to sustainability[53] and its impact on inclusive growth[54,55].

Effective policymaking requires sufficient, accurate and high-quality data. With insufficient data, there is high probability that the policymaking will be misguided. The framework for multidimensional sustainable development is broadly based on such dimensions as health, education, income, insecurity, environment, social connections,

---

[k] See Morris D. Morris[39] and Dasgupta and Weale[40] for academic discussion on the issue of development.
[l] UNDP[41] and the World Bank[42].

governance and personal activities including work. These dimensions are supposed to be used to evaluate the society's overall well-being and/or quality of life.[m]

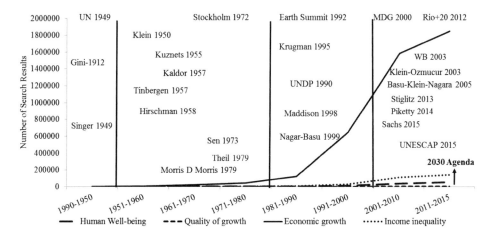

Fig. 3. Tracking Global Research: Economic Growth versus Sustainable Development.

Notes: Total number of articles on issue of "Income inequality", "Human well-being", and "Quality of growth" and "Economic growth".
Source: Computed from Google Scholar site (https://scholar.google.com/), accessed on 12 June 2015.

The multidimensional sustainable development framework in a broad sense includes three parameters, namely (a) emphasize inclusive economic growth, decent employment and social protection; (b) allocate more resources, both financial and human, for delivering essential services and ensuring access for all; and (c) strengthen political will and improve the international policy environment. As indicated in Fig. 4, there are two key factors that policymakers must focus on: (a) a better understanding of policy linkages across various sectors within the national development plan; and (b) developing a robust set of indicators to support evidence-based policymaking for an improved monitoring framework and follow-up mechanisms.

Based on these ideas and concepts, a framework for multidimensional sustainable development needs to address the following global development challenges: (a) rising inequality, poverty eradication and promotion of shared prosperity; (b) opportunities to access productive public services, including expanding choices for a decent job; and (c) freedom to choose various options for improving efficiency of the public administration and governance mechanisms for inclusiveness and sustainability.

In this chapter, the measurement of the sustainable development index (SDI) is composed of two key pillars: (a) a development index (DI) that includes economic, social and environmental dimensions of development; and (b) a policy and institutional

---

[m] 2030 Agenda for Sustainable Development includes 17 goals, 169 targets and more than 200 indicators.

index (PII) that includes both the dimensions of policies and institutional aspects. Klein emphasized that there had to be a clear and robust position in linking policy framework to evidence-based policymaking with a view to improve the development outcomes. Simply speaking, national economic policy measures must lead to an improvement in productive capacity to support economic activities. If policymakers initiate strategic and forward-looking economic policy measures, society will experience not only increased economic activity but also increased choices and thereby improved access to social and environmental aspects of sustainable development.

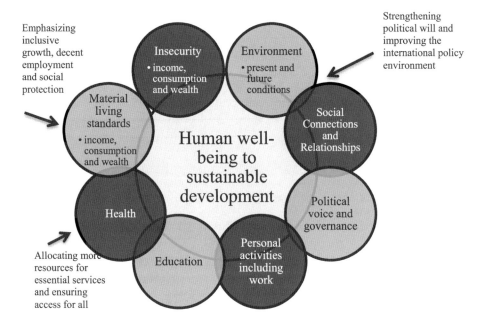

Fig. 4. Framework for Multidimensional Sustainable Development.

Notes: Some elements of the framework are reflected in various documents, such as in Stiglitz, Sen and Fitoussi[33], United Nations Open Working Group Report[56] and United Nations Secretary General Synthesis Report[57].
Sources: Based on Nagar and Basu[58] and Basu, Klein and Nagar[36].

2.2. *Measurement framework*

A measurement framework comprised of an appropriate set of methodologies serves as an important tool for helping policymakers understand better the issues at stake. During my interactions with Klein, we often discussed the need to have in place measurement frameworks that are robust and statistically sound. Initially with Nagar, and then with Klein, I devised a global modelling framework to measure the human well-being and/or quality of life to be used for developing an in-depth understanding of the process and outcomes of development.

Standard models aim to estimate the multidimensional concepts, such as well-being and/or quality of life by using, for example, the following methods: (a) statistical averages: it entails taking a simple average of indicators to obtain overall scores of indices; or (b) the Borda Method: this is an ordinal rule in which each indicator is ranked to obtain aggregate scores, and give an overall ranking[59]. Along with these methods, researchers also use several other econometric models, in line with the traditions initiated by (a) Joreskog and Goldberger[60] for the MIMIC (multiple indicators and multiple causes) models and (b) Joreskog[61] for the structural equation model (SEM). MIMIC models include exogenous variables that "cause" and influence the latent factor, while SEM accounts for the interactions among the different dimensions, and the influence of the surrounding environment.[n] These model structures are used for estimating composite measures, which are applied by researchers to identify connections among the various factors of sustainable development that affect policymaking. Even though these estimation methods and model structure differ, the analytical results indicate co-movement of outcomes.

During my research collaboration with Nagar in the summer of 1999, I developed a methodology to construct a composite index based on a multivariate statistical technique of principal component analysis. Subsequently, Klein coined the proposed quantitative technique as the Nagar-Basu methodology.[o] The composite index is obtained as a weighted average of the principal components as the number of casual variables, and derives coefficients (weights) of the causal variables. So, the weights of the indicators of development are derived from the data and not fixed arbitrarily[58]. Interestingly, during the early 2000s, Klein encouraged his students and associates to develop a high-frequency current quarter model (CQM) for emerging economies that incorporated techniques of the Nagar-Basu methodology to estimate high-frequency GDP growth forecasts and other economic variables[64]. This macroeconomic modelling framework for forecasting and policy simulation has indeed evolved immensely since the initial attempts by Klein in 1950s.

Furthermore, the key advantage of this methodology is its capability to define a composite measure that is able to account for interactions and interdependence between the identified set of dimensions and variables to construct a composite measure, such as the quality of life and/or sustainable development. During my joint research collaboration with Klein and Nagar in 2004, we expanded the scope of this methodology to incorporate a time-series data component for various dimensions of sustainable development. The earlier version of the model technique used the cross-section data. In this paper, I propose to present two examples by using the principal component method as a modelling tool to examine the usefulness of the technique for analyzing the impact of policy intervention on development.

---

[n] See Krishnakumar and Nagar[62] for further description of these methods.
[o] See Klein and Ozmurcur[63].

2.3. *Principal component method*

As in Nagar and Basu[58], I propose that human well-being and/or sustainable development is, in fact, a latent variable which cannot be measured directly in a straight forward manner. However, I assume that it is linearly determined by many exogenous variables say, $X_1, \ldots, X_K$. The variation in these variables is supposed to explain the variation in composite measures. According to the estimator, if the latent variable (say, y) can be measured, I can get an optimal linear combination of $X_1, \ldots, X_K$ to obtain an optimal estimator of $E(y/x_1, \ldots x_K)$. However, in the absence of the measurement of y, what is that linear combination of $X_1, \ldots, X_K$ which can account for the explained part of the total variation in y due to $X_1, \ldots, X_K$?

In this methodology, I propose to replace the set of indicators by an equal number of their principal components (PC), so that 100 per cent of the variation in indicators is accounted for by their PCs. Now to compute PCs, I apply the following steps:

1) the variables can be normalized either by max-min type $x_{kt} = \frac{X_{kt} - minX_{kt}}{max\,X_{kt} - minX_{kt}}$ or

by mean-SD type $x_{kt} = \frac{X_{kt} - \bar{X}_k}{s_{xk}}$, where maximum X_k and minimum X_k, are the values of X_k for k=1, 2,……n . However, normalization should not affect the results-correlation coefficient is unaffected by change of origin or scale.

2) Solve the determinantal equation, $|R - \lambda I| = 0\ for\ \lambda$ where R is a $K \times K$ matrix; this provides a Kth degree polynomial equation in λ and hence K roots. These roots are called eigenvalues of R. Let us arrange λ in descending order of magnitude, as $\lambda_1)\lambda_2)\ldots\ldots)\lambda_k$.

3) Now, corresponding to each value of λ, I solve the matrix equation$(R - \lambda I)\alpha = 0$ for the $K \times 1$ eigenvectors α, subject to the condition that $\alpha'\alpha = 1$. Then we write the characteristic vectors as

$$\alpha_1 = \begin{pmatrix} \alpha_{11} \\ \vdots \\ \alpha_{ik} \end{pmatrix}, \ldots\ldots\ldots\ldots, \alpha_k = \begin{pmatrix} \alpha_{k1} \\ \vdots \\ \alpha_{kk} \end{pmatrix}, \tag{1}$$

which correspond to $\lambda = \lambda_1 = \ldots\ldots\ldots, \lambda_k$ respectively.

4) Then, I obtain the principal components as:

$$\left.\begin{aligned} P_{1t} &= \alpha_1^{(1)} X_{1t} + \ldots\ldots + \alpha_k^{(1)} X_{1t} \\ P_{2t} &= \alpha_1^{(2)} X_{1t} + \ldots\ldots + \alpha_k^{(2)} X_{kt} \\ &\vdots \\ P_{Kt} &= \alpha_1^{(K)} X_{1t} + \ldots\ldots + \alpha_K^{(K)} X_{Kt} \end{aligned}\right\} \tag{2}$$

These linear functions of $X_{1t}, \ldots\ldots, X_{Kt}$ constitute a canonical form. Thus, I compute all these PCs using elements of successive eigenvectors corresponding to eigenvalues, $\lambda_1, \lambda_2, \ldots\ldots \lambda_k$, respectively.

5) Finally, I estimate the Y (human well-being and/or sustainable development) as the weighted average of the PCs, thus:

$$\hat{Y} = \frac{P_1\lambda_1 + P_2\lambda_2 + \ldots\ldots + P_k\lambda_k}{\lambda_1 + \lambda_2 + \ldots\ldots + \lambda_k} \qquad (3)$$

where the weights are the eigenvalues of the correlation matrix R and is known that $\lambda_1 = \text{var}P_1, \ldots\ldots \lambda_k = \text{var}P_k$.

So, the final composite measure to capture the multidimensional aspect of human well-being and/or sustainable development, which is a weighted sum of a normalized version of these selected indicators, where respective weights are obtained from the analysis of principal components. Hence, I attach highest weights to the first principal component, because they account for the largest proportion of total variation in all indicator variables. Similarly, the second principal component accounts for the second largest and therefore, the second largest weight is attached to this, and so on[65].

The methodology was also developed to ascertain the importance of different factors that used for determining the composite measure. For example, in determining the order of dominance in HDI, Nagar and I argued that GDP per capita was the most dominant factor, followed by life expectancy at birth, the combined gross enrolment ratio, and the adult literacy rate (Nagar and Basu, 1999)[34]. The method was further contextualized by Klein and many of his associates and students in the early 2000s at the University of Pennsylvania for producing results for a high-frequency CQM to prepare short-run GDP growth forecasts instead of using a structural model[66].

The composite index, which can be compared over years, aims to provide policymakers with a set of quantitative measures to systematically consider the linkages between various aspects of development via-a-vis policy and institutional measures. In doing so, the conceptual framework could be developed to serve as: a monitoring mechanism to track trends in sustainable development; a diagnostic device to identify broad areas of gaps in various dimensions; and a policy tool whereby implications of economic shocks can be analysed systematically[67].

2.4. *Data*

One of the critical elements of a good policymaking is to gather meaningful and reliable data on indicators, both subjective and objective, of various dimensions of sustainable development. In many cases, policymakers are interested in using subjective indicators that encompass different aspects (cognitive evaluations of one's life, happiness, satisfaction, positive emotions such as joy and pride, and negative emotions such as pain and worry) of the multidimensional development, and are drawn from household and/or opinion surveys. On the other hand, traditionally, objective variables include GDP, social (health and, education), infrastructure (roads, railways, ports and information and communications technology), institutions (rights, freedom, voices, accountability and effectiveness), and are drawn from national statistical books and other international/institutional data sources.

This chapter is based on two sets of results, (a) comparative estimates of sustainable development measures in China and India and (b) linkages of policies aimed at achieving sustainable development at the cross-country level. For the first set of results, the data for China and India are based on 22 indicators and grouped into four dimensions, as in the Fig. 5.

These indicators are spanned over a 25-year period, from 1980 to 2004. This means that at the national level, the analysis includes 25 observations. The time series data are long enough to sufficiently grasp the changes at the national level with respect to the evolution of sustainable development.

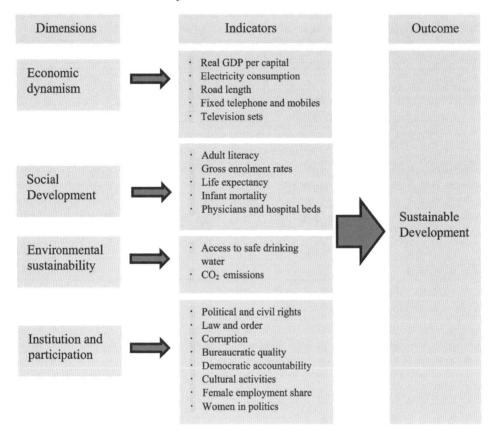

Fig. 5. Dimensions and Indicators of Sustainable Development Framework.

Source: Framework based on Basu, Klein and Nagar[36].

In the case of the policy and development linkages at the global level, the analysis includes 175 countries of which 52 are in Africa, 52 in Asia and the Pacific, 33 in Latin America and the Caribbean, 38 in Europe, members of the Commonwealth of Independent States or in North America, respectively. Also, countries can further be classified under the categories of 25 developed, 100 developing, 25 emerging and 15 transition economies, which spanned for the period 1995 to 2007. The data were further grouped in four non-overlapping time periods, namely, 1995-1997, 1998-2000, 2001-2003 and 2004-2007. To prepare the measure of development, the index includes 18 indicators. In the case of measuring the level of policy and institutions, the analysis includes 34 indicators. Most of the country level indicators are obtained from United Nations databases, the World Bank, the International Monetary Fund and national statistical sources.

3.   Results

In this section, I revisit the results of the research collaboration with Klein and Nagar for the Project LINK meeting in 2005, which was held at the United Nations headquarters.[p] The comparative analysis of the Chinese and Indian development stories was captured as a part of the research, which intended to guide policymaking. The key objectives were to help identify the year-to-year change in development, and give an estimate of the growth rate of development at the national level. By using a time series profile, I look at the individual country, and accordingly trace out its own growth and development performance in comparison to the base period. For example, by fixing the base year, say, 1980=100, the composite measure gives an estimate of the annual changes at the national level over the period, and its trend helps to estimate the annual average percentage change of the composite measure. In Nagar and Basu[57], the analysis focused on a cross-section type of analysis of composite measures, which intended to provide a relative position of countries in a given period of time.

3.1.   *National level estimation of sustainable development: A case of China and India*

The estimation of sustainable development and/or quality of life is based on four dimensions, as in Fig. 5, economic dynamism, social development, environmental sustainability, and institutions and participation. For each dimension, we select multiple indicators that reflect its link with these dimensions.

Here, the analysis provides an estimate of a variant of sustainable development for China and India during the period 1980-2004. The composite measure is based on the methodology described in section 2.2. The results of this year-to-year change of measure are informative, as one can trace association of the rise of the composite measure with the changes in economic reform policies and other policy and institutional changes. A careful

---

[p] Initiated in 1968 under the auspices of the U.S. Social Science Research Council and the leadership of Lawrence R. Klein, Project LINK is a large cooperative, non-governmental, international research consortium. It is based on a world-wide network of participants in more than 60 countries in the industrial and developing world, and it is internationally recognized as a leading centre of quantitative international economic analysis. The activities of Project LINK are coordinated jointly by the Project LINK Research Centre at the University of Toronto and the Department for Economic and Social Affairs of the United Nations. More information is available at http://projects. chass.utoronto.ca/link/desc0305.htm .

look at the measure definitely corresponds to the turning points of these two economies. Now, I convert these index, can be termed as a sustainable development index (SDI), scores into a form of an index number with a common base of 1980=100.

This procedure helps in determining the speed of improvements of SDI over the time period. Another advantage of converting them into an index number is that the rate of annual average change of SDI and its dimensions can be estimated by taking the logarithmic values of SDI of China and India, a semilog-linear regression on chronological time (time=1980 to 2004, 25 observations, namely time=1, 2,…25) can be formed. The trend coefficient in the regressions estimate gives annual average rates of growth of SDI for China and India, respectively, which take the following form:

$$\log(SDI) = \alpha + \beta^*(time) + \varepsilon \tag{4}$$

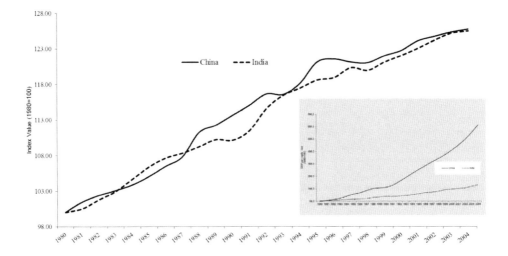

Fig. 6. Estimating Sustainable Development in China and India.

Source: Results based on Basu, Klein and Nagar[36].

The results indicate that, on average, SDI grew at a slightly greater pace in China as compared to India over the same time period. However, when comparing GDP per capita of the two countries, the results were very different, (Fig. 6). GDP per capita grew much more rapidly in China in comparison with India. So, the analysis shows that by including aspects of social, environmental and policy and institutional measures, a different overall picture of development is indicated. A key lesson from this analysis is that growth and development discussions need to take into account the overall direction of policymaking. A general critique against the economists is their inability to guide playmakers on adequately placing weights on sequencing — economic growth first and then development or some realistic mix of the two aspects.

3.2.   *Linking policies and institutions to development*

At the cross-country level, I use a similar conceptual framework as in section 2.1. To measure the development, as in the case of China and India, this analysis includes three dimensions, namely (a) economic dynamism, (b) social development and (c) environmental sustainability. In total, I use 18 indicators for the estimation of the development index[69,q].

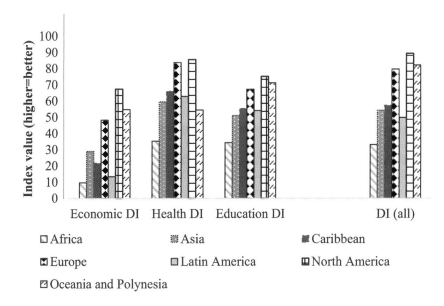

Fig. 7. Estimating Development: A Global Analysis.

Note: DI denotes development index.
Source: Results based on Basu[14,68].

The policy and institution measure, can be termed as policy and institution index (PII), is based on four dimensions, namely (a) trade policies: it captures indicators, such as tariff, peaks (international and national peaks) and specific rates; (b) macroeconomic policies: it captures indicators, such as inflation, real exchange rates, current account & public debt; (c) financial market policies: it captures liquid liabilities, financial system deposits and private credit; and (d) institution building policies: it captures economic, social and political aspects of institutors. In total, the analysis includes 11 indicators for measuring policy and 23 indicators for measuring the institutions.

---

q The analysis used in the paper was very much influenced and shaped by Klein during a visit to the University of Pennsylvania in 2009.

The results indicate that, on average, the DI level varies across regions, as well as in all three dimensions during the period 1995 to 2007. For the overall DI, among regions, North American countries are leading, followed by Oceania and Polynesia, and European countries. The scores of Asian countries and Caribbean and Latin American countries are comparable while African countries lag substantially behind other regions (Fig. 7). An overall analysis of the three dimensions of the development index reveals that the relatively high score of North American countries reflects high average scores for the economic, health and education dimensions. African countries lag behind other developing countries on all three dimensions of the development index.

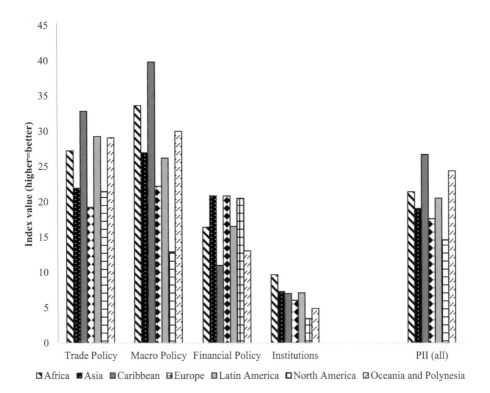

Fig. 8. Estimating Variability in Policy and Institution.

Note: PII denotes policy and institution index.
Source: Results based on Basu[14,68].

Another way to judge the policy consistency is to compute the coefficient of variation of across the four dimensions of the PII levels. The findings indicate that policy and institutional measures across regions have been stable. So, in interpreting the score across these dimensions of PII, it's clear that policymakers have invested time and efforts across regions to ensure policy coherence with regard to macroeconomic policies through inflation stability and trade policy reforms by reducing across the board cuts in rates of tariffs or in aspects related to securing institutional changes (Fig. 8).

For policymakers, perhaps, the most critical piece of evidence is that the countries with the highest development index score also tend to score uniformly well in terms of the level of individual dimensions in PII. In particular, countries with the best development index scores display a low variability of scores among the four dimensions of PII. Importantly, the observed tendency is that the variability in the components of PII decreases with higher development index scores. The highest variability is found among countries with the lowest development index scores, as shown in Fig. 9. Therefore, the better performing countries with regard to development show consistency and coherence in policy and institutional measures and have a solid performance in social, education and health outcomes.

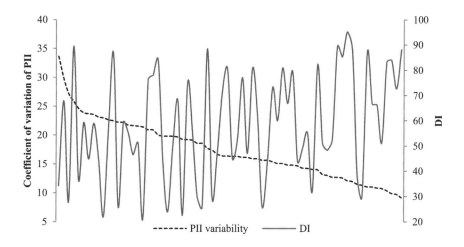

Fig. 9. Link Policy Variability to Development Outcomes.

Note: DI denotes development index and PII denotes policy and institution index.
Source: Results based on Basu[14,68].

4.   Global Policymaking: Some Reflections

For most students of economics, Klein is best known for creating the modern global macroeconometric modelling framework and technique for forecasting and policy analysis. As the Nobel Committee wrote in 1980: "Few, if any, research workers in the empirical field of economic science have had so many successors and such a large impact as Lawrence Klein"[69]. The aim of this chapter is to reflect on my interactions with Klein on various aspects of measuring human well-being and/or quality of life within the context of sustainable development. I was fortunate enough to work with him on proposing new ways to measure human well-being and/or quality of life, which now further enhance our understanding of the sustainable development framework with far- reaching implications for global policymaking.

In this chapter, I have shown with evidence that to effectively pursue inclusive economic growth strategies, policymakers need to focus on strategic interventions for coherence across macroeconomic, structural, and institutional policies in an integrated manner. There is need to promote a set of deliverables and meaningful policy proposals for implementing sustainable development at various levels. The model set out in this chapter shows ways in which researchers can use the quantitative assessment tool to estimate interlinkages among dimensions of development, as well as to estimate economic growth prospects and for conducting a scenario analysis.

The discussions also intend to encourage policymakers to strengthen interministerial coordination and ensure policy coherence at multiple levels in order to sustain investment in economic activities with due attention to inclusiveness and sustainability. In the words of Klein[7], "The level of investment can be stimulated most directly by outright government investment. There are many socially useful projects which need to be undertaken".

In moving forward, the analysis notes several key lessons:

a) There is a clear policy implication of inverse-relationship between policy variability and development outcomes. A disproportionate emphasis on a limited number of policy and institutional targets is likely to yield only marginal welfare gains in the medium-term to long-term. At the national level, policymakers should identify a set of strategies that would facilitate designing successful sustainable development plans.

b) There is an increasing understanding of the need to expand the scope and the number of policy planning choices. Policymakers are expected to focus on balancing multiple long-term development goals within a coherent overall national policy and institutional strategic framework.

c) The analysis emphasizes an economic policy mix that can provide stimulus for removing inefficient resource allocation, ineffective regulations and other domestic policy controls that routinely hinder the economic growth potential at the national level.

These lessons are very much in line with what Klein[3] observed: "the economy definitely needs guidance — even leadership — and it is up to professional economists to provide public policymakers with the right information to deliver such leadership. As for the methods of doing this, I see no alternative to the quantitative approach of econometrics, but I do realize that all policy issues are not quantitative and measurable. At times, subjective decisions must also be made".

The most important role of the policymakers, emphasized by Klein throughout his professional career, is to undertake strategic interventions with a vision to change the path of economic process and development aspirations. Working with Klein in developing measures of development and building a macroeconometric forecasting model have been instrumental in strengthening my conviction that it's imperative to mix economic theory with empirical tools to sharpen our understanding of the current discourse on global interdependence. As a way forward, policymakers should be encouraged to take a holistic and pragmatic view to better understand the nuances of the development process and prospects, as well as its far-reaching socioeconomic and environmental implications to the global development.

Finally, the analysis in this chapter support my view that our engagement with policymakers must continue and shed light on the most challenging issue of the economics profession — the art of policymaking for advancing the agenda of sustainable development — a theme that was prevalent in all of the contributions of Lawrence R. Klein to global economic modelling.

References

1. United Nations, *Developing Countries in International Trade 2005: Trade and Development Index*. (UNCTAD, United Nations, New York and Geneva, 2005).

2. United Nations, *Transforming our World: 2030 Agenda for Sustainable Development*. A/Res/70/1 (United Nations, New York, 2015).

3. L. R. Klein, *My Professional Life Philosophy* in *Eminent Economists: Their Life Philosophies*, ed. Michael Szenberg (Cambridge University Press, Cambridge, UK, 1992), pp. 180-189.

4. L. R. Klein, International policy coordination: Experience and prospects. *Indian Economic Review*, **32**(1), (1997).

5. L. R. Klein, Peacekeeping operations: From the birth of the United Nations onward. *The Economics of Peace and Security Journal* **1**(2), (2006).

6. L. R. Klein, Shift in the world economic center of gravity from G7 to G20. *Journal of Policy Modeling* **35**(3), (2009a).

7. L. R. Klein, *The Keynesian Revolution* (Macmillan, New York, 1947).

8. J. E. Stiglitz, *Globalization and its Discontents* (Norton, New York, 2002).

9. J. Tinbergen, *On the Theory of Economic Policy* (North-Holland Publishing Company, Amsterdam, 1952).

10. A. L. Nagar, *Stochastic Simulation of the Brookings Econometric Model*, in *The Brookings Model: Some Further Results*, eds. J. S. Duesenberry, G. Fromm, L. R. Klein, and E. Kuh, (Rand McNally & Company, Chicago, 1969), pp. 425-456.

11. A. L. Nagar and S. R. Basu, Weighting socio-economic indicators of human development: A latent variable approach, *Handbook of Applied Econometrics and Statistical Inference* (Marcel Dekker, New York, 2002).

12. S. R. Basu, *Does Governance Matter? Some Evidence from Indian States*. Presentation at Spring Meeting of Young Economist, Paris (2002).

13. M. Agarwal and S. R. Basu, *Development strategy and regional inequality in India*, in *India's North East: Developmental Issues in a Historical Perspective*, ed. A. Barua (Manohar Publishing Ltd, New Delhi, 2005).

14. S. R. Basu, A new way to link development to institutions, policies and geography, *Policy Issues in International Trade and Commodities*, UNCTAD/ITCD/TAB/38, (United Nations, New York and Geneva, 2008).

15. S. R. Basu and M. Das, Institutional quality and development revisited: A nonparametric approach. *Policy Issues in International Trade and Commodities*, UNCTAD/ITCD/TAB/43, (United Nations, New York and Geneva, 2010).

16. A. Sengupta. *Conceptualizing the right to development for the twenty-first century* in *Realizing the Right to Development: Essays in Commemoration of 25 Years of the United Nations Declaration on the Right to Development* (United Nations, New York, 2013).

17. A. Sengupta and S. R. Basu, Constructing the indicators for the right to development. *A background paper of a study for the Nobel Symposium Book Project on The Right to Development and Human Rights in Development*, (United Nations, Geneva, 2007).

18. C. Gini, *Variabilit`a e Mutabilit`a*, (Tipografia di Paolo Cuppini, Bologna, 1912).

19. A. K. Sen, Real national income. *Review of Economic Studies* **43**, 19-39 (1976).

20. J. E. Stiglitz, *The Price of Inequality: How Today's Divided Society Endangers Our Future* (W. W. Norton, New York, 2012).

21. T. Piketty, *Capital in the 21st Century* (Harvard University Press, Massachusetts, 2014).

22. M. Shashoua, and S. R. Basu, *Polarizing World: GDP, Development and Beyond.* MPDD Working Paper WP/15/13 (2015).

23. United Nations, *United Nations Development Programme Human Development Report* (United Nations, New York, 2014).

24. United Nations ESCAP, *Economic and Social Survey of Asia and the Pacific. Making Growth More Inclusive for Sustainable Development* (United Nations, Bangkok, 2015).

25. S. R. Basu, Comparing China and India: Is the dividend of economic reforms polarized? *European Journal of Comparative Economics* **6**(1), 57-99 (2009a).

26. A. Smith, *An Inquiry into the Nature and Causes of the Wealth of Nations* (W. Strahan and T. Cadell, London, 1776).

27. D. Ricardo, *The Principles of Political Economy and Taxation* (John Murray, London, 1817).

28. J. M. Keynes, *The General Theory of Employment, Interest and Money* (London, 1936).

29. P. M. Romer, Increasing returns and long run growth, *Journal of Political Economy* **92** (1986).

30. R. E. Lucas, On the mechanisms of economic development, *Journal of Monetary Economics* **22**, (1988).

31. G. M. Grossman and E. Helpman, *Innovation and Growth in the Global Economy* (MIT Press, Massachusetts, 1991).

32. J. Stiglitz, A. K. Sen and J. Fitoussi, *Report by the Commission on the Measurement of Economic Performance and Social Progress* (2009), http://www.stiglitz-sen-fitoussi.fr/en/index.htm.

33. United Nations, *Development Countries in International Trade 2007: Trade and Development Index* (UNCTAD, New York and Geneva, 2007).

34. S. R. Basu, S. Fan and X. Zhang, *Welfare Comparison Beyond GDP: An Illustration from China and India,* HEI Working Paper 08-2007, (Graduate Institute of International Studies, Geneva, 2007).

35. A. L. Nagar and S. R. Basu. *Weighting Socio-economic Indicators of Human Development (A Latent Variable Approach)*, National Institute of Public Finance and Policy, New Delhi (1999).

36. S. R. Basu, L. R. Klein and A. L. Nagar, *Quality of Life: Comparing India and China.* Paper presentation at the Project LINK UNDESA Expert Group Meeting on the World Economy (United Nations, Geneva, 2005).

37. A. K. Sen, *Development as Freedom* (Oxford University Press, 1999).

38. United Nations, *International Definition and Measurement of Standards and Levels of Living* (United Nations, New York, 1954).

39. D. Morris, *Measuring the Condition of the Words' Poor: The Physical Quality of Life Index* (Pergamon. New York, 1979).

40. P. Dasgupta and M. Weale, On measuring the quality of life, *World Development* **20**(1), 119-131 (1992).

41. United Nations Development Programme, Human Development Report. (United Nations, New York, 1990).

42. World Bank, *Where is the Wealth of Nations? Measuring Capital in the 21st Century* (The World Bank, Washington D.C., 2006).

43. H. W. Singer, Economic progress in underdeveloped countries, *Social Research: An International Quarterly of Political and Social Science* **16**(1), 1-11 (1949).

44. L. R. Klein, *Economic Fluctuations in the United States, 1921-1941,* CC Monograph no. 11, (John Wiley & Sons, New York, 1950).

45. S. Kuznetz, Economic growth and income inequality. *The American Economic Review* **45**(1), (1955).

46. N. Kaldor, A model of economic growth. *Economic Journal* **67**(268), 591-624 (1957).

47. J. Tinbergen, Welfare economics and income distribution, *American Economic Review* **57**(2), (1957).

48. A. Hirschman, *The Strategy of Economic Development* (Yale University, New Haven, 1958).

49. A. K. Sen, *On Economic Inequality* (Clarendon Press. Oxford, 1973).

50. H. Theil, World income inequality. *Economics Letters* **2**(1), 99-102 (1979).

51. P. Krugman, *Growing World Trade: Causes and Consequences.* BPEA, no. 1, 327-77 (1995).

52. A. Maddison, *Chinese Economic Performance in the Long Run* (OECD, Development Studies Center, Paris, 1998).

53. World Bank, *World Development Report 2003: Sustainable Development in a Dynamic World—Transforming Institutions, Growth, and Quality of Life* (The World Bank, Washington D.C., 2003).
54. J. D. Sachs, *The Age of Sustainable Development* (Columbia University Press, 2015).
55. UNESCAP, *Economic and Social Survey of Asia and the Pacific 2015: Making Growth More Inclusive for Sustainable Development.* UNECAP, Bangkok, 2015).
56. A. L. Nagar and S. R. Basu, Infrastructure development index: An analysis for 17 major Indian states, 1990-91 to 1996-97, *Journal of Combinatorics, Information and System Sciences* **27**(1-4), 185-203 (2002).
57. United Nations, *Report of the Open Working Group of the General Assembly on Sustainable Development Goals* (2014a), http://www.unesco.org/new/fileadmin/MULTIMEDIA/FIELD/Santiago/pdf/Open-Working-Group.pdf
58. United Nations, *The Road to Dignity by 2030: Ending Poverty, Transforming All Lives and Protecting the Planet.* Synthesis report of the Secretary-General on the post-2015 sustainable development agenda (2014b).
59. J. C. Borda, *Memoire sur les Elections au Scrutin; Memoires de l'Academie Royale des Sciences* (1781); English translation by Alfred de Grazia (1953). Mathematical Derivation of an Election System.
60. K. Joreskog and A. Goldberger, Estimation of a model with multiple indicators and multiple causes of a single latent variable. *Journal of the American Statistical Association* **70**(351), 631-639 (1975).
61. K. Joreskog, *A General Method for Estimating a Linear Structural Equation System* in *Structural Equation Models in the Social Sciences*, eds. A. S. Goldberger and O. D. Duncan (Seminar Press, New York, 1973).
62. J. Krishnakumar and A. L. Nagar, On exact statistical properties of multidimensional indices based on principal components, factor analysis, mimic and structural equation models. *Social Indicators Research* **86**(3), 481-496 (2008).
63. L. R. Klein and S. Ozmucur, The estimation of China's economic growth, *Journal of Economic and Social Measurement* **62**, (2002/2003).
64. L. R. Klein, *The Making of National Economic Forecasts* (Edward Elgar, London, 2009b).
65. A. L. Nagar and S. R. Basu, Statistical properties of a composite index as estimate of a single latent variable, *Journal of Quantitative Economics* **2**(2), 19-27 (2004).
66. S. R. Basu, *Economic Growth Story in India: Past, Present and Prospects for Future*, in *The Making of National Economic Forecasts* (ed.) Lawrence R. Klein, (Edward Elgar, London, 2009b).
67. United Nations, *Developing Countries in International Trade 2007: Trade and Development Index* (UNCTAD, New York and Geneva, 2007).
68. S. R. Basu, *Measuring Policies, Institutions and Development in a Multispeed World.* Paper presentation at the Project LINK UN DESA Expert Group Meeting on the World Economy, New York, USA, October (2011). The presentation is available online at http://projects.chass.utoronto.ca/link/meeting/materials/22.pdf

69. The Nobel Committee (1980). *Press Release*, 15 October 1980. The Sveriges Riksbank Prize in Economic Sciences in Memory of Alfred Nobel 1980. The press release is available from http://www.nobelprize.org/nobel_prizes/economic-sciences/laureates/1980/press.html.

Damaging austerity policies[a]

Franjo Štiblar

Member EIPF and Chair, Department of Law and Economics
School of Law and EIPF, University of Ljubljana, Slovenia
E-mail: franjo.stiblar@pf.uni-lj.si

The economic policy of complete austerity (where monetary and restrictive fiscal policies are implemented at the same time) is damaging for Europe, the EU and particularly the peripheral Eurozone members, for the basis of the monetary union and de facto for the entire EU project. Recent partial corrections based only on a relaxation of monetary policy (negative interest rates and quantitative easing) but with further fiscal consolidation at the same time do not help to mediate economic growth, and in fact increase inequality with negative political implications. This paper explains why austerity policies fail on two fronts: as a coherent set of economic ideas and as an economic policy. Austerity is a dangerous doctrine, as it has pushed millions of people, especially in the EU, into unnecessary distress. The experience of different countries with austerity led to catastrophic results in the 1930 and 1980s as well as during the recent global financial crisis. The panel econometric analysis shows that monetary and fiscal austerity measures as applied had a significant negative impact on GDP growth. There are better ways of managing a crisis other than through austerity, as austerity leads to internal devaluation and deflation. The best solution is to prioritize economic growth, which requires the simultaneous implementation of fiscal and monetary stimuli. This approach is the exact opposite to an austerity doctrine.

The paper deals only indirectly with global economic modeling, but it is in line with Professor L. R. Klein's view that economists need to be involved in current economic policy discussions. Crucial to his advisory role to President Carter was regular engagement in debates on the situation in American and the global economy, including the situation in Japan, and transition countries. It was his thinking that the work of macroeconomists should be applied to solving current practical problems of a particular country and the global economy.

Keywords: Austerity, fiscal policy, monetary policy.

1. Introduction

The neoclassical assumptions of perfectly efficient markets and ultra-rational behavior of individuals represented an illustration of neoliberal economic policy. The rigid reliance on these resulted in a global financial crisis with a huge negative impact on the real sector in the form of the Great Recession of 2008. A strong fiscal and monetary stimulus protected the world economy from the brink of disaster and renewed the popularity of the ideas of J.M. Keynes[1]. The quick intervention and subsequent success made serious structural reforms in the financial sector redundant, as in previous instances of similar interventions. Unfortunately, a side effect of this sort of intervention is that it encourages the next

---

[a] An earlier version of this paper was presented at the Global Economic Modeling conference, June 10-13, 2015 at the Rotman School of Management in Toronto, Canada, and updated in early 2016.

financial crisis in the making, which according to the dominant orthodoxy is an inevitable feature of the capitalist economy.

In order to effectively navigate crises, different countries applied different economic policy measures[2]. Most developed countries continued with growth-supportive fiscal and monetary stimulus that enabled them to reboot their economic activity. In these countries, by 2014, their GDP by far exceeded the pre-crisis level, unemployment rates were halved and inflation remained positive. On the contrary, the EU, especially the Eurozone, followed the opposite approach – austerity – which had a significantly negative impact on economic activity and brought suffering to its citizens.[b] Among other things, inequality increased enormously.[c]

Most Anglo-Saxon media and scientists as well as the rest of the world (including China and Japan) are critical of the EU policy stance and believe that austerity policies are detrimental and as such unsustainable. However, the German-led ordo-liberal doctrine in the EU and the Eurozone remains stubborn in its application of austerity policies even in the face of evidence of their catastrophic consequences: seven years after the crisis had begun, GDP has still not returned to the pre-crisis level. As the EU GDP growth remains weak (close to recession), unemployment rates have doubled, and the ghost of deflation looms across the EU region.

The heterodox theoretical literature asserts that austerity is a dangerous economic policy based on the neo-liberal doctrine[10], but few empirical studies have supported this criticism with empirical results. This article attempts to achieve just that, however as an early example and on a small scale. First, the basic theoretical arguments on the roots of the austerity idea through history are presented. Second, the negative experiences that various countries had with austerity in history are summarized. Third, the recent discussion on austerity in the literature is reviewed. Fourth, a cross-country econometric analysis was conducted in order to prove that the austerity policy during the last financial crisis (2008-2014) had a negative impact on EU (Eurozone) countries that implemented it. Fifth, the results are applied to Slovenia as a case study. The recommendation of this study is to abandon the damaging austerity policy approach in order to elevate EU countries from the crisis, bring an end to citizens' unnecessary distress, and at the same time enable other countries in the world to grow faster (through the EU as an export destination).

2.   Theory (Historical Background Summary)[d]

Post-WWII Germany provided support for austerity arguments in the form of ordo-liberalism, the instruction sheet for how to run a late-developer, high-savings, high-technology, export-driven economy[10]. However, these were extreme conditions that were at the time experienced by Germany, and they are not experienced today by Eurozone economies and most other countries in the world. For the majority, austerity does not work

---

[b]More on that, for instance: Krugman[3]; Rodrik[4]; Shiller[5]; Smithers[6]; Stiglitz[7].
[c]More on that: Piketty[8] and Stiglitz[9].
[d]About historical aspects, see Medema & Samuels[12].

and, if applied, leads to great problems. What are the roots of the German position? The idea has its early roots in the liberal approach of Hume, Smith[11] and Locke in the 18th century, for whom savings came before spending. It was developed further by Ricardo[13] and John Stuart Mill[14] in the late 19th century. In the UK, Mills ideas were adopted by the new liberals[15], while Ricardo was followed by the neo-liberals[16,17]. Mill saw an important role of the state in providing a framework and conditions for social protection and a good living environment (later adopted by the Keynesian tradition). Ricardo was of the opinion that the state must not interfere with the economy. Schumpeter[18] did not follow Keynes[19]. The Austrian School of Economics with von Mises and Hayek[20] continued along Ricardo's lines and their impact on the economic policy contributed to the Great Depression in late 1920s[21]. In practice, the interventionist approach following the ideas of John Maynard Keynes[19] and applied with Roosevelt's New Deal helped to prevent the economy from collapsing. The state had an important role in the economy for 40 years with no major crises occurring, however, business cycles remained a regular feature.

In the 1970s, the old liberal approach once again became popular[22,23] and as the state retreated from controls of the economy this led to enormous financial deregulation, privatization and marketization in all spheres of life[24]. Notably, the IMF applied it with the Pollak[25] model. With this change, the financial and real sector crises returned. Several smaller crises occurred before the major financial crisis in 2008, but in 2008 there was a huge impact on the real sector which led to the Great Recession of the late 2000s. Two major economic policy approaches were applied in order to get the economy out of the crisis. Most countries, following the lead of the United States, used direct monetary intervention (quantitative easing) once the usual interest rate policy proved to be insufficient in restarting economic growth, with the fiscal stimulus via government spending as an initial input. The positive results in their economic performance are now clearly recognized. On the other hand, the EU and especially the Eurozone quickly abandoned both monetary and fiscal stimuli and opted for the economic policy of austerity. Germany led this approach based on its post-WWI hyperinflation experience and its ordo-liberal approach that was theoretically developed at the beginning of the 20th century and later applied in practice. The ordo-liberals use the state only as an institutional framework for the economy, while the Austrians want to abolish it once and for all.

The Washington Consensus[26] was a set of policy prescriptions in the neoliberal tradition initially aimed at developing countries, but also applied to developed economies during the recent crisis, especially to countries on the EU and Eurozone periphery[27,28]. There are five main ways of getting out of a financial crisis: inflate, deflate, devaluate, financial repression and default. As the other options were not viable, internal devaluation and deflation (i.e. austerity) were implemented to deal with the financial crises in the Eurozone, since placing priority on the renewal of GDP growth was not considered[10]. The extreme theoretical case for austerity is the notion of expansionary contraction, which was "invented" by Italian economists at Bocconi University. Following Einaudi in the early 20th century the new major proponents were Alesina and his cooperators at the turn of the millennium[29-32]. It became the "ultimate idea" in the EU in 2010, but was rejected by many, including the IMF (who in 2011, under O. Blanchard, proved that the fiscal multiplier was on average larger than one) and later even Bocconi. In the fashion of ultra-rationality based on the expected utility framework they claimed that the slump was the right time to cut the spending side of the budget (be austere) and that this should be done decisively. Because the state can positively affect the expectations of future available personal income (as economic agents expect tax cuts following cuts in government expenditures), decisive cuts will make people spend, invest more and thus increase GDP by increasing the total final demand.

In practice, the doctrine of expansionary contraction on which austerity is based led to severe damage in the EU[34,e] The fiscal consolidation pact is based on it and it is still valid. If it holds true, then cutting the budget deficit (i.e. fiscal consolidation) while applying monetary restriction will lead to GDP growth. This will be tested in the subsequent empirical analysis.

3. Experience of Different Countries in the Past

The history of austerity is summarized along three historical avenues:[f]

1. During and in the wake of the Great Depression 1920s-1930s

2. In Western Europe and Australia during the 1980s

3. In Europe during the Great Recession 2008-today

3.1. *During and in the wake of the Great Depression 1920s–1930s*

Austerity policies were applied in the USA, Great Britain, Sweden, Germany (with chancellor Brüning's mistake that brought Hitler into power), Japan (austerity and military expansion) and France. Apart from a few short-term expansions in the early 1920s when countries were not based on the gold standard, not only did the application of austerity not work, it made the depression deeper, longer and laid the foundation for WWII. The country cases show that a specific form of austerity sometimes worked when applied as a combination of devaluation and wage cuts that were implemented with agreement from trade unions, but only in a single country, and not for the entire group of countries (beggar-thy-neighbor policies).

3.2. *In Western Europe and Australia during the 1980s*

In the 1980s new cases of expansionary austerity could be noticed in Denmark, Ireland, Australia and Sweden. None of these cases validated the expectation of creating GDP expansion by cutting the budget, and for that reason the empirical work on austerity switched from country level to large-scale world analyses.

---

[e]One does not need to look at Greece to see the results of austerity. Other PIIGS members as well as the EU members from Eastern Europe are also good examples.
[f] A detailed analysis can be found in Blyth[10], chapters 6 and 7.

3.3. *In Europe during the Great Recession 2008–today.*

When austerity programs in the PIIGS (Portugal, Ireland, Italy, Greece and Spain) did not provide the expected positive results after years of application, the proponents of austerity turned to a new group of countries REBLL (Romania, Estonia, Latvia, Lithuania, Bulgaria) in order to validate their assertions[35]. Failure in the first group of countries was explained with the assertion that austerity measures were not deep and long enough, thus more radical cuts were applied to the second group of countries. In 2009 the REBLL countries experienced an average GDP slump of 10% and, in order to save the banks, they applied the usual austerity measures which led to high interest rates, unemployment and the transformation of private bank debt into public debt. Austerity failed to work as planned in two areas: private sector wages were not cut deeply enough, and the government deficit was not cut as abruptly as it was supposed to. The external demand helped these countries out of the slump, but that was not the case for all PIIGS as a group. In addition, the political environment allowed pressure to be put on the public in the REBLL countries, but this could not be implemented with the same harshness across the PIIGS.

As a counter example, a small country, Iceland, applied measures opposite to austerity during the 2008 crisis and achieved positive outcomes. It allowed its banks to go bankrupt (and jailed some bankers), devalued its currency, put up capital controls, and bolstered welfare measures. As a non-EU state Iceland could choose its own path out of the crisis with measures that were not available to EU countries due to the EU policies led by Germany.

4.   Recent Literature on Austerity

Most of the literature focuses merely on the effects of fiscal austerity (fiscal consolidation) that result from economic activity, while this paper understands austerity in a broader sense and includes monetary austerity (bank credit crunch) as well as fiscal austerity (budget consolidation via decreasing government expenditures).

The historical development of the notion of austerity and its practical application was summarized in the previous sections. At this point I present the recent literature on austerity, which appeared in the aftermath of the recent global financial crisis. Recent scholarly and policy discussions on the subject are described by Monastiriotis[36]. The discussion turned heated by the blog on the subject that was opened by the CEPR and by the conference on austerity that was organized by the University of Cambridge Economic Review. Some of the most recent views on austerity from 2015 are presented at the end of this section.

4.1. *Austerity and debt sustainability*

In his article on the conditional link between fiscal austerity and debt sustainability Monastiriotis[36] reviewed the current status of the austerity debate, on which he followed up with the introduction of his two additional explanatory variables that explain this relation. These are trade openness and quality of government. The central dispute occurs between the mainstream orthodox proponents of austerity (austerity works) and the heterodox opponents of austerity (austerity does not work). The controversy centers on the size of the fiscal multiplier: if it is less than one, austerity works. If it is bigger than one, austerity is self-defeating because of the so-called "snowball effect", as the fiscal effort reduces GDP by more than the resulting savings.

The debate started in 2011 with an empirical study by IMF researchers who ascertained that the multiplier ranged between 0.9 and 1.5. Yet in 2013 Blanchard and Leigh from the IMF admitted that the IMF's initial projections of the fiscal multiplier were not way off the mark. However, by that time the "austerity trap" idea already gained the attention of the economic community. This idea is rooted in two premises: 1) primary surpluses are necessary for the reduction of debt, and 2) fiscal consolidation deprives the economy of some of its key growth drivers (fiscal stimulation and/or private consumption). The size of the multiplier depends on the specific assumptions regarding the response of economic agents to the changes in government spending and taxation, and the speed with which prices and wages adjust to the changing supply and demand conditions. Keynesians consider wages and prices to be sticky, while the expectations are adaptive so that the fiscal multipliers are above 1. On the other hand, neoclassical economists believe that prices adjust instantaneously, that economic agents are (ultra)rational and fully informed, thus making the government spending immediately discounted ("Ricardian equivalence") and leading the fiscal multiplier to near zero[36]. However, nobody asked whether these neo-classicist assumptions, which are introduced and necessary in order to create a perfect mathematical model, are realistic. Unwilling to give up this mainstream orthodoxy, neo-classicists used empirical examples to indicate that the debate on the size of the multiplier is inconclusive, as it is time and country dependent[38,39]. With the lack of empirical data, they frequently merely simulate calibrated data.

Other factors such as the role of the market and the macroeconomic environment[40-42], which determine the multiplier and make it endogenous, were introduced[43]. The literature also mentions other factors, such as the overall situation in the economy, the exchange rate regime, the state of public finances, the room for monetary expansion, and the severity of credit constraints. Less open economies with worse governments have a higher fiscal multiplier[36].

Two strands of the debate emerged from these works[36]. One points out the danger of the "austerity trap" and propagates a policy shift towards fiscal stimulus[44]. The other seeks to identify the specific conditions under which fiscal consolidation becomes painful or self-defeating[45]. Martin Wolf's commentary in the Financial Times[46] on the negative correlation between the forecasted GDP growth and the structural fiscal tightening as well as Krugman's estimate of the multiplier equaling 1.25 (2012) added heat to this debate.

4.2. *CEPR Vox blog*

4.2.1. *Barry Eichengreen*

Barry Eichengreen[47] questions the confidence and feeds the crisis. Fiscal consolidation is hard, but structural reforms are harder. EU institutions need to be reformed and to a certain degree this has been established by 2015. In order for the EU to draw a line under its crisis the author proposes the following:

1. Make the detailed results of bank stress tests public and recapitalize the banks (done),
2. Provide greater clarity as regards their 440 billion € special purpose vehicle (done),
3. Resolve the Greek situation (currently underway),
4. Support growth by devaluating the Euro.

He also proposed quantitative easing, which was finally introduced in March 2015.

4.2.2. *Paul Krugman*

Paul Krugman[48] explained the introduction of the new model oriented towards dealing with debt, deleveraging and the liquidity trap. It is in line with the New Keynesian models, which have two and not merely a single representative agent: borrower and creditor. Besides the paradox of thrift, he also envisages the paradox of toil and the paradox of flexibility. Compared to aggregate net worth, the overall level of debt makes no difference on the global level. Deleveraging should take place only once the crisis has ended and growth had returned.

4.2.3. *Alesina*

According to Alesina[32], a famous proponent of austerity based upon the doctrine of expansionary fiscal consolidation, the important austerity question is not how much austerity, but how to deal with it. He prefers public spending cuts to tax increases, as only the former lead to a decline in the debt-to GDP ratio.

4.2.4. *Giancarlo Corsetti*

Giancarlo Corsetti[49] discusses whether austerity has gone too far. By comparing the failure of Italy with the success of UK, he classifies countries in three categories: high risk premium, low risk premium and in between. By 2012 the fiscal policy debate has gone through several phases. First, a fiscal stimulus was required in 2008 in order to prevent a return of the Great Depression; secondly, a shift towards a fiscal consolidation was made in 2010, and after 2012 calls for fiscal austerity became unfashionable once again. Fiscal tightening is self-defeating in the liquidity trap. Growth can re-emerge only with an unconstrained monetary policy and fiscal expansion. The sovereign-risk channel transmission has two implications:

- if the sovereign risk is already high, fiscal multipliers are lower than normal;
- highly indebted economies become vulnerable to self-fulfilling economic fluctuations.

Strongly capitalized banks and monetary policy support help overcome the crisis.

4.2.5. *Rethinking austerity*

In June 2012 CEPR VoxEU started a new blog "Rethinking austerity". The blog emphasizes the three issues that need to be addressed (in line with Corsetti): the fiscal multiplier, the impact the fiscal reform has on uncertainty and what comes after fiscal consolidation. His general lessons are that debt consolidation is not the same across the various countries and that the impact of the fiscal reform is hard to assess.

4.2.6. *Eichengreen and O'Rourke*

According to Eichengreen and O'Rourke[50] the IMF multiplier estimates of 0.9 - 1.7 are confirmed by their independent panel data research.

4.2.7. *de Grauwe and Ji*

For Paul de Grauwe and Yuemei Ji[51] the Eurozone policy seems driven by market sentiment. Fear and panic led to excessive and possible self-defeating austerity in the south while failing to induce offsetting stimulus in the north. The resulting deflation bias produced the double-dip recession and perhaps more dire consequences.

4.2.8. *Laurence Ball*

Laurence Ball[52] concluded that the "great recession (reinforced by austerity) will cause long-term damage". It will damage labor productivity, thereby reducing its potential output (what Blanchard and Summers would call "hysteresis"). In most countries the loss of potential output has been almost as great as the loss of the actual output. In countries hardest hit by the recession, the growth rate of potential output is much lower today than it was in 2008 (the present analysis will indirectly result in the same). The recession decreases potential output as it sharply reduces capital accumulation, has long-term effects on employment, and may slow the growth of total factor productivity.

4.3. **The newest views from 2015**

4.3.1. *ECB economists*

The ECB economists have recently discovered that austerity works[53]. Simulations (not calculations) that use plausible assumptions suggest that frontloading consolidation reduces the total consolidation effort and stabilizes the debt ratio faster, although it implies larger short-term reductions in output (social costs are not considered and there is a question of political sustainability). Simulations (not actual data) are used to prove the desired outcome that has yet to be confirmed in real life. Lithuania was used as an example and the Greek position on austerity was attacked. Blyth[54] exposed the crucial problems with using the Baltic States as arguments for austerity.

4.3.2. *Caggiano and Castelnuovo*

Giovanni Caggiano and Efrem Castelnuovo[55] discuss government multipliers and the business cycle. There is no consensus with regards to the size of multipliers, as linear models are used, and multipliers in a recession tend to be larger than during periods of full potential growth. They established that government spending is highly effective when most necessary, which is during deep recessions. One-size-fits-all recommendations are not appropriate.

4.3.3. *Thomas Piketty*

In his interview for FT[56], Thomas Piketty asserted that Europe had chosen the wrong path. With regard to the growing inequality he proposes a global wealth tax, or at least a higher top income tax rate. Europe has chosen the wrong path of eternal penitence and it would be a disaster to force Greece out of the Eurozone. The Eurozone crisis also reflects a deeply flawed governance, in which two leaders have the power to decide everything. From the macroeconomic point, Greece is insignificant.

4.3.4. *Reinhart and Rogoff*

Early studies were initiated by the controversial findings of Reinhart and Rogoff[57], who stated that there is a historical limit to fiscal expansion, and they estimated it at around 90% of GDP. This was soon discredited by revelations focusing on their data manipulations[58-60]. Some studies found the critical point to be at different sizes of debt-to-GDP ratio, even at 20% to 60%[61]. Others linked the counter-cyclical behavior of the fiscal multiplier to the monetary policy aggregates[40], which is also the substance of this work.

4.3.5. *Gros and Blyth*

The heterodox view that austerity is self-defeating at least in the short-run, as it reduces the denominator GDP more than the numerator debt, was supported by Daniel Gros[62], Mark Blyth[10], and articles in the 2012 special issue of the Cambridge Journal of Economics.

4.4.   The goal of this research study

In contrast to the above studies, this empirical study includes all of the 42 largest countries in the world plus Slovenia and analyzes the period between the start and the aftermath of the global financial crisis (2008-2014). In addition, while the debate in the literature is centered only on fiscal policy, and rarely includes monetary conditions, this study also includes monetary (banking) austerity in the form of a domestic credit crunch and treats it on par with fiscal austerity. Thus, our study is globally (macro) oriented in three senses: it encompasses the whole world, the entire crisis period and the full breadth of the austerity experience. In order to achieve this goal, numerous specific details needed to be sacrificed with the intention of obtaining the global picture of the austerity phenomenon. Additional factors were identified when the results were applied to Slovenia. Similar to other studies in the literature, these were introduced in order to explain the difference between the estimated and actual values of the country's macroeconomic variables (confidence, economic climate, changes in the economic and political institutional structure during the analyzed period).

Thus, this empirical study is much more global and all-embracing than other studies in the literature. In order to obtain a general overall picture, one has to make numerous methodological compromises, but the results are encouraging and make the effort worthwhile.

5. Empirical Analysis: The Impact of Austerity on the Economic Performance

The question was raised as to how successful were austerity measures in elevating countries from the slump during the latest global financial crisis and great recession 2008-2014. The empirical study analyzes the impact the austerity measures had on the economic performance of a country during the latest global financial crisis.

The basic hypothesis of the supporters of austerity is that it works (restrictive monetary and fiscal policies lead to an improved economic performance due to expectations), while the null hypothesis is that it does not work. The model specification for null hypothesis is as follows:

5.1. Model

(1) $P = f(M, F)$, where $\partial P / \partial M > 0$ and $\partial P / \partial F < 0$

(2) $U = g(M)$, where $\partial U / \partial M < 0$

(3) $Inf = h(M, F)$, where $\partial Inf / \partial M > 0$ and $\partial Inf / \partial F < 0$,

where: P = GDP growth, U = unemployment rate, Inf = inflation rate

M = monetary stimulus, F = fiscal stimulus (deficit), ∂ = partial derivative.

5.2. Methodology

The non-observables of the austerity policy are restrictive monetary policy and restrictive fiscal policy, while the observables are changes in the share of credits to GDP for monetary policy and budget deficit to GDP for fiscal policy. The non-observables for economic performance are economic growth, unemployment and inflation, while the related observables are GDP growth, unemployment rate and inflation rate.

For each independent and dependent variable the changes during the global crisis between 2008/9 and 2013/14 were calculated as first differences d (for variables "without memory" according to the system theory)[g] or growth coefficients k (for variables "with memory"), using the system theory.[h]

The impact of austerity on the macroeconomic performance of 43 countries was analyzed:

- by comparing the average values of variables in the observation period, for eight country groupings,
- with a cross section regression analysis for the world's 42 most important countries, measured by GDP, plus Slovenia.

Eight variables included in analysis are:

- k(d)GDP = growth coefficient GDP2012/ GDP2008, (higher number, better GDP growth),
- k(d)unempl = growth coefficient of the unemployment rate 2014/2009, expressed in % (an increase represents an increase in the unemployment rate),
- dinfl = difference in inflation rate between 2014 -2009, expressed in % (a higher number represents higher inflation),
- d(k)BOG = difference or growth coefficient in budget /GDP 2014/ 2009, expressed in %, (a positive indicates a decreasing deficit),
- d(k)BOP = difference or growth coefficient in current account/GDP 2014/ 2009, expressed in %, (a positive indicates decreasing deficit),
- d(k)kred = difference and growth coefficient in loans to private sector/GDP 2013/ 2009, (higher number represents a higher growth of domestic credit in GDP),
- dbalance = dbog + dbop, expressed in % (higher number indicates decreasing deficits),
- kexrate = growth coefficient of the domestic currency/USD 2014/2009 (a higher number indicates greater depreciation of the domestic currency when compared to USD).

The 42 countries in the sample, aggregated into eight groups, are:

- Euro area = Eurozone members (not used in regression)
- € 9 = 9 Euro area members: DEU, FRA, ITA, SVN, AUT, BEL, GRC, NLD, DNK
- EU - € = five EU members but not EA members: CES, HUN, POL, SWE, GBR
- ANS = 4 Anglo-Saxon countries: USA, GBR, CAN, AUS
- BRICs 5 = emerging economies: BRA, RUS, IND, CHI, SAF
- LAM = 6 Latin American countries BRA, ARG, CHI, COL, MEC, VEN
- ASI 13 = Asian countries: CHI, IND, TUR, JAP, HON, INE, MAL, PAK, SIN, SKO,

---

[g] This idea was suggested to me by Robert Volčjak.
[h] All data relate to 2009 and 2014, except KKRED (2008 and 2013, and KGDP (2008 and 2012), which are exceptions made due to the lack of availability of latest data.

Štiblar

TAI, THA, SAR
- Oil 4 = oil exporters: RUS, NOR, VEN, SAR.[i]

5.3. *Results*

5.3.1. *Comparison of period 2008–2014 average values of variables by country groupings*

Table 1 depicts the average values of variables that were calculated for country groupings in the observed period 2008-2014. Besides the geographical criterion the other major criterion for aggregation was the difference in economic policy measures applied in order to get out of the crisis. We have observed different approaches ranging from the austerity-oriented EU policy to the more growth-supportive policy of the Anglo-Saxon countries, as well as the policies of other countries in Asia, Latin America, BRICs and oil exporters. The average values of the groupings confirm our hypothesis: the EU, and especially its euro area sub-group, introduced the austerity type restrictive monetary and fiscal policies which led to miniscule GDP growth, higher unemployment and an overall deflationary situation.

Table 1. Comparison of the Average Values of Variables by Country Groupings

Country group	Dinfl	Dbog	Dbop	Dbalance	Kgdp	Kkred	Kunempl	Kexrate
all 43	0.909	2.237	0.005	2.242	1.186	1.121	0.951	1.083
Eurozone	0.300	3.900	3.000	6.900	0.900	0.969	1.173	1.068
€ 9	0.078	3.300	4.100	7.400	0.879	0.997	1.371	1.068
EU- € 5	-1.680	3.000	0.380	3.380	0.919	0.957	0.844	0.851
ANS 4	1.000	5.200	-0.138	5.075	1.163	1.022	0.805	0.922
BRICS 5	-0.680	2.38	-3.760	-1.380	1.462	1.216	0.744	1.168
LAM 6	6.217	-0.517	-1.850	-2.367	1.356	1.299	0.774	1.426
ASI 13	1.092	2.492	-1.585	0.908	1.381	1.251	0.788	1.048
oil 4	7.125	2.350	2.400	4.750	1.235	1.155	0.992	1.403
Slov. SLN	-0.500	1.700	7.600	9.300	0.831	0.849	1.508	1.068
Rank SLN	30.	25.	2.	5.	41.	40.	4.	15.

Sources: World Bank Data, The Economist, EIPF, SURS.

Rank correlation coefficients were calculated for eight groups within which we measured the correlation of three dependent variables (GDP, unemployment and inflation) with two independent variables (credit growth, budget deficit).

---

[i] Some countries appear in more than one group

- Rank correlation: rR (GDP, KRE) = 0.81; rR (GDP, BOG) = -0.65
- rR (infl, KRE) = 0.62; rR (infl, BOG) = -0.43
- rR (unempl, KRE) = -0.71; rR (unempl, BOG) = 0.50

It indicates that country groups with larger credit expansions were positively correlated with higher GDP growth and higher inflation, but negatively with changes in the unemployment rate. In addition, a lower budget deficit in a country group was negatively correlated with GDP growth and the inflation rate, but positively with a higher unemployment rate.

5.3.2. *Regression: The impact of austerity on economic activity*

An economic policy reduced-form model was used to test the impact of austerity policy measures on the economic performance of different countries. Obviously, better results would have been achieved if a full-fledged production function for economic growth as the dependent variable would have been specified, alongside the usual unemployment and inflation macroeconomic functions. However, the primary goal of this study is to identify the impact of individual economic policy measures on the economic performance of a country and additional explanatory variables would blur the impact of the original economic policy variable. Thus; better statistical significance of the estimated equations is intentionally sacrificed for their improved substantive meaning.

Table 2. Estimation Results

Y	= a	+	b1 x	X1	+	b2	x	X2	R2	F	
KBDP	= 1.21	+	0.0038 x	DKRED	-	0.027 x DBOG			0.19	4.70	eq1
	(24.1)		(2.044)			(-2.12)					
KNEZAP	= 1.41	-	0.413 x	KKRED					0.068	2.95	eq2
	(5.11)		(-1.72)								
DINFL	= -3.42		-0.633 x	DBOG	+	5.13 x KKRED			0.16	3.73	eq3
	(-0.91)		(-2.23)			(1.59)					

5.4. *Statistical significance*

a) The differences in the GDP of the 43 countries in the sample required a test for the heteroskedasticity for three estimated equations. The White Test statistics F-values are not significant, which means that the null hypothesis of homoskedasticity cannot be rejected, or, in other words, that the error term is not heteroskedastic.

The White test values of F-values for heteroskedasticity of the estimated equations:

Equation	F-degrees of freedom	F-value
Eq1	F (2, 40)	1.049
Eq2	F (1,41)	0.071
Eq3	F (2,40)	0.1421

b) The values of Students t-distribution for significance of regression coefficients for 40 degrees of freedom are:

$t = 1.303 p = 0.2$
$t = 1.684 p = 0.1$
$t = 2.021 p = 0.05$
$t = 2.423 p = 0.02$
$t = 2.704 p = 0.01$
$t = 3.551 p = 0.001$

Most regression coefficients in these three equations are statistically significant at a level of $p = 5\%$, while the regression coefficient of the KKRED variable is significant only at a level of $p = 10\%$.

c) The values for F-statistics for the significance of the estimated regression equations are:

$F (2, 40) = 3.23$ for $p = 0.05$
$F (2, 40) = 4.05$ for $p = 0.025$

Thus, the first and third equation are statistically significant at a satisfactory level of 5%, and the second equation at a level slightly below that.

d) The coefficients of determination R2 have low values for all three equations (0.068, 0.16, 0.19), but these specified policy evaluation models intentionally avoid the inclusion of the explanatory variables of traditional production function, labor equation or inflation. The primary goal of this exercise is not to achieve high statistical significance, but to identify and measure the impact of the austerity policy variables on the country's economic performance.

5.5. *Interpretation*

The estimated equations in Table 2 show for the 43 countries included in the sample that higher growth of credits/GDP and higher growth of budget deficit/GDP between the start and the wake of the global financial crisis led to an increase (positive change) in GDP growth. The decline in the unemployment rate was positively influenced by the credit/GDP growth. Inflation grew with higher credit/GDP growth and higher budget deficit/GDP growth. The economic policy measures of austerity as a way out of the crisis (monetary with a restriction of credit growth, fiscal with a constraint on the budget deficit) had a negative impact on the economic performance: lower GDP growth, higher unemployment rate and lower inflation (which in fact could be treated as a negative outcome in the current deflationary environment). Although the identified impact of the policy variables is not very strong, it exists and is moderately statistically significant. Austerity is indeed damaging[10]!

5.6.   Implications for Slovenia (Case study)

Among the 43 countries in the sample, Slovenia is one of those that strictly applied the austerity measures[63]. The values of its variables in the sample give it the following rankings:
a)   Regarding the economic policy variables: with respect to the decrease in the budget deficit it was only 25th, to the growth of bank loans only 40th, to the increase of the current account surplus it was 2nd, to the improvement of combined two balances it was 5th, and with respect to the euro depreciation compared to USD it was 15th-24th.
b)   Regarding the economic performance variables: the country had the fourth-largest decline of GDP, the decline of inflation was below average (rank 30th), while the rise in the unemployment rate was fourth largest.
    In summary, Slovenia implemented above average restrictive austerity policy measures (more monetary than fiscal) which resulted in a catastrophic performance. With such a policy it was impossible for the country to get out of the abyss[64,65].

5.7.   The difference between actual and estimated values of economic performance variables

Variable for Slovenia		actual value	−	estimated value	= difference
GDP growth	(e.2)	0.831		1.115	-0.284
change in unemployment rate	(e.3)	1.508		1.059	0.449
change in inflation rate	(e.4)	-0.500		-0.141	-0.359

If the estimated equations are representative of the general rule for all countries, then Slovenia differs from that rule: GDP decreased significantly more, unemployment increased significantly more, while the inflation rate declined significantly more than what the estimated equations (rule) would suggest. Hence, the worse than expected economic performance of Slovenia during the crisis has to be the result of other factors in addition to restrictive austerity policy measures. These could include psychological pessimism, political uncertainty, weak legislature and administrative inefficiency, the enormous banking crisis. By improving some of them Slovenia achieved an above average GDP growth of 2.6% in 2014, with a small decline in the unemployment rate, but with a looming deflation.

6. Conclusion

The idea of austerity, especially in its most extreme form of an expansionary contraction, proved to be wrong in theory, as well as in the practical application in several countries in the past, as well as in its current less than successful attempts in getting the Eurozone countries out of the recent great recession. The empirical analysis in this study shows that when applied as a way out of the 2008 crisis, the austerity based monetary and fiscal restrictions led to a GDP slump, an increase in unemployment and threatened with deflation. The social consequences of such a dangerous policy are well known: millions of people in the EU are pushed into poverty and suffering, being punished for the sins of other, financial and economic, political elites.

Finally, with the ECB's introduction of quantitative easing the first cracks started to appear in the stubborn wall of European austerity. However, this is a necessary but not sufficient condition to overcome these damaging economic policies and return growth to the EU economy. The addition of a fiscal stimulus would represent a sufficient condition with using the additional liquidity trough government expenditures as an initial impetus. For this to happen, Juncker's proposed EU investment stimulus is by no means large enough to do the job. More should be done on the fiscal side to return the EU economy to its historical growth track and to save the EU idea and the Euro monetary union from collapsing.

References

1. R. Skidelsky, *Keynes: The Return of Master,* (Public Affairs, New York, 2009).
2. S. J. Slivia, Why do German and U.S reactions to the financial crisis differ, *German Politics and Society* **29**(4), 2011.
3. P. Krugman, *The Return of Depression Economics and the Crisis of 2008*, (Penguin Group, USA, 2010).
4. D. Rodrik, *The Globalization Paradox: Democracy and the Future of the World Economy,* (Oxford University Press, Oxford, 2012).
5. R. Shiller, *Irrational Exuberance*, (Broadway Books, USA, 2009).
6. A. Smithers, *The Road to Recovery*, (John Willey and Sons, United Kingdom, 2013).
7. J. Stiglitz, *Stiglitz Report*, (United Nations, New York, 2010).
8. T. Piketty, *Capital in the Twenty-First Century* (Harvard University Press, Cambridge, MA, 2013).
9. J. Stiglitz, *The Price of Inequality: How Today's Divided Society Endangers Our Future,* (W. W. Norton & Company, New York, 2012).
10. M. Blyth, *Austerity: The History of a Dangerous Idea* (Oxford University Press, United Kingdom, 2012, revised version 2015).
11. A. Smith, *An Inquiry into the Nature and Causes of Wealth of Nations*, eds. R. H. Campbell and A. S. Skinner, (Liberty Fund, Indianapolis, 1981).
12. D. Medema and W. Samuels (eds.), *The History of Economic Thought: A Reader*, (Routledge, NY, 2012).

13. D. Ricardo, *Principles of Political Economy and Taxation* (Prometheus, New York, 1996).
14. J. S. Mill, *Principles of Political Economy*, Book V (Longmans, Green and Co., London, 1989).
15. J. Allet, *The New Liberalism* (University of Toronto Press, Toronto,1978).
16. C. J. Friedrich, The political thought of Neo-Liberalism, *American Political Science Review* **49**(2), 509-525 (1955).
17. R. Ptak, *Neoliberalism in Germany: Revisiting the Ordoliberal Foundations of the Social Market Economy* in *The Road from Mont Pelerin: The Making of Neoliberal Through Collective*, eds. P. Mirowski and D. Plehwe (Harvard University Press, Cambridge, 2009).
18. J. A. Schumpeter, *Capitalism, Socialism and Democracy* (Harper, New York, 1942).
19. J. M. Keynes, *The General Theory of Employment, Interest and Money,* (A Harvest Book, Harcourt Inc, 1964).
20. F. Hayek, The Road to Serfdom, (Chicago University Press, Chicago, 1994).
21. P. J. Boettke (ed.), *The Elgar Companion to Austrian Economics*, (Edward Elgar, USA, 1994).
22. M. Friedman, The Role of Monetary Policy, American Economic Review **58**(1), 1-17 (1968).
23. M. Friedman, *Capitalism and Freedom*, (Chicago University Press, Chicago, 2002).
24. M. Sandel, *What Money Can't Buy: The Moral Limits of Markets*, (Farrar, Straus and Giroux, New York, 2010.
25. J. J. Polak, The IMF monetary model: A hardy perennial, *Finance and Development Dec* (1997).
26. J. Williamson, *A Short History of Washington Consensus*, Fundacion CIDOB, Barcelona (2004).
27. D. Rodrik, Goodbye Washington consensus, hello Washington confusion? A review of the World Bank's economic growth in the 1990s: Learning from a decade of reform, *Journal of Economic Literature* **44**(4), 973-987 (2006).
28. J. Schambaugh, *The Euro's Three Crises,* Brooking Papers on Economic Activity (Brookings Institution, Washington DC, Spring 2012).
29. A. Alesina and G. Tabellini, *A Positive Theory of Fiscal Deficits and Government Debt in a Democracy*, NBER Working Paper 2308, (NBER, Cambridge, 1987).
30. A. Alesina and S. Ardagna, *Tales of Fiscal Adjustment* (NBER, Cambridge, 1998).
31. A. Alesina, S. Ardagna, R. Perotti and F. Schiantarelli, Fiscal policy, profits and investment, *American Economic Review* 92(3), (2002).
32. A. Alesina, Fiscal adjustment: lesson from history, *Ecofin* (Madrid, 2010).
33. A. Alesina, The Austerity Question: "How" is as Important as "How Much", Vox CEPR,4/2014.
34. J. Guajardo, D. Leigh and A. Pescatori, *Expansionary Austerity: New International Evidence*, IMF Working Paper 11/158, (IMF, Washington, 2011).
35. G. Soros, *The Tragedy of the European Union* (Public Affairs, New York, 2014).
36. C. Lagarde, *Latvia and the Baltics: A Story of Recovery (*Riga, June 2012).

37. V. Monasteriotis, (When) does austerity work? On the conditional link between fiscal austerity and debt sustainability, *Cyprus Economic Policy Review* **8**(1), 71-92 (2014).
38. O. L. Blanchard, *2011 in Review: Four Hard Truths*, IMF Direct, December (2011).
39. M. Chinn, *Fiscal Multipliers*, in *The New Palgrave Dictionary of Economics*, eds. S. Darlauf and L. Blume, (Palgrave Macmillan, 2013).
40. A. Auerbach, and Y. Gorodnichenko, *Fiscal Multipliers in Recession and Expansion*, in *Fiscal Policy after the Financial Crisis*, eds. A. Alesina and F. Giavazzi, (NBER, Cambridge, MA, 2013).
41. L. Christiano, M. Eichenbaum, and S. Rebelo, When is the government spending multiplier large? *Journal of Political Economy* 119(78), 78-121 (2011).
42. L. Eyraud, and A. Weber, *The Challenge of Debt Reduction During Fiscal Consolidation*, IMF Working Paper 13/67 (IMF, Washington, 2013).
43. K. Kuester, G. Mueller, G. Corsetti and A. Meier, *Sovereign Risk, Fiscal Policy and Macroeconomic Stability*, IMF Working Paper 12/33, (IMF, Washington, 2012).
44. R. Bachmann, E. Sims, Confidence and the transmission of government spending shocks, *Journal of Monetary Economics* 59(3), 235-49 (2012).
45. P. Krugman, *The ECB and the Austerity Trap*, Opinion Pages, New York Times, March 31, 2013.
46. A. Minshima, M. Poplawski-Ribeiro, A. Weber, *Size of Fiscal Multipliers*, in *Post-crisis Fiscal Policy*, eds. C. Cotarelli, P. Gerson and A. Senhadji, (MIT Press, Cambridge, MA, 2014).
47. M. Wolf, Martin Wolf's exchange, *The Financial Times*, (2012), http://blogs.ft.com/martin-wolf-exchange/.
48. B. Eichengreen, *Drawing a Line Under Europe's Crisis*, VOX, CEPR, June 17, 2010.
49. P. Krugman, *Debt, Deleveraging and the Liquidity Trap*, VOX CEPR, November 18, 2010.
50. G. Corsetti, *Has Austerity Gone Too Far?* VOX CEPR, April 2, 2012.
51. B. Eischengreen, and K. H. O'Rouke, *Gauging the Multiplier Lessons from History*, VOX CEPR, October 23, 2012.
52. P. De Grauwe, and Y. Ji, *Panic-Driven Austerity in The Eurozone And Its Implications*, VOX CEPR, February 21, 2013.
53. L. Ball, *The Great Recession's Long-term Damage*, VOX CEPR, July 1, 2014.
54. Real Time Economics, *The Wall Street Journal* (2015), http://blogs.wsj.com/economics/
55. M. Blyth, *Great Transformations* (Cambridge University Press, UK, 2002).
56. G. Caggiano and E. Castelnuovo, *Government Spending Multipliers and The Business Cycle*, VOX CEPR, June 23, 2015.
57. A.-S. Chassany, Lunch with the FT: Thomas Piketty, *The Financial Times*, (June 26, 2015), https://www.ft.com/content/7ca6cfc2-1b39-11e5-a130-2e7db721f996
58. C. Reinhart and K. Rogoff, *This Time is Different: Eight Centuries of Financial Folly* (Princeton University Press, New Jersey, 2009).

59. T. Herdon, M. Ash and R. Pollin, Does high public debt consistently stifle economic growth? A critique of Reinhart and Rogoff, *Cambridge Journal of Economics* **38**(2), (2013).

60. A. Dube, *A Note on Debt, Growth and Causality*, mimeo (2014).

61. M. Kimball, and Y. Wang, *After Crunching Reinhart And Rogoff Data, We've Concluded That High Debt Does Not Slow Growth, Qartz*, May 29, 2013, http://qz.com/88781/after-crunching-reinhart-and-rogoffs-data-weve-concluded-that-high-debt-does-not-cause-low-growth/

62. B. Egeert, Public Debt, Economic Growth and Nonlinear Effects: Myth or Reality? OECD Working Paper 993 (OECD, Paris, 2012).

63. D. Gros, *Can Austerity Be Self-Defeating?* Economic Policy CEPS Commentaries (2011).

64. F. Štiblar, *Svetovna kriza in Slovenci – Kako jo preživeti?* ZRC SAZU, (2008).

65. F. Štiblar, *Introduction of Euro in Slovenia*, in *Financialization in South East Europe* eds. D. Radošević and Vidošević (Peter Lang, 2015).

66. F. Štiblar, *Škodljivost zategovanja pasu*, GG, EIPF, (Ljubljana, 2015).